Religion and Its Impact on Organizational Behavior

Ebtihaj Al-Aali
University of Bahrain, Bahrain

Meryem Masmoudi
University of Bahrain, Bahrain

Gardenia Jassim AlSaffar
Royal Bahrain Hospital, Bahrain

A volume in the Advances in Human Resources Management and Organizational Development (AHRMOD) Book Series

IGI Global
PUBLISHER of TIMELY KNOWLEDGE

Published in the United States of America by
IGI Global
Business Science Reference (an imprint of IGI Global)
701 E. Chocolate Avenue
Hershey PA, USA 17033
Tel: 717-533-8845
Fax: 717-533-8661
E-mail: cust@igi-global.com
Web site: http://www.igi-global.com

Library of Congress Cataloging-in-Publication Data

Names: Al-Aali, Ebtihaj Ahmed, 1957- editor. | Masmoudi, Meryem, 1979- editor. | Alsaffar, Gardenia, 1980- editor.
Title: Religion and its impact on organizational behavior / Ebtihaj Ahmed Al-Aali, Meryem Masmoudi, and Gardenia Alsaffar, editors.
Description: Hershey, PA : Business Science Reference, [2022] | Includes bibliographical references and index. | Summary: "This book bridges the gap between religious ideas, concepts and procedures and contemporary field of studies in behavior in organizations"-- Provided by publisher.
Identifiers: LCCN 2021046495 (print) | LCCN 2021046496 (ebook) | ISBN 9781799893196 (hardcover) | ISBN 9781799893202 (paperback) | ISBN 9781799893219 (ebook)
Subjects: LCSH: Organizational behavior--Religious aspects. | Business ethics. | Leadership--Religious aspects.
Classification: LCC HD58.7 .R4545 2022 (print) | LCC HD58.7 (ebook) | DDC 302.3/5--dc23/eng/20111105
LC record available at https://lccn.loc.gov/2021046495
LC ebook record available at https://lccn.loc.gov/2021046496

This book is published in the IGI Global book series Advances in Human Resources Management and Organizational Development (AHRMOD) (ISSN: 2327-3372; eISSN: 2327-3380)

British Cataloguing in Publication Data
A Cataloguing in Publication record for this book is available from the British Library.

Advances in Human Resources Management and Organizational Development (AHRMOD) Book Series

ISSN:2327-3372
EISSN:2327-3380

Patricia Ordóñez de Pablos
Universidad de Oviedo, Spain

MISSION

A solid foundation is essential to the development and success of any organization and can be accomplished through the effective and careful management of an organization's human capital. Research in human resources management and organizational development is necessary in providing business leaders with the tools and methodologies which will assist in the development and maintenance of their organizational structure.

The **Advances in Human Resources Management and Organizational Development (AHRMOD) Book Series** aims to publish the latest research on all aspects of human resources as well as the latest methodologies, tools, and theories regarding organizational development and sustainability. The **AHRMOD Book Series** intends to provide business professionals, managers, researchers, and students with the necessary resources to effectively develop and implement organizational strategies.

COVERAGE

- Human Relations Movement
- Upward Feedback
- Personnel Retention
- Outsourcing HR
- Change Management
- Training and Development
- Human Resources Development
- Workplace Discrimination
- Workplace Culture
- Skills Management

IGI Global is currently accepting manuscripts for publication within this series. To submit a proposal for a volume in this series, please contact our Acquisition Editors at Acquisitions@igi-global.com or visit: http://www.igi-global.com/publish/.

The Advances in Human Resources Management and Organizational Development (AHRMOD) Book Series (ISSN 2327-3372) is published by IGI Global, 701 E. Chocolate Avenue, Hershey, PA 17033-1240, USA, www.igi-global.com. This series is composed of titles available for purchase individually; each title is edited to be contextually exclusive from any other title within the series. For pricing and ordering information please visit http://www.igi-global.com/book-series/advances-human-resources-management-organizational/73670. Postmaster: Send all address changes to above address.

Titles in this Series

For a list of additional titles in this series, please visit:
https://www.igi-global.com/book-series/advances-human-resources-management-organizational/73670

Analyzing Telework, Trustworthiness, and Performance Using Leader-Member Exchange COVID-19 Perspective
Michael A. Brown Sr. (Right Fit Communications LLC, USA)
Business Science Reference • ©2022 • 263pp • H/C (ISBN: 9781799889502) • US $215.00

Future Advancements for CSR and the Sustainable Development Goals in a Post-COVID-19 World
Andrea Pérez (University of Cantabria, Spain)
Business Science Reference • ©2022 • 355pp • H/C (ISBN: 9781799880653) • US $225.00

Building Competencies for Organizational Success Emerging Research and Opportunities
Donta S. Harper (University of Washington, USA)
Business Science Reference • ©2021 • 217pp • H/C (ISBN: 9781799865162) • US $195.00

Role of Leadership in Facilitating Healing and Renewal in Times of Organizational Trauma and Change
Lynda Byrd-Poller (Thomas Nelson Community College, USA) Jennifer L. Farmer (Renewed Mindset LLC, USA) and Valerie Ford (ISP Global Communications LLC, USA)
Business Science Reference • ©2021 • 291pp • H/C (ISBN: 9781799870166) • US $195.00

Impact of Infodemic on Organizational Performance
Muhammad Waseem Bari (Government College University, Faisalabad, Pakistan) and Emilia Alaverdov (Georgian Technical University, Georgia)
Business Science Reference • ©2021 • 380pp • H/C (ISBN: 9781799871644) • US $195.00

Handbook of Research on Advancements in Organizational Data Collection and Measurements Strategies for Addressing Attitudes, Beliefs, and Behaviors
Mihai C. Bocarnea (Regent University, USA) Bruce E. Winston (Regent University, USA) and Debra Dean (Regent University, USA)
Business Science Reference • ©2021 • 400pp • H/C (ISBN: 9781799876656) • US $295.00

For an entire list of titles in this series, please visit:
https://www.igi-global.com/book-series/advances-human-resources-management-organizational/73670

IGI Global
PUBLISHER of TIMELY KNOWLEDGE

701 East Chocolate Avenue, Hershey, PA 17033, USA
Tel: 717-533-8845 x100 • Fax: 717-533-8661
E-Mail: cust@igi-global.com • www.igi-global.com

Editorial Advisory Board

Table of Contents

Detailed Table of Contents

It is crucial to grasp individual behaviour in organizations. This can shed light on evaluation of organizational outcomes. The evaluation can assist in deciding changes required. This chapter investigates organizational behaviour models. The investigation aims to develop a better comprehension of human behaviour. The chapter examines the most reviewed organizational behaviour models. These models are the human relation, the system perspective, productivity perspective, the human resource approach, the contingency approach, and finally, the situation approach. These models are argued to be elementalistic. The elementalism leads to perceive humans and their behaviour in a partial manner. The Aristotelian structure of language underpinning Indo-European languages upholds such elementalism. The structure is built on three laws. These are "is" of identity, two value orientation, and excluding middle stance. The chapter presents some principles of Islam to transform organizational behaviour models. The model enriched by Islam is argued to be in flux.

Although spirituality in the workplace has recently received extensive attention from many researchers in the field of management, it has often been interchanged with the term religion. Yet religion is neglected. According to Vitell, religion contributes to setting a framework for moral and ethical behavior in a business context, creating a spiritual workplace that is aligned with organizational goals and has a positive

Religion is a cornerstone of any society as it affects politics, law, economics, science, and is reflected throughout history in arts and more. In contrast, spirituality is an individual practice with the aim of mindfulness and having a sense of peace and purpose. This research aims to investigate the influence of religion and spirituality on organizational behavior in organizations in Bahrain specifically with regard to managing individuals in Bahrain. A sample of 46 valid responses was reached due to the sensitivity of the topic. Nationality was found to have a statistically significant effect on 'behavior-based religion'. Principal component analysis found two distinctive factors among the religion values indicators being referred to as 'behavior-based religion' and 'belief of religion'.

Since the early 1980s researchers have shown increased interest in integrating spirituality and leadership. Spirituality has emerged as a discrete construct underlying the essence of effective leadership, and the negotiating ability has been regarded as one of its core descriptors. The study, on which the present chapter is based, attempts to ascertain the relationship between spirituality and leaders' negotiating ability. The sample for this study consisted of 450 leaders and 904 subordinates working across different service and manufacturing sectors in India. With the help of a mixed-method research design, data was gathered employing several tools. Leaders' spirituality has been measured through MacDonald's spirituality inventory and their negotiating ability through Rai's model. The study reveals that leaders' negotiating ability is a function of spirituality, and a proper understanding of spirituality improves negotiating abilities of leaders. It offers workable suggestions and outlines the implications of the results for policy and practice.

This chapter is an exploratory study that explores the issues of the religious fact in Bahraini banks. The chapter will produce an understanding of this phenomenon, the

Preface

This book elaborates on the issue of religion and its impacts on human behaviour in organisations. This is the era of Organisations. Starting from nursery to age of retirement, individuals' experience different types of organisational requirements. Religion is a major part in shaping such experiences. Organisations do not exist in vacuum. They are shaped by the environments which at they operate. Religions are embedded by values , ethics and principles. Faith is the underlying act for accepting religious values, ethics and principles. Faith as well can not be subjected for studying in relation to this book for two reasons. The first is that faith is immersed in believes and values which is not the focus of this book. The second is that behaviours reflecting faiths overlap making it hard to separate. This book therefore attempts to study the impacts of certain religious principles on human behaviour in organisations.

The book revolves around eight themes as follows:

- Reflections on literature of theories of human behaviour in the light of organisational behavioural models
- Inculcation of Islamic values in teaching
- Impacts of religion and spirituality on behaviour in organisations
- Religion in the work place: the case of Bahraini Islamic banks
- Spirituality and negotiating abilities of leaders
- Islamic work ethics
- Synergy between religion, spirituality, and organisational behaviour
- Job demand theory and mental health

Chapter 1 examines models of organisational behaviour. The chapter argues that such models are characterized by partially. This is due to the partial and elementalistic views of humans and therefore realities. The chapter calls to revise the present literature in relation to models of organizational behaviour. The revision aims to reflect the totality nature of humans and organisation. An alternative tentative model based on some Islamic principles is elaborated on. The research illustrates the unique abilities of self-referential of humans. Such abilities enable individuals to self-reflect and self-correct.

Chapter 2 then attempts to highlight the differences between religion and spirituality which are used interchangeably. The chapter investigates the impacts of religion and spirituality on four areas in Organizations. These areas are corporate cultures, leadership, employees well beings and future concerns and issues. It is argued that business ethics and values should be directed towards motivating employees. The chapter explains that in global environments of today cultures and values should not be favouring specific beliefs.

In Chapter 3, the authors argue that work ethics are based on religious beliefs. It is stated that Islamic work ethics are on rise. This justifies, according to authors, conducting their research in order to understand and analysis studies in relation to Islamic work ethics. They illustrate that such studies have been in rise during the last five years. Most of the studies were conducted on employees then managers. The findings show as well that the majority of the studies on Islamic work ethics were conducted in Pakistan. Only one study was conducted on Israel at which the majority are non-Muslims. The paper calls to conduct more research on Islamic work ethics.

The author in Chapter 4 scans the literature of positive psychology. This chapter demonstrates the relationship between employees behaviour, meaningful of work and positive psychology. The chapter, according to the author, provides guidelines for managers to draw upon to enhance performance and to increase productivity.

The authors of Chapter 5 illustrate that religion has been over looked in relation to managing individuals in organizations. The findings of this chapter argue that religion has no relationship to human resources activities in organisations. However, it is found that some religious values are still affecting working relationships.

In Chapter 6, the authors based on their empirical research conclude that negotiating abilities of leaders are functions of spirituality. They add that organizational spiritual philosophy should be reflected on all organizational activities, policies, functions, and processes. This according to authors guide subordinate behaviour in a positive direction.

Chapter 7 is an exploratory research examining impacts of religion on workplace in Bahraini banks. The findings of the research reveals the existence of religious symbols and practices in the workplace. However, such existence does not lead to difficulties in management. The author argues that understanding the effects of religion on daily practices in workplace can assist business managers to develop a better strategies corresponding to local and multinational values. Businesses then will be more able to deal with the issues related to diversity.

The authors of Chapter 8 state that the workplace spirituality and leadership share a positive relationship based on literature reviewed. Leaders' behavior, attitudes and different personalities issues can be improved once work spirituality is enhanced.

Leaders then can have positive impacts on all aspects related to individuals' lives and organisations as well.

The authors of Chapter 9 study leadership styles in Islamic banks. The chapter as well aims to link leadership styles to sources of power used. The chapter employs qualitative methodology. The chapter illustrates that two interviewees followed Strategic. Leadership styles. This leadership utilises legitimate and expertise sources of power. Only one interviewee exhibits features of transformational leadership which is relying on referent source of power.

Chapter 10 illustrates that students' behavior and ethics are enhanced when Islamic values are infused in teaching. Interviews were conducted. Analysis of collected information reveals that Islamic value-based teaching, environments, parents and peers are the factors playing major roles in building students' characters. The chapter recommends to prepare value-based curriculum to enable students to deal with the present and future situations locally and internationally

The last chapter investigates the job demand and resources theory on employee mental health. The spiritual resources impact on employee exhaustion and on employees ill-health are examined as well. Job demand and resources theory with reference to spiritual resources do not predict employee ill-health and employee exhaustion. The chapter also shows that the impacts of job-demand and resources on employees vary based on cultural differences.

Ebtihaj Al-Aali

Meryem Masmoudi

Gardenia Jassim AlSaffar

Chapter 1 Human Behaviour in Organizations: An Enhancement Perspective

Ebtihaj Ahmed Al-Aali
University of Bahrain, Bahrain

ABSTRACT

It is crucial to grasp individual behaviour in organizations. This can shed light on evaluation of organizational outcomes. The evaluation can assist in deciding changes required. This chapter investigates organizational behaviour models. The investigation aims to develop a better comprehension of human behaviour. The chapter examines the most reviewed organizational behaviour models. These models are the human relation, the system perspective, productivity perspective, the human resource approach, the contingency approach, and finally, the situation approach. These models are argued to be elementalistic. The elementalism leads to perceive humans and their behaviour in a partial manner. The Aristotelian structure of language underpinning Indo-European languages upholds such elementalism. The structure is built on three laws. These are "is" of identity, two value orientation, and excluding middle stance. The chapter presents some principles of Islam to transform organizational behaviour models. The model enriched by Islam is argued to be in flux.

INTRODUCTION

Employees are humans working in organizations. Varying situations in organizations lead employees to behave differently. Besides, every employee may act in different manner at a given situation. This illustrates the importance of the discipline of

DOI: 10.4018/978-1-7998-9319-6.ch001

organizational behaviour. The paper argues that the present contextual perspectives and its related literature on organizational behaviour overlook the holistic nature of humans. This leads literature to be elementalistic making it hard to deal with continuous changes . Therefore there is a need to have a comprehensive contextual perspective inducing the evolution of thorough literature. This paper consists of five sections. The first examines the evolution of management theories focusing on organizational Behaviour. The second elaborates on contextual models of organizational behaviour. The third presents the Islamic principals to promote a perspective as an alternative to organizational behaviour models. Impacts of the alternative perspective on leadership/management are illustrated in section four. The summary of the discussion of this paper is stated in the final section.

EMERGENCE OF ORGANIZATIONAL BEHAVIOR

This section describes the evolution of management theories leading to the development of organizational behaviour as a discipline. The characteristics of the discipline are stated.

EVOLUTION OF MANAGEMENT THEORIES

Theories of management describe the approaches to accomplish work in organizations. The choice between approaches for applying theories depends on the demands of every situation . Some of the theories were developed in the 18th or 19th centuries. However principals of such theories may be still related to the present. Management theories provide guidelines to decision-making processes, enhancing collaboration between workers and leaders to increase productivity and improving objectivity.

A brief review of management theories t is presented as an introduction to the discussion of organizational behaviour discipline. kinicki and Williams (2020) state that theories of management can be classified as historical and contemporary. Historical theories are based on principles of the Scientific management of Taylor. Taylor is to study methods to accomplish work and to improve productivity. Administrative management of Henry Fayol and Weber focus on examining the entire organizations. The last historical theory focuses on quantitative methods aiming to study principles of management issues. This ear lasted from 1911-1950s (Indeed Career Guide,2021) Ivancevich, Konopaske, Matteson (2014). This includes as well behavioural perspective focusing on human relation. Human relation attempts to understand how to motivate employees in order to enhance performance. Contemporary theories according to Kinicki and Williams (2020) are built on three different views. These are the system, the contingency and quality management ;1960s-the present. The system assumes an organization is a system consisting of sub systems. The contingency postulates that managers' behaviour is contingent on external environment and employees. Quality management aims at continuously training of employees and improving quality procedures. These three views are named as Contextual perspectives by Moorhead and Griffin (2013) . This is to say that every group of theories of organizational behaviour are based on one of these perspectives. Organizational behaviour as a discipline is stated to emerge in 1960s. Organizational behaviour focuses on examining behaviour of individuals in organizational contexts, the interactions between individuals and organizations and studying the organization itself (Borkowski, 2005) . The discipline of organizational behaviour displays two characteristics. The first illustrates that many disciplines contribute to the field of organizational behaviour. Organizational behaviour is based on interdisciplinary findings. These disciplines are medicine, economics, engineering, political science, anthropology, psychology and sociology. The second is that organizational behaviour theories are descriptive in nature. This is due to the unique nature of human behaviour (iEduNote.com.2021). This is a reason to argue that organizational behaviour is a field of a study and not just a discipline based on science (the intactone,2018). The field of study examines issues and problems related to humans in organizations.

CONTEXTUAL PERSPECTIVES/ MODELS OF ORGANIZATIONAL BEHAVIOR

Theories related to examining organizations, human behaviour in organizations, and the interactions between humans and Organizations rely on certain perspectives. These perspectives are the results of experts' research in the field of organizational behaviour. The perspectives are named differently by various authors. They are called for example contextual by Jones (2006), McShane & Von Glinow (2010), Moorhead and Griffin (2011), Models and approaches by Theintactone (2018), overarching perspectives by Kinicki & Williams (2020),and Approaches to Organizational Behaviour by IEduNote (2021). Discussions of these contextual perspectives is needed to exhibit the characteristics of each . Below is the discussion of the main six contextual perspectives frequently examined by literature.

THE HUMAN RELATION PERSPECTIVE

It is sometimes named as the supportive contextual approach (Wibowo, (2017). The role of leaders in the context is to provide support to employees to get the best of their performance. The authority is still within the hand of leaders . The purpose of this approach is to attain organizational goals through employees. So employees are seen as means to achieve the objectives. Employees are assumed to be passive reacting to external triggers.

THE SYSTEM PERSPECTIVE

This perspective assumes that an organization consists of interrelated subsystems. Every subsystem is a unit by itself and is a part of the broader system (Moorhead & Griffin (2011)). An organization as system interacts with the external environment. Employees are important to accomplish organizational goals however they represent a subsystem i.e. input element. This organizational subsystem is controlled and monitored by leaders. Once again passivity of employees is underpinning this perspective. Besides elementalism thinking is the underlined theme for theories of this perspective. Employees are seen as means to achieve goals. They are input to the broader system.

PRODUCTIVITY APPROACH

This perspective employs quantitative methods. The perspective measures productivity in term of economic ratio ; i.e. input to output. Economic gains refer to the traditional meaning of productivity (iEduNote,2021)). Human and social factors besides economic gains shape decisions in organizations. This enhances the contemporary definition of productivity. Humans i.e. employees are employed to enhance productivity. They are input to productivity. Elementalisic thinking prevails as a base for this perspective.

THE HUMAN RESOURCES APPROACH

This approach acknowledges the importance of employees' contribution to the success of organizations. The roles of managers is to change their styles based on the situation (theintactine, 2021). The purpose of this change is to allow employees to work at their best toward the achievement of organizational goals. Humans/

employees are viewed as a resource to achieve organizational goals. Employees are not seen in a totality stance. They are important cause they can contribute to the accomplishments of organizational goals. Elementalism dominates this approach although it acknowledges the importance of employees. This acknowledgment however is to enhance organizational performance.

THE CONTINGENCY APPROACH

The contingency approach states that a given behaviour can not be right for all the situations. The external environment and the internal processes shape management roles.

The Contingency approach states that management roles are contingent upon their situations. The management roles are functions of environment, skills to analyze the changes, human skills to deal with employees through selecting the suitable communication methods (Godon,2021).

The contingency approach is argued to be an extension of the system approach. However it differs in respect to illustrating the impact of structure on management. This in turn affects managers' behaviour on employees (Pearsonhighhered,2019)). The system approach examines the impact of structure on behaviour. The contingency approach highlights the importance of external factors on organizational structure and behavior.

Managers change their behaviour based on contingency approach to get the advantages of the situations which employees are part of. This exhibits that employees are seen based on elementalistic view . Employees are thought of as means to achieve organizational goals. Employees/humans are not viewed in holistic beings. They are an aspect of the contingent situation.

THE SITUATIONAL APPROACH

Though the contingency and situational approaches are similar for disapproving universality of managers' roles and situations, they differ in terms of managers' reactions. Managers based on contingency perspective are said to match their behavior to the situation. Managers adapt their styles according to the situational approach. (https://askinglot.com/what-is-the-difference-between-situational-and-contingency-theory, 2020)).

The situational model argues that employees interact continuously with their situations. This leads behaviours of leaders and employees to change all the time. The situational model is ahead of previous perspectives for assuming that behavior is not constant. However it lacks corresponding to the totality nature of individuals and situations. Humans are only thought of as employees interacting on a continuous basis in a given organizational setting.

The above six perspectives are discussed in the literature by different scholars as mentioned above. Though these perspectives vary in term of focus they are all characterised by elementalism . This is the result of the focus of study of organizational behavior as a discipline . The focus consists of three elements individuals behaviour, interactions of individuals and organizations and the study of the organization itself. However, these perspectives are not viewed on flux. The elements of behaviour either are examined by quantitative or qualitative methodologies. Computer stimulation is employed as well to study operations of organizations and employees' behaviour. The following discussion supports and justifies the earlier arguments that contextual organizational models are elementalistic and based on partially.

Weick (2021) contends that individuals in organizations create situations that they react to. They do not adapt to existing situations. He adds that stability leading to order based on constant perspectives i.e. organisational behaviour models, separates between employees, managers and organisations. This is a phenomenon which he describes as separation between the knower and known in an organization. This is a function of either-or thinking as a reflection of Aristotelian structure of Indo-European languages(Al-Meraie, 1984)).

Weick (2021) objects such separation though he has attached no name to it. He elaborates as well on the word recurring requirements in relation to jobs, functions and processes. He explains that such recurring of jobs, functions and processes is never the same. Weick (2021) once again attributes no causes to such never the same recurring. Whyte (1965) and Al-A'ali (1999) argue that this assumption of similar recurring is underpinned by organisational conformity requirements. Such conformity reflects the nature of "is" of identity of Aristotelian structure of language. These two laws of Aristotle lead to the third law of Aristotelian structure of language that assume no middle ground between ideas examined. Each Contextual perspectives discussed above excludes the other one . This implies that each focuses on one aspect of the totality being of humans and organizations. Weick (2021) states that Perspective based on one of the formal definitions is " a mental view of the relative importance of things". This formal definition refers to a degree of stable relationships. Weick (2021) however, promotes different definition reflecting transient nature . His perspective consists of five elements; faith, evidence, action, guesses and unknowable. He adds that creating perspectives are on-going processes helping to bridge the gap between previous and present experiences . He develops his perspective based on five sources. These are "experiences, formal education, research sites, texts, events, and dispositions". He argued that a perspective should be based on hunches and flux. This is to enable bridging the gap between past and ongoing perspectives. He elaborates on what so named " A COMMUNITY OF PERSPECTIVES ". This entails increase meanings through subjecting present propositions to revision and replacement. The community perspectives, according to Weick, may instigate search for wisdom by implying opposing values such as knowledge and doubt, detachment and emotions and actions and inaction. He states that "Drop your tool" reflects a way of thinking relinquishing old and present styles of actions and thoughts. These old styles preclude developing new views and perspectives. In conclusion he argues that the present perspectives of Organizational Behavior are fragmented. They are as well stable and not dealing with flux nature of reality. His argument to use the community of perspective is still trapped by the laws underpinning Aristotelian structure of language. His perspective is be based on opposing assumptions as he mentioned. The totality and complementary nature of humans and organizations is neglected.

The argument against organizational behavior models presents the three laws of Aristotelian style of thinking; the law of "is" of identity, the two value orientation and the law of excluding the middle or the non-contradiction. Weick 's (2021) analysis is a step ahead toward diagnosing the present perspectives of organizational behaviour. However Weick (2021) seems to overlook the underpinning logic for such elementalistic thinking.

Wibowo (2017) explains that a model illustrates a simplification of description of a system or a plan. He examines organizational behaviour models as management mechanisms. His review examines five models. The first is autocracy referring to power kept by the managers. The second is the Custodial depending on economic incentives given to employees working on individuals basis and not as a team. This model is stated to reflect Theories Y of McGregor (1967). This is one aspect of human relation model mentioned earlier. The supportive model revolves around leadership. The human relation model mentioned above is called occasionally supportive perspective. The leader role is not restricted to provide economic incentives. The leader role is to support, respect and guide employees. The fourth is the Collegial model. This model aims to enhance employees contribution to organizations. Employees are assumed to be committed and self-disciplined. Leaders are to motivate employees to achieve self-actualization. This is argued to be compatible to Human Resources Model discussed earlier. The last model is the system model. The leaders should possess a proper understanding of the organization and have better comprehension of external environment. Employees' needs are considered to enhance trust and commitment. This model is elaborated on by literature of organizational behaviour as shown above. Employees are still thought of as means to achieve organizational goals. Environment is said to be an external factor affecting the organization. This exhibits partiality underlining this model. Wibowo (2017) concludes stating that organizations are in state of change. He adds that the state of changes makes non of the models reviewed to fit all the situations. He argues that the suitable model is a combination of the five models of organizational behaviour. Wibowo 's argument of a combining of models does not overcome elementalism of organizational behaviour models. This is because each model is based on different assumptions. Besides the additive thinking employed i.e. combining models, will not lead to develop a holistic organizational behaviour model.

Weick (2021) and Wibowo (2017) illustrate partially and elementalism of organizational behaviour models . They however have not elaborated on the causes leading to such elementalism and partially.

The organizational models illustrated above exhibit management behavior leading to the development of certain ethics. These ethics are conformity based on scientism, belongingness and togetherness according to whyte 's analysis (1965). Individuals are seen to be passive. This neglects individuals uniqueness. It is the group which is superior to them. Groups are capable to handling all organizational matters . Zohar (1997) analysis of Organizations is computable with Whyte (1965). This is described as an organizational predicament by Al-Meraie (1984). Elementalism and passivity of employees are the major characteristics of organizational behavior models. Al-A'Ali (1991) adds that such elementalism is embedded in Morgan 's analysis of organizational metaphors. She states that the metaphors are based on elementalistic assumptions of humans. Each of these metaphors is said to be referring to different organizational models. This is highlighted by McEachern (1984). He contends that "...what happens in organizations depend on their sustenance more than on the pattern of theorists " (P.1). He adds that assumptions about humans and their organizations should be explicit. The models of organizational behaviour and the analysis of Weick (2021) and Wibowo (2017) mentioned above do not examine such assumptions.

This paper argues that elementalism and employees passivity due to dualism characterize organizational behaviour models. This reflects the Aristotelian laws underlying the structure of of Indo-European languages. The laws are of "is" of identity, the two values orientation and the non contradiction. This actuates Organizational models to promote elementalistic focus based on partial assumptions about humans. The following section elucidate on alternative perspective in relation to models of organizational behaviour and it's possible impacts on management.

AN ALTERNATIVE PERSPECTIVE TO ORGANIZATIONAL BEHAVIOUR MODELS: AN ISLAMIC PERSPECTIVE

The section is to to illustrates the Islamic perspective as an alternative to organizational behaviour models discussed above.

Religions are not sciences and are not subject for testing. This is due to the faiths and believes embedded in their teachings. However some of their ideas and principles can be used to enhance organizational practices. These ideas and principles promote different styles of thinking in comparison to those of human sciences (Al-A'ali,1995)).

This section presents a perspective based on Islamic ideas and principles arguing to be an alternative to the elementalistic organisational behavior models. Islam is related to Arabic nations and as any other religion has spread globally. Arabs are Semitic nations. The structure of their Semitic language is different from Indo-European languages. Al-Meraie (1984)states that Arabic is a non-linear language. This means that Arabic is a Nonconcatenative morphology. (Glottipedia, 2009). Al-Meraie (1984) illustrates that metaphors i.e. models of organisational behaviour based on Aristotelian structure of Indo-European languages, overlooks differences. This is due to the three laws of Aristotelian structure of language. These are "is" of identity, two values orientation and non-contradiction. These laws highlight elementalism and passivity due to dualism. Metaphors are used differently based on Arabic language. Three issues exhibit the differences. The first issue illustrated by Al-Meraie (1984) is that objects perceived in the light of metaphors i.e models are seen in term of differences and not similarities. The second issues states that similarities between objects/existents should not be in an exhaustive and universal views. The last issue is to focus attention on prominent characteristics of objects/existents. The features of Arabic language for being non-linear and its unique perception of metaphors perception leads to the evolution of unparalleled assumptions about humans. Humans are the highest class of substances according to Islam. Substances are atoms, inorganic existents, plants, animals and human beings. Mahgniya (1982) based on his analysis, elaborates on the three major existents. The first is materialistic objects existing externally. The second is mental existents reflecting individuals perceptions of external objects. This is argued to be the most powerful. The third mirrors feelings and emotions of individuals. It is the artistic existent. Humans are on continuous movements representing all these three existents in a holistic manner . Haji (1986) then expounds that knowledge acquisition based on islam follows synergetic paths. The first path is being horizontal leading to add new fields of study as required. The second path is vertical causing to re innovate and modify old and present postulations as needed. These two paths reflect the continuous movement of humans' knowledge. Such movements are characterized by holistic perspective. This is to say that neither qualitative and nor quantitative methodologies can be employed solely to acquire knowledge . These methodologies complement each other in a synergetic manner. This is different from elementalisic knowledge accumulated based on organizational models. The alternative model of organizational behaviour in Islam is argued to be on flux.

In conclusion the alternative model based on Islamic principles discussed above is on flux. It acknowledges that humans and situations are continuously changing. Humans' situations, perceptions and feelings are seen in a wholistic view. No dualism is assumed. Humans are seen to have active roles in life. They are not passive. Knowledge sought and acquired by humans are not elementalisic . The two paths, assumed by Islam, to acquire knowledge complement each other on a synergetic basis. Horizontal and vertical knowledge lead to introduce new fields of study or to transform existing ones. The section follows is to present the transformation of leadership roles based on Islamic suggested model.

IMPACTS OF ISLAMIC PERSPECTIVE ON LEADERSHIP AND EMPLOYEES BEHAVIOR

Roles of leaders and managers based on organizational behaviour models vary. Such Roles swing between the leaders being the sole decision makers or leaders allowing employees a degree of participation. The participation is assumed to achieve organizational goals on one hand and to motivate employees on the other hand. Dualism underpins all organizational behavior models. Human behaviour is seen through action and reaction based on reciprocal relationships.

Islam perspective of individuals and society including organizations is based on infusion. Individuals, organizations and society are on continuous transactions. They influence and are influenced by each others. Islam deals with the problems of the the linear relationships of leaders-employees represented through action and reaction based on organizational models (Al-A'ali, (1993). Kinicki and Williams (2020) states that leadership revolves around the power to influence employees. Such influence makes employees achieve organizational goals willingly. This illustrates the assumptions of such dualism and linear relationships. This dualism depicts employees passivity (whyte (1965)). McEachern 's (1984) argument however states that influence in relationships is not linear. To him influence is exercised by Both leaders and employees. It based on socialisation processes. The continuous transactions argued by Islam and stated earlier reveal that leaders and employees hold theories tentatively based on horizontal and vertical progression of knowledge acquired. Such continuous transactions consider values and uniqueness of individuals. Leaders-employees relationships are not predetermined or envisaged. The predetermined relationships are the result of the dualism and passivity assumptions of organizational behavior models.

Individuals, based on Islam, are not passive (Al-A'ali, 1995)). They are active players in life as well in organizations. This is based on two principles. The first is related to individuals abilities to be self-referential leading to self-reflexiveness and self-correctiveness. The second confirms that individuals acquire knowledge through two paths. These two paths complement each other in a synergetic way. These paths are horizontal and vertical knowledge acquisition paths explained earlier by Haji (1986). This implies that theories are tentatively held.

These two principles transform roles of leaders and managers. The transformation occurs to managerial functions in general. In this paper such transformation is elaborated on in relation to planning and decision-making, motivation, and controlling. Below is the discussion exhibiting transformation of selected managerial functions.

Planning consists of roles to setting organizational goals and choosing methods and procedures to achieving them. These roles are mainly assigned to leaders and managers as predetermined by organizational behavior models (Ebert & Griffin, 2019). This demonstrates the dualism assumption and shows employees' passivity. Dualism and passivity perspective in viewing employees may hinder the accomplishment of goals sought. The hindrance may be caused by employees' hidden resistance. The resistance is a resultant to employees' unwillingness to identify with goals set by management. Islam acknowledges the abilities of employees to be self-referential and to develop self-reflexiveness and then to acquire self-correctiveness. These abilities can enable employees to grasp the requirements of organisations and their surroundings. Employees contribution to the goals setting can enhance self -identification and then improve commitment to goals. Some models of organizational behaviour stated above allow employees to participate to planning and decision making processes. However such participation as mentioned aims mainly to achieve organizational goals. Therefore participation based on such models represents elementalisic thinking. Individuals in organizations are only seen as employees. This is incompatible with Islamic view of individuals. Islam state that individuals are capable of making decisions serving organisations and their needs simultaneously (Al-A'ali, (1995)). Individuals are equipped as well with abilities to acquire knowledge horizontally and vertically as mentioned earlier. So employees can enrich the roles of planning and improve methods of implementation on continuous basis.

Ebert and Griffin (2019) state that forces leading individuals to behave in certain ways are classified as motivators. They add that motivation is triggered by external factors. This implies that leaders/managers play major roles in deciding methods to motivate their employees. Internally motivated employees, based on organizational theories, have to be granted the freedom by their leaders to accomplish their work. Dualism underlines motivation theories therefore. Islam as mentioned above leads to transform the organizational behaviour models. The transformation has introduced a different definition of motivation. The definition leads to new applications to motivate employees. Employees based on Islamic perspective are internally motivated (Al-A'ali, 1995)). Individuals' abilities of self-referential, self-reflexiveness and self correctiveness are the major motivators. The is upheld by the synergetic transactions between the three major existents; materialistic objects, mental and artistic. No dualism is assumed.

Controlling as a managerial function aims at dealing with uncertainty and change, errors discovery, cost reduction, productivity increasing and value adding, seizing opportunities, feedback providing and teamwork building and enhancing decision making (kinicki & Williams, 2020)). Islam deals with these aims of controlling through the three abilities of humans stated above. Self referential ability based on self reflexiveness learning can enhance capacity to discover errors made. This can lead to create new methods to produce products. The methods equipped by self correctiveness can lead to add value, reduce the cost, increase productivity and then seizing new opportunities. Feedback is not hierarchical (Al-A'ali, 1999)). Employees continuously reflect on their own work, with their own team and with their managers. Knowledge then is acquired horizontally and vertically as mentioned by Haji (1986). Islam view of change is characterised by being on flux. Al-A'ali (1995) argues that change is an on ongoing process in Islam. Transactions between all existents are continuous. Al-A'ali (1995) illustrates that elementalism underlines organizational views of change. She states that the holistic perspective of humans and existents in Islam leads to the evolution of wholistic perspective of change. The attributes of self referential, self reflexiveness and self correctiveness of humans can overcome resistance of change. Resistance is instigated by the elementalistic view of humans based on models of organizational behaviour The elementalistic views of humans lead to the evolution of partial perspectives of organizational change (Al-A'ali,1995)). Passivity and dualism are the consequences for such views. Change according to organizational theories is not on flux . Al-A'ali (1995) argues passivity assumed of organizational behavior models neglects the benefits of allowing employees to envisage and implement changes. She (1995) adds that Islam upholds the perspective of active roles of individuals in general. These active roles equipped individuals to enacting realities i.e. changes in their life and in organizations. Therefore employees' resistance to changes is minimised and if not eliminated.

CONCLUSION

Organizations are made of individuals working together to achieve predetermined goals and objectives. Behaviour of these individuals decide the levels and quality of performance desired. Many models for organizational behaviour have been postulated to understand humans/individuals behaviour in organizations. The most examined models are human relation, system perspective, productivity perspective, human resource models, contingency and situational. The paper illustrates that these models of behaviour are elementalistic . The elementalism is a function of

Aristotelian structure underlining Indo-European languages. The elementalism neglects the holistic nature of humans and their surroundings. Such elementalism leads to the evolution of assumption of passivity of humans. Dualism is an outcome of elementalism as well. The paper argues that there is a need for a new model. The new model has to correspond to two factors. The first is that the new model has to reflect the holistic nature of humans and their surroundings. The second then states that individuals are self-referential making them able to self-reflect and self-correct. These two factors lead to transform the roles of leaders/managers. The transformation can have positive impacts on organizations, leaders and employees.

REFERENCES

Al-A'ali, E. (1991). *The phenomenon of women in Management: An alternative perspective and its implication in the case of Bahrain* (Unpublished PhD thesis). University of Lancaster.

Al-A'ali, E. (1993). Assumptions Concerning Sicial Sciences: A comparative Perspective. American Journal of Islamic Sciences, 10(4), 485-490.

Al-A'ali, E. (1995). *Organisational change: A transformational perspective. In 1st Annual Asian Academy of Management.* Creating Management Synergy in Asian Economies.

Al-A'ali, E. (1996). *Some Fundamentals features of Arabic-Islamic culture and it's possible contribution to world peace in Creative Peace Through Encounter of World Cultures* (H. Beck & G. Schmirber, Eds.). Sri Satguru Publications.

Al-A'ali, E. (1999). Training in Organizations Training: An Enhancement View. In *1999 International Performance Improvement Conference and Exposition*. Omnipress.

Al-Meraie, A. M. (1984). *Prisoners of Aristotle*. Epistemics Institute Press.

Borkowski, N. (2005). *Overview and History of Organizational Behavior.* In N. Borkowski (Ed.), *Organizational Behavior in Health Care* (pp. 3–13). Jones and Bartlett publishers.

Haj, J. (1986). *Nadhrayat Al-Mahraifah Fi Al-islam* [An Epistemological Theory in Islam]. Al-Alfaen Press.

Ivancevich, J. M., Konopaske, R., & Matteson, M. T. (2014). *Organizational Behavior & Management*. McGraw-Hill Irwin.

Johns, G. (2006). The essential impact of context on organizational behavior. *Academy of Management Review*, *31*(2), 386–408.

Kinicki, A., & Williams, B. K. (2020). Management (9th ed.). New York: McGraw-Hill Education.

Mahgniya, M. J. (1982). *Ma'lam Al-Falsafa Al-Isslammiyyah [The major features of Islamic philosophy]*. Al-Hilal Library.

McEachern, A. (1984). *Organizational Illusions*. Shale Books.

McShane, S. L., & Von Glinow, M. A. (2010). *Organizational Behavior*. McGraw-Hill Irwin.

Moorhead, G., & Griffin, R. S. (2011). Organizational Behavior (11th ed.). Academic Press.

Weick, K. E. (2021). Perspective Construction in Organizational Behavior. *Annual Review of Organizational Psychology and Organizational Behavior, 4*, 1-17. Retrieved from https://www.annualreviews.org/doi/full/10.1146/annurev-orgpsych-032516-113043

Whyte, W. H. (1965). *The Organization Man*. Penguin Books Ltd.

Wibowo, G. (2017). Comparison of the Models of Organizational Behavior: A Review. *Management and Economics Research Journal, 2*, 32-40.

Zohar, D. (1997). *Rewiring the Corporate Brain*. Bevrett-Koehler Publishing.

ADDITIONAL READING

Bois, S. (1970). *Breeds of Men*. Harper and Row Publisher.

Boys, S. (1978). *The Art of Awareness* (3rd ed.). Wm. C. Brown Company.

Burrell, G., & Morgan, G. (1979). *Sociological paradigms and Organizational Analysis*. Gower publishing Company Ltd.

Hawking, S. W. (1988). *A brief History of Time London*. Bantam Press.

Hayakawa, S. I. (1954). What is Meant by Aristotelian Structure of Language. In S. I. Hayakawa (Ed.), *Language, Meaning and Maturity*. Harper and Row Publishers.

Johnson, W. (1946). *People in Quandaries*. Harper and Row Publisher.

Korzybski, A. (1923). *Manhood of Humanity*. The International Non-Aristotelian Library Publishing Company, Institute of General Semantics Distributors.

Maxwell, N. (1984). *From knowledge to wisdom*. Basil Blackwell Ltd.

Morgan, G. (1983). Towards a More Reflective Social Science. In G. Morgan (Ed.), *Beyond Method*. Sage Publications.

Morgan, G. (1986). *Images of Organizations*. Sage Publications Ltd.

Polanyi, M. (1959). *The Study of Men*. The University of Chicago Press.

Williams, W. J. (1972). General Semantics and the Social Sciences. New York: Philosophical. *The Library*.

Williams, W. J. (1978). *Uncommon Sense and Dimensional Awareness*. University Publishers.

Williams, W. J. (1985). *The Miracle of Abduction*. Epistemics Institute Press Inc.

KEY TERMS AND DEFINITIONS

Aristotelian Structure of Language: It is the structure underpinning Indo-European languages. The structure is based on three laws. The first is the law of "is" of identity. The second is the two-value orientation. The third then is the non-middle stance or non-contradiction principle.

Dualism: It is the division of an object and idea into opposed parts.

Horizontal Knowledge: It the addition of new field of study as required.

Humans: The definition of humans in Islam is argued to be holistic. They are at the highest rank of existents. They are equipped with three types of abilities. These are self-referential, self-reflexiveness, and self-correctiveness.

Islam: The paper focuses on some principles of Islam to enhance organizational behaviour theories. The paper is not studying Islam as a religion.

Organizational Behaviour Models: These models reflect assumptions underlying theories related to every model.

Self-Correctiveness: It is the ability to direct and redirect evolution of beings and knowledge generated.

Self-Referential: This is the ability of humans to generate and regenerate of their beings to evolve and transform.

Self-Reflexiveness: This ability is linked with self-referential ability. It illustrates that evolution of self and knowledge based on self-referential is not static. Self and knowledge evolution is subjected for reflection to evolve.

Vertical Knowledge: It is the transformation of theories and principles of a given field of study as needed.

Chapter 2
Do Religion and Spirituality in the Workplace Matter?
Concepts, Perspectives, and Implications

Bradley Saunders
https://orcid.org/0000-0002-2037-9113
American University of Bahrain, Bahrain

Hanan Naser
https://orcid.org/0000-0002-9062-0603
American University of Bahrain, Bahrain

Fatema Alaali
American University of Bahrain, Bahrain

ABSTRACT

Although spirituality in the workplace has recently received extensive attention from many researchers in the field of management, it has often been interchanged with the term religion. Yet religion is neglected. According to Vitell, religion contributes to setting a framework for moral and ethical behavior in a business context, creating a spiritual workplace that is aligned with organizational goals and has a positive impact on productivity and profitability. Therefore, there is a need to conduct more investigations not only to explain the core concept of each, but also to evaluate the effectiveness of each and their integration in the workplace. This chapter addresses the increased demand to better conceptualize, define, and contrast the concepts of religion and spirituality in the workplace. In addition, the impact of leaders' life standards and personal values on behavior in the workplace are examined, with attention on the discussion of the impact of religion and spirituality.

DOI: 10.4018/978-1-7998-9319-6.ch002

INTRODUCTION

Over its long history, the study of management and of organizations has not dedicated much attention to religion (Kim, Fisher & McCalman, 2009). The secular nature of daily activities in modern commercial organizations seems far removed from religious considerations. Indeed, the objectives of the study of the two areas have, it has been claimed, diverged to such a point that they cannot co-exist in harmony (Wicks, 2014). This discord between religion and commerce has arisen as a result of several factors. The growth of rationalism coincided with the rise of Scientific Management and consequently research into the rational planning and development of work activities was influenced by secular thinking (Peltonen, 2020). This led to a movement away from faith-based views towards a system based on rational cause and effect governed by empirical scientific methods. Religion was regarded no longer as a central pillar of thinking but considered rather to be merely a private affair with no logical role to play in research into the activities of large corporations which aspire to be objective, scientific, and value-free (Kim, Fisher & McCalman, 2009).

The infrequency with which religious concepts are mentioned in the management and organizational literature can also be attributed to a prevailing view of religion as a taboo topic (Sandelands, 2003; Chan-Serafin, Brief & George, 2013). As a result of different viewpoints among different religions, discussion of religious matters can be divisive and therefore is often avoided (Van Buren et al, 2020).

Recently, however, some have challenged the view that religion and management are incompatible entities, advocating the integration of spirituality and religion research into the study of organizational practice, highlighting connections between religion and aspects of organizational life. Of the various topics discussed in the literature, this chapter focuses on four discrete yet closely related topics: leadership, corporate culture, ethics and employee well-being.

This chapter examines the potential impact of religion in these areas, addresses some of the key questions and issues related to the topic, points out some possible areas of concern, and discusses future directions of research in this area.

The chapter begins by defining and contrasting the concepts of religion and spirituality. This is followed by an examination of the impact of leaders' life standards and personal values on behaviour in the workplace and a discussion on the search for an integrative, holistic model of leadership incorporating intellectual, emotional, spiritual, and behavioral aspects. It then addresses the impact of religious diversity in the workplace in the light of increasing globalization and increased workforce diversity in effectively recognising the needs and challenges of all groups of employees and thereby enhancing employee engagement. Next, the impact of leadership practices on organizational culture is examined. Attention then turns to the impact of religion and spirituality on Business Ethics, addressing ethical standards, self-identity and the relationship between intrapersonal religiosity and ethical behaviour. Subsequently, the role played by religion and spirituality in coping with adversity and stressors in the workplace is examined.

BACKGROUND

Defining Religion and Spirituality

Despite its presence in their everyday lives, individuals' ability to explain what religion is stems from their cultural experiences and therefore does not address general issues underlying all religious thinking (Rodrigues & Harding, 2008; Schilderman, 2014). Consequently, it is far from straightforward to come up with a universal definition of religion. Although certain religions have aspects in common (e.g. monotheistic religions share a belief in a divine being), basing a definition solely on those common aspects would fail to include other religious traditions which do not include those aspects. To define religion as believing in a divine being – or even in divine beings – would account for monotheistic and polytheistic religions. However, other non-theistic religions such as Buddhism would be excluded (Neo, 2018). Peltonen (2020) supports this view and adds that the fact that major religions such as Christianity and Islam have diverged to form distinct branches with differing viewpoints on key issues further complicates any attempt to agree on a universal definition.

Other studies define religiosity or religion as a structure of beliefs and practices (Rodrigues & Harding, 2008). Hence, there are intrinsic and extrinsic forms of religiosity. Intrinsic religiosity refers to believing in a religion and having an identity defined by the religion, while extrinsic religiosity refers to the use of religion in practices that benefit society (Chowdhury & Fernando, 2013).

The term spirituality is often used synonymously with the term religiosity as either explaining the relationship between God and oneself or the interconnection among souls (Ashmos & Duchon, 2000; Korac-Kakabadse et al.,2002). In contrast, Zellars et al. (2010) distinguish between spirituality as a wide term that embeds one's beliefs and values, and religiosity as a narrow concept that may focus on specific rituals, prayers, ideas, rules, and codes. Religion may demonstrate a path for spirituality as claimed by Dent et al. (2005) and accordingly incorporate a set of rules and practices which may vary among different religions.

Both religiosity and spirituality are multidimensional, but it is worth noting that psychologists have defined them in many ways (Zinnbauer & Pargament, 2005). Spirituality is not explicitly separated from religiosity but it is more concerned about the quality of human spirit including the different positive concepts such as care, forgiveness, love, patience, and others that allow one to blend smoothly with one's environment (Hill et al., 2000; Snyder & Lopez, 2009).

RELIGION AND SPIRITUALITY IN THE WORKPLACE

The focus of this chapter is on identifying ways in which religion and spirituality could be put into practice and used to serve organizational goals. In particular, attention is directed to the role leaders' actions and thinking play in formulating and shaping a corporate culture which will foster ethical behavior and so enhance employees' sense of personal well-being.

Clearly, any examination of organizational goals and the policies put in place in order to achieve them, needs to take into account the nature of the leadership within the organization. This requires an examination of leadership. Leadership is by its very nature forward-looking; it sets out a mission and vision and a way to achieve these (Kotter, 1996). Among the most basic requirements of a leader is the ability to drive change and optimize its impact on the organization's stakeholders. Leadership has been defined as the ability to lift other workers, build their capacity, and help them to excel beyond limits (Drucker, 1985). Accordingly, leadership ability can significantly influence an organization's level of success. Yet in order to achieve these goals, a leader is exposed to the temptation to act unethically, for example by valuing personal gain over the group's best interests, by abusing his/her power to harm potential rivals, or by turning a blind eye to questionable, but profitable business practices. Ciulla (2005) describes a successful leader as someone who does the right thing but also does it in the right way and for the right reasons.

In examining and evaluating a leader's performance, to what extent do religion and spirituality play a role in influencing a leader to 'do the right thing'? How have factors such as globalization, rapid changes in technology, and social unrest made leadership more challenging (Gardner & Schermerhorn, 2004)? There is a need to develop a leadership model that accounts for more meaningful aspects of individuals (Fernandez, 2004). In the words of Antoine de Saint-Exupéry: 'If you want to build a ship, don't drum up the men to gather wood, divide the work and give orders. Instead, teach them to yearn for the vast and endless sea.'

Kouzes et al. (2004) have explained how life standards and personal values can be incorporated to form a credible leader. They argued that whenever a leader is found to be highly aware of her/himself and accordingly acts authentically, then other employees can be empowered to achieve both personal and organizational success. This reflects that such leaders are focused and committed not only for their personal development but also committed to continued learning to strengthen their own capabilities and those of their followers. In other words, such leaders are concerned in building an organizational culture that is associated with a normative sense of goodness (spirituality) and incorporates humanitarian concerns and outcomes. Fry (2003) has claimed that creating a spiritual workplace that is aligned with organizational goals has a positive impact on productivity and profitability.

Despite the growing literature in this field, Dugan and Komives (2011) claim that leadership theory has a clear shortage, complex, generally constructed and is endlessly evolving.

Spiritual Leadership

Due to the shortage in the majority of earlier studies in the field, Gill (2006) has suggested building an integrative, holistic model of leadership taking into consideration four key dimensions of leadership studies including intellectual, emotional, spiritual, and behavioral (Bryman, 2011). Accordingly, the theory of spiritual leadership has evolved and received much attention from researchers in the field of management. In religion and philosophy, spirit is an intangible material of a human being and can still function even after death (Baloğlu & Karadağ, 2009). Fairholm (1996) was the first researcher to connect the term spirit with leadership and was followed by many studies aiming to frame and to better explain the role and impact of spirituality in the context of the workplace (Dent et al., 2005; Fry, 2005). Fairholm (1996) argued that the power of the spirit not only keeps people alive, but also strengthens the deep connection with the self which enables individuals to empower creativity, permeate the entire system and accordingly improve the quality of organizational output (Fawcett et al., 2008). Studies such as Dent et al. (2005) proposed that building a positive and strong spiritual leadership foundation in the workplace is important to earn workers' spiritual satisfaction, which in turn will lead to enhanced productivity.

According to Fry et al. (2005), spiritual leadership emerges from the interaction of noble love, vision, and hope/faith in organizational members. It can be described as a causal leadership for organizational transformation intended to build an intrinsically motivated learning organization. The primary development of the theory of spiritual leadership is attributed to the demand for excellence in organizational commitment, a higher level of productivity, and better well-being for employees. The operation of spiritual leadership includes the required values, attitudes, and behaviors that may foster one's own and others' motivation, so they have a sense of spiritual survival through calling and membership (belonging). This will satisfy the essential needs of both leader and follower for spiritual survival and also facilitate the creation of congruence of vision and value across the individual, empowered team, and organization (Malone & Fry, 2003).

Although there is a growing literature that tackles the issue of spirituality, low attention has been paid to religiosity in leadership. Some studies have linked it directly with spirituality, arguing that religiosity in leadership is considered as spiritual leadership (Sanders, 1988). For example, Sanders (1988) suggested that spiritual leadership reflects the acknowledgement of and confidence in God. it is motivated by the love of God which can be reflected by following God's path (Barton & Ford, 2008), It is therefore a result of having faith in God and being religious and accordingly such leadership is according to God's calling.

Workplaces are generally composed of individuals – both leaders and followers – of different faiths. According to Pew Forum's U.S. Religious Landscape Survey (2008), 89% of respondents report religious/ spiritual diversity among their organization's employees. The same instrument revealed a very high degree of cooperation (98%) among employees belonging to different religious groups (SHRM, 2008). These results would seem to support the claim that the desire for an inclusive and welcoming work environment is more influential in employees' day-to-day workplace interactions than the religious differences that set them apart. This in turn supports the theory that religion and spirituality can enhance employee satisfaction and productivity in the workplace. Cavanagh (1999) suggests that people should extract their core values from their religions to better communicate with other workers. In addition, it has been suggested that leaders should take on the role of spiritual guides rather than religious guides (Hicks, 2003). Goethals and Sorenson (2006) have expanded this argument noting that managing or leading on a religious basis in the workplace can easily lead to conflicts. They have also claimed that an equal emphasis on all different religions is unachievable, therefore the best way to manage or lead in the workplace is by respecting each other's beliefs and depending on shared core values. Based on these statements, it is revealed that differentiating between the terms of religiousness and spirituality is a necessity and it will be essential for the organization.

Researchers have exerted a great deal of effort in investigating not only leadership concepts, but also the impact of leadership practices on organizational culture (McKee, 2003; Verschoor, 2006). Bodinson (2005) claimed that leadership is the only thing that can develop organizational culture. Despite the numerous studies that have extensively attempted to define organizational culture and its features, there is no clear agreement on what culture is the best at generating improvements in organizational output.

Unsurprisingly, people define culture in many ways. For example, Kilmann et al. (1985) suggest that culture is `philosophy, ideology, values, beliefs, assumptions, and norms shared together.' They have also claimed that the intangible power of culture plays a significant role in driving workers' actions in the workplace. Other studies explained the different components of organizational culture such as ideas, cognition, and/or the holistic nature of culture (Ajiferuke & Boddewyn, 1970; Sackmann, 1991). Based on theoretical studies, organizational culture is a result of dynamic interactions of employee movements, behavior, and attitude. It brings together the basic assumptions that are built to overcome external and internal challenges.

In line with the above, scientists have introduced two different theories that describe the openness of an organizational culture. The first is called open system theory, which simply describes the culture of an organization that interacts with its surroundings (Katz & Kahn, 1978), while the second is opposite to the first and is called closed system theory (Cole, 1993). According to Katz & Khan (1978), an organization can simply be described as an energic system that depends on its inputs where the environment is supporting the open system and ensuring that inputs have gone through different activities and interactions with individuals to yield outputs. In terms of functioning, an open system does not operate in isolation as it is interdependent and interacts with the greater system (environment) via management subsystems such as production, support, maintenance, adaptation, and management. Other scholars have shown interest to more sensitive aspects of organizational culture such as administration of culture, power of culture, culture changes, and others (Cameron & Ettington, 1988; Lundberg, 1988; Smart & Hamm, 1992).

There are three main factors that determine the orientation of culture in an organization. Defining, communicating, and supporting these three factors - attribution to workplace, organizational climate and core values - can make a significant impact on productivity. In addition, once a people-centered culture is born in an organization, workers' capacity and productivity both expand leading to more organizational success (Neal & Griffin, 1999).

Success Culture

Since organizational culture plays a significant role in fostering workers' creativity and passion, organizations would be well advised to pay a good deal of attention to investing in their culture. This will allow workers to feel that they are valued, and their existence has a purpose (King & Nicol, 1999). Otherwise, both organizational structure and culture may inhibit workers' development, which will result in a non-productive environment (Jaques, 1976). In other words, both workers and organizations can shine in a people-centered culture.

Spirituality in Culture

Since the 1990s, both religion and spirituality in the workplace have been extensively investigated by extensive studies (Cash et al., 2000). Studies argued that elements of organizational spirituality and a culture of success can both push the organizational environment from being limiting into inspiring (Konz & Ryan, 1999). Many organizations in the US, UK, and the Netherlands have expressed an interest in discussing the impact of spirituality in the workplace (Auper & Houtman, 2006). For example, many US business organizations have shown growing interest in global views and practices of the New Age and accordingly large companies such as Guinness, General Dynamics, and Boeing Aerospace have received in-company training (Auper & Houtman, 2006). In the Netherlands, the list of companies that have received in-company training is lengthy and includes major Dutch banks and insurance companies such as ABN Amro, ING, Rabobank, and Zwitserleven and Delta Lioyd, in addition to IT companies such as IBM Nederland and CMG (Auper & Houtman, 2006). The focus of many studies is built on finding out how different traditions of spirituality can be implemented in the workplace for efficient management (Brown, 2003).

To emphasize the interest in spirituality in organizations, researchers have developed different arguments in the area. Fry et al. (2011) have paid considerable attention to spiritual solutions that may improve unstable social and business changes. Another strand in the literature has emphasized how global changes have influenced spiritual awareness (Duchon & Plowman, 2005). Accordingly, many organizations have concluded that a humanistic workplace generates a win-win situation among employees and organizations. To have productive and creative workers, organizations should ensure workers' happiness and satisfaction (Garcia-Zamor, 2003).

Since both religion and spirituality were always connected to each other in the literature, the impact of religion on organizational culture cannot be neglected. Many studies have investigated the relationship between religion and work attitudes such as that of motivation, satisfaction, and commitment (Parboteeah et al., 2010).

Having a glance at the global population, it is revealed that 72% of the global population in 2004 were practicing different beliefs under one of the most popular religious systems such as Judaism, Christianity, Islam, Hinduism, and Buddhism. On the other hand, many were atheists and non-religious people. Therefore, it can be assumed that a similar breakdown of religious to non-religious people occurs in organizations, which will influence organizational culture (Mazur, 2015). The spillover of workers' religious views, behavior and preferences directly influence engagement within organizational life as well as decision making towards organizational investments. For instance, faith-based mutual funds built on the ethical basics of a specific religion should be very critical in choosing suitable securities and excluding firms that violate their beliefs. So, investors in such cases take decisions and actions that are in line with their faith. Others develop organizational set up, regulations, and core business under the influence of religions such as Islamic Banking which is built on Sharia and prohibit Reba which is the inflated interest associated with financial loans (Gellman, 2013).

Through the creation of diverse groups in an organization, many benefits may be derived because of having uniquely talented workers with different experiences, backgrounds, and potential to compete in a global market. Van Buren et al. (2020) claimed that promoting religious and ethical values, integrity and ethical conduct are all benefits for any organization. This can play a significant positive role as a driver in social, environmental, and governance challenges.

Ethics

In the last two decades, the world has witnessed a number of instances of business malfeasance that resulted in corporate scandals such as Enron, Worldcom, Parmalat, ComRoad and the Volkswagen emissions scandal, among others. These scandals happened through different paths such as keeping huge debts off balance sheets, reporting fake earnings, falsifying revenues or creating fake assets. Most of these events have led to large financial losses for the stockholders and investors and to the companies filing for bankruptcy. The dominant component among these scandals is the unethical action taken by managers, accountants, bankers and lawyers.

Business Ethics points to the principled perspectives of an organization or entrepreneurship that are involved in their attitude or clearly articulated in their governing codes (Cowton & Crisp, 1998). Several studies show that the presence of a code of ethics promotes ethical behavior in organizations (Adams, Tashchian & Shore 2001; Downe, Cowell & Morgan, 2016). However, the efficiency of codes depends on the organizational culture (Ethics Resource Center 2005).

The significance of the ethical climate in encouraging ethical behavior has been emphasized in numerous studies (Racelis, 2010; Lu & Lin, 2014). The term ethical climate has been defined as "the shared perception of what is correct behavior and how ethical situations should be handled in an organization" (Victor & Cullen, 1987: 51). Ethical climates evolve as a consequence of an organization's formation and implementation of policies. They can have a significant impact on the ethical decision making of employees and their subsequent attitudes and behavior (Newman et al., 2018). The existence of an ethical climate in organizational policies, the hiring procedure and the compensation structure will encourage employees to operate more efficiently and work on better relationships with their clients (Weeks et al., 2004). Luria & Yagil (2008) examined the relationship between ethical climate and service outcomes in restaurants. Their research set out to identify the reasons behind the positive impact of ethical climate on service performance. Their findings state that ethical climate is composed of perception of responsibility, trust and high moral criterion. Such perceptions positively affect employees' adherence to service quality, which has a positive impact on organizational performance.

Weaver & Agle (2002) introduced a framework for the role of religion in fostering the ethical behavior in an organization. They state that religion will have an impact on employee behavior if self-identity, role expectations and identity prominence are aligned with a religious identity. For instance, if the religion prompts obeying parents, then the expected role could be a "responsible child". In addition, an employee would accept the role prescribed by the religion if s/he identifies her/himself with a religious identity. Moreover, if the identity is prominent so that many reminders of the religion exist in the work environment, the employee will perform according to the role expectations.

Religiosity was defined by McDaniel and Burnett (1990) as the belief in God complemented by an adherence to all the principles set forth by God. Vitell (2009) stated that religion contributes to setting a framework for moral and ethical behavior in a business context. This does not indicate that religion is the only origin for morality but an essential one. Wiebe & Fleck (1980) conclude that religious people have a higher level of moral standards, commitment and responsibility in contrast to non-religious people. Epstein (2002) noted that the role of religion in business ethical behavior was not examined empirically until the mid-1990s. The results of the empirical studies that investigate the relationship between religion and ethical behavior are not consistent. A large number of studies found a significant positive impact of religion on ethical decision making (Conroy & Emerson, 2004; Phau & Kea, 2007;Fernando & Chowdhury, 2010; Ho, 2010). However, several other papers found an insignificant impact of religion on ethical behavior (Oumlil & Balloun, 2009). Religiosity is found to support an individual's commitment to moral self-improvement, but it is not related to better ethics (Kurpis et al., 2008).

It is interesting to note that India, with its strong religious background, was ranked the most corrupt country in the Asian Pacific area in 2017. Goel & Misra (2020) examined the relationship between religiosity and attitude towards business ethics. Their results show that religious individuals have an ethical path towards business matters. Moreover, they found that only intrapersonal religiosity (an individual's metaphysical belief) has an impact on attitude towards business ethics. This suggests that pursuing religious beliefs is more essential than just attending religious events.

Employee Well-Being

Employee well-being is the comprehensive quality of experiences and performance of an employee (Warr, 1987). This holistic description is based on three core dimensions: psychological wellbeing, physical wellbeing and social wellbeing. Psychological and physical wellbeing are features of the individual employee, whereas social wellbeing concentrates on communication between employees (Grant, Christianson & Price, 2007). Harter et al. (2002) state that employees spend a considerable part of their life at the workplace, therefore employers should promote employees' wellbeing at the workplace. Bakke (2005) relates employees' wellbeing to a work environment that makes work exciting, rewarding, stimulating and enjoyable.

It has been agreed that workplace spirituality enhances employees' well-being in the workplace. Spirituality is described as having two dimensions: vertical and horizontal. The vertical dimension reflects a deep relation with God, and this can be shown by silence before the start of meetings, meditation training and supporting employees to be granted breaks for spiritual conduct as applied at Intel, Microsoft and Boeing. The horizontal dimension involves actions done for society improvement, such as helping others and serving people (Altaf & Awan, 2011). Workplace spirituality refers to the achievement of both the vertical and horizontal dimensions (Hungelmann et al., 1985). Achieving both sides may result in employee satisfaction as well as a higher level of productivity, morale and competition.

The Attraction-Selection-Attrition (ASA) theory developed by Schneider (1987) proposes that employees are attracted to organizations which recognize their identity, values, principles, faith and interest. The major assumptions of the ASA theory are: 1) Attraction: employees are enticed to join organizations whose workers have the same identity, interests, values and other characteristics; 2) Selection: organizations appoint individuals with analogous proficiencies and competencies as their existing members; and 3) Attrition: in the long term, members who are not meeting the expectation of the organization will most probably leave.

Lee et al. (2003) employed the spillover theory (Diener, 2009; Wilensky, 1960) to explain the impact of spiritual values on life satisfaction. They state that there are two forms of spillover: vertical and horizontal spillover. The vertical spillover suggests that satisfaction in one life domain has a vertical spillover to the most subordinate domain, life satisfaction. For instance, spiritual satisfaction affects life satisfaction positively (Paloutzian, 1996). This can be explained through providing a purposeful objective in life and social support. This relationship is strengthened when an individual is intrinsically religious or affiliated with a religious group. The horizontal spillover shows that satisfaction in one life domain leads to satisfaction in a neighboring life domain (Diener, 2009). For instance, spiritual satisfaction may affect job satisfaction positively as the spirituality implants meaning into work (Emmons, 1999).

Several studies have empirically examined the relationship between spirituality and religiosity on people's well-being. Koburtay & Alzoubi (2021) examined the spirituality fit between employees and their workplaces. Their results indicate that investing in spirituality of employees positively affects their well-being and accordingly affects the organization's position positively. Hashemi et el. (2020) investigated the input of religious identity and other factors on the psychological well-being of Middle Eastern migrants in Australia. They note that "engagement in religious activities, and belief in [Allah] provide individuals with a sense of significance, positive emotions, self-esteem, positive relations, sense of meaning, and purpose in life". Karakas (2010) reviewed about 140 articles about workplace spirituality. They introduced three aspects about the way that spirituality supports workers and benefits organizational achievement: 1) spirituality boosts workers' well-being and their life quality; 2) spirituality adds an aim and meaning for employees' work; 3) spirituality strengthens interrelations among employees. Koburtay & Syed

(2021) studied the effect of adhering to religious regulations and providing spiritual facilities on the psychological well-being of hotel workers. Their results show that not adhering to religious regulations negatively influences employees' well-being whereas spiritual facilities reinforce their well-being. Haldorai et al. (2020) stated that workplace spirituality helps workers recognize their major purpose in life, strengthen relationships with their colleagues and align their beliefs with the organization's values. Reinforcing workplace spirituality will help employees meaningfully engage in their work as well as act efficiently in teams. According to Altaf & Awan (2011), when employees are experiencing spirituality in the work environment, they will have better interaction and communication. Communication enhancement between employees may reinforce trust among them and help them face their workload and avoid work stress and burnout.

SOLUTIONS AND RECOMMENDATIONS

Leadership

Since spirituality plays a vital role in creating a positive, creative, and productive environment in the workplace, organizations should gradually introduce it in steps or stages to allow for sustainable organizational development. At all stages, spirituality is a key motivator for both employers and employees. It shows that business ethics, values, and culture of care are all aligned, allowing employees to remain motivated and enabling them to continue to pursue the employer's path.

It is very important to expand employees' knowledge and allow them to differentiate between religiosity and spirituality. This process encourages those of different faiths to overlook differences and emphasise commonalities. It can be done via many different approaches such as counseling, discussions, seminars, or training.

Organizations should not only emphasize the concept of spirituality, but also grant recognition to different practices, thereby signaling that they respect them and consequently enhancing the impact of organizational policies on employees, groups, leadership, culture, and productivity.

Culture

Organizations should strive to enhance the relationship between workers, managers and other stakeholders. Having informal communication channels can help in improving openness and accordingly influence creativity and innovations in the organization. Clarity in communication will lead to better awareness and so help to minimize conflict and reduce the need for costly and time consuming conflict resolution measures.

In order for employees to feel that they are valued, that their existence is meaningful, and that they serve a purpose, organizations should engage employees in a variety of different activities, encourage collaborative work across departments, host celebrations of a range of religious festivals and allow employees to organize faith-based informal gatherings. Doing so will not only foster a sense of community and help employees to pursue a unified vision which gives their work a purpose, but also it will play a significant role in boosting employee morale, making them feel recognized and satisfied. Ensuring employees' happiness by enabling them to engage in meaningful work should be an organizational objective as productive and loyal workers are the main output of such a culture. Another way of increasing employee motivation and productivity is by providing dedicated quiet areas for meditation and prayer.

However, the decision to allow religious activities such as prayer and scripture study in the workplace may have a negative impact by generating proselytism. This can be partially offset by anti-harassment training (SHRM, 2008).

A culture which values a spiritual component should be consistently clear and transparent (Warrick, 2017). For example the staffing process - from the point of view of both the employer and the candidates - should be built on clarity and transparency. On the one hand, the employer should have a clear vision, mission, objectives, and values in order to build trust. On the other hand, candidates' values and objectives should be tested from the point of staffing. The impact of having common objectives and values cannot be neglected. The nature of the job, duties, and responsibilities should also be clear from the beginning.

As research into spirituality in the workplace has shown, people have emotional and cognitive needs which they bring with them into the workplace. The quest for spirituality fulfilment requires meaningful work, meaningful interactions with others and self-development. Consequently, employers should consider the benefits of providing their employees with considerable learning opportunities which may directly influence their contribution to organizational goals, allow them to remain focused on their profession, and open doors for future career developments. Being appreciated, recognized, and valued for individual or group success can work as a vital booster for individual and organizational development, thereby improving retention.

Ethics

Organizations whose employees are in continuous interaction with customers should give more attention to workplace spirituality and create an ethical climate.

By promoting workplace spirituality, employees may be inherently stimulated and may function with their entire ability. Accordingly, a workplace that is centered on spirituality may boost employees' attitudes and increase their productivity by engaging meaningfully in their work and making a difference through their distinctive input. Moreover, workplace spirituality highlights teamwork that is translated into good relations with coworkers and work-related society.

There are various channels to foster ethical behavior in any organization. Golestanipour (2016) states that an ethical leader using spirituality in the organization will have intrinsic motivation and will be a source of motivation for his/her team. An ethical leader will be honest with the employees, offer them essential and adequate support, reward ethical behavior and penalize unethical behavior. Managers may maintain an ethical environment through conducting regular workshops to strengthen ethical behavior among employees. Institutionalizing ethical conduct will stimulate employees to keep up standards. Leaders may use different simulation practices such as role plays and videos to illustrate the effect of unethical behavior on employees and the organization.

To enhance ethical behavior, HR can link employees' performance evaluations and their remunerations to their ethical behavior. HR managers can anonymously gather feedback from employees about ethical and unethical workplace issues. Furthermore, organizations should offer counseling services to guide employees when they are involved in unethical conduct as a result of work circumstances such as when confronted by an uncooperative colleague or an impolite client (Haldorai et al., 2020).

Well-being

Karakas (2010) claims that integrating spirituality in the workplace and supporting employees in practicing their spiritual beliefs boosts employees' well-being. He proposes a number of practices in order to incorporate spirituality in the workplace: 1) arrangements for spiritual requests (managers should respond to the different spiritual requests as long as they do not limit the freedom of others (Cavanagh, 1999); 2) respect for diversity, (Hicks (2003) claimed that managers should work on providing a respectful `and indulgent environment so that workers are free to discuss their own beliefs and ideas on spirituality) and 3) freedom of expression (employees should be able to express their feelings and values regardless of fear in a positive atmosphere (Krishnakumar & Neck, 2002)).

HR managers should be asked to develop procedures and regulations to restrain any form of religious discrimination. They need to carefully examine existing policies in order to identify any potential for discrimination to occur unintentionally. For example, an organization's dress policy may require employees to be clean shaven and so unintentionally discriminate against Sikhs or shift schedules may require Christian employees to work on a Sunday. Care should be taken to ensure equity of treatment for different religions in such cases.

FUTURE RESEARCH DIRECTIONS

As highlighted above, there has been a paucity of studies into the role religion can play in organasational success and more studies into the impact of religion and spirituality on the performance of organizations is required. In particular there is a need for studies into the impact of religion and spirituality on leadership, ethics, corporate culture and employee well-being. Suggested topics of study include:

- the impact of external factors such as globalization, rapid changes in technology, and social unrest on the application of a spiritual leadership approach in organizations
- the effects of religious diversity in the workplace on the psychological well-being of expatriate workers working in a country with a dominant religion different to their own, such as non-Muslims working in Middle Eastern countries
- the efficiency of codes of ethics in supporting spiritual aspects of an organizational culture
- the role played by religion and spirituality in coping with adversity and stressors in the workplace

Whilst the above is not intended to constitute an exhaustive list, it highlights some areas of potential interest for management researchers wishing to explore the interconnections between religion and spirituality and organizational performance.

CONCLUSION

Although there would appear to be a disconnect between the interpretation and implementation of religious teachings and the commercial pursuit of profit, several recent studies have stressed the interconnections between the two. Long regarded as a taboo topic, religion and spirituality can be seen to be a driving force in setting out a roadmap towards the achievement of organizational goals and the empowerment of employees. A distinction was made between religion as a narrow concept with a focus on practices and rules, and spirituality as a broad term referring to more general beliefs and values which influence our interconnections with others.

In the analysis of leadership, the powerful impact of a spiritual leadership approach on the spiritual satisfaction of organizational members was shown to result in better productivity. However, care must be taken not to be seen to favour a particular faith, which would lead to conflicts. Thus a spiritual rather than a religious approach is preferable to ensure that shared core values and beliefs of the employees are respected. This is of particular importance in today's increasingly globalized workplace in which a highly diverse workforce brings different religious and cultural aspects to be considered.

One major impact of leadership is the forging and maintenance of an organizational culture and here too religion and spirituality play a role by instilling employees with the sense that their work is meaningful and enabling them to benefit from the existence of communities within the workplace allowing them to share spiritual activities and discussions with others of a similar outlook. This increases satisfaction by reducing the gap between the issues of concern to employees outside of the workplace and those that they encounter in the workplace.

A series of high profile scandals arising from unethical business behaviour raises many questions. Given that a central feature of religion is the existence of a set of rules to eradicate unethical conduct, can a spiritual leadership approach help to prevent such events from happening? To what extent do ethical codes of conduct and ethical climates play a role in this respect? Research to date has been inconclusive.

Integrating spirituality in the workplace improves employees' psychological, physical and social well-being. This will enable them to meaningfully engage in their work and function efficiently in teams. Organizations should strive to accommodate spiritual requests and foster a respectful and open environment in which workers are free to discuss their beliefs. Organizations should restrain any form of religious discrimination, whether intentional or not and ensure equity of treatment for different faiths.

REFERENCES

Adams, J. S., Tashchian, A., & Shore, T. H. (2001). Codes of ethics as signals for ethical behavior. *Journal of Business Ethics*, *29*(3), 199–211. doi:10.1023/A:1026576421399

Ajiferuke, M., & Boddewyn, J. (1970). "Culture" and other explanatory variables in comparative management studies. *Academy of Management Journal*, *13*(2), 153–163.

Altaf, A., & Awan, M. A. (2011). Moderating affect of workplace spirituality on the relationship of job overload and job satisfaction. *Journal of Business Ethics*, *104*(1), 93–99. doi:10.100710551-011-0891-0

Ashmos, D. P., & Duchon, D. (2000). Spirituality at work: A conceptualization and measure. *Journal of Management Inquiry*, *9*(2), 134–145. doi:10.1177/105649260092008

Auper, S., & Houtman, D. (2006). Oriental religion in the secular west: Globalization, new age, and the reenchantment of the world. *Globalization and Social Change*, 82.

Bakke, D. W. (2005). Joy at Work: A Revolutionary Approach to Fun on the Job. Penguin Group Inc.

Baloğlu, N., & Karadağ, E. (2009). A theoretical analysis about spiritual leadership. *Kuram ve Uygulamada Eğitim Yönetimi*, *58*, 165–190.

Bodinson, G. W. (2005). Change healthcare organizations from good to great. *Quality Progress*, *38*(11), 22.

Brown, R. B. (2003). Organizational spirituality: The sceptic's version. *Organization*, *10*(2), 393–400. doi:10.1177/1350508403010002013

Bryman, A. (Ed.). (2011). *The SAGE handbook of leadership*. Sage Publications.

Cameron, K. S., & Ettington, D. R. (1988). The conceptual foundations of organizational culture. In J. Smart (Ed.), *Higher education handbook of theory and research* (pp. 356–396). Agathon Press.

Cash, K. C., Gray, G. R., & Rood, S. A. (2000). A Framework for Accommodating Religion and Spirituality in the Workplace [and Executive Commentary]. *The Academy of Management Executive*, 124-134.

Cavanagh, G. F. (1999). Spirituality for managers: Context and critique. *Journal of Organizational Change Management*, *12*(3), 186–199. doi:10.1108/09534819910273793

Chan-Serafin, S., Brief, A. P., & George, J. M. (2013). Perspective—How does religion matter and why? Religion and the organizational sciences. *Organization Science*, *24*(5), 1585–1600. doi:10.1287/orsc.1120.0797

Chowdhury, R. M., & Fernando, M. (2013). The role of spiritual well-being and materialism in determining consumers' ethical beliefs: An empirical study with Australian consumers. *Journal of Business Ethics*, *113*(1), 61–79. doi:10.100710551-012-1282-x

Ciulla, J. B. (2005). Integrating leadership with ethics: Is good leadership contrary to human nature. *Handbook on responsible leadership and governance in global business*, 159-179.

Cole, G. A. (1993). *Management Theory and Practice*. DP Publication Ltd.

Conroy, S. J., & Emerson, T. L. (2004). Business ethics and religion: Religiosity as a predictor of ethical awareness among students. *Journal of Business Ethics*, *50*(4), 383–396. doi:10.1023/B:BUSI.0000025040.41263.09

Cowton, C., & Crisp, R. (1998). *Business ethics: perspectives on the practice of theory*. Oxford University Press.

Dent, E. B., Higgins, M. E., & Wharff, D. M. (2005). Spirituality and leadership: An empirical review of definitions, distinctions, and embedded assumptions. *The Leadership Quarterly*, *16*(5), 625–653. doi:10.1016/j.leaqua.2005.07.002

Diener, E. (2009). Subjective well-being. *The science of well-being*, 11-58.

Downe, J., Cowell, R., & Morgan, K. (2016). What determines ethical behavior in public organizations: Is it rules or leadership? *Public Administration Review*, *76*(6), 898–909. doi:10.1111/puar.12562

Drucker, P. F. (1985). The discipline of innovation. *Harvard Business Review*, *63*(3), 67–72. PMID:10272260

Duchon, D., & Plowman, D. A. (2005). Nurturing the spirit at work: Impact on work unit performance. *The Leadership Quarterly*, *16*(5), 807–833. doi:10.1016/j.leaqua.2005.07.008

Dugan, J. P., & Komives, S. R. (2011). Leadership theories. *The handbook for student leadership development*, 35-57.

Emmons, R. A. (1999). Religion in the psychology of personality: An introduction. *Journal of Personality*, *67*(6), 874–888. doi:10.1111/1467-6494.00076

Epstein, E. M. (2002). Religion and business–the critical role of religious traditions in management education. *Journal of Business Ethics*, *38*(1), 91–96. doi:10.1023/A:1015712827640

Ethics Resource Center. (2005). *The 2005 National Business Ethics Survey*. Ethics Resource Center.

Fairholm, G. W. (1996). Spiritual leadership: Fulfilling whole-self needs at work. *Leadership and Organization Development Journal*, *17*(5), 11–17. doi:10.1108/01437739610127469

Fawcett, S. E., Brau, J. C., Rhoads, G. K., Whitlark, D., & Fawcett, A. M. (2008). Spirituality and organizational culture: Cultivating the ABCs of an inspiring workplace. *International Journal of Public Administration*, *31*(4), 420–438. doi:10.1080/01900690701590819

Fernandez, J. A. (2004). The gentleman's code of Confucius: Leadership by values. *Organizational Dynamics*, *33*(1), 21–21. doi:10.1016/j.orgdyn.2003.11.007

Fernando, M., & Chowdhury, R. M. (2010). The relationship between spiritual well-being and ethical orientations in decision making: An empirical study with business executives in Australia. *Journal of Business Ethics*, *95*(2), 211–225. doi:10.100710551-009-0355-y

Fry, L. W. (2003). Toward a theory of spiritual leadership. *The Leadership Quarterly*, *14*(6), 693–727. doi:10.1016/j.leaqua.2003.09.001

Fry, L. W. (2005). Introduction to the leadership quarterly special issue: Toward a paradigm of spiritual leadership. *The Leadership Quarterly*, *16*(5), 619–622. doi:10.1016/j.leaqua.2005.07.001

Fry, L. W., Hannah, S. T., Noel, M., & Walumbwa, F. O. (2011). Impact of spiritual leadership on unit performance. *The Leadership Quarterly*, *22*(2), 259–270. doi:10.1016/j.leaqua.2011.02.002

Fry, L. W., Vitucci, S., & Cedillo, M. (2005). Spiritual leadership and army transformation: Theory, measurement, and establishing a baseline. *The Leadership Quarterly*, *16*(5), 835–862. doi:10.1016/j.leaqua.2005.07.012

Garcia-Zamor, J. C. (2003). Workplace spirituality and organizational performance. *Public Administration Review*, *63*(3), 355–363. doi:10.1111/1540-6210.00295

Gardner, W. L., & Schermerhorn, J. R. Jr. (2004). Unleashing individual potential. *Organizational Dynamics*, *3*(33), 270–281. doi:10.1016/j.orgdyn.2004.06.004

Gellman, L. (2013). Investing as a religious practice. *The Wall Street Journal*.

Gill, R. (2006). Theory and practice of leadership. *Sage (Atlanta, Ga.)*.

Goel, P., & Misra, R. (2020). It's not inter-religiosity but intra-religiosity that really matters in attitude towards business ethics: Evidence from India. *International Journal of Ethics and Systems*, *36*(2), 167–184. doi:10.1108/IJOES-10-2018-0153

Golestanipour, M. (2016). Simple and multiple relationships between ethical leadership, transformational leadership and ethical climate and organizational spirituality among the employees of the Iran national steel industrial group. *Review of European Studies*, *8*(2), 183. doi:10.5539/res.v8n2p183

Grant, A. M., Christianson, M. K., & Price, R. H. (2007). Happiness, health, or relationships? Managerial practices and employee well-being tradeoffs. *The Academy of Management Perspectives*, *21*(3), 51–63. doi:10.5465/amp.2007.26421238

Haldorai, K., Kim, W. G., Chang, H. S., & Li, J. J. (2020). Workplace spirituality as a mediator between ethical climate and workplace deviant behavior. *International Journal of Hospitality Management*, *86*, 102372. doi:10.1016/j.ijhm.2019.102372

Harter, J. K., Schmidt, F. L., & Hayes, T. L. (2002). Business-unit-level relationship between employee satisfaction, employee engagement, and business outcomes: A meta-analysis. *The Journal of Applied Psychology*, *87*(2), 268–279. doi:10.1037/0021-9010.87.2.268 PMID:12002955

Hashemi, N., Marzban, M., Sebar, B., & Harris, N. (2020). Religious identity and psychological well-being among middle-eastern migrants in Australia: The mediating role of perceived social support, social connectedness, and perceived discrimination. *Psychology of Religion and Spirituality*, *12*(4), 475–486. doi:10.1037/rel0000287

Hicks, D. A. (2003). *Religion and the workplace: Pluralism, spirituality, leadership*. Cambridge University Press. doi:10.1017/CBO9780511615474

Hill, P. C., Pargament, K. I., Hood, R. W., McCullough, J. M. E., Swyers, J. P., Larson, D. B., & Zinnbauer, B. J. (2000). Conceptualizing religion and spirituality: Points of commonality, points of departure. *Journal for the Theory of Social Behaviour*, *30*(1), 51–77. doi:10.1111/1468-5914.00119

Ho, J. A. (2010). Ethical perception: Are differences between ethnic groups situation dependent? *Business Ethics (Oxford, England)*, *19*(2), 154–182. doi:10.1111/j.1467-8608.2010.01583.x

Hungelmann, J., Kenkel-Rossi, E., Klassen, L., & Stollenwerk, R. M. (1985). Spiritual well-being in older adults: Harmonious interconnectedness. *Journal of Religion and Health*, *24*(2), 147–153. doi:10.1007/BF01532258 PMID:24306074

Jaques, E. (1976). *A general theory of bureaucracy*. Halsted Press.

Karakas, F. (2010). Spirituality and performance in organizations: A literature review. *Journal of Business Ethics*, *94*(1), 89–106. doi:10.100710551-009-0251-5

Katz, D., & Kahn, R. L. (1978). *The social psychology of organizations* (Vol. 2). Wiley.

Kilmann, R. H., Saxton, M. J., & Serpa, R. (1985). *Gaining control of the corporate culture*. Jossey-Bass.

Kim, D., Fisher, D., & McCalman, D. (2009). Modernism, Christianity, and business ethics: A worldview perspective. *Journal of Business Ethics*, *90*(1), 115–121. doi:10.100710551-009-0031-2

King, S., & Nicol, D. M. (1999). Organizational enhancement through recognition of individual spirituality: Reflections of Jaques and Jung. *Journal of Organizational Change Management*, *12*(3), 234–243. doi:10.1108/09534819910274026

Koburtay, T., & Alzoubi, A. (2021). The linkages between person-organization spirituality fit and workers' psychological well-being. *The Journal of Social Psychology*, *161*(1), 103–118. doi:10.1080/00224545.2020.1778618 PMID:32538323

Koburtay, T., & Syed, J. (2021). Do religion and spirituality matter for hotel workers' well-being and guests' happiness? An update of the Attraction-Selection-Attrition theory. *International Journal of Hospitality Management*, *95*, 102951. doi:10.1016/j.ijhm.2021.102951

Konz, G. N., & Ryan, F. X. (1999). Maintaining an organizational spirituality: No easy task. *Journal of Organizational Change Management*, *12*(3), 200–210. doi:10.1108/09534819910273865

Korac-Kakabadse, N., Kouzmin, A., & Kakabadse, A. (2002). Spirituality and leadership praxis. *Journal of Managerial Psychology*, *17*(3), 165–182. doi:10.1108/02683940210423079

Kotter, J. P. (1996). Why transformation efforts fail. *Harvard Business Review*.

Kouzes, J. M., Posner, B. Z., & Maxwell, J. C. (2004). *Christian reflections on the leadership challenge*. Jossey-Bass.

Krishnakumar, S., & Neck, C. P. (2002). The "what", "why" and "how" of spirituality in the workplace. *Journal of Managerial Psychology*, *17*(3), 153–164. doi:10.1108/02683940210423060

Kurpis, L. V., Beqiri, M. S., & Helgeson, J. G. (2008). The effects of commitment to moral self-improvement and religiosity on ethics of business students. *Journal of Business Ethics*, *80*(3), 447–463. doi:10.100710551-007-9430-4

Lee, D. J., Sirgy, M. J., Efraty, D., & Siegel, P. (2003). A study of quality of work life, spiritual well-being, and life satisfaction. Handbook of workplace spirituality and organizational performance, 209-230.

Lu, C. S., & Lin, C. C. (2014). The effects of ethical leadership and ethical climate on employee ethical behavior in the international port context. *Journal of Business Ethics, 124*(2), 209–223. doi:10.100710551-013-1868-y

Lundberg, C. C. (1988). Working with culture. *Journal of Organizational Change Management, 1*(2), 38–47. doi:10.1108/eb025598

Luria, G., & Yagil, D. (2008). Procedural justice, ethical climate and service outcomes in restaurants. *International Journal of Hospitality Management, 27*(2), 276–283. doi:10.1016/j.ijhm.2007.07.022

Malone, P. F., & Fry, L. W. (2003). *Transforming schools through spiritual leadership: A field experiment*. Academy of Management.

Mazur, B. (2015). Basic assumptions of organizational culture in religiously diverse environments. *International Journal of Contemporary Management, 14*(3), 115–132.

McDaniel, S. W., & Burnett, J. J. (1990). Consumer religiosity and retail store evaluative criteria. *Journal of the Academy of Marketing Science, 18*(2), 101–112. doi:10.1007/BF02726426

McKee, A., & Morey, A. (2003). *Primal Leadership*. Macmillan Audio.

Neal, A., & Griffin, M. A. (1999). Developing a model of individual performance for human resource management. *Asia Pacific Journal of Human Resources, 37*(2), 44–59. doi:10.1177/103841119903700205

Neo, J. L. (2018). Definitional imbroglios: A critique of the definition of religion and essential practice tests in religious freedom adjudication. *International Journal of Constitutional Law, 16*(2), 574–595. doi:10.1093/icon/moy055

Newman, A., Herman, H. M., Schwarz, G., & Nielsen, I. (2018). The effects of employees' creative self-efficacy on innovative behavior: The role of entrepreneurial leadership. *Journal of Business Research, 89*, 1–9. doi:10.1016/j.jbusres.2018.04.001

Oumlil, A. B., & Balloun, J. L. (2009). Ethical decision-making differences between American and Moroccan managers. *Journal of Business Ethics, 84*(4), 457–478. doi:10.100710551-008-9719-y

Paloutzian, R. F. (1996). Understanding Religious Conversion (Book). *The International Journal for the Psychology of Religion*, *6*(3), 225–227. doi:10.120715327582ijpr0603_9

Parboteeah, K. P., Chen, H. C., Lin, Y. T., Chen, I. H., Lee, A. Y., & Chung, A. (2010). Establishing organizational ethical climates: How do managerial practices work? *Journal of Business Ethics*, *97*(4), 599–611. doi:10.100710551-010-0527-9

Peltonen, T. (2020). *16 The Role of Religion in Cross-Cultural Management: Three Perspectives*. The SAGE Handbook of Contemporary Cross-Cultural Management.

Phau, I., & Kea, G. (2007). Attitudes of university students toward business ethics: A cross-national investigation of Australia, Singapore and Hong Kong. *Journal of Business Ethics*, *72*(1), 61–75. doi:10.100710551-006-9156-8

Racelis, A. D. (2010). Relationship between employee perceptions of corporate ethics and organizational culture: An exploratory study. *Asia Pacific Management Review, 15*(2).

Rodrigues, H. P., & Harding, J. S. (2008). *Introduction to the Study of Religion*. Routledge. doi:10.4324/9780203891728

Sackmann, S. A. (1991). Uncovering culture in organizations. *The Journal of Applied Behavioral Science*, *27*(3), 295–317. doi:10.1177/0021886391273005

Sandelands, L. E. (2003). The argument for God from organization studies. *Journal of Management Inquiry*, *12*(2), 168–177. doi:10.1177/1056492603012002008

Sanders, J. O. (1988). *Christian spiritual leadership*. Ae Chan Co.

Schilderman, H. (2014). Religion as concept and measure. *Journal of Empirical Theology*, *27*(1), 1–16. doi:10.1163/15709256-12341298

Schneider, B. (1987). The people make the place. *Personnel Psychology*, *40*(3), 437–453. doi:10.1111/j.1744-6570.1987.tb00609.x

Smart, J. C., & Hamm, R. E. (1992). *Organizational Culture and Effectiveness in Two-Year Colleges.* AIR 1992 Annual Forum Paper.

Snyder, C. R., & Lopez, S. J. (Eds.). (2009). *Handbook of positive psychology*. Oxford university press.

Society for Human Resource Management. (2008). *Religion and Corporate Culture: Accommodating Religious Diversity in the Workplace*. SHRM.

Van Buren, H. J. III, Syed, J., & Mir, R. (2020). Religion as a macro social force affecting business: Concepts, questions, and future research. *Business & Society, 59*(5), 799–822. doi:10.1177/0007650319845097

Verschoor, C. C. (2006). Strong ethics is a critical quality of leadership. *Strategic Finance*, 19-21.

Victor, B., & Cullen, J. B. (1987). A theory and measure of ethical climate in organizations. *Research in Corporate Social Performance and Policy, 9*, 51-71.

Vitell, S. J. (2009). The role of religiosity in business and consumer ethics: A review of the literature. *Journal of Business Ethics, 90*(2), 155–167. doi:10.100710551-010-0382-8

Warr, P. (1987). *Work, unemployment, and mental health.* Oxford University Press.

Warrick, D. D. (2017). What leaders need to know about organizational culture. *Business Horizons, 60*(3), 395–404. doi:10.1016/j.bushor.2017.01.011

Weaver, G. R., & Agle, B. R. (2002). Religiosity and ethical behavior in organizations: A symbolic interactionist perspective. *Academy of Management Review, 27*(1), 77–97. doi:10.2307/4134370

Weeks, W. A., Loe, T. W., Chonko, L. B., & Wakefield, K. (2004). The effect of perceived ethical climate on the search for sales force excellence. *Journal of Personal Selling & Sales Management, 24*(3), 199–214.

Wicks, A. (2014). Stakeholder theory and spirituality. *Journal of Management, Spirituality & Religion, 11*(4), 294–306. doi:10.1080/14766086.2014.917984

Wiebe, K. F., & Fleck, J. R. (1980). Personality correlates of intrinsic, extrinsic, and nonreligious orientations. *The Journal of Psychology, 105*(2), 181–187. doi:10.1080/00223980.1980.9915149

Wilensky, H. L. (1960). Work, careers and social integration. *International Social Science Journal, 12*(4), 543–560.

Zellars, K. L., Perrewé, P. L., & Brees, J. R. (2010). The multiple roles of spirituality in occupational stress and well-being. In *Handbook of workplace spirituality and organizational performance* (pp. 243–256). Routledge.

Zinnbauer, B. J., & Pargament, K. I. (2005). Religiousness and spirituality. Handbook of the psychology of religion and spirituality, 21-42.

ADDITIONAL READING

Badshah, S. (2012). Historical study of leadership theories. *Journal of Strategic Human Resource Management*, *1*(1), 49.

Conger, J. A., & Kanungo, R. N. (1988). The empowerment process: Integrating theory and practice. *Academy of Management Review*, *13*(3), 471–482. doi:10.2307/258093

Daft, R. L. (1999). *Leadership: Theory and practice*. Harcourt College Pub.

Dean, D. J. (2017). *Religion and spirituality in the workplace: A quantitative evaluation of job satisfaction and organizational commitment* (Doctoral dissertation). Regent University.

House, R. J. (1996). Path-goal theory of leadership: Lessons, legacy, and a reformulated theory. *The Leadership Quarterly*, *7*(3), 323–352. doi:10.1016/S1048-9843(96)90024-7

Judge, T. A., Bono, J. E., Ilies, R., & Gerhardt, M. W. (2002). Personality and leadership: A qualitative and quantitative review. *The Journal of Applied Psychology*, *87*(4), 765–780. doi:10.1037/0021-9010.87.4.765 PMID:12184579

Ouchi, W. G. (1981). Organizational paradigms: A commentary on Japanese management and Theory Z organizations. *Organizational Dynamics*, *9*(4), 36–43. doi:10.1016/0090-2616(81)90024-3

KEY TERMS AND DEFINITIONS

Code of Ethics: A set of principles formulated to help employees to conduct business honestly and with integrity.

Employee Wellbeing: The all-round sense of happiness and security felt by an employee in the workplace.

Ethical Climate: An agreed view of the right way to behave in an organization when facing ethical choices.

Humanistic Workplace: A working environment which regards human interactions and relationships as crucial to organizational success.

Organizational Culture: A shared system of attitudes and beliefs evolving over time in an organization.

Shariah: A set of religious guidelines in Islam.

Spiritual Request: An employee-initiated appeal for special treatment based on his/her religious beliefs.

Chapter 3
Islamic Work Ethic:
A Content-Analysis Based Literature Review

Burak Özdemir
Kastamonu University, Turkey

Hamid Murad Özcan
Eskisehir Osmangazi University, Turkey

ABSTRACT

Islamic work ethic (IWE) has been on the rise in the last 10 years and started to attract the attention of researchers. This study examines the development of IWE studies. In this direction, studies with the theme of Islamic work ethic were determined by examining the studies published in the Web of Science database. How IWE research has changed and developed was interpreted by the content analysis method. For that purpose, scientific publications were analyzed in terms of publication year, type of study, research design, sample type, sample size, data collection method, country where the study was carried out, variable types, antecedents and consequences of the IWE by descriptive review model When past studies were examined, it was seen that there was no study examining the literature on IWE in the context of content analysis. This study aims to fill this gap in the literature, to evaluate the situation of the IWE phenomenon in the literature, and to reveal which variables it is associated with.

INTRODUCTION

Work ethic is a phenomenon that expresses the application of ethical norms and rules in business life, and it expresses the right and wrong in the production, sales and

DOI: 10.4018/978-1-7998-9319-6.ch003

consumption processes in the business world. The question of what is right and what is wrong is an ethical issue. In most definitions of work ethic, rules on right-wrong in the operation of specific situations are associated with principles and standards and turns into ethical principles and standards that guide the behavior of employees in the business world (Ferrell, Linda and John, 2004). As such, work ethic deals with the responsibilities of the business world and employees within the framework of principles and standards. It is possible to define business ethics as a code of conduct which is based on being right and fair and goes beyond obedience to legal regulations (McNamara, 1998). Additionally, work ethic examines and discusses how to behave ethically in communications between employees, shareholders, competitors who are stakeholders of business life, and makes suggestions on these issues (Bektaş and Köseoğlu, 2008). In general, work ethic refers to adopting honest, reliable, respectful and fair-minded behaviors in all economic activities and to display a supportive attitude in relations with society (Özgener, 2009). In other words, work ethic presents a working perspective that constructs the ethical dimension of business life.

Considering the contribution of the employees in the productivity increase in the enterprises, the importance of business ethics emerges once again and it becomes impossible to think of productivity and business ethics separately. There are studies in the literature showing that there is a positive relationship between a strong work ethic and worker productivity (Siegel, 1983). In addition to ensuring employee satisfaction according to work ethic values, employees need to comply with certain work ethic values. Studies show that the incidence of unethical behaviors in the organization affects the development and conformity of the ethical environment in the organization (Cullen, Parboteeah and Victor, 2003). These behaviors, which are expressed as harmful, not only reduce employee performance but also impose a serious cost on the business. Preventing these unethical behaviors will be possible by establishing a correct ethical understanding within the organization. Thus, while creating a working environment whose moral values are based on trust, the performance of the organization will also be increased (Becker and Huselid, 1999).

Based on all this information, considering that various organizational and individual consequences of work ethic are frequently examined in the literature (Kumar and Rose, 2009) and it is considered that work ethic is an important field of research in the context of organizational behavior discipline, this study aims to examine the position of Islamic work ethic in the literature.

BACKGROUND

It is not an ordinary situation that the ethical approach has come to the fore and the need for it has intensified in recent years. The increase in behaviors and practices contrary to ethical values in management and business life, and the prevalence of irregularities, corruptions and degenerations show the importance of work ethic (Saylı, Ağca, Kızıldağ and Yaşar Uğurlu, 2009). The fact that there are many studies in the literature between work ethic and organizational behaviors is an indicator of this situation. Studies focus on how ethical standards that guide the behavior of individuals in the business world can be applied to behaviors and organizational policies.

Emergence of Work Ethic

Merrens and Garrett (1975) found that workers with a strong Protestant ethic work and produce more. Their research has revealed that work ethic has a relatively large impact on time spent on the task. While Greenberg (1977) found that the work ethic has a moderate and lasting effect on the task, Blood (1969) reported that there is a correlation between work ethic and job satisfaction. Looking at more recent studies, it is seen that there are significant and positive relationships between work ethic and work performance. Practices related to work ethic vary according to personal characteristics and work groups and are effective in showing positive behaviors and attitudes of employees (Schwepker, 2001). Eren and Hayatoğlu (2011) investigated the relationship between ethical behavior and performance in their studies and found that work ethic has a significant effect on trust in management and job performance. Similarly, another study found significant relationships between work ethic, trust in the organization, and job performance (Büte, 2011). As stated by many studies, it is seen that work ethic has a positive effect on organizational commitment, organizational justice, job satisfaction, job performance and the tendency to stay in the organization (Cullen et al., 2003; Schwepker, 2001). According to a study, consumers prefer the products of businesses that do good things for the society and bear responsibility if there is no difference in quality and price. According to this, as organizations contribute to society and act in line with ethical values, they get more in return commercially (Baltaş, 2002). On the other hand Çelik (2010) found that business ethics practices increase employee satisfaction.

According to Marx, what individuals are is related to how they produce as much as what they produce in their production, i.e., what individuals are depends on the conditions of their production (Marx and Engels, 1992). Here comes the issue of work ethic. Belief systems have a great role in shaping work ethic and business life. Especially before the industrial revolution, work ethic is a concept that is built on traditions and religious values. This is why religions are the main factor that shapes and develops work ethic (Zaim, 2012). Christianity is a monotheistic religion that has a significant impact on work ethic. German sociologist Weber, discussed the issue of work ethic in the context of religious elements and sought an answer to the question: "To what extent did religious understandings affect the economic understanding of various societies?" (Aron, 2007). Weber states that modern culture, as a rational and rational way of life, founded on the idea of ethic and profession, which is one of the basic elements of the modern capitalist spirit, emerged from the Protestant morality of Christian culture. During the Middle Ages, the church's regulations on work ethics did not have a restrictive effect on work activities, but the prohibition of interest created tension between the church and the world of economy (Bakirov, 2005). This tension tended to fade with the emergence of the Protestant sect. Because in Protestantism the right of interest of the person who invested capital was considered religiously appropriate and legalized (Özgener, 2009). It is now possible to see that all the chains of this spirit have been broken and united only with worldly passions, with this greed for gain, which has stripped away the religious and ethical meaning of the Christian Protestant spirit (Şengül, 2017). In Islam, on the other hand, since there is no psychological uncertainty or sense of sinfulness as in Christianity, Muslims do not try to be successful by working too hard for salvation (Bayat, 1992). Work in the Islamic understanding of work differs from the principle that work in the Protestant concept is a value. Weber attributes the lack of the spirit of capitalism in Islam, as in the Protestant understanding, to the influence of the Sufi tradition of Muslim societies (Arslan, 2001). While accumulating wealth in Protestant ethic is encouraged to elevate God's glory, in Islam this is condemned in the Koran and hadiths. Worldly asceticism and therefore working hard only to amass wealth by neglecting the Hereafter is not encouraged in Islam contrary to the Protestant work ethic. It is clear that Islam does not recommend worldly asceticism. What matters in Islam is the afterlife, that is, the Hereafter. This world, on the other hand, is temporary (Kurt, 2009). However, the IWE includes dimensions that are not explicitly emphasized in the Protestant Work Ethic. In particular, there is an emphasis in Islamic work ethic on intention rather than outcome as a measure of ethic. For example, gambling or the alcohol trade may yield money but are seen as an unethical enterprise. Serving others and society is considered an integral part of the IWE, and the growing possibility of deceptive working life in Christianity, Judaism and Islam. Islam is one of the religions emphasizing the behavior makes it a necessity for those taking any action to be transparent. In this context, the idea that "all risks belong to the buyer" is strongly rejected with the understanding that "the one who deceives us is not from us" (Ali, 2005).

As mentioned before, the most basic principles of work ethic take their source from religion. There are many ethical principles that regulate importance of work ethic (Aktan, 1999). The aims of Islam are not primarily materialistic, but are based on the well-being of humanity and the fulfillment of spiritual needs such as a good life, brotherhood, social and economic justice (Chapra, 1992).

Evolution of IWE

Trying to create an IWE corresponds to the 1980s. Although Nasr's work (Nasr, 1984) can be stated as the first study on the IWE, it should be stated that the most important and prominent studies on the IWE are those of Ali (Ali 1988, 1992; Ali and Azim, 1994). According to Ali (1988), since the treatise of Max Weber on Protestant morality, productivity problems and economic development problems and their relation to religious beliefs have gained increasing popularity. The discussion of most of these issues is related to Judeo-Christian morality. Although many other religious and ethnic groups have achieved prosperity and tremendous economic achievements at some point in their history (e.g., the Jains in India; the Saritri Muslims in Java), their contributions have been almost completely ignored in management literature. Ali (1992) stated that the phenomenon of individualism can also be added to this and emphasized that, although it is frequently included in Western studies, it is important and needed to examine work ethic and individualism in non-Western societies. At this point, he pointed out that the IWE is an important concept that should be emphasized.

Unlike Protestantism, Islam is a collective religion and this affects the concept of work. The unity of the Muslim, which is evident in the expression "Islamic Ummah", is one of the most important principles emphasized in Islam. Economic activity in Islam, which is of no use to the Islamic ummah, is strictly prohibited, especially if this activity seriously harms other religious brothers. Thus, the only economic activity that benefits the Islamic Ummah and gives potency and power to the Islamic Ummah is right (Chanzanagh and Akbarnejad, 2011). The IWE has its roots in the Koran and hadith. The Koran generally speaks of honesty and justice in trade and the fair distribution of wealth in society. The Koran encourages the acquisition of skills and technology and does not approve of laziness. While Islamic work ethic considers dedication to work to be a virtue, it emphasizes collaboration and consultation at work (Abbasi, Rehman and Bibi, 2011).

According to Islamic understanding; work concept provides independence, self-esteem, satisfaction, success, happiness, pride and business development to the individual. It is claimed that this provides an increase in the society and its welfare (Ali, 1988). In this context, when it comes to working life in Islamic culture, it is aimed to add moral depth to the soul of the person and to earn income by entering the working life without cutting off the relationship with the world (Kitagava, 1985).

The practices of the religion of Islam on work ethic are as old as the emergence of religion. Because the prophet of the religion of Islam was a merchant, and both the holy book of the religion, the Koran, the hadiths, including the words of the prophet, and the sunnah, which includes the behavior of the prophet, cover many provisions on the subject of work ethic. In the sources of the religion of Islam, business operations were encouraged and it was stated that honesty should be taken as a basis, not only against Muslims, but also against all humanity (Özgener, 2009).

The IWE is an orientation related to work. Work is both a virtue related to the individual's needs and one of the elements necessary to achieve balance in private and public life. The basis of the IWE is for the individual to realize himself. Its main foundation and source is the Koran (Ali, 1992).

The moral values of Muslim societies are determined by the Koran and the Sunnah. The basis of Islam is broterhood and togetherness but not materialism. Also it emphasizes being a good person, living well, socio-economic justice and the balance between body and spirit (Rice, 1999).

It is possible to talk about three basic areas of both general work ethic and the IWE; oriented towards profession and colleague, society and customer, and goods and services. Accordingly, the employee should do his job right and the employer should give the employee's due, thus everyone should instill confidence in his colleagues. Likewise, professional experts should see the customer not as a factor to be exploited, but as someone trying to meet their needs. In addition to these, it is one of the requirements of work ethic that the quality of service provided and the goods produced should not harm material and moral values. It is not possible to mention that attitudes and behaviors contrary to these three principles of work ethic are moral (Karagül, 2012). The basis of the IWE is the inevitable spiritual character of all human actions and the responsibility that a person bears not only towards the employee or employer, but also towards the work itself. This means that the worker should do his job as perfectly as he can (Nasr, 2009).

The IWE commands hard work. The saying "Service to the people is service to God" is an indication of this. However, this hard work should not lead believers to a materialist lifestyle (Tabakoğlu, 1996). In Islam, working is flexible. Therefore, although Islamic working methods are mainly based on principles arising from the God's messages, practices vary according to time and place. The principles of Islamic economics are based on the rightful due. These principles can be summarized as avoiding waste, ensuring economic and political independence, expanding property, social justice and welfare (Tabakoğlu, 2008). In Islam, trade is based on rules. For example, while participating in trade, the person should act fairly, keep the measure and weighing correctly, and avoid making inaccurate measurements. There is a great warning for those who cheat in measuring and weighing and those who do not act in accordance with the rules (Dökmen and Yeşilyurt, 2015). A verse from the Koran says; "Do what you do well. Allah loves those who do their job well." In other words, the God ordered people to do their job in the best way possible (Murat, Dursun and Şen, 2016). Therefore, it is possible to say that the ethical responsibilities of the individual towards himself and other people are also responsibilities towards the God. One of the most important principles of Islamic ethics is keeping one's word.

Every promise, whether given to people or to the God, makes people obliged and responsible (Durmuş, 2002).

The religion of Islam has individualistic elements, but this individualism differs from secular individualism. Islam does not have an individualistic ideology in a secular sense. More like Protestantism, it is a communitarian religion with a strong emphasis on individual responsibility. Many Islamic scholars have seen the prohibition of interest and zakat as the communal and egalitarian aspect of Islam (Mannan, 1986). Many contemporary Islamic theologians see it as a positive attitude for a Muslim to become rich by working hard and legitimately. Because in this way, the person will engage in many charitable activities for Islam, create employment and help the development of the Islamic society (Türkdoğan, 1996).

The religion of Islam states that the most precious and halal food of man is what he earns by working properly. Everyone must do their best while working. Every person should do his job to the best of his ability by doing right by his profession and art. On the other hand, the religion of Islam demands that the jobs be given on the basis of meritocracy to the most competent people who can perform in the best way. For this reason, the Prophet of Islam, Muhammad said: "When the jobs are given to incompetent people, wait for the Day of Judgment!" Undoubtedly, competent people fulfill their obligations in the best way possible. This automatically creates the quality that will satisfy everyone in production. Thereby the quality of the good or service increases the demand and brings profit to the producer (Kayadibi, 2007).

When we look at the work ethic in today's Islamic society, we certainly will not find the aforementioned qualities and features everywhere, especially in most management approaches. So much so that in the recent generations in most Islamic countries, particularly in crowded city centers, the spirituality of workers and the moral dimension of work has weakened and almost disappeared (Nasr, 2009). Nevertheless, it must be remembered that the moral principles, hard work, and commitment to the economic development of the Muslim community in the past had the promise of strengthening trade and economic progress in today's world (Ali and Al-Owaihan, 2008).

IWE and Organizational Behavior

For more than a decade materialism has been a major factor for employee performance in organizations. However, over the past 15 to 20 years, this trend has changed tremendously in a way that the substance of belief and religiosity has came to the forefront in the field of management and organization (Khan & Arshad, 2016). As a reflection of this, the relationship between IWE and employee attitudes and behaviors in the organizational context has started to be examined in the literature (Yousef, 2000; Rokhman, 2010; Hayati and Caniago, 2012; Düşmezkalender, Secilmis and

Yilmaz, 2020; Saban, Basalamah, Gani and Rahman, 2020; Qasim, Irshad, Majeed and Rizvi, 2021; Ahmad, Islam and Kaleem, 2021; Al-Shamali, Irani, Haffar, Al-Shamali and Al-Shamali, 2021; Ahmed, Arshad, Mahmood and Barkat, 2021).

IWE has serious positive or negative effects on organizations, as does general work ethic. Studies in the literature confirm this. The IWE positively affects employee performance, the quality of work and productivity (Syarif, Rahmawati and Fasa, 2019). Yousef (2000), found that the IWE positively affects attitudes towards organizational change and organizational commitment. The same author found in another study that IWE increases organizational commitment and plays a moderator role in the relationship between organizational commitment and job satisfaction (Yousef, 2001). As a result of another study, it was seen that the IWE increased organizational commitment and job performance (Hayati and Caniago, 2012). According to the results of a study examining the organizational consequences of the IWE, while the IWE positively affecting job satisfaction and organizational commitment, it has no effect against turnover intention (Rokhman, 2010).

There are also more recent studies on the subject. In a study conducted on service sector employees in Pakistan, it was found that IWE positively affects task performance and psychological capital (Qasim et al., 2021). Another study was conducted in Pakistan and the results show that IWE moderates the relationship between social cynicism and perceived bullying (Ahmad et al., 2021). In other words, the more IWE rules in a workplace, the less bullying behaviour occurs. The results of a study on bank employees in Kuwait show that IWE negatively affects organizational deviance and continuance commitment to change (Al-Shamali et al., 2021). A similar finding emerged as a result of a study conducted on hotel businesses in Turkey. According to the research, while IWE reduces deviant organizational behavior, it positively affects person organization fit (Düşmezkalender et al., 2020). Similarly, in the hotel industry the relationship between IWE and job satisfaction and employee performance was examined. Results from the study conducted in Indonesia show that IWE increases job satisfaction and employee performance (Saban et al., 2020). In another study, it was concluded that IWE positively affects employee loyalty (Ahmed et al., 2021).

These studies, which can be increased in number, show that the IWE has an important place for organizations in Islamic societies or in the presence of Muslim employees. In this context, this study was carried out considering that examining the place of IWE in the literature is important for researchers and practitioners in the future. From this point of view, in the study, it is aimed to provide descriptive information about the identity of the articles examining the IWE, such as research design, study type, sample structure and some other features. In line with this purpose, answers to the following questions are sought:

- What is the publication year distribution of articles on IWE in Web of Science database?
- What is the study type distribution of articles on IWE in Web of Science database?
- What is the research design distribution of articles on IWE in Web of Science database?
- What is the sample type distribution of articles on IWE in Web of Science database?
- What is the study size distribution of articles on IWE in Web of Science database?
- What is the data collection method distribution of articles on IWE in Web of Science database?
- What is the distribution of the articles on IWE in the Web of Science database regarding the countries where they were published?
- What type of variable is IWE mostly used in articles in Web of Science database?
- What are the antecedents of IWE in articles in Web of Science database?
- What are the consequences of IWE in articles in Web of Science database?

METHODOLOGY

This study is carried out with descriptive review model. Descriptive reviews introduce some quantification, often a frequency analysis of a body of research. In the descriptive review model, it is aimed to systematically search for the largest number of studies about the phenomenon under investigation. In this direction, each selected study is coded according to certain research characteristics. Publication year, research method, basic approach and symbolic research findings are some of them. The findings obtained with the descriptive review aim to explain the state of the research area (King and He, 2005).

Sample of the Study

The study sample consists of all studies written on the IWE in journals indexed in Web of Science database. A search was made in the relevant journals with the word "Islamic work ethic". The search is limited by filtering by titles, articles, early access and review articles. 32 studies determined in this direction constitute the sample of the research.

Data Collection and Survey Process

The data were obtained by document analysis. The data obtained from 32 studies were coded according to the content analysis coding method (Krippendorff, 2004). The coding process was carried out under 10 headings. These are: year of publication, type of study (empirical/conceptual), research design (quantitative/qualitative/mixed), sample type, sample size, data collection method, country where the study was carried out, variable types, antecedents and consequences of the concept. Microsoft Excel was used in coding processes.

Analysis and Findings

Content analysis can be used with a wide variety of data sources, including textual data, visual stimuli (e.g., photos/videos) and audio data. Additionally, the technique is quite flexible in that it can be empirically or theoretically guided (Stemler, 2015). The most distinctive feature of content analysis is that it is objective, systematic and quantitative (Kassarjian, 1977). Also these features are more prone to quantitative content analysis (White and Marsh, 2006). In this study, content analysis was applied to the research data.

Investigator triangulation, inter-coder reliability and intra-coder reliability are used for the validity and reliability of content analysis. It is stated that the use of triangulation has the potential to increase the validity of the study, reduce researcher bias, and provide multiple perspectives on the phenomenon (Renz, Carrington and Badger, 2018). In this study, investigator triangulation technique was used. In the investigator triangulation technique, two or more coders/evaluators classify the data, calculate a reliability index and report it (Turner and Turner, 2009). Moreover, in this reporting process, inter-coder reliability and intra-coder reliability were used.

Cohen's Kappa formula, which is widely used in Content Analysis, was used to calculate how much of the observed agreement among the coders was random, in other words, to calculate the reliability between coders. The inter-coder reliability was found to be, 88 according to the Cohen's Kappa formula. Perreault and Leigh's (1989) reliability index formula was used to express how compatible the encodings of the coders were with each other (Rust and Cooil, 1994). When the data were replaced in the formula, it was determined that the consistency between the coders was, 97. Finally, in order to check the reliability of the coders, the coding was repeated two weeks later and the percentage of agreement was found to be 99%-99%.

According to Table 1, the first publication about the IWE was made in 1988. It was determined that 2 studies (6.2%) were published between 1988-1998, 4 studies (12.5%) between 1999-2009 and 21 studies (65.7%) between 2010-2020. The

Table 1. Distribution of the studies by years

Year	n	(%)	Year	n	(%)
1988	1	3,1	2016	3	9,4
1992	1	3,1	2017	1	3,1
2000	1	3,1	2018	3	9,4
2001	1	3,1	2019	9	28,1
2009	2	6,3	2020	2	6,5
2011	1	3,1	2021-...	5	15,6
2012	1	3,1	Total	32	100
2015	1	3,1			

number of studies published and accepted for publication in 2021 was determined as 5 (15.6%). Most publications on the IWE were made in 2019.

Table 2 shows the frequency of empirical and conceptual studies. According to Table 2, 30 studies (93.7%) are empirical studies and 2 studies (6.3%) are conceptual. Thus, it is understood that empirical studies are in the majority in the literature.

Table 2. Distribution of the studies by type of study

	Empirical	Conceptual	Total
n	30	2	32
%	93,7	6,3	100

When Table 3 was evaluated, it was determined that 29 of the studies (96.7%) were conducted in a quantitative research design. One of the studies (3.3%) is in qualitative research design. It is seen that quantitative research design is preferred more in empirical studies.

Table 3. Distribution of empirical studies by research design

	Quantitative	Qualitative	Mixed	Total
n	29	1	-	30
%	96,7	3,3	-	31

Based on Table 4, it was determined that the samples consisting of employees (n=16) were the most preferred in the studies. This is followed by administrators (n=5), employees and managers (n=3), nurses (n=2) and students (n=2). However, there is one study that takes the chairmans (n=1) as a sample.

Table 4. Distribution of the studies by main population

Main Population	n	%
Students	2	6,9
Chairmans	1	3,4
Nurses	2	6,9
Employees	16	55,2
Employees and managers	3	10,3
Managers	5	17,2
Toplam	29	100

According to the sample size findings in Table 5, it is seen that the sample size between 201-300 (n=9) is mostly used in the studies. However, sample sizes between 301-400 (n=7), 101-200 (n=4), 401-500 (n=4) and 51-100 (n=2) were also frequently used in studies. In addition, it was determined that there was one

Table 5. Distribution of the studies by sample sizes

Sample Size	n	%
25-50	1*	3,4
51-100	2	6,9
101-200	4	13,8
201-300	9	31
301-400	7	24,1
401-500	4	13,8
501-600	-	-
601-700	-	-
701-800	1	3,4
801-..	1	3,4
Total	29	100
***1 study is in qualitative research design**		

study each conducted using sample sizes of 25-50 (n=1), 701-801 (n=1), 801 and above (n=1). The study in which a sample size of 25-50 was used was carried out in a qualitative research design different from the others.

Table 6 provides information on which countries were preferred for the samples included in the studies. Accordingly, 13 studies were carried out in Pakistan, 3 studies in Malaysia, 3 studies in Turkey, 2 studies in Saudi Arabia, 2 studies in United Arab Emirates and 2 studies in Iran. Israel, Indonesia, Iraq and the other were identified as one each.

Table 6. Distribution of the studies by countries

Country	n	%	Country	n	%
Pakistan	13	44,8	Other	1*	3,4
Malaysia	3	10,3	Israel	1	3,4
Turkey	3	10,3	Indonesia	1	3,4
Saudi Arabia	2	6,8	Iraq	1	3,4
United Arab Emirates	2	6,8	Total	29	100
Iran	2	6,8			
* In the related study, it is stated as Arab students.					

According to Table 7, in 27 studies (90%) data were obtained by questionnaire method. The number of studies using in-depth interviews was 1 (3.3%), the number of studies in which document review was preferred was 1 (3.3%), and the number of studies using content analysis was 1 (3.3%). It is seen that data is collected mostly with questionnaires among empirical research.

Table 7. Distribution of empirical studies by data collection method

Data Collection Method	n	%
Survey method	27	90
In-depth interviews	1	3,3
Document Review	1	3,3
Content Analysis	1	3,3
Total	30	100

Table 8 shows the rate of use of the IWE as variable types in research. When the table is examined, it is seen that the IWE is mostly preferred as independent variable (n=14) and moderator variable (n=13) in studies. However, the IWE has never been used as a mediator variable and dependent variable in studies.

Table 8. Use of the IWE as variable types in empirical studies

Variable Type	n	%
IWE as an independent variable	14	51,85
IWE as a dependent variable	-	-
IWE as a moderator variable	13	48,15
IWE as a mediator variable	-	-
Total	27	100

Table 9 contains information on the antecedents and consequences of the IWE. According to Table 9, it is seen that the antecedents of the IWE were not included in the studies, but rather its consequences. At this point, job satisfaction (n=7), organizational commitment (n=5) and helping behavior (n=3) were the most studied consequences. Innovation capability (n=2), turnover intention (n=2), job involvement (n=2), employee performance (n=2), deviant work behavior (n=2) and knowledge sharing behavior (n=2) follow them. Emergence of pious or devout business people, attitudes toward organizational change, organizational networks, adaptive performance, innovative work behavior, perceived organizational justice, psychological ownership, work engagement, negligent behavior, intrinsic motivation, work satisfaction, employees' public service motivation, psychological well-being, moral identity, employee voice, employee loyalty, accountability in Islamic social enterprise, financial governance in Islamic social enterprise and person-organization fit have once found their place in the studies as consequences of the IWE.

FUTURE RESEARCH DIRECTIONS

With this study, it is aimed to draw attention to the use of the IWE in the literature. After this study, the researchers had the opportunity to see the existing structure in the literature, based on the IWE's examinations in Web of Science database. For future studies, recommendations can be given to researchers to examine the IWE in different samples or in more than one sample group. Finally, considering that

Table 9. Antecedents and Consequences of the IWE in studies

Antecedents	n	%
-	-	-
Consequences	**N**	**%**
Job satisfaction	7	15,2
Organizational commitment	5	10,8
Helping behavior	3	6,5
Innovation capability	2	4,3
Turnover intention	2	4,3
Job involvement	2	4,3
Employee performance	2	4,3
Deviant work behavior	2	4,3
Knowledge sharing behavior	2	4,3
Emergence of pious or devout business people	1	2,2
Attitudes toward organizational change	1	2,2
Organizational networks	1	2,2
Adaptive performance	1	2,2
Innovative work behaviour	1	2,2
Percieved organizational justice	1	2,2
Psychological ownership	1	2,2
Work engagement	1	2,2
Negligent behavior	1	2,2
Intrinsic motivation	1	2,2
Work satisfaction	1	2,2
Employees' public service motivation	1	2,2
Psychological Well-Being	1	2,2
Moral identity	1	2,2
Employee voice	1	2,2
Employee loyalty	1	2,2
Accountability in Islamic social enterprise	1	2,2
Financial governance in Islamic social enterprise	1	2,2
Person-organization fit	1	2,2
Total	46	100

the IWE has been studied intensively in societies that have adopted the religion of Islam, it will also contribute to the literature to examine the employees who have accepted the religion of Islam in different societies.

CONCLUSION

This study was designed upon seeing that the IWE literature was not examined in the context of content analysis when past studies on the IWE were examined. Thus, it is aimed to fill this gap in the literature and to guide researchers who want to study on the IWE. The study was carried out with this motivation and an evaluation was carried out on the studies about the IWE in Web of Science database.

According to the findings obtained from the study, it is seen that at least one study about the IWE was published almost every year in the last 10 years. The IWE has been extensively studied in the Web of Science database, especially in the last 5 years. This is proof that the concept arouses curiosity in the eyes of researchers. Considering that Web of Science is an important database (the world's most trusted publisher-independent global citation database), it is possible to state that studies on the IWE are expected to increase in the field. It is seen that the type of research carried out is mostly empirical research. One reason for this can be considered as the role played by the Protestant work ethic in the emergence of the IWE. The historically intense study of Protestant work ethic has actually helped to develop the foundations and conceptual framework of the IWE. In line with the rapid conceptual maturation of IWE, it can be stated that researchers mostly focus on the reflections of the concept in the field research. Job satisfaction, organizational commitment, helping behavior, innovation capability, turnover intention, job involvement, employee performance, deviant work behavior, knowledge sharing behavior were the mostly studied reflections of IWE in that field research. It has been determined that more quantitative research design is applied in empirical studies. In particular, the scale created by Ali (1988) has been used in many studies and has helped to measure the concept. However, it should be noted that qualitative research is needed to better understand the IWE phenomenon in the field. It can be stated that qualitative research will help to understand the phenomenon in depth, especially in different cultures where the religion of Islam is dominant.

It has been determined that the sample structure in the studies was mainly based on the employees and then the managers. Again, it is seen that specific samples (eg nurses) were used in the context of the researched subject in the studies. Data were obtained from these samples, mostly through questionnaires. As the sample size, it is seen that the samples determined between 201-300 people and between 301-400 people were preferred. A striking point is that the studies were mostly carried out on samples from Pakistan. The only study that did not have a majority of the population adopting the religion of Islam was carried out in Israel. This is also an indication of the IWE has not been studied enough in Western countries.

REFERENCES

Abbasi, A. S., Rehman, K. U., & Bibi, A. (2011). Islamic work ethics: How it affects business performance. *Actual Problems of Economics*, *12*, 312–322.

Ahmad, S., Islam, T., & Kaleem, A. (2021). Workplace bullying in Pakistan: Mapping the implications of social cynicism and the moderation of Islamic work ethic. In P. D'Cruz, E. Noronha, & A. Mendonca (Eds.), *Asian Perspectives on Workplace Bullying and Harassment*. Springer. doi:10.1007/978-981-16-2362-2_4

Ahmed, A., Arshad, M. A., Mahmood, A., & Barkat, W. (2021). The impact of spiritual values on employees loyalty: The moderating role of Islamic work ethic. *International Journal of Ethics and Systems*, *37*(3), 341–355. doi:10.1108/IJOES-09-2020-0147

Aktan, C. (1999). *Ahlak ve ahlak felsefesi*. ARI Düşünce ve Toplumsal Gelişim Derneği Yayınları.

Al-Shamali, A., Irani, Z., Haffar, M., Al-Shamali, S., & Al-Shamali, F. (2021). The influence of Islamic Work Ethic on employees' responses to change in Kuwaiti Islamic banks. *International Business Review*, *30*(5), 1–11. doi:10.1016/j.ibusrev.2021.101817

Ali, A. (1988). Scaling an Islamic work ethic. *The Journal of Social Psychology*, *128*(5), 575–583. doi:10.1080/00224545.1988.9922911

Ali, A. (1992). The Islamic work ethic in Arabia. *The Journal of Social Psychology*, *126*(5), 507–519.

Ali, A., & Al-Owaiah, A. (2008). Islamic work ethic: A critical review. *Cross Cultural Management*, *15*(1), 5–19. doi:10.1108/13527600810848791

Ali, A., & Azim, A. (1994). Islamic work ethic and organization in development. *Proceedings of 23rd International Congress of Applied Psychology*.

Ali, J. A. (2005). *Islamic perspectives on management and organization*. Edward Elgar Publishing. doi:10.1080/14766080509518602

Aron, R. (2007). *Sosyolojik düşüncenin evreleri* (A. Korkmaz, Trans.). Kırmızı Yayınları. (Original work published 1967)

Arslan, M. (2001). The work ethic values of Protestant British, Catholic Irish and Muslim Turkish managers. *Journal of Business Ethics, 31*(4), 321–339. doi:10.1023/A:1010787528465

Bakirov, R. (2005). *İşletmelerde iş ahlakı ve sosyal sorumluluk* (Unpublished master's thesis). Gazi University Institution of Social Sciences, Ankara, Turkey.

Baltaş, A. (2002). İş hayatı, sorumluluk ve ahlak. *Activeline, 23*.

Bauer, M. W. (2003). Classical content analysis: A review. In M. W. Bauer & G. Gaskell (Eds.), *Qualitative researching with text, image and sound*. Sage Publication.

Bayat, A. (1992). The work ethic in Islam: A comparison with protestantism. *The Islamic Quarterly, 36*(1), 5–27.

Becker, B. E., & Huselid, M. A. (1999). Overview: Strategic human resource management in five leading firms. *Human Resource Management Journal, 38*(4), 287–301. doi:10.1002/(SICI)1099-050X(199924)38:4<287::AID-HRM2>3.0.CO;2-L

Bektaş, Ç., & Köseoğlu, M. A. (2008). Business ethics and its prevalence process. *Suleyman Demirel University Journal of Faculty of Economics and Administrative Sciences, 13*(1), 145–158.

Blood, M. R. (1969). Work values and job satisfaction. *The Journal of Applied Psychology, 53*(6), 456–459. doi:10.1037/h0028653

Büte, M. (2011). The relationship between the effects of nepotism on the employees and human resource practices: A research on Turkish public banks. *Ataturk University Journal of Social Sciences, 15*(1), 383–404.

Çelik, S. (2010). The relationship of the application of business ethics with employee satisfaction. *Turkish Journal of Business Ethics, 3*(5), 21–40.

Chanzanagh, H. E., & Akbernejad, M. (2011). The meaning and dimensions of Islamic work ethic: Initial validation of a multidimensional IWE in Iranian society. *Social and Behavioral Sciences, 30*, 916–924. doi:10.1016/j.sbspro.2011.10.178

Chapra, M. (1992). *Islam and the economic challenge*. International Institute of Islamic Thought.

Cullen, J. B., Parboteeah, K. P., & Victor, B. (2003). The effects of ethical climates on organizational commitment: A two-study analysis. *Journal of Business Ethics, 46*(2), 127–141. doi:10.1023/A:1025089819456

Dökmen, G., & Yeşilyurt, Ş. (2015). Islamic finance system in the context of religion and economy: The comparison with today's fiscal system. In *International Congress on Islamic Economics and Finance* (pp. 331-347). Academic Press.

Durmuş, Z. (2002). Kur'ân'a göre insanın ilişkilerinde sorumlu olduğu temel ahlâkî ilke: Ahde vefâ. *Dinbilimleri Akademik Araştırma Dergisi*, *2*(2), 77–95.

Düşmezkalender, E., Secilmis, C., & Yilmaz, V. (2020). The effect of Islamic work ethic on person-organization fit and workplace deviance in hotels. *International Journal of Islamic and Middle Eastern Finance and Management*, *14*(1), 164–182. doi:10.1108/IMEFM-05-2019-0198

Eren, S. S., & Hayatoğlu, Ö. (2011). The effect of ethical climate on salesperson's job attitudes, and job performance: An application in pharmaceutical sector. *ZKU Journal of Social Sciences*, *7*(14), 109–128.

Ferrell, O. C., Linda, F., & Fraedrich, J. F. (2004). *Business ethics: Ethical decision making and cases*. South-Western Cengage Learning.

Greenberg, J. (1977). The Protestant work ethic and reactions to negative performance evaluations on a laboratory task. *The Journal of Applied Psychology*, *62*(6), 682–690. doi:10.1037/0021-9010.62.6.682

Hayati, K., & Caniago, I. (2012). Islamic work ethic: The role of intrinsic motivation, job satisfaction, organizational commitment and job performance. *Procedia: Social and Behavioral Sciences*, *65*(3), 1102–1106. doi:10.1016/j.sbspro.2014.05.148

Karagül, M. (2012). Akhism and social capital context of the business ethic and production. *Akademik Bakış Dergisi*, *32*, 1–16.

Kassarjian, H. H. (1977). Content analysis in consumer research. *The Journal of Consumer Research*, *4*(1), 8–18. doi:10.1086/208674

Kayadibi, F. (2007). The dinamic forces of development in Islam. *Darulfunun İlahiyat*, *15*, 1–24.

Khan, K., & Arshad, M. (2016). Impact of Islamic Work Ethics on employees' behavior: Case of Kabul based organizations, Afghanistan. *Abasyn Journal of Social Sciences*, *9*(2), 366–375.

King, W., & He, J. (2005). Understanding the role and methods of meta-analysis in IS research. *Communications of the Association for Information Systems*, *16*, 665–686. doi:10.17705/1CAIS.01632

Kitagava, J. (1985). *Comparative work ethics*. Library of Congress.

Krippendorff, K. (2004). Reliability in content analysis: Some common misconceptions and recommendations. *Human Communication Research*, *30*(3), 411–433. doi:10.1111/j.1468-2958.2004.tb00738.x

Kumar, N., & Rose, R. C. (2010). Examining the link between Islamic work ethic and innovation capability. *Journal of Management Development*, *29*(1), 79–93. doi:10.1108/02621711011009081

Kurt, A. (2009). *İslam çalışma ahlakı*. Emin Yayınları.

Mannan, M. A. (1986). *Islamic economics: Foundations of Islamic economics: Theory and practice*. Hodder and Stoughton.

Marx, K., & Engels, F. (1992). *Alman İdeolojisi* (S. Belli, Trans.). Sol Yayınları. (Original work published 1932)

McNamara, T. (1998). Policy and social considerations in language assessment. *Annual Review of Applied Linguistics*, *18*, 304–319. doi:10.1017/S0267190500003603

Merrens, M. R., & Garrett, J. B. (1975). The Protestant Ethic Scale as a predictor of repetitive work performance. *The Journal of Applied Psychology*, *60*(1), 125–127. doi:10.1037/h0076297 PMID:1110253

Murat, G., Dursun, S., & Şen, M. (2016). A view of industrial relations from Islamic perspective. *Ataturk University Journal of Economics & Administrative Sciences*, *30*(5), 1031–1046.

Nasr, S. H. (1984). Islamic work ethics. *Hamdard Islamicus*, *7*(4), 25–35.

Nasr, S. H. (2009). Islamic work ethic. *Turkish Journal of Business Ethic*, *2*(3), 143–151.

Özgener, Ş. (2009). *İş ahlakının temelleri yönetsel bir yaklaşım* (2nd ed.). Nobel Yayınları.

Perreault, W. D. Jr, & Leigh, L. E. (1989). Reliability of nominal data based on qualitative judgments. *JMR, Journal of Marketing Research*, *26*(2), 135–148. doi:10.1177/002224378902600201

Qasim, M., Irshad, M., Majeed, M., & Rizvi, S. T. H. (2021). Examining impact of Islamic work ethic on task performance: Mediating effect of psychological capital and a moderating role of ethical leadership. *Journal of Business Ethics*, 1–13. doi:10.100710551-021-04916-y

Renz, S. M., Carrington, J. M., & Badger, T. A. (2018). Two strategies for qualitative content analysis: An intramethod approach to triangulation. *Qualitative Health Research*, *28*(5), 824–831. doi:10.1177/1049732317753586 PMID:29424274

Rice, G. (1999). Islamic ethics and the implications for business. *Journal of Business Ethics*, *18*(4), 345–358. doi:10.1023/A:1005711414306

Rokhman, W. (2010). The effect of Islamic work ethics on work outcomes. *JBO - Electronic Journal of Business Ethics and Organization Studies*, *15*(1), 21-27.

Rust, R. T., & Cooil, B. (1994). Reliability measures for qualitative data: Theory and implications. *JMR, Journal of Marketing Research*, *31*(1), 1–14. doi:10.1177/002224379403100101

Saban, D., Basalamah, S., Gani, A., & Rahman, Z. (2020). Impact of Islamic work ethics, competencies, compensation, work culture on job satisfaction and employee performance: The case of four star hotels. *European Journal of Business & Management Research*, *5*(1), 1–8. doi:10.24018/ejbmr.2020.5.1.181

Saylı, H., Ağca, V., Kızıldağ, D., & Yaşar Uğurlu, Ö. (2009). Ethics, corporate reputation and business performance relationships: A research in the fırst 500 big firms in Turkey. *Suleyman Demirel University The Journal of Faculty of Economics and Administrative Sciences*, *14*(2), 171–180.

Schwepker, C. H. Jr. (2001). Ethical climate's relationship to job satisfaction: Organizational commitment and turnover intention in the sales force. *Journal of Business Research*, *54*(1), 39–52. doi:10.1016/S0148-2963(00)00125-9

Şengül, F. N. (2017). *A study on Islamic work ethic and economy from sociology of religion* (Unpublished master's thesis). Yıldırım Beyazıt University, Ankara, Turkey.

Stemler, S. E. (2015). Content analysis. In R. Scott & S. Kosslyn (Eds.), *Emerging trends in the social and behavioral sciences*. John Wiley & Sons. doi:10.1002/9781118900772.etrds0053

Syarif, A. H., Rahmawati, A., & Fasa, M. I. (2019). The effect of Islamic work ethic and productivity on work quality through the employee performance. *Review of Islamic Economics and Finance*, *2*(2), 92–101. doi:10.17509/rief.v2i1.22375

Tabakoğlu, A. (1996). *İslâm ve ekonomik hayat*. Ankara, Turkey: Diyanet işleri Başkanlığı Yayınları.

Tabakoğlu, A. (2008). Ahilik ve iş ahlakı. İstanbul Ticaret Odası İGİAD İş Ahlakı Sempozyumu, 31, 37-52.

Türkdoğan, O. (1996). *İslâm ekonomik sistemi ve Weberci görüşler*. Turan Yayıncılık.

Turner, P., & Turner, S. (2009). Triangulation in practice. *Virtual Reality (Waltham Cross), 13*(3), 171–181. doi:10.100710055-009-0117-2

White, M. D., & Marsh, E. E. (2006). Content analysis: A flexible methodology. *Library Trends, 55*(1), 22–24. doi:10.1353/lib.2006.0053

Yıldırım, A., & Şimşek, H. (2003). *Sosyal bilimlerde nitel araştırma yöntemleri*. Seçkin Yayıncılık.

Yousef, D. A. (2000). Organizational commitment as a mediator of the relationship between Islamic work ethic and attitudes toward organizational change. *Human Relations, 53*(4), 513–537. doi:10.1177/0018726700534003

Yousef, D. A. (2001). Islamic work ethic – A moderator between organizational commitment and job satisfaction in a cross-cultural context. *Personnel Review, 30*(2), 152–169. doi:10.1108/00483480110380325

Zaim, H. (2012). *İş hayatında erdemli insan*. Empati Matbaacılık.

ADDITIONAL READING

Alam, M. A., & Talib, N. (2015). Islamic work ethics and individualism in managing a globalized workplace: Does religiosity and nationality matter? *Journal of Management & Organization, 22*(4), 566–582. doi:10.1017/jmo.2015.54

Ali, A. (1988). Scaling an Islamic work ethic. *The Journal of Social Psychology, 128*(5), 575–583. doi:10.1080/00224545.1988.9922911

Ali, A. (1992). The Islamic work ethic in Arabia. *The Journal of Social Psychology, 126*(5), 507–519.

Ali, A. J., & Al-Owaihan, A. (2008). Islamic work ethic: A critical review. *Cross Cultural Management, 15*(1), 5–19. doi:10.1108/13527600810848791

Ali, J. A. (2005). *Islamic perspectives on management and organization*. Edward Elgar Publishing. doi:10.1080/14766080509518602

Ayob, M. A. S., Sairi, F. M., Soh, N. S. M. & Aziz, A. A. (2021). A review on literature of Islamic work ethics in Malaysia between 2010-2020. *Library Philosophy and Practice*, 1-10.

Bayat, A. (1992). The work ethic in Islam: A comparison with protestantism. *The Islamic Quarterly*, *36*(1), 5–27.

Kitagava, J. (1985). *Comparative work ethics*. Library of Congress.

Nasr, S. H. (1984). Islamic work ethics. *Hamdard Islamicus*, *7*(4), 25–35.

Rice, G. (1999). Islamic ethics and the implications for business. *Journal of Business Ethics*, *18*(4), 345–358. doi:10.1023/A:1005711414306

KEY TERMS AND DEFINITIONS

Allah: How Muslims call God.

Hadith: Words and actions of the Prophet of Islam, Muhammad.

Halal: One that is not contrary to the rules of Islam, that is not forbidden in terms of religion.

Islamic Ummah: All of the Muslims gathered around the Prophet Muhammad, believing in him and practicing what he did and said.

Koran: The basic book of Islam, which contains the basic principles of the religion of Islam and the commandments of the God sent to the Prophet Muhammad.

Protestantism: The sect that emerged as a result of the reform movement in Christianity.

Sunnah: Behaviors of the Prophet Muhammad that are deemed necessary to be followed by Muslims.

Zakat: One of the five pillars of Islam, which orders the distribution of one-fortieth of the wealth and money owned by the rich.

Chapter 4
Authenticity, Religiosity, and Organizational Opportunity:
Exploring the Synergies Between Religion, Spirituality, and Organizational Behavior

Ryan H. Sharp
Brigham Young University, USA

ABSTRACT

A relatively recent emphasis on increased authenticity in the workplace has opened conversations that have previously been considered out-of-bounds within organizational dialogue. With this emphasis has come an invitation for employees to bring their "whole self" to work. An individual's religious beliefs and spiritual inclinations are often at the heart of their so-called true self. Thus, as organizations have encouraged greater authenticity, discussions regarding religiosity and spirituality have followed. While there are some inherent dangers in incorporating religiosity and spirituality into the workplace, the primary purpose of this chapter is to show three natural ways in which these important parts of an individual's identity can be—or already are being—situated into existing and accepted areas of research. Thus, this theoretical piece provides a brief examination of the literature in the fields of positive organizational behavior, meaningful work, and employee engagement and will, in the process, analyze areas of crossover between these and religiosity and spirituality.

DOI: 10.4018/978-1-7998-9319-6.ch004

INTRODUCTION

A relatively recent emphasis on increased authenticity in the workplace has opened conversations that have previously been considered out-of-bounds within organizational dialogue. With this emphasis has come an invitation for employees to bring their "whole self" to work. For an individual to be authentic requires "the unobstructed operation of one's true- or core-self in one's daily enterprise" (Kernis & Goldman, 2006, p. 294). Others have described authenticity as "acting in accord with the true self, expressing oneself in ways that are consistent with inner thoughts and feelings" (Harter, 2005, p. 382), "or acting in accord with one's core values, beliefs, self-representations, and motivations" (Hewlin, Karelaia, Kouchaki, & Sedikides, 2020, p. 80). An individual's religious beliefs and spiritual inclinations are often at the heart of their so-called true self. Thus, as organizations have encouraged greater authenticity, discussions regarding religiosity and spirituality have followed.

Even though "religious identity is tied to an array of important workplace outcomes, . . . the intersection of religion and the workplace is not widely studied in either HR or organizational research" (Heliot, Gleibs, Coyle, Rousseau, & Rojon, 2019, p. 154). Some argue that much of what has been written implies that managers and scholars alike are positive toward spirituality but negative toward religion (Mitroff & Denton, 1999). For them, religion is inherently divisive, partisan, and rigid. Leadership scholar Dr. Douglas Hicks (2002) cautioned against this overly simplistic dichotomy when he wrote:

Even as they criticize the framework of a secular workplace, these scholars tend to accept uncritically a strict distinction between spirituality and religion. In this frequently repeated view, religion is institutional, dogmatic, and rigid; spirituality is personal, emotional, and adaptable to an individual's needs. Authors have relied upon this dichotomy to offer a simplistic solution to the secular framework: spiritual language, symbols, and rituals should be acceptable in the workplace, but religious talk and action remain unacceptable. (p. 380)

While there are some reasons a distinction between religiosity and spiritually is merited, both often play an important role in an individual's whole self. A study done by the Pew Research Center (2015) showed that the majority of Americans (77 percent of all adults) identify with some religious faith. Consequently, for much of the workforce, an invitation to bring one's true self to the organization includes bringing religious beliefs and values. As one executive summarized, "Being religious, being observant, being ultra-Orthodox is something that is inside you in everything you do—in your business, in your meetings, in your interactions, in your food" (Kleinhandler, 2016). While there are some inherent dangers in incorporating religiosity and spirituality into the workplace, the primary purpose of this article is to show three natural ways in which these important parts of an individual's identity can be—or already are being—situated into existing and accepted areas of research. Thus, this theoretical piece will provide a brief examination of the literature in the fields of Positive Organizational Behavior, meaningful work, and employee engagement and will, in the process, analyze areas of crossover between these and religiosity and spirituality.

Positive Organizational Behavior

On September 11, 1999, Dr. Martin Seligman met with a large group of scholars in Lincoln, Nebraska, for what would become a historic academic summit. The purpose: "To create a scientific monument . . . that would bring the light of science to bear on the question of what are the best things in life? How can we achieve these things? How can we help our fellow human beings to achieve them?" (Seligman, 1999). Seligman's professional mission became to accentuate positive qualities and focus on what actions and attributes produce positively minded individuals, families, and communities (Seligman & Csikszentmihalyi, 2000).

One of the scholars who attended that first positive psychology summit was Dr. Fred Luthans. Luthans was a pioneer in the field of organizational behavior and had dedicated more than thirty years to this discipline. Sitting in that meeting in Lincoln, Nebraska, Luthans felt a spark come to his mind as he determined that this concept of positive psychology was exactly what the field of management needed. This experience became the genesis for what he would appropriately call Positive Organizational Behavior (POB).

Positive organizational behavior is gaining momentum and has recently attracted the interest and engagement of scholars around the world (Luthans, 2002; Wright, 2003; Nelson & Cooper, 2007; Chen & Silverthorne, 2008; Karimi & Alipour, 2011). The work happening in this new discipline stands on the shoulders of the positive psychology movement (Lazarus, 2003), which argues that "what is good about life is as genuine as what is bad and therefore deserves equal attention" (Peterson, 2006, p. 4). POB takes this assumption and expands its implications to the workplace, studying, among other things, how various organizations and organizational leaders are able to create a positive environment that leads to greater employee satisfaction, engagement, and productivity (Seligman & Csikszentmihalyi, 2000; Clapp-Smith, Vogelgesang, & Avey, 2009; Gardner, Cogliser, Davis, & Dickens, 2011;). Thus, Luthans argued that the point of emphasis within POB should be the study of "positively oriented human strengths and psychological capacities that can be measured, developed, and effectively managed for performance improvement in today's workplace" (Luthans, 2002a, p. 59).

It should be noted that such an approach is not without its critics. Some have argued that POB is simply a rehashing of some old-school self-help books focusing on the power of a positive mental attitude (Miller, 2008). However, POB scholars have established rigorous criteria for inclusion in this discipline (Luthans, 2002b; Luthans & Avolio, 2009; Luthans & Youseff, 2007). In addition to the requirement that it be positively oriented, the three requirements for a psychological resource capacity to fit within the defined POB framework: "1. Must be based on theory, research, and valid measurement; 2. Must be 'state-like' (as opposed to more fixed 'trait-like') and thus be open to development; 3. Must have performance impact" (Luthans & Avolio, 2009, p. 299). The primary purpose of these guidelines is to validate studies through rigor, data, and the peer review process. These guidelines also ensure that attention is being given to constucts which can be measured, validated, and quantitatively generalized rather than a trait in which one has very little control.

First, the need for a foundation of theory, research, and valid measurement ensures a marked distinction between POB research and popular culture's self-help and personal development literature. Specifically, POB provides scientific data to substantiate its claims. Second, the need for the construct to be state-like, suggests a division between psychological traits and states. In contrast to a "trait-like" capacity, which is relatively stable, "state-like" qualities have the capacity to be acquired, developed, and refined (Avey, Luthans, & Mhatre, 2008). Some scholars have argued that this distinction between traits and states is fruitless (Allen & Potkay, 1981). However, the opportunity to influence and change is what allows leaders to have a positive influence on the psychosocial capacity of their organizations through worksite interventions, on-the-job trainings, and self-development opportunities (Luthans, 2002b).

After spending over a decade studying personality traits, psychology scholars have identified five primary traits, appropriately called "the big five" (Ozer & Benet-Martínez, 2006). Personality traits include such things as conscientiousness, emotional stability, extroversion, agreeableness, and openness to experience (Luthans & Youseff, 2007). It is these so-called "trait-like" capacities that are at the center of the consulting paradigm used by the Gallup Organization as it seeks to identify and manage the strengths or natural talents of individual employees. Helping individuals identify and use these strengths on a consistent basis has proven to help individuals find greater satisfaction and meaning in their work (Luthans, 2002a; Buckingham & Coffman, 1999; Buckingham & Clifton, 2001).

If these psychological traits are "stable across time and context" (Avey et al., 2008), then state-like qualities become the amendable, clinical material of POB and the means by which it is measured, tested, and improved. While there is great value in organizational leaders helping individuals understand the personality traits that are their greatest strengths, the focus of POB, is the ability to help individuals acquire, develop, and refine positive states and thus help them become more productive in their work and find greater satisfaction in doing so (Judge et al., 2002).

While this trait-like versus state-like dialogue has sometimes been viewed in dichotomous terms, recent studies have pointed to a continuum approach (Avey et al., 2008; Luthans et al., 2008). Such an approach allows for the reality that some traits are more developable than others and, conversely, that some states are less malleable than others. Thus, "perhaps the optimal method of considering states and traits in the domain of POB is the degree of stability, rather than the potentially limiting dichotomous thinking of a stable trait versus an unstable state" (Avey et al., 2008, p. 707).

It is within this framework, and with the "state-like" definitional requirement of POB, that scholars have focused in on the following four constructs: self-efficacy, hope, optimism, and resilience (Youseff & Luthans, 2007). These four constructs best meet the inclusion criteria of being substantiated by valid research measures, being state-like, and demonstrating performance impact (Avey et al., 2008). The combination of these constructs constitutes what POB scholars identify as psychological capital, or PsyCap. The following section will define each of these four constructs but will also show how scholars have explored their association with either religiosity or spirituality.

Psychological Capital

Organizational leaders spend significant time seeking to identify a competitive advantage. To this end, both scholars and managers have emphasized various ways of understanding, developing, and maximizing capital. Studies have focused on economic capital (primarily interested in *what you have* in terms of financials and assets and how to leverage these), human capital (focusing on *what you know* and what skills you have developed to contribute to the mission of the organization), social capital (concerned about *who you know* and how those relationships can better stimulate growth and success in an organization), and psychological capital (which has as its primary focus *who someone is* and how that will help them thrive in the workplace). With regard to psychological capital, one study suggested that "beyond human and social capital, psychological capital presents a comprehensible theoretical framework to understand the value of human beings by focusing on psychological capacities of individuals in organizational psychology" (Oruc & Kutanis, 2015, p. 1). We will look briefly at each of the four components of PsyCap (Self-Efficacy, Hope, Optimism, and Resilience)

Self-Efficacy

Self-efficacy, PsyCap's first core construct, has been described as "one's conviction (or confidence) about his or her abilities to mobilize the motivation, cognitive resources, and courses of action needed to successfully execute a specific task within a given context" (Stajovic & Luthans, 1998). Albert Bandura (1994) suggested that "self-efficacy beliefs determine how people feel, think, motivate themselves and behave. Such beliefs produce these diverse effects through four major processes. They include cognitive, motivational, affective and selection processes" (p. 71). Self-Efficacy has been called the "best fit" in meeting the definitional criteria of PsyCap (Luthans, 2002) and has the most established and substantiated research support (Bandura, 1997; Maurer & Pierce, 1998; Parker, 1998). Scholars have identified the following ways self-efficacy can be developed:

1. Performance accomplishments: An individual's personal successful experiences can lead to greater self-efficacy.
2. Vicarious experiences: Observing another person who successfully accomplishes a task can lead to greater self-efficacy.
3. Verbal persuasion: Encouraging words and constructive feedback, particularly from leaders, can instill greater self-efficacy.
4. Physiological states: An individual's personal emotional state can impact self-efficacy, both positively and negatively. The way in which we interpret and respond to these emotions can improve self-efficacy.

Several scholars have reported a significant positive association between religiosity and self-efficacy (Bryd, 2012; Bryd, Hageman, & Isle, 2007; Watson, Morris, & Hood, 1988; Wright, 2010). Shameem Fatima and colleagues looked specifically at religiosity as religious coping and religious practices (Fatima, Sharif, & Khalid, 2018). In this same study they showed that this correlation is particularly beneficial to emerging adults and that "the salience of self-efficacy may be translated into increased sense of autonomy, environmental mastery, personal growth, life purpose, positive relations, and self-acceptance" (Fatima et al., 2018, p. 120). Interestingly, one study showed differences in the degree to which religiosity impacts self-efficacy based on which religion an individual belongs to (Nie, 2019).

Hope

At the heart of PsyCap's second core capacity, hope, is what some scholars have called "willpower" and "waypower." Youseff and Luthans (2007) suggest that "hope's agency or 'willpower' component provides the determination to achieve goals, whereas its pathways or 'waypower' component promotes the creation of alternative paths to replace those that may have been blocked in the process of pursuing those goals" (p. 778). Thus, hope is focused on an individual's efforts toward attaining their personal goals and then making a conscious effort to produce a pathway in order to achieve those goals (Youseff & Luthans, 2007; Snyder, Irving, & Anderson, 1991). Furthermore, "hope has been shown to be adaptable and to relate to performance in various domains, including the workplace" (Luthans, Avolio, Walumbwa, & Li, 2005; Luthans & Jensen, 2002; Luthans, Van Wyk, & Walumbwa, 2004; Youseff & Luthans, 2007).

While the concept of hope is already deeply entrenched in a religious context, particularly within Christianity, the academic construct of hope brings additional spiritual and religious relevance. For example, religiosity has been shown "to be a strong predictor of behavior and health. Religious involvement can provide comfort, meaning and hope during time of adversity" (Abdel-Khalek, 2014). Several studies have shown that individuals who are committed to religious beliefs demonstrated significantly higher scores on hope (Hwang et al., 1996; Pourghaznein et al., 2003). An additional correlation between religiosity, spirituality, and hope is more practical. Some scholars have defined hope as "a positive motivational state that is based on an interactively derived sense of successful (1) agency (goal-directed energy) and (2) pathways (planning to meet goals)" (Snyder, Irving, & Anderson, 1991, p. 287). Drawing on this idea, Luthans and his colleagues provided several opportunities in which leaders and managers can effectively use hope within their organizations. They suggest leaders:

- "Set specific, challenging goals and align those goals with the organization's most important objectives.
- Stimulate and set the context for their followers to determine their own goals, establish higher standards, and stretch their limits.
- Accept and respect their followers as individuals, support their self-set goals, and reward their creative pathways, even if nontraditional and unusual.
- Be compassionate, stable, trustworthy, and hopeful" (Ideas in this list taken from Luthans et al., 2015, p. 93).

When leaders seek to increase opportunities for employees to bring their whole self to the workplace, they provide a space where employees can draw upon the religious or spiritual influences in their lives. When individuals are given this opportunity, their personal development goals become more authentic and they can find fresh pathways to problem-solving that have not been previously explored.

Optimism

Optimism, the third core capacity of PsyCap, focuses on "making an internal, relatively stable, and global attribution regarding positive events such as goal achievement, and an external, relatively unstable, and specific cause for negative events like a failed attempt at reaching a goal" (Luthans et al., 2008). Additionally, optimism includes the reasons and attributions an individual uses to explain why specific events, positive and negative, occur in the past, present, and future (Seligman, 1998). Luthans and his colleagues argue that optimists "adopt problem-focused coping, especially when the situation is within their control. They frame the situation more positively, but they tend to accept the realities of the situation that they cannot control" (Luthans et al., 2015, p. 117). Research has shown that optimism as a psychological capacity is positively correlated with performance, satisfaction, and happiness (Luthans et al., 2008; Seligman, Steen, Park, & Person, 2005; Youssef & Luthans, 2007).

Regarding the intersection between religion and optimism, a growing number of studies have shown that religiosity is positively correlated with optimism and negatively with pessimism (Abdel-Khalek & Lester, 2006). Scholars have shown that "people with deep religious beliefs and confidence in their hearts can show patience and behave rationally when dealing with problems" (Homaei, Bozorgi, Ghahfarokhi1, & Hosseinpour, 2016, p. 58). Articulating a relevant connection between religiosity, optimism, and self-efficacy, it has been suggested that "people who believe in their own strengths and think of themselves as people who can control situations effectively, face problems in a more positive and productive way" (Homaei et al., 2016, p. 58). In an organizational setting, such control and patience can prove to be a great strength.

Resilience

The final construct in PsyCap is resilience. Resilience "refers to a class of phenomena characterized by patterns of positive adaptation in the context of significant adversity or risk" (Masten & Reed, 2002). While some scholars have defined resilience as the ability to "bounce back" from challenges (Luthans, 2002a; Masten & Reed, 2002), Richardson (2002) developed a model that suggests that individuals can improve their resiliency in successive progression through a disruption and reintegration process. Not only does he suggest that this process results in "growth, knowledge, self-understanding, and increased strength of resilient qualities" (p. 310), he also postulates that these disruptive and adversarial experiences can lead to an individual's personal development and growth.

Perhaps more than any of the other constructs within PsyCap, the relationship between resilience and religiosity and spirituality is the most established. While studies have confirmed that religiosity is significantly correlated with increased resilience, scholars have also demonstrated resiliency's positive effect on overall mental health, including fewer depressive symptoms (Fradelos et al., 2018).

Others have identified a positive relationship between spirituality and resilience and that relationship's effect on quality of life (Momeni, 2012). Importantly, research has demonstrated the developmental influence of religiosity through a spiritual-religious intervention that positively impacted the resilience scores of its participants (Saeidi, Pour Ebrahim, Bagherian, & Mansour, 2010). The positive relationship between religious beliefs and resilience have likewise been confirmed internationally (Javanmard, 2013). The most obvious factor in this relationship is in the role of religion to help individuals deal with adversity, setbacks, and tragedy. Thus, to fully integrate the complete authentic self in the workplace necessitates a space wherein a person's religious beliefs and spiritual proclivities can be called upon.

These four constructs that make up PsyCap—self-efficacy, hope, optimism, and resilience—have a synergistic relationship with one another and have been shown to increase the influence of each other. Additionally, while each of them has individually been shown to have a positive relationship with religiosity or spirituality, scholars have recently explored the connections between religiosity, spirituality, and the overall construct of PsyCap.

Religiosity, Spirituality, and Psychological Capital

Over the past decade, research surrounding PsyCap has grown exponentially. According to Görgens-Ekermans and Herbert (2013), PsyCap has been studied in China, India, Canada, the United Kingdom, Portugal, and South Africa, and scholars have since studied it in parts of Australia (Dawkins, Martin, Scott, & Sanderson, 2015). Work site interventions focused on developing and strengthening PsyCap can assist in generating greater employee satisfaction and fulfillment and have already been positively connected to the following desirable outcomes: employees' attitudes, employee behavior, job performance and productivity, safety, commitment to organizational missions, well-being, organizational identity and citizenship, perceived supervisor support, work happiness, and a decreased level of job stress (Avey, Reichard, Luthans, & Mhatre 2011; Cheung et al., 2011; Luthans, Youssef, Sweetman, & Harms, 2013; Norman, Avey, Nimnicht, & Pigeon, 2010; Roberts, Scherer, & Bowyer, 2011; Wright & Cropanzano, 2004; Youseff & Luthans, 2007).

Until recently, however, any connection to spirituality or religious beliefs had been absent in the literature. Then Elif Baykal and Cemal Zehir (2018) looked at the relationship between spiritual leadership and PsyCap. In this study, PsyCap effectively acts as a mediator between spiritual leadership and employee performance. Additionally, it shows that spiritual leadership actually increases PsyCap (Baykal,

2018). Summarizing important implications of their study and opportunities for organizational application, they postulate that managers

> *could be more successful in directing their organizations towards organizational goals when they touch their followers' souls and minds. Being led by spiritual leadership contributes to a considerable increase in the psychological capacities of followers and this situation results in higher levels of performance. Hence, we propose that managers should give importance to workplace spirituality and serve as a mechanism that supplies the necessary atmosphere for the spiritual growth of their followers. (Baykal, 2018, p. 136)*

In addition to these findings, another study showed a positive relationship between PsyCap and spiritual intelligence. Spiritual intelligence was described as "the evergrowing awareness of the matter, body, mind, and soul. . . . [It] tends to be used to refer to the ability to apply spiritual resources, values, and qualities, thus enhancing daily functioning and comfort (physical and mental health)" (Pakdaman & Balideh, 2020, p. 127). These same researchers argue that individuals are more likely to meet their organizational responsibilities if they are enabled to draw strength and support from their spiritual capacities. Furthermore, Pakdaman and Balideh postulate that the synergy between PsyCap and spirituality will improve employee performance and job satisfaction.

Luthans and his colleagues seemed to recognize the possible relationship between PsyCap and spirituality. In their summative treatment entitled "Psychological Capital and Beyond," Luthans, Youssef-Morgan, and Avolio (2015) analyze each of the four stated elements of PsyCap. While they determined that these four constructs of PsyCap best fit their inclusion criteria, they indicated that those constructs were not meant to represent an exhaustive list. Indeed, they suggested that

> *the rich emerging body of knowledge on positive psychology and positive organizational scholarship presents a wide range of positively oriented, unique individual, group, and organizational resources, strengths, and virtues. Many of these positive constructs appear highly promising in terms of both their theoretical foundations and potential applicability to the workplace. Some have also been shown to be measurable and developmental—meaning as states we can change them for the better!*

One of their suggested areas of possible inclusion within the PsyCap framework is spirituality. In their treatment of spirituality, they acknowledge the reality that has already been mentioned in this paper—that religion and spirituality have largely been neglected in management and organizational behavior literature. However, they summarized areas where some progress has been made (Luthans et al., 2015, p. 214):

- "Positive psychology and positive organizational scholarship recognize the role of spirituality.
- "The Academy of Management now has a division on Management, Spirituality, and Religion.
- "There are also dedicated journals (e.g., APA's Psychology of Religion and Spirituality is currently on its sixth volume), journal special issues (e.g., Leadership Quarterly, October 2005 issue), and a Handbook of Workplace Spirituality and Organizational Performance."

The already established correlation between PsyCap and spirituality and the expansion of research in "management, spirituality, and religion" combine to provide opportunities for further exploration, including studying PsyCap with religiosity.

Meaningful Work

Studs Terkel suggested that "working is about the search for daily meaning as well as daily bread, for recognition as well as cash. For astonishment rather than torpor; in short for a sort of life rather than a Monday through Friday sort of dying" (Terkel, 1975, p. 1). The academic interest on meaningful work originated from philosophical discussions on finding greater meaning in life. Individuals seek this type of meaning and purpose in their personal life and families lives but also in their work (Steger, Oishi, & Kashdan, 2009; Csikszentmihalyi, 1990; Seligman, 2002).

A recent review of empirical literature on meaningful work recognized a natural correlation with spirituality. In this review, Catherine Bailey and her colleagues made the following observation:

A number of researchers have used the theoretical work of Ashmos and Duchon (2000) in the domain of workplace spirituality to conceptualize meaningfulness. Scholars in this tradition have recognized "that employees have an inner life that nourishes and is nourished by meaningful work that takes place in the context of community" (Duchon & Plowman, 2005, p. 809). The workplace spirituality approach suggests that organizations can enable human flourishing by providing a setting in which individuals' spiritual needs for an inner life, meaningful work, and community can be met. (Bailey et al., 2019)

Because many employees spend about a third of their time at work, their jobs often become the setting in which they find purpose and meaning. Furthermore, this professional context also often encourages a drive towards personal development (Meyers, 2007; Van Zyl, Deacon, & Rothmann, 2010; Cameron, Dutton, & Quinn, 2003). It was recently suggested that, "evidence has been brought forward to suggest that money is losing its power as a central motivator partially due to the general population realising that above a minimum level necessary for survival, money adds little to their subjective well-being" (Geldenhuys, Karolina, & Venter, 2014). One scholar defined meaningfulness as "the value of a work goal or purpose, judged to *the individual's own* ideals or standards" (May et al., 2004, p. 11). These definitions put the bulk of the responsibility on the shoulders of the individual to understand and determine what is important to them and then to find work that aligns with those ideals.

Religion, Meaningful Work, and Work as a Calling

Within the literature of meaningful work and this emphasis on individuality is the idea of work as a calling (Duffy et al., 2014; Bunderson & Thompson, 2009; Berkelaaar & Buzzanell, 2015; Steger et al., 2010; Elangovan et al., 2010; Hunter et al., 2010). Bunderson and Thompson (2009) argue that one of the underlying assumptions in professional callings is that "work done solely for economic or career advancement reasons is unlikely to inspire a sense of significance, purpose, or transcendent meaning. When viewed as one's calling, however, work assumes both personal and social significance." This sense of purpose and significance is what defines meaningful work. A basic framework that has been proposed in determining whether or not an occupation is truly a "vocation" (from the Latin *voco,* meaning "to call") consists of the following three ideas: (1) the individual must be drawn to pursue it, (2) they must expect it to be intrinsically enjoyable and meaningful, and (3) they must see their work as a central part of his or her identity (Wrzesniewski et al. 1997; see also Forest, Mageau, Sarrazin, & Morin, 2012; Kram, Wasserman, & Yip, 2012; Vallerand & Houlfort, 2003). While the literature in work as a calling has relevance in a secular context, it necessarily recognizes its roots are from a religious framework. Commenting on the evolution of the idea of work as a calling, two leading scholars explained the following:

In he Protestant Reformation, the term "calling" was used to refer either to a specific call to the ministry or to the universal call of the gospel (see Weber, 1930, for a detailed history of the term). Martin Luther broadened the definition of calling to refer to any station that one might occupy in the world of productive work and suggested that through faithful execution of one's duties in that station, one both pleased God and contributed to the general welfare of humankind. So by working diligently to make shoes that will cover and warm human feet, the cobbler serves God in his or her station with just as much divine approbation as the person whose station it is to preach the word of God. With the specific exceptions of the prostitute, the usurer, and the totally cloistered monk (Luther, 1883: 317), all work can be a divine calling by which a person "participates in God's ongoing providence for the human race" (Hardy, 1990: 47), and "every legitimate calling has exactly the same worth in the sight of God" (Weber, 1930: 41). Luther's concept of calling elevated work by transforming it from a necessary evil into a divine offering. (Bunderson & Thompson, 2009, 32–33)

One way in which both scholars and managers can integrate religion and spirituality into the workplace is by leaning into this natural relationship. Many employees see higher purpose in their work, so an overt effort to both study and magnify this purpose for them could lead to greater authenticity in the workplace. This effort could lead to other positive outcomes such as increased job satisfaction (Duffy & Sedlacek, 2007), improved work engagement (Geldenhuys et al., 2014; Fairlie, 2011; Hoole, 2015), greater life satisfaction (Wrzesniewski et al., 1997), less significant job stress (Oates et al., 2005), and greater work-life balance (Munn, 2013).

Building on Luther's efforts to demonstrate the concept of work as a calling, John Calvin taught, "For as God bestows any ability or gift upon any of us, he binds us to such as have need of us and as we are able to help" (Calvin, 1574, p. 307). Thus, for Calvin, each individual has a responsibility to identify the gifts and talents God has bestowed upon them and then to find ways to use these gifts in the service of others. Thompson and Bunderson (2009) further explained, "It acknowledges that individuals are differentially suited for these various specializations by virtue of their particular talents and station in life. And it places on individuals a solemn obligation to seek their calling and to make whatever sacrifices might be required to diligently and faithfully fulfil the duties associated with it for the glory of God and the welfare of the human family" (p. 34). An effort to identify and focus on the development of unique talents and strengths is at the heart of the work of Marcus Buckingham and his colleagues with the strengths movement (1999). For individuals who are spiritually oriented, this process is one way in which they rely on a higher power in their own personal and professional development.

Workplace spirituality has been described as "the acknowledgment that workers have an internal life that nurtures and is nurtured by meaningful work that happens in the work community. Employees allocate as much significance between the pursuit of paychecks and the attainment of meaningful work, thus enabling a holistic fulfillment as an individual who is connected to others and to the transcendent" (Yunan, Ahmad, & Omar, 2017, p. 62). Thus, encouraging employees to bring their best, authentic selves to the workplace presupposes the freedom to involve the religious and spiritual elements of their lives in their career choices, in their efforts in the organization, and in their own personal improvement.

Employee Engagement

Having explored the spiritual implications of meaningful work, this section will analyze the literature in employee engagement and will discuss similarities and distinctions between the two fields. Additionally, it will introduce ways in which religiosity and spirituality can be useful in increasing employee engagement.

While some have suggested that there is no agreed-upon definition of employee engagement (Bakker, 2011; Gruman & Saks, 2011; Shuck & Wollard, 2010), an analysis of the literature suggests that the basic anatomy of the constructs seem to be generally accepted and widely used. Most scholars conceptualize it as a positive, fulfilling, work-related state of mind characterized by vigor, dedication, and absorption (Schaufeli, Salanova, González-Romá, & Bakker, 2002; Schaufeli, Bakker, & Salanova, 2006; Macey & Schneider, 2008). In this definition, *vigor* represents high levels of energy, resilience, persistence, and willingness to invest in one's work; *dedication* is characterized by a sense of enthusiasm, inspiration, challenge, and pride in one's work; and *absorption* is a total immersion and concentration on one's work (Schaufeli & Bakker, 2004).

The Towers Perrin Talent Report (2003) suggests that engagement is directly tied to meaningful work experience. It postulates that organizations who effectively provide work that is perceived as meaningful will naturally lead to greater employee engagement (Townsend & Gebhardt, 2008). While the engagement literature strives to identify traits that make work universally engaging, the meaningful work literature strives to identify how people differ in what they find meaningful. Some scholars argue that engagement refers specifically to the individual employee's "involvement and satisfaction as well as enthusiasm for work" (Harter et al., 2002, p. 269). While some have suggested the need to distinguish engagement from many of the positive attributes mentioned earlier in this paper, others argue that when various biases are accounted for in the data, a few of these attributes (including satisfaction, commitment, and engagement) seem to be measuring the same thing (Harter & Schmidt, 2008).

Scholars have suggested that some of the connections between engagement and concepts such as ability to thrive, zest, vitality, and even satisfaction might be suspect considering their close definitional relationship, but significant findings show that engagement is positively correlated to financial results (Xanthopoulou, Bakker, Demerouti, & Schaufeli, 2009; Macey & Schneider, 2008), job performance (Bakker & Bal, 2010; Halbesleben & Wheeler, 2008), loyalty, turnover, safety (Harter, Schmidt, & Hayes, 2002), and client satisfaction (Salanova, Agut, & Peiró, 2005). Such findings have fueled the popularity of engagement tools in major consulting firms along with the larger corporate landscape (Harter, Schmidt, & Hayes, 2002).

Analyzing the Relationship between Employee Engagement and Meaningful Work

Overlap

One of the primary areas of overlap between employee engagement and meaningful work is their placement in the positive organizational framework. Scholars focusing on meaningful work (including work as a calling, compassion at work, work centrality, etc.) are emphasizing the many positive benefits of a workforce that draws strength from its employees' purpose (Geldenhuys et al., 2014). Similarly, research surrounding employee engagement is interested in its positive effect on the employee, the leaders, and the overall organization. Both are interested in helping employees be more productive, more fulfilled, more loyal, safer, and more committed to the organization's mission, all while finding greater life satisfaction. It is also interesting to note that while both constructs are framed in a positive way, they have also been studied as mediators against negative outcomes such as job stress, burnout, turnover, and so on.

The three basic components discussed in work engagement are vigor, dedication, and absorption. For the purposes of demonstrating overlap, we will look more closely at what scholars have said regarding dedication. Dedication is the emotional part of engagement that some have called putting one's heart into the job (Schaufeli et al., 2002). Perhaps more directly correlated is a description used by Chughtai and Buckley (2008) when they expressed that the dedication component of engagement typifies an individual's strong sense of identification with their work. Another scholar added that dedication involves "a strong involvement in one's work and a sense of significance and pride" (Fairlie, 2011). These ideas sound much like what researchers focusing on meaningful work describe as an individual seeing their work as "a central part of his or her identity" (Wrzesniewski et al., 1997) and what Bunderson and Thompson (2009) label as "significance" and "purpose."

Perhaps the strongest evidence of overlap is in the literature where both employee engagement and meaningful work are studied together and where scholars identify a strong relationship between the two (Lips-Wiersma & Morris, 2009; Geldenhuys et al., 2014; Hoole & Bonnema, 2015; Fairlie, 2011). One study showed that "meaningful work characteristics had the strongest relationship with engagement" and was also the "strongest unique predictor of engagement" (Fairlie, 2011, p. 516).

Distinctions

While there are many other areas of overlap in the literature, it is also important to analyze the distinguishing features that differentiate the two concepts. One of the key differences between these two constructs is that meaningful work seems most interested in the "what," the "where," and the "why" of work, while engagement focuses more on the "how." Said differently, meaningful work really wants to understand *what* an individual is doing for work, *where* they are doing it, and *why* they have decided to pursue that occupation. Engagement also clearly draws upon the idea of *why* an individual is in a certain job, but scholars are more interested in *how* that job is being performed (vigor, dedication, absorption) and how employees can become even more productive in their work.

Some scholars studying what would traditionally be called work engagement have suggested a new approach to this concept. In 2005 Gretchen Spreitzer and her colleagues introduced "a socially embedded model of thriving at work." In this article they said, "Employees vary in the degree to which they languish or thrive at work. Whereas languishing captures the subjective experience of being stuck, caught in [a] rut, or failing to make progress (Keyes 2002), thriving captures the opposite. When people are thriving, they feel progress and momentum, marked both by a sense of learning (greater understanding and knowledge) and a sense of vitality (aliveness)" (Spreitzer et al., 2005, p. 537). *Vitality* denotes positive feelings of aliveness, spirit, and energy (Peterson & Seligman, 2004).

Learning represents a commitment to personal and professional development and growth. Speaking on the importance of thriving containing both vitality and learning, it was suggested that "one can envision employees who show vitality at work, but over time, this vitality will likely fade if they do not have opportunities for learning and growth, which replenish their vitality. By the same token, one can envision employees who are constantly learning at work but lack the vitality to apply their new knowledge and skills over time. The two components of thriving interact to create an overall sense of forward momentum and progress at work that is not captured by either vitality or learning alone" (Paterson, Luthans, & Jeung, 2013, p. 435).

Thus, while meaningful work and work as a calling focus on individuals being guided to work that matches their passion and purpose, engagement wants to know how productive, energetic, dedicated, and absorbed the individual is once they launch into their chosen work. In a way, meaningful work creates the ideal context in which engagement can succeed. Another important distinction is that it could be possible for an employee to demonstrate high work engagement while being in a job that is not considered "meaningful" (Steger et al., 2012).

Job crafting can play a major role in helping employees to find greater engagement even when their work calling has gone unanswered (Berg et al., 2010). As Berg and his colleagues describe, in these situations "people do not simply accept the tasks and roles that managers outline for them. Instead, they actively shape their lives at work to incorporate or emphasize aspects of their unanswered callings. . . . Job crafting captures the ways in which employees actively change the behavioral, relational, and cognitive boundaries of their jobs to alter their experiences and identities at work" (Berg et al., 2010, p. 979). In short, engagement may be more about techniques for enhancing one's job, whereas meaningful work strives to understand the purposes and personality that make one's job inherently meaningful. After all, "engaging" is something you do to someone else. "Finding meaning" is something one can do only autonomously.

Religiosity, Spirituality, and Employee Engagement

Recent work done by Petchsawang and McLean (2017) argue for a relationship between workplace spirituality and employee engagement. They suggest that the correlation is primarily based on spillover theory, which says that individuals who are satisfied with their personal spiritual life are more likely to be satisfied in their work life (Kolodinsky et al., 2008). In their contribution to *The Palgrave Handbook of Workplace Spirituality and Fulfillment*, Manish Gupta and Sitamma Mikkilineni elaborate on this theory. They summarize that

when employees are happy at work, they invest their personal energies fully in their work role. Spirituality at work influences the perceptions of employees about their organization positively. However, it is important that organizations support the cultivation of employees' spiritual well-being to enable them to engage themselves and outperform in the workplace. This support is majorly in terms of allowing individuals to attain their own spirituality which leads to higher intrinsic motivation, greater organizational commitment, and enhanced creativity. All this in turn leads to higher engagement at work. (Gupta et al., 2018, p. 686)

Others have similarly found correlations between spirituality and employee engagement (Kahn 1990; Roof 2015; Saks 2011). Spirituality in the workplace can increase an individual's sense of completion and wholeness and can likewise improve connectedness at work (Milliman et al., 2003; Gupta et al., 2018). In addition to the overlap already discussed, the construct of thriving could also find synergy when analyzed through the lens of spirituality. The two components of thriving are an individual's sense of vitality and a commitment to learning and growth.

It is important to note that, like the idea of work as a calling, the construct of vitality also has a spiritual heritage. In their Oxford handbook of character strengths and attributes, Christopher Peterson and Martin Seligman (2004) explained, "Concepts of organismic energy and vitality have been central topics in a variety of Eastern philosophies and healing traditions. Prominent among them is the ancient Chinese concept of chi . . . [and] a similar concept in Japan, Ki, [referring] to the energy and power one has available to draw on and is related to physical, mental, and spiritual health" (p. 275). With increased emphasis on employee health and wellness, leaders can find ways to help individuals increase vitality and thus improve productivity and job satisfaction (Palmer, Dankoski, Smith, Brutkiewicz, & Bogdewic, 2011).

Similarly, while a commitment to learning, growth, and development is not unique to the religious space, there are subfields in religious studies—particularly in biblical studies—committed to spiritual formation and growth. In Christianity, this emphasis is largely derived from the biblical teachings of Jesus but are also found in his writings from his early followers (Ward, 2003). A thorough academic treatment of spiritual formation emphasized various facets of development (Boa, 2001). In addition to spiritual formation, studies have shown a relationship between religiosity, learning engagement, and academic performance (Khalid, Mirza, Bin-Feng, & Saed, 2020). Thus, spirituality seems to bring an innate emphasis on progression, and religiosity is positively correlated to learning and growth.

CONCLUSION

There has been a traditional assumption that the separation between church and state makes any discussion about religion or spirituality inappropriate in research in organizational behavior. However, with the recent emphasis on authenticity in the workplace and the encouragement for an employee to bring their "whole self" to work, scholars are finding it easier to discuss the influences of religion and spirituality in the workplace. Two such scholars defined workplace spirituality as "the recognition that employees have an inner life that nourishes and is nourished by meaningful work that takes place in the context of community" (Ashmos & Duchon, 2000, p. 137). Others have defined religiosity as "a particular institutionalized or personal system of beliefs, values, and practices relating to the divine—a level of reality or power that is regarded as the source or ultimate transcending yet immanent in the realm of human experience" (Worden, 2005, p. 221). Scholars have shown that as employees are encouraged to draw upon this powerful part of their inner life, they are often more productive and engaged in their work.

This article has demonstrated ways scholars have found to integrate religiosity and spirituality with organizational behavior. Furthermore, it showed areas of future research where scholars can continue to establish the relationship. While there are opportunities to explore religiosity and spirituality in myriad aspects of the fields of organizational behavior and human resource management, a few have already proven to be natural entry points, including positive organizational behavior, meaningful work, and employee engagement.

In the *Oxford Handbook of Positive Organizational Scholarship,* Sandelands (2012) argued that "lacking an idea of the human spirit, business science cannot account for the trust that makes business possible" (p. 1001). He continued. "If today's literature on spirituality in business is united about anything, it is in the claim that there is 'something more' to the human person; namely his or her human essence or spirit. . . . Perhaps this literature evinces its subject, finding inspiration in its study of 'spirit'" (p. 1002).

For scholars, it seems appropriate to cite the biblical passage that states, "Behold, I say unto you, lift up your eyes, and look on the fields; for they are white already to harvest" (John 4:35). Indeed, the deep correlations and influences of religion on organizational behavior remains a largely underexplored field of study that promises to yield important fruit in the years to come. For leaders and managers, as has been demonstrated throughout this paper, the existing literature in these important areas of study has already shown ways in which religion and spirituality can significantly improve organizational culture, employee engagement, and productivity. Leaders can continue to find ways to enable individuals to bring their complete selves to the workplace and to engage with their colleagues in authentic and meaningful ways.

REFERENCES

Abdel-Khalek, A., & Lester, D. (2006). Optimism and Pessimism in Kuwaiti and American College Students. *The International Journal of Social Psychiatry*, *52*(2), 110–126. doi:10.1177/0020764006062092 PMID:16615244

Abdel-Khalek, A. M. (2014). Religiosity, health and happiness: Significant relations in adolescents from Qatar. *The International Journal of Social Psychiatry*, *60*(7), 656–661. doi:10.1177/0020764013511792 PMID:24327187

Allen, B. P., & Potkay, C. R. (1981). On the arbitrary distinction between states and traits. *Journal of Personality and Social Psychology*, *41*(5), 916–928. doi:10.1037/0022-3514.41.5.916

Ashmos, D. P., & Duchon, D. (2000). Spirituality at work: A conceptualization and measure. *Journal of Management Inquiry*, *9*(2), 134–145. doi:10.1177/105649260092008

Avey, J., Luthans, F., & Mhatre, K. (2008). A call for longitudinal research in positive organizational behavior. *Journal of Organizational Behavior*, *29*(5), 705–711. doi:10.1002/job.517

Avey, J. B., Luthans, F., & Jensen, S. (2009). Psychological capital: A positive resource for combating employee stress and turnover. *Human Resource Management*, *48*(5), 677–693. doi:10.1002/hrm.20294

Avolio, B., & Gardner, W. (2005). Authentic leadership development: Getting to the root of positive forms of leadership. *The Leadership Quarterly*, *16*(3), 315–338. doi:10.1016/j.leaqua.2005.03.001

Bailey, C., Yeoman, R., Madden, A., Thompson, M., & Kerridge, G. (2019). A Review of the Empirical Literature on Meaningful Work: Progress and Research Agenda. *Human Resource Development Review*, *18*(1), 83–113. doi:10.1177/1534484318804653

Bakker, A. (2011). An evidence-based model of work engagement. *Current Directions in Psychological Science*, *20*(4), 265–269. doi:10.1177/0963721411414534

Bandura, A. (1994). Self-efficacy. In V. S. Ramachaudran (Ed.), *Encyclopedia of human behavior* (Vol. 4, pp. 71–81). Academic Press.

Bandura, A. (1997). *Self-efficacy: The exercise of control*. Freeman.

Baykal, E., & Zehir, C. (2018). Mediating effect of psychological capital on the relationship between spiritual leadership and performance. *E+M. Ekonomie a Management*, *21*(3), 124–140. doi:10.15240/tul/001/2018-3-008

Berg, J., Grant, A., & Johnson, V. (2010). When Callings Are Calling: Crafting Work and Leisure in Pursuit of Unanswered Occupational Callings. *Organization Science*, *21*(5), 973–994. doi:10.1287/orsc.1090.0497

Berkelaar, B. L., & Buzzanell, P. M. (2015). Bait and switch or double-edged sword? The (sometimes) failed promises of calling. *Human Relations*, *68*(1), 157–178. doi:10.1177/0018726714526265

Boa, K. (2001). *Conformed to His image: Biblical and practical approaches to spiritual formation*. Zondervan.

Bryd, K., Hageman, A., & Isle, D. (2007). Intrinsic motivation and subjective well-being: The unique contribution of intrinsic religious motivation. *The International Journal for the Psychology of Religion*, *17*(2), 41–156. doi:10.1080/10508610701244155

Buckingham, M., & Clifton, D. (2001). *Now, discover your strengths*. The Free Press.

Buckingham, M., & Coffman, C. (1999). *First, break all the rules*. Simon & Schuster.

Bunderson, J. S., & Thompson, J. A. (2009). The call of the wild: Zookeepers, callings, and the dual edges of deeply meaningful work. *Administrative Science Quarterly*, *54*(1), 32–57. doi:10.2189/asqu.2009.54.1.32

Byrne, P. P. (2012). *The relationship between religiosity, general self-efficacy and locus of control* (Diploma thesis). School of Arts, Dublin Business School.

Calvin, J. (1574). *Sermons of M. John Calvin upon the Epistle of Saint Paul to the Galatians*. Lucas Harison and George Bishop.

Cameron, K., Dutton, J., Quinn, R., & Wrzesniewski, A. (2003). *Developing a discipline of positive organizational scholarship. Positive Organizational Scholarship*. Berrett-Koehler.

Cameron, K. S., & Spreitzer, G. M. (Eds.). (2012). *The Oxford Handbook of Positive Organizational Scholarship*. Oxford University Press.

Cheung, F., Tang, C. S., & Tang, S. (2011). Psychological capital as a moderator between emotional labor, burnout, and job satisfaction among school teachers in China. *International Journal of Stress Management*, *18*(4), 348–371. doi:10.1037/a0025787

Chughtai, A. A., & Buckley, F. (2008). Work Engagement and its Relationship with State and Trait Trust: A Conceptual Analysis. *Journal of Behavioral and Applied Management*, *10*, 47. doi:10.21818/001c.17170

Dawkins, S., Martin, A., Scott, J., & Sanderson, K. (2015). Advancing conceptualization and measurement of psychological capital as a collective construct. *Human Relations*, *68*(6), 925–949. doi:10.1177/0018726714549645

Donaldson, S., Dollwet, M., & Rao, M. (2014). Happiness, excellence, and optimal human functioning revisited: Examining the peer-reviewed literature linked to positive psychology. *The Journal of Positive Psychology*, *10*(3), 185–195. doi:10.1080/17439760.2014.943801

Duffy, R., Allan, B., Autin, K., & Douglass, R. (2014). Living a Calling and Work Well-Being: A Longitudinal Study. *Journal of Counseling Psychology*, *61*(4), 605–615. doi:10.1037/cou0000042 PMID:25181588

Duffy, R. D., & Sedlacek, W. E. (2007). The presence of and search for a calling: Connections to career development. *Journal of Vocational Behavior*, *70*(3), 590–601. doi:10.1016/j.jvb.2007.03.007

Elangovan, A. R., Pinder, C., & McLean, M. (2010). Callings and organizational behavior. *Journal of Vocational Behavior, 76*(3), 428–440. doi:10.1016/j.jvb.2009.10.009

Fairlie, P. (2011). Meaningful Work, Employee Engagement, and Other Key Employee Outcomes: Implications for Human Resource Development. *Advances in Developing Human Resources, 13*(4), 508–525. doi:10.1177/1523422311431679

Fatima, S., Sharif, S., & Khalid, I. (2018). How does religiosity enhance psychological well-being? Roles of self-efficacy and perceived social support. *Psychology of Religion and Spirituality, 10*(2), 119–127. doi:10.1037/rel0000168

Forest, J., Mageau, G.A., Sarrazin, C., & Morin, E.M. (2011). "Work is my passion": The different affective, behavioural, and cognitive consequences of harmonious and obsessive passion toward work. *Canadian Journal of Administrative Sciences-revue Canadienne Des Sciences De L Administration, 28*, 27–40.

Fradelos, E. C., Latsou, D., Mitsi, D., Tsaras, K., Lekka, D., Lavdaniti, M., Tzavella, F., & Papathanasiou, I. V. (2018). Assessment of the relation between religiosity, mental health, and psychological resilience in breast cancer patients. *Contemporary Oncology (Poznan, Poland), 22*(3), 172–177. doi:10.5114/wo.2018.78947 PMID:30455589

Gardner, W., Cogliser, C., Davis, K., & Dickens, M. (2011). Authentic leadership: A review of the literature and research agenda. *The Leadership Quarterly, 22*(6), 1120–1145. doi:10.1016/j.leaqua.2011.09.007

Geldenhuys, M., Łaba, K., & Venter, C. M. (2014). Meaningful work, work engagement and organisational commitment. *SA Journal of Industrial Psychology, 40*(1). Advance online publication. doi:10.4102ajip.v40i1.1098

Görgens-Ekermans, G., & Herbert, M. (2013). Psychological capital: Internal and external validity of the Psychological Capital Questionnaire (PCQ-24) on a South African sample. *SA Journal of Industrial Psychology, 39*(2).

Gruman, J. A., & Saks, A. M. (2011). Performance management and employee engagement. *Human Resource Management Review, 21*(2), 123–136. doi:10.1016/j.hrmr.2010.09.004

Gupta, M., & Mikkilineni, S. (2018). Spirituality and Employee Engagement at Work. In S. Dhiman, G. Roberts, & J. Crossman (Eds.), The Palgrave Handbook of Workplace Spirituality and Fulfillment. Academic Press.

Halbesleben, J. R. B., & Bowler, W. M. (2007). Emotional exhaustion and job performance: The mediating role of motivation. *The Journal of Applied Psychology, 91*(1), 93–106. doi:10.1037/0021-9010.92.1.93 PMID:17227154

Harter, J. K., Schmidt, F. L., Asplund, J. W., Killham, E. A., & Agrawal, S. (2010). Causal Impact of Employee Work Perceptions on the Bottom Line of Organizations. *Perspectives on Psychological Science, 5*(4), 378–389. doi:10.1177/1745691610374589 PMID:26162184

Héliot, Y. F., Gleibs, I. H., Coyle, A., Rousseau, D. M., & Rojon, C. (2020). Religious identity in the workplace: A systematic review, research agenda, and practical implications. *Human Resource Management, 59*(2), 153–173. doi:10.1002/hrm.21983

Hewlin, P. F., Karelaia, N., Kouchaki, M., & Sedikides, C. (2020). Authenticity at work: Its shapes, triggers, and consequences. *Organizational Behavior and Human Decision Processes, 158*, 80–82. doi:10.1016/j.obhdp.2020.01.010

Hicks, D. A. (2002). Spiritual and religious diversity in the workplace. *The Leadership Quarterly, 13*(4), 379–396. doi:10.1016/S1048-9843(02)00124-8

Homaei, R., Bozorgi, Z. D., Ghahfarokhi, M. S., & Hosseinpour, S. (2016). Relationship between Optimism, Religiosity and Self-Esteem with Marital Satisfaction and Life Satisfaction. *International Education Studies, 9*(6), 53–61. doi:10.5539/ies.v9n6p53

Hoole, C., & Bonnema, J. (2015). Work engagement and meaningful work across generational cohorts. *SA Journal of Human Resource Management, 13*(1). Advance online publication. doi:10.4102ajhrm.v13i1.681

Hunter, I., Dika, B., & Banning, J. (2010). College students' perceptions of calling in work and life: A qualitative analysis. *Journal of Vocational Behavior, 76*(2), 178–186. doi:10.1016/j.jvb.2009.10.008

Hwang, R., Ku, N., Mao, H., & Lo, S. (1996). Hope and related factors of breast cancer women. *Nurs Res (China), 4*(1), 35–46.

Ilies, T., Morgeson, F., & Nahrgang, J. (2005). Authentic leadership and eudaemonic well-being: Understanding leader–follower outcomes. *The Leadership Quarterly, 16*(3), 373–394. doi:10.1016/j.leaqua.2005.03.002

Javanmard, G. (2013). Religious Beliefs and Resilience in Academic Students. *Procedia: Social and Behavioral Sciences, 84*, 744–748. doi:10.1016/j.sbspro.2013.06.638

Judge, T., Heller, D., & Mount, M. (2002). Five-factor model of personality and job satisfaction: A meta-analysis. *The Journal of Applied Psychology*, *87*(3), 530–541. doi:10.1037/0021-9010.87.3.530 PMID:12090610

Kahn, W. (1990). Psychological Conditions of Personal Engagement and Disengagement at Work. *Academy of Management Journal*, *33*(4), 692–724.

Kernis, M. H., & Goldman, B. M. (2006). A multicomponent conceptualization of authenticity: Theory and research. In M. P. Zanna (Ed.), Advances in experimental social psychology (Vol. 38, pp. 283–357). doi:10.1016/S0065-2601(06)38006-9

Keyes, C. L. M. (2002). The mental health continuum: From languishing to flourishing in life. *Journal of Health and Social Behavior*, *43*(2), 207–222. doi:10.2307/3090197 PMID:12096700

Khalid, F., Mirza, S. S., Bin-Feng, C., & Saeed, N. (2020). Learning Engagements and the Role of Religion. *SAGE Open*, *10*(1). Advance online publication. doi:10.1177/2158244019901256

Kleinhandler, C. (2016). *Haredi Jewish start-up founder from Israel*. BBC Online. Retrieved from https://www.bbc.co.uk/news/magazine-37300929

Kolodinsky, R., Giacalone, R., & Jurkiewicz, C. (2008). Workplace Values and Outcomes: Exploring Personal, Organizational, and Interactive Workplace Spirituality. *Journal of Business Ethics*, *81*(2), 465–480. doi:10.100710551-007-9507-0

Kram, K. E., Wasserman, I. C., & Yip, J. (2012). Metaphors of Identity and Professional Practice: Learning From the Scholar–Practitioner. *The Journal of Applied Behavioral Science*, *48*(3), 304–341. doi:10.1177/0021886312439097

Lips-Wiersma, M., & Morrise, L. (2009). Discriminating between 'meaningful work' and the 'management of meaning. *Journal of Business Ethics*, *88*(3), 491–511. doi:10.100710551-009-0118-9

Luthans, F. (2002a). Positive organizational behavior: Developing and managing psychological strengths. *The Academy of Management Executive*, *16*(1), 57–72. doi:10.5465/ame.2002.6640181

Luthans, F. (2002b). The need for and meaning of positive organizational behavior. *Journal of Organizational Behavior*, *23*(6), 695–706. doi:10.1002/job.165

Luthans, F., & Avolio, B. (2009). The "point" of positive organizational behavior. *Journal of Organizational Behavior*, *30*(2), 291–307. doi:10.1002/job.589

Luthans, F., Van Wyk, R., & Walumbwa, F. (2004). Recognition and development of hope for South African organizational leaders. *Leadership and Organization Development Journal*, *25*(6), 512–527. doi:10.1108/01437730410556752

Luthans, F., & Youssef, C. M. (2007). Emerging positive organizational behavior. *Journal of Management*, *33*(3), 321–349. doi:10.1177/0149206307300814

Luthans, F., Youssef, C. M., Sweetman, D. S., & Harms, P. D. (2013). Meeting the leadership challenge of employee well-being through relationship PsyCap and health PsyCap. *Journal of Leadership & Organizational Studies*, *20*(1), 118–133. doi:10.1177/1548051812465893

Luthans, F., Youssef-Morgan, C. M., & Avolio, B. J. (2015). *Psychological Capital and Beyond*. Oxford University Press.

Macey, W. H., & Schneider, B. (2008). The meaning of employee engagement. *Industrial and Organizational Psychology: Perspectives on Science and Practice*, *1*(1), 3–30. doi:10.1111/j.1754-9434.2007.0002.x

Masten, A. S., & Reed, M. G. (2002). Resilience in development. In C. R. Snyder & S. J. Lopez (Eds.), *Handbook of positive psychology* (pp. 74–80). Oxford University Press.

Maurer, T. J., & Pierce, H. R. (1998). A comparison of Likert scale and traditional measures of self-efficacy. *The Journal of Applied Psychology*, *83*(2), 324–329. doi:10.1037/0021-9010.83.2.324

May, D. R., Gilson, R. L., & Harter, L. M. (2004). The Psychological Conditions of Meaningfulness, Safety and Availability and the Engagement of the Human Spirit at Work. *Journal of Occupational and Organizational Psychology*, *77*(1), 11–37. doi:10.1348/096317904322915892

Meyers, C. (2007). *Industrial psychology*. Garnsey Press.

Miller, A. (2008). A critique of positive psychology—Or 'the new science of happiness.'. *Journal of Philosophy of Education*, *42*(3-4), 591–608. doi:10.1111/j.1467-9752.2008.00646.x

Milliman, J., Ferguson, J., Trickett, D., & Condemi, B. (1999). Spirit and community at Southwest Airlines. *Journal of Organizational Change Management*, *12*(3), 221–233. doi:10.1108/09534819910273928

Mitroff, I., & Denton, E. A. (1999). A Study of Spirituality in the Workplace. *Sloan Management Review*, *40*, 83–92.

Momeni, K., & Shahbazi Rad, A. (2012). Relationship of spirituality, resiliency, and coping strategies with quality of life in university students. *Journal of Behavioral Science.*, *6*, 1–2.

Munn, S. L. (2013). Unveiling the Work–Life System: The Influence of Work–Life Balance on Meaningful Work. *Advances in Developing Human Resources*, *15*(4), 401–417. doi:10.1177/1523422313498567

Nie, F. (2019). Religion and self-efficacy: A multilevel approach. *Mental Health, Religion & Culture*, *22*(3), 279–292. doi:10.1080/13674676.2019.1612337

Norman, S., Avey, J., Nimnicht, J., & Pigeon, N. G. (2010). The interactive effects of psychological capital and organizational identity on employee citizenship and deviance behaviors. *Journal of Leadership & Organizational Studies*, *17*(4), 380–391. doi:10.1177/1548051809353764

Oates, K. L. M., Hall, M. E. L., & Anderson, T. L. (2005). Calling and conflict: A qualitative exploration of interrole conflict and the sanctification of work in Christian mothers in academia. *Journal of Psychology and Theology*, *33*(3), 210–223. doi:10.1177/009164710503300306

Oruc, E., & Kutanis, O. (2015). The views of academic staff on psychological capital: A qualitative study in Turkey. *International Journal of Scientific Research and Innovative Technology*, *2*(5), 1–9.

Ozer, D. J., & Benet-Martínez, V. (2006). Personality and the prediction of consequential outcomes. *Annual Review of Psychology*, *57*(1), 401–421. doi:10.1146/annurev.psych.57.102904.190127 PMID:16318601

Pakdaman, M., & Balideh, M. (2020). The Study of the Effect of Psychological Capital and Spiritual Intelligence on the Performance of Individuals: A Review Study. *Archives of Pharmacy Practice (Mumbai)*, *11*(S1), 126–136.

Parker, S. (1998). Enhancing role breadth self-efficacy: The roles of job enrichment and other organizational interventions. *The Journal of Applied Psychology*, *6*(6), 835–852. doi:10.1037/0021-9010.83.6.835 PMID:9885197

Paterson, T., Luthans, F., & Jeung, W. (2014). Thriving at work: Impact of psychological capital and supervisor support. *Journal of Organizational Behavior*, *35*(3), 434–446. doi:10.1002/job.1907

Petchsawang, P., & McLean, G. N. (2017). Workplace spirituality, mindfulness meditation, and work engagement. *Journal of Management, Spirituality & Religion*, *14*(3), 216–244. doi:10.1080/14766086.2017.1291360

Peterson, C., & Seligman, M. E. P. (2004). *Character strengths and virtues: A classification and handbook.* New York: Oxford University Press.

Pew Research Center. (2015). *America's changing religious landscape.* Pew Research Publications.

Pourghaznein, T., Hoshmand, P., Talasaz Firouzi, E., & Esmailli, H. (2003). The sources of inspiration and the level of hope among cancer patients. *Majallah-i Ravanpizishki va Ravanshinasi-i Balini-i Iran, 8*(4), 82–87.

Richardson, G. (2002). The metatheory of resilience and resiliency. *Journal of Clinical Psychology, 58*(3), 307–321. doi:10.1002/jclp.10020 PMID:11836712

Richardson, G., Neiger, B., Jensen, S., & Kumpfer, K. (1990). The resiliency model. *Health Education, 21*(6), 33–39. doi:10.1080/00970050.1990.10614589

Roberts, S., Scherer, L., & Bowyer, C. (2011). Job Stress and Incivility: What Role Does Psychological Capital Play? *Journal of Leadership & Organizational Studies, 18*(4), 449–458. doi:10.1177/1548051811409044

Roof, R. (2015). The association of individual spirituality on employee engagement: The Spirit at work. *Journal of Business Ethics, 130*(3), 585–599. doi:10.100710551-014-2246-0

Saeidi, M. S., Pour Ebrahim, T., Bagherian, F., & Mansour, L. (2010). The relationship between spirituality and resilience of families, the quality of communication in family mediation. *J Manag Syst, 2*, 63–79.

Saks, A. M. (2006). Antecedents and consequences of employee engagement. *Journal of Managerial Psychology, 21*(7), 600–619. doi:10.1108/02683940610690169

Salanova, M., Agut, S., & Peiró, J. M. (2005, November). Linking Organizational Resources and Work Engagement to Employee Performance and Customer Loyalty: The Mediation of Service Climate. *The Journal of Applied Psychology, 90*(6), 1217–1227. doi:10.1037/0021-9010.90.6.1217 PMID:16316275

Sandelands, L. (2012). God we trust: A comparison of spiritualities at work. Academic Press.

Schaufeli, W. B., & Bakker, A. B. (2004). Job demands, job resources, and their relationship with burnout and engagement: A multi-sample study. *Journal of Organizational Behavior, 25*(3), 293–437. doi:10.1002/job.248

Schaufeli, W. B., Bakker, A. B., & Salanova, M. (2006). The Measurement of Work Engagement With a Short Questionnaire: A Cross-National Study. *Educational and Psychological Measurement*, *66*(4), 701–716. doi:10.1177/0013164405282471

Schaufeli, W. B., Salanova, M., González-Romá, V., & Bakker, A. B. (2002). The measurement of engagement and burnout: A two sample confirmatory factor analytic approach. *Journal of Happiness Studies: An Interdisciplinary Forum on Subjective Well-Being*, *3*(1), 71–92. doi:10.1023/A:1015630930326

Seligman, M. E. P. (1999). *Seligman speech at Lincoln Summit.* Retrieved from https://www.sas.upenn.edu/psych/seligman/lincspeech.htm

Seligman, M. E. P., & Csikszentmihalyi, M. (2000). Positive psychology: An introduction. *The American Psychologist*, *55*(1), 5–14. doi:10.1037/0003-066X.55.1.5 PMID:11392865

Seligman, M. E. P., Steen, T., Park, N., & Person, C. (2005). Positive psychology progress: Empirical validation of interventions. *The American Psychologist*, *60*(5), 410–421. doi:10.1037/0003-066X.60.5.410 PMID:16045394

Shuck, B., & Wollard, K. (2010). Employee engagement and HRD: A seminal review of the foundations. *Human Resource Development Review*, *9*(1), 89–110. doi:10.1177/1534484309353560

Snyder, C. R., Irving, L. M., & Anderson, J. R. (1991). *Hope and health: Measuring the will and the way. In The handbook of social and clinical psychology: The health perspective.* Pergamon Press.

Snyder, C. R., Shorey, H. S., Cheavens, J., Pulvers, K. M., Adams, V. H., & Wiklund, C. (2002). Hope and academic success in college. *Journal of Educational Psychology*, *94*(4), 820–826. doi:10.1037/0022-0663.94.4.820

Spreitzer, G., Sutcliffe, K., Dutton, J., Sonenshein, S., & Grant, A. (2005). A Socially Embedded Model of Thriving at Work. *Organization Science*, *16*(5), 537–549. doi:10.1287/orsc.1050.0153

Stajkovic, A. D., & Luthans, F. (1998). Self-Efficacy and Work-Related Performance: A Meta-Analysis. *Psychological Bulletin*, *124*(2), 240–261. doi:10.1037/0033-2909.124.2.240

Steger, M. F., & Dik, B. J. (2009). If one is looking for meaning in life, does it help to find meaning at work? *Applied Psychology. Health and Well-Being*, *1*(3), 303–320. doi:10.1111/j.1758-0854.2009.01018.x

Steger, M. F., Dik, B. J., & Duffy, R. D. (2012). Measuring Meaningful Work: The Work and Meaning Inventory (WAMI). *Journal of Career Assessment, 20*(3), 322–337. doi:10.1177/1069072711436160

Terkel, S. (1972). *Working*. Avon Books.

Townsend, P., & Gebhardt, J. E. (2008). Employee engagement—Completely. *Human Resource Management International Digest, 16*(3), 22–24. doi:10.1108/09670730810869529

Vallerand, R. J., & Houlfort, N. (2003). Passion at Work: Toward a New Conceptualization. In S. W. Gilliland, D. D. Steiner, & D. P. Skarlicki (Eds.), *Emerging Perspective on Values in Organizations* (pp. 175–204). Information Age Publishing.

Van Zyl, L. E., Deacon, E., & Rothmann, S. (2010). Towards happiness: Experience of work-role fit, meaningfulness, and work engagement of industrial/organisational psychologists in South Africa. *SA Journal of Industrial Psychology, 36*(1), 1–10. doi:10.4102ajip.v36i1.890

Ward, B. (2003). *The Desert Fathers: Sayings of the early Christian monks*. Penguin Books.

Watson, P., Morris, R., & Hood, R. Jr. (1988). Sin and self-functioning: II. Grace, guilt, and psychological adjustment. *Journal of Psychology and Theology, 16*(3), 270–281. doi:10.1177/009164718801600306

Worden, S. (2005). Religion in Strategic Leadership: A Positivistic, Normative/Theological, and Strategic Analysis. *Journal of Business Ethics, 57*(3), 221–239. doi:10.100710551-004-6943-y

Wright, K. K. (2010). *An examination of the relationship between teacher efficacy and teacher religiosity* (Ph.D. Thesis). University of North Texas.

Wright, T. A. (2003). Positive organizational behavior: An idea whose time has truly come. *Journal of Organizational Behavior, 24*(4), 437–442. doi:10.1002/job.197

Wrzesniewski, A., McCauley, C., Rozin, P., & Schwartz, B. (1997). Jobs, Careers, And Callings: People's Relations To Their Work. *Journal of Research in Personality, 31*(1), 21–33. doi:10.1006/jrpe.1997.2162

Xanthopoulou, D., Bakker, A. B., & Fischbach, A. (2013). Work engagement among employees facing emotional demands: The role of personal resources. *Journal of Personnel Psychology, 12*(2), 74–84. doi:10.1027/1866-5888/a000085

Youseff, C., & Luthans, F. (2007). Positive organizational behavior in the workplace: The impact of hope, optimism, and resilience. *Journal of Management*, *33*(5), 774–800. doi:10.1177/0149206307305562

Yunan, W., Ahmad, A., & Omar, Z. (2017). The Experience of Workplace Spirituality: Do Age and Educational Attainment Matter? *International Journal of Academic Research in Business & Social Sciences*, *7*(7), 61–69. doi:10.6007/IJARBSS/v7-i7/3078

Chapter 5
The Influence of Religion and Spirituality on Managing Individuals in Organizations:
Reflections From the Kingdom of Bahrain

Nehal Fareed El Naggar
Royal University for Women, Bahrain

Jalal Nasser
JAFCON Consultants for Productivity Improvement, Bahrain

ABSTRACT

Religion is a cornerstone of any society as it affects politics, law, economics, science, and is reflected throughout history in arts and more. In contrast, spirituality is an individual practice with the aim of mindfulness and having a sense of peace and purpose. This research aims to investigate the influence of religion and spirituality on organizational behavior in organizations in Bahrain specifically with regard to managing individuals in Bahrain. A sample of 46 valid responses was reached due to the sensitivity of the topic. Nationality was found to have a statistically significant effect on 'behavior-based religion'. Principal component analysis found two distinctive factors among the religion values indicators being referred to as 'behavior-based religion' and 'belief of religion'.

DOI: 10.4018/978-1-7998-9319-6.ch005

1 INTRODUCTION

Religion is never the problem; it's the people who use it to gain power. Julian Casablancas (n.d.)

Religion and spirituality are part of the daily life of individuals and from this perspective, Managers and organizations must provide considerable attention to this while managing individuals especially when coming from different backgrounds, cultures and ethnicities.

SHRM (2008) stated that as the focus on diversity and inclusion grows, so does the visibility of faith and religious practices in the workplace. Religion and spirituality, for many employees, are no longer a part of their lives that they leave at home as religion is probably the strongest belief system that existed for so many years. Such beliefs influence individual and organizational behavior. Spirituality for these employees is a way of life; their religion and spirituality define who they are and determine their actions.

The issue addressed in this chapter is about exploring the influence of religion, if there is any, on managing individuals working in Bahrain. This topic was under-researched especially in Bahrain and the GCC. The main research objective is to investigate the influence of religious values indicators on managing individuals as it is a major topic of organizational behavior. The sub-objectives include the following:

- To measure the religion values indicators levels among a representative sample of employees working in Bahrain
- To understand the tendency to manage individuals differently as per their religion or ethnicity measured on the main six Human Resources functions (Recruitment, Training, Salary and Pay, Performance Appraisal, Motivation and Work Relationships) as part of the overall organizational behavior.
- To assess the relation between the self-reported religion values indicators and the perception of managing individuals which is an indicator of organizational behavior

The importance of this topic is that it contributes to the literature. And as Alkhatib & Arnout (2019) stated that it is necessary to direct research and studies to know the contribution of religiosity in predict leadership organizational behaviors to detect the obstacles that decrease the success and effectiveness of leaders in achieving the objectives of the institution and plan the developmental training program that based on religion to increase the leaders' success and efficiency."

Majority of studies in this topic addressed religion and spirituality with caution, and when addressed, it has been addressed from leadership or as an ethical drive of business. (Frunza, S., 2017). In contrast several researchers referred to the importance of studying religion especially in organizations and in managing people, especially with the relatively low number of research addressing religion and spirituality. (Ysseldyk et al., 2010) stated that "there is a significant body of work connecting religion and business ethics, and the notion of workplace spirituality has also generated considerable attention". He added that- according to his review- very few articles in the mainstream management literature identified the topic of religion where most focused-on religion in the west and very few examined different faiths or parts of the world.

In accordance, it is important to research this topic from the employees' point of view as well as the management of the companies and organizations operating in Bahrain. Both the employees and the management teams would be informed better with the findings of this research topic.

Given the intense role that religion and culture play in societies and organizations, it is surprising that management researchers have not explored the influence of religion and culture on organizations behavior in a more meaningful and determined way. This is probably the topic is deemed too sensitive. Whatever the reason is, this chapter aims to shed light on one research in this area that we hope it would be the start of several studies to follow. The chapter started with the above introduction section and continues with an overview on Bahrain being the scope of this chapter followed by a section about previous studies followed by a brief section of the methods and approaches used to address the relation between religion values indicators and the perception of employees toward the managing of them in their organizations. Main findings will be discussed followed by conclusions and implications.

2 OVERVIEW ON BAHRAIN

According to the CIA World Factbook, "The Kingdom of Bahrain is an archipelago of 33 islands covering a total area of 741 square kilometers in the Arabian Gulf, located east of the Kingdom of Saudi Arabia and northwest of Qatar. The capital of Bahrain is Manama, and the estimated population is 1,526,929 which is considered to be the smallest population of the Gulf States, but urbanization rate exceeds 90% with a 0.9% growth rate." (July 2021 est.)

The majority of these people are Arabs; there are many temporary and permanent immigrant workers, in contrast one-third of the population is foreign-born. Nineteen percent of the population is Asian, 10 percent is non-Bahraini Arab, and 8 percent is Irani. There are significantly more men than women. The population is growing rapidly with a high birth rate and a low death rate. One-third of the people are less than fifteen years old. Tables and Figures will be presented in the following sections.

2.1 The Scene in Bahrain

Bahrain Open Data Portal data shows the demographic of Bahrain population as per the latest census of the year 2020. The total population in 2020 was 1.5 million approximately. The main religion in Bahrain is Islam, where Muslims represent 74% of the total population. Among Bahrainis, Muslims are the great majority (99.68%). However, among non-Bahrainis, Muslims are half of the population (50.87%).

Bahrain Open Data Portal data also shows the distribution of Bahrain population by age group, nationality and sex as per census 2020. It can be observed that the working population taking from 15-19 years to 60-64 years represents 76.71% of the total population. This working population represents 88.27% in non-Bahrainis and 63.91% in Bahrainis suggesting that non-Bahrainis are mainly workers.

Figures 1 to 3 shows the population pyramid by age group, nationality and sex. The total population in Bahrain tends to be represented by male slightly more when compared to female. While the Bahraini populations seems to have almost equal representation by both sexes, the non-Bahraini population seems to have more male representation when compared to female to a great extent. This might suggest that the non-Bahrainis are mainly male who are living alone either they are single or left their families at home country.

Figure 1 represents the population pyramid for Bahrain illustrating the age and sex structure of the whole population. As shown above, the population is distributed along the horizontal axis. The males are represented on the left and the females on the right over 5-year age groups. The youngest age groups at the bottom and the oldest at the top.

As for the Religious Beliefs, seventy percent of the population is Shi'a Muslim, 15 percent is Sunni Muslim, and the remaining 15 percent is Christian or Jewish or follows indigenous practices. Muslims believe in the equality of all people before Allah.

The Bahrain 2020 International Religious Freedom Report by the United Nations referred to the constitution that declares Islam to be the official religion and sharia to be a principal source for legislation. It provides for freedom of conscience, the inviolability of places of worship, and freedom to perform religious rites. The constitution guarantees the right to express and publish opinions, provided these do not infringe on the "fundamental beliefs of Islamic doctrine."

2.2 Religions in Bahrain

Labour Market Regulatory Authority (LMRA) Open Data Portal shows the top 20 nationalities of non-Bahraini workers as per the latest available data of March 2021. These nationalities are proxy of religion. India is the top nationality which

Figure 1. Population pyramid of total population (2020)
source: Information & eGovernment Authority

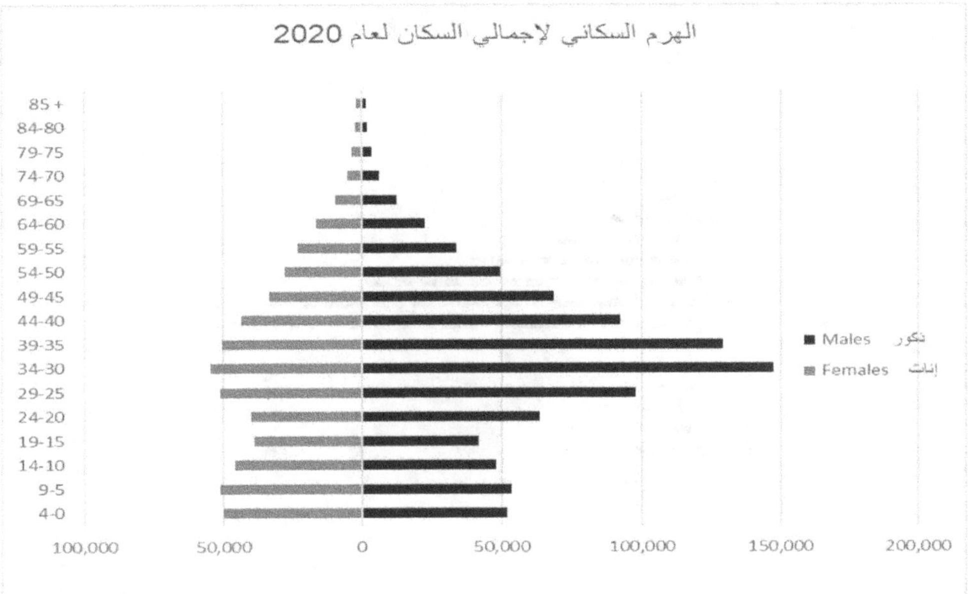

Figure 2. Population pyramid of Bahraini population (2020)
source: Information & eGovernment Authority

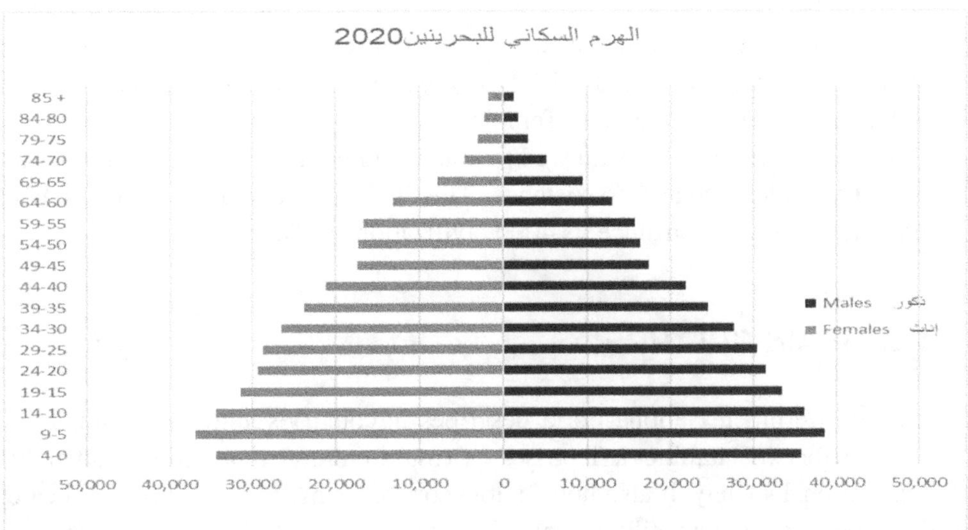

Figure 3. Population pyramid of non-Bahraini population (2020)
source: Information & eGovernment Authority

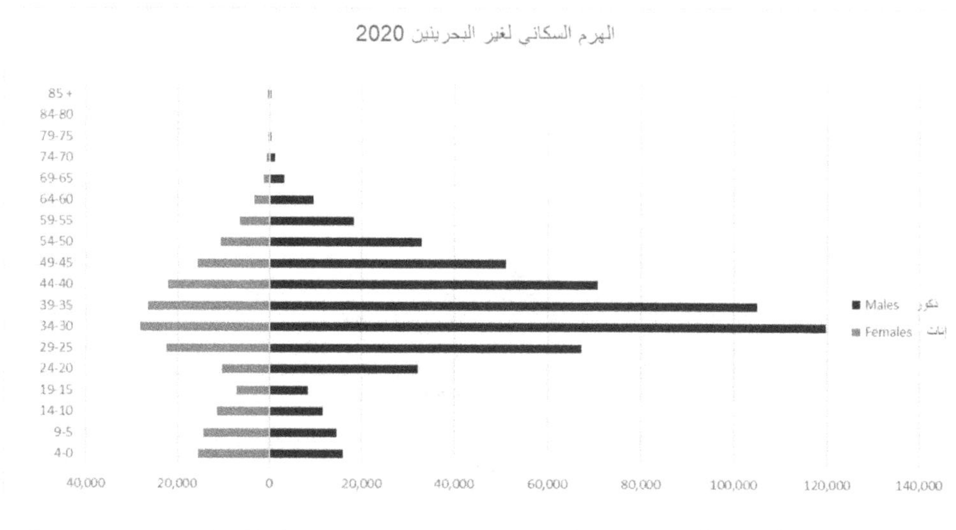

suggests the main religions of India including: Muslims, Hindus, Christians, Sikhs and other religions. Philippines's nationality would also suggest Christians including Roman Catholic, Christians cults and Protestants. United Kingdom nationality would suggest Christians too.

2.3 Practicing non-Muslim religions in Bahrain

In the capital of Bahrain, Manama, churches can be easily observed located not far away from mosques. Also, the Jewish Synagogue is located in the capital Manama as well as the Hindu Shri Krishna Temple.

Non-Muslim religions are allowed to practice in public in Bahrain. This shows the country's tolerance and coexistence. This is deeply rooted in the only island among the MENA region since its 4000 civilizations of Dilmun.

2.4 BAHRAIN CULTURE

Bahrain eGovernment National Portal describes the country's culture as "an attractive destination for expat families as it possesses a multi-cultural, multi-ethnic and multi-denominational society. It also holds a low cost of living, high-quality healthcare, and excellent education facilities that offer a diversity of international curriculums.

The Kingdom is a cosmopolitan capital city, an attractive liberal lifestyle with a rich history and culture - from historical monuments such as AlKhamis Mosque established back in 692 A.D. to the Bahrain International Circuit which is one of the most modernized and advanced Formula One racetracks in the World.

Like the rest of the Gulf monarchies, Bahrain has long been influenced by strong religious and societal views. And Despite working within the boundaries of fast moving internationalized organizations, Managers and leaders in Bahrain continues to demonstrate the Islamic influence on their attitudes toward work (Jonathan et al. 2009).

In contrast, according to the eGovernment National Portal, "Bahrain is known in the Gulf for being open and tolerant. Bahraini men and women socialize and congregate at local cafes as well as restaurants. Expatriates mix with Bahraini nationals across all social settings; leading people from all over the Gulf to visit the Kingdom for the purpose of relaxation and enjoyment."

2.5 BAHRAIN LABOR LAW

Bahrain Labor Law covers religion, gender and culture aspects of employment in the private sector.

As for women employment, according to Article 29 female workers are subject to all of the provisions governing the employment as the male workers without discrimination in similar situations while providing women maternity leaves. In contrast Article 30 governs the women employment at night which is a cultural aspect of women work unless there is a necessity or special occasions in which females may work at night. The law as well prohibits some jobs where females are prohibited as well as

by stating: The Minister shall issue a decision determining the cases, works and occasions in which women may not be employed at night. Article 31 is also related to the culturally accepted work in which the employment of women is prohibited, stating: The Minister shall issue, after taking the opinion of the concerned authorities, a decision determining the works in which the employment of women is prohibited.

Moreover, Bahrain Labor Law prohibited discrimination in employees' wages in Article 39 of the law stating that Discrimination in wages based on sex, origin, language, religion or ideology shall be prohibited.

Another aspect of the culture dimensions for workers is related to leave. The Bahrain Labor Law article 63 states few types of leave that are culturally oriented out of which that Muslim female worker shall be entitled to a one month paid leave in the event of death of her spouse, moreover she is entitled to complete the Idda period (grievance) of three months and ten days from her annual leave, and in the event the balance of her annual leave is insufficient she may take an unpaid leave.

Article 64 mentioned that Friday is a special day for Muslims as a leave with full pay. Non-Muslims consequently take Friday with full pay as the Main Holiday in the country.

In addition, Article 67 provides Muslim workers who spent five consecutive years in the service of his employer a fourteen day leave with full pay to perform his Hajj (Pilgrimage) obligation. This leave shall be granted once to the worker during his period of service unless he benefited from it from during his service for another employer.

2.6 BAHRAIN ON INGLEHART–WELZEL CULTURAL MAP

World Values Survey (WVS) website describe it as "an international research program devoted to the scientific and academic study of social, political, economic, religious and cultural values of people in the world. The project's goal is to assess which impact values stability or change over time has on the social, political and economic development of countries and societies." WVS has over the years demonstrated that people's beliefs play a key role in economic development, the emergence and flourishing of democratic institutions, the rise of gender equality, and the extent to which societies have effective government.

The data of WVS are kept available for researchers. WVS data was utilized by political scientists Ronald Inglehart and Christian Welzel asserts that there are two major dimensions of cross-cultural variation in the world:

1. Traditional values versus Secular-rational values and
2. Survival values versus Self-expression values.

Figure 3 shows the latest version available of Inglehart–Welzel Cultural Map (2017-2021). As Bahrain WVS data is not available till now, it can be induced using this cultural map that it belongs to the African-Islamic cluster found at the bottom left corner. The African-Islamic cluster includes countries that are like Bahrain such as the neighbor countries: Saudi Arabia and Qatar. The two dimensions of this cluster which Bahrain is expected to be part of are: negative values of Traditional values versus Secular-rational values dimension and negative values of Survival values versus Self-expression values dimension.

Thus, Inglehart–Welzel Cultural Map suggests that Bahrain culture tends to be a traditional society and thrives to survive.

The main characteristics of traditional society within the Inglehart–Welzel Cultural Map includes the following:

- religion is very important
- the importance of the family is a major theme
- have high levels of national pride
- favor more respect for authority

The main characteristics of survival society within the Inglehart–Welzel Cultural Map includes the following:

- have relatively low levels of subjective well-being
- relatively intolerant of outgroups
- low on support for gender equality

Knowing the tolerance and coexistence of Bahrain as a country since the civilization of Dilmun more than 4000 years ago till now, one would expect that it scores high on the survival society dimension.

This section provided a brief of Bahrain's population demographics in terms of religion, religion groups, practice of religion, the culture and the labor law aspects

Figure 4. Inglehart–Welzel Cultural Map - Cultural map - WVS wave 7 (2017-2021)
Source: World Values Survey Organization

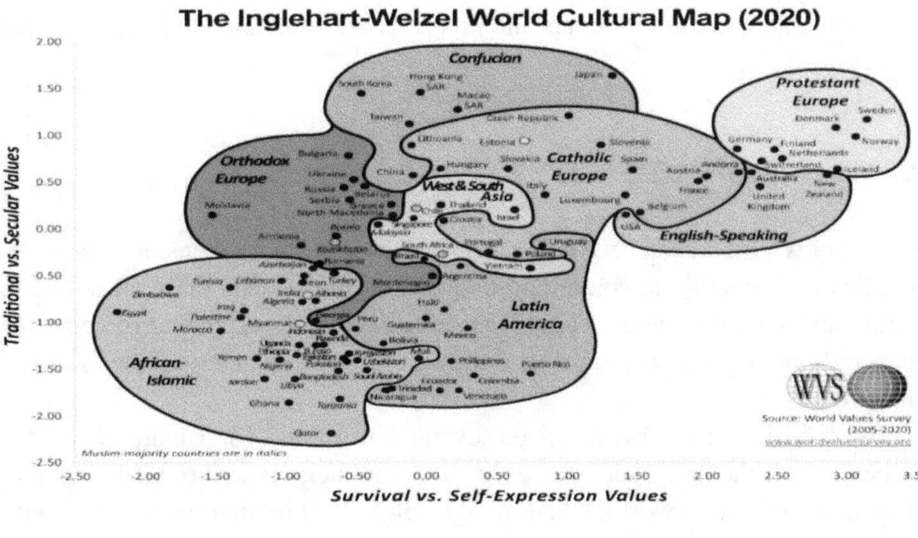

related to religion. The section concluded with the position of Bahrain on the cultural map two dimensions: traditional values vs. secular-rational values and survival values versus self-expression values.

3 OVERVIEW ON RELIGION AND SPIRITUALITY

Throughout the literature, Religion was found to have different definitions and notions; for example, as per the U.S. Equal Employment Opportunity Commission, "Religious observances or practices include, for example, attending worship services, praying, wearing religious garb or symbols, displaying religious objects, adhering to certain dietary rules, proselytizing or other forms of religious expression, or refraining from certain activities."

3.1 WHAT IS RELIGION?

Religion is a system of meanings and beliefs that is translated into set of behaviors and actions.

According to the Random House Dictionary of the English Language (1979), "religion is a concern over what exists beyond the visible world (operating through faith and intuition, as opposed to reason), it includes the idea of the existence of a single being, a group of beings, an eternal principle, or transcendental spiritual entity that has created the world, that governs it, that controls its destinies, or that intervenes occasionally in the natural course of its history", Moreover it refers to a specific fundamental set of beliefs and practices generally agreed upon by a group of people.

3.2 WHAT IS SPIRITUALITY?

Spirituality is a broad perspective with various aspects and dimensions. In general, it implies a connection to something bigger than individuals that makes one feel stability and serenity. Spencer (2012) stated that "the development of spirituality is generally recognized as requiring some sort of practice or discipline in order to make progress".

Love & Talbot in 1999 synthesized several definitions of spirituality taken from the literature of theology, social science, and other helping and fields like nursing, counseling, and social work). Accordingly, spirituality in internal process seeking a state of wholeness, peace and acceptance while connecting with one's locus of centricity and others. Simple stated, spirituality is the process of deriving meaning, purpose, and direction in one's life

Adawiyah, et al. (2017) referred to role of workplace spirituality that supports the job, institutional and spiritual partnership. They added that the concept of spirituality has triggered positive attitudes and behaviors. The main outcome of their research is the necessity to promote positive employees' work behaviors. Moreover, spirituality in the workplace should be taken into consideration and applied on individual, group and organizational levels.

3.3 THE EFFECT OF RELIGION ON ORGANIZATIONS

Religious beliefs and affiliations can affect organizational practices when employees bring their religious commitments and practices into the workplace. It is even more significant in the degrees of religious accommodation from organizations and managers when dealing with individuals and employees from different cultures, ethnicities, or religion.

Religion can influence employees' behavior with colleagues, subordinates, and managers. This results mainly on the religious beliefs, commitments and practices employees bring to the workplace and the general perception and tolerance of diversity.

Worden, S. (2005) emphasized on the importance of religion in organization, and managing people and in leadership; he stated, "with regard to the environment, how a society views the particular organization, religion, and the relation of business to religion would impact the extent to which society tolerates the application of religion in business leadership."

Although religious behavior and viewpoints can result in conflict at work, religion can also inspire positive virtues to emerge in the workplace. For example, religion can positively influence a worker's loyalty, morale, and communication (Askeland & Døhlie, 2015).

Etherington, Matt. (2019) conducted a very interesting study religious self-identity as he explored the work perspective of two individuals who self-identify as religious and are employed in non-religious work responsibilities. based on the perceptions and experiences of two male participants -a Muslim and a Christian- this narrative study examines how religion affects intentions, perceptions, and work behavior and how their religion intersects with their working lives. With a focus on diversity and inclusion in the workplace, this study distinguishes religion as an important workplace issue.

Marques et al. (2005) mentioned in their research that applying a spiritual mindset in a workplace should encourage creativity and innovativeness within the workers leading to increased productivity. This by time will develop a sense of interconnectedness among individuals and between individuals and their management.

3.4 RELIGION IN ORGANIZATION AND MANAGING INDIVIDUALS

According to Hastings, "One way that organizations convey their sensitivity to employee beliefs is by adapting the work environment to enable employees to practice their beliefs during the workday" (Hastings, 2021).

Similarly, the Title VII of the Civil Rights Act of 1964 requires employers to "reasonably accommodate employees' sincerely held religious beliefs, observances and practices when requested, unless accommodation would impose an undue hardship on business operations".

Zinnbauer et al., (1999) stated that "Both religion and spirituality have been characterized here as dynamic processes interconnected with all types and levels of experience including the ordinary as well as the extraordinary, the social and situational as well as the personal. The challenge for researchers is to capture religion and spirituality "in motion" within the larger context of personal and social interactions." And this signifies this study within organizations in Bahrain and confirms the need for further similar studies.

4 CONCEPTUAL FRAMEWORK AND METHODS

The conceptual framework below shows visually the relationships that will be empirically tested (Figure 5). This conceptual framework can be considered as a visual reflection of the chapter title. The explanatory variables are represented by religion values, the moderating variables are represented by the Firm and Personal Characteristics and the response variables are represented by the organization behavior and the Human Resources practices in managing individuals in organizations.

The null and research hypotheses associated with the conceptual framework includes the following:

$H_{(^\circ 1)}$: religion values are not a statistically significant explanatory variable of managing individuals

***$H_{(^\circ 2)}$*:** firm characteristics do not moderate the relationship between religion values and managing individuals

***$H_{(^\circ 3)}$*:** personal characteristics do not moderate the relationship between religion values and managing individuals

Figure 5. Research Variables and Conceptual Framework
Source: Developed by the researchers

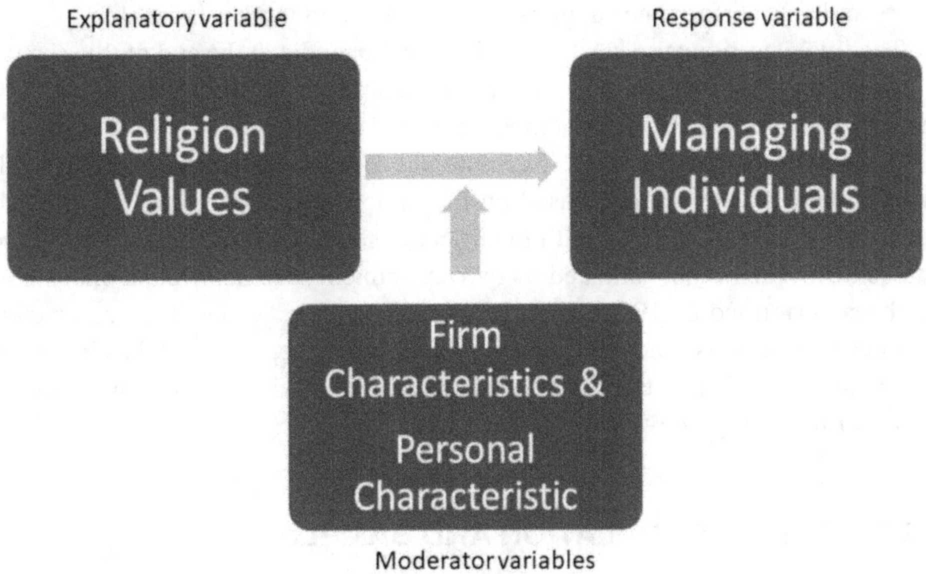

In contrast, the Research Hypotheses of the above null hypotheses are:

H_{r1}: religion values are a statistically significant explanatory variable of managing individuals
H_{r2}: firm characteristics moderate the relationship between religion values and managing individuals
H_{r3}: personal characteristics moderate the relationship between religion values and managing individuals

4.1 QUESTIONNAIRE DEVELOPMENT

In order to assess the hypotheses implied by the conceptual framework, a data collection form or questionnaire was needed to be developed. The questionnaire was designed in four sections following a filtering question that asks the respondent to report the sector they work in or otherwise.

A summary of the questionnaire questions and sources is shown in Table 1. The religion values indicators were adopted from the World Values Survey questionnaire wave 6 for the year 2010-2012 and Religious Commitments and Clinical Practices: A National Physician Survey, The University of Chicago.

The managing individuals' questions were developed by the authors with reference to the main functions of Human Resources functions, including recruitment, training, salary and pay, performance appraisal, motivation and work relationship.

The final questionnaire can be found in the Appendix at the end of this chapter.

The research design for this research is quantitative design. Accordingly, the main methodology used is a structured validated questionnaire.

Google Form was used to distribute the questionnaire electronically. The questionnaire was developed based on the reviewed literature and relied on the work of Curlin et al. in 2007 with modifications to match the research objectives and context. Then it got validated by two academic researchers, and a pilot survey has been performed on 10 respondents, there was no major feedback received on the questions phrases. The pilot reliability level was acceptable (Alpha Cronbach's Coefficient = .992) and the principal component analysis extracted into only one factor for managing individuals.

4.2 TARGETED POPULATION AND SAMPLE

For a further description of the framework adopted in this chapter, the population targeted was defined as all employees from any religion who are working in the private or public sector in the Kingdom of Bahrain. Convenient sampling method was followed as it was convenient for the time allowed and the purpose of this research. A sample of 30 or more would be convenient due to the time and sensitivity of the topic. This sample threshold can be considered as good enough in Statistics.

4.3 STATISTICAL PACKAGE AND METHODS

IBM SPSS version 28 was used to perform the statistical analysis. Descriptive and Inferential statistical methods were performed. Descriptive methods included: frequency tables, mean and median values computation, standard deviation computation and box plots. **Box plot:** was used to detect outliers if any and to examine the variability.

Inferential analysis methods were correlation and regression. **Correlation:** was used to test for relationship among two quantitative variables. It tests the null hypothesis that the two variables are not correlated. The correlation coefficient for a statistically significant correlation found provides the direction of the correlation (positive or negative) based on the sign and provides the strength of the correlation based on the numeric absolute value of the coefficient. Closer to zero indicates a poor correlation while close to 1, indicates a strong correlation.

Table 1. Questionnaire questions and sources

Item or Section	Number of Questions	Questions	Source
Filtering item	1	sector of respondent's work	Authors
Section 1: Firm Characteristics	5	Firm size	Authors
		Diversity in workforce	
		Diversity in management	
		Years since existence	
		Management team is formed of one or mix of religions	
Section 2: Individual Characteristics	5	Sex	Authors
		Age	
		Education	
		Marital status	
		Nationality	
Section 3: Religion Values Indicators	5	believe in: God, Life after death, Hell, Heaven	WVS, wave 6
		How important is God in your life? 10-point scale	
		To what extent do you consider yourself a spiritual person? 4-point scale	Religious Commitments and Clinical Practices: A National Physician Survey, The University of Chicago
		To what extent do you consider yourself a religious person? 4-point scale	
		How important would you say your religion is in your own life? 5-point scale	
Section 4: Managing Individuals – Organizational Behaviour	6	Recruitment is managed with no religion focus, i.e. same management for different religion; 3-point scale	Authors
		Training is managed with no religion focus, i.e. same management for different religion; 3-point scale	
		Salary and pay is provided with no religion focus, i.e. same packages for different religion; 3-point scale	
		Performance appraisal is measured and managed with no religion focus, i.e. same management for different religion; 3-point scale	
		Motivation is provided with no religion focus, i.e. same management for different religion; 3-point scale	
		Work relationship is with no religion focus, i.e. same for different religion; 3-point scale	

Regression: was used to test the effect of religion values indicator being an explanatory or independent variable on managing individuals being the dependent variable. The null hypothesis to confirm a statistically significant effect by the explanatory/independent variable is the regression coefficient of the explanatory/independent variable is equal to zero.

In addition, reliability was assessed using Cronbach's Alpha coefficient method. Factor analysis was performed using Principal Component Method.

Reliability analysis: Alpha Cronbach's Coefficient was used to assess the internal consistency of the managing individual items as they were measured using the same 4-point scale. The rule for an acceptable reliable measure generally adopted by researchers is any

Principal Component Analysis: was used to reduce the dimensions for religion values indicators and the managing individual items. Principal Component Analysis is also known as Factor Analysis. It is useful to discover the dimensions (or factors) within the set of variables. It saves the factors for regression use.

Kolmogorov-Smirnov normality test was used to check normality assumption.

4.4 STATISTICAL SIGNIFICANCE

The hypotheses were tested on the following statistical significance levels:

- Statistically significant at 5% significance level, when the p-value computed from the statistical method is less than 0.05. This was denoted by "*". The null hypothesis is rejected, and the alternative hypothesis is concluded with 95% confidence level.
- Statistically significant at 1% significance level, when the p-value computed from the statistical method is less than 0.01. This was denoted by "**". The null hypothesis is rejected, and the alternative hypothesis is concluded with 99% confidence level.0

Any p-value equal or greater than 0.05 was considered as not statistically significant at 5%. The null hypothesis was not rejected, and it was concluded with 95% confidence level.

In the previous sub-sections, a brief of the main methods and approaches employed as part of the empirical process in order to test the hypotheses was formulated.

The next section demonstrates the key findings and results revealed based on the analysis.

5 KEY FINDINGS AND DISCUSSION

5.1 Firm Characteristics

Table 2 shows the firm characteristics distribution as reported by the surveyed sample respondents. The distribution of sectors shows that services and government sectors were the largest among the surveyed sample. Respondents surveyed are working in large and medium companies. The diversity in workforce and management both measured in number of nationalities was mainly 5 or more nationalities. Majority of respondent's firms existed more than 10 years ago. Management team of the surveyed respondents' firms were formed of a mix of religions. There was noticed portion of respondents who preferred not to answer the question regarding number of religions in management team as religion is not among the consideration in their firms.

Table 2. Firm characteristics distribution

Sector	services sector	manufacturing sector	agriculture sector	government sector	none of the above/I don't work now
	47.8%	8.7%	2.2%	32.6%	8.7%
Firm size	Micro	Small	Medium	Large	
	10.9%	6.5%	13.0%	69.6%	
Diversity in workforce	1 nationality only	2 nationalities only	3 nationalities only	4 nationalities only	5 or more nationalities only
	13.0%	0.0%	6.5%	8.7%	71.7%
Diversity in management	1 nationality only	2 nationalities only	3 nationalities only	4 nationalities only	5 or more nationalities only
	23.9%	13.0%	8.7%	10.9%	43.5%
Years since existence	3 years or less	4 to 10 years	more than 10 years		
	8.70%	10.90%	80.40%		
Number of religions in management team	management team is formed of only one religion	management team is formed of a mix of religions	prefer not to answer as religion is not among the consideration in my firm		
	28.30%	37.00%	34.80%		

5.2 INDIVIDUAL CHARACTERISTICS

Table 3 shows the individual characteristics distribution as reported by the surveyed sample respondents. The distribution of sex shows that female respondents were slightly more. Majority of respondents were in the age between 33 years and more. Most of the respondents holds bachelor or master's degrees. Majority of respondents were married. Majority of respondents were Bahrainis.

Table 3. Individual characteristics distribution

Sex	male	female			
	43.5%	56.5%			
Age	18 – 22 years	23 – 27 years	28 – 32 years	33 – 37 years	38 and more
	0.00%	4.30%	15.20%	37.00%	43.40%
Education	secondary or below	diploma	bachelor	master	PhD
	0.0%	4.3%	41.3%	43.5%	10.9%
Marital status	single	married	widow/divorce		
	30.4%	65.2%	4.3%		
Nationality	Bahraini	Non-Bahraini			
	80.4%	19.6%			

5.3 RELIGION VALUES INDICATORS

Table 4 shows the religion values indicators distribution as self-reported by the surveyed sample respondents. Respondents reported high level of believing in God, Life after death, Hell and Heaven. Great majority of respondents reported that God is very important in their life. Majority of respondents indicated they are moderately spiritual and moderately religious. Majority of respondents stated that religion is the most important in their life.

5.4 FIRMS TENDENCY OF RELIGION FOCUS IN MANAGING INDIVIDUALS

Table 5 shows the summary statistics and distribution of the tendency of religion in managing individuals as self-reported by the surveyed sample respondents. The

Table 4. Religion values indicators distribution

Do you believe in (Yes%)	God	Life after death	Hell	Heaven	
	93.5%	82.6%	87.0%	91.3%	
Importance of God in your life	Not at all important	2	7	8	Very important
	2.2%	2.2%	2.2%	2.2%	91.3%
Extent of being a spiritual person	Not spiritual at all	Slightly spiritual	Moderately spiritual	Very spiritual	
	4.3%	8.7%	47.8%	39.1%	
Extent of being a religious person	Not religious at all	Slightly religious	Moderately religious	Very religious	
	10.9%	8.7%	63.0%	17.4%	
Importance of your religion in your own life	Not applicable. I have no religion	Not very important	Fairly important	Very important	The most important
	6.5%	0.0%	19.6%	26.1%	47.8%

mean values of the six variables measured ranged from 1.83 to 2.00, which indicates a moderate tendency of managing individuals with no religion focus.

5.5 RELIABILITY ANALYSIS

There were 6 questions under the Managing Individuals measure. These were found reliable (Alpha Cronbach's Coefficient = .972 > 0.7). This reliable level indicated the clarity of this measure and internal consistency level.

5.6 PRINCIPAL COMPONENT ANALYSIS

Principal Component Analysis was performed for Religion Values Indicators and Managing Individuals using Varimax rotation method. It was found that religion values indicators which are a total of 8 questions is extracted into two dimensions (or factors). The first factor was labeled 'behavior based on religion' which consists of the following questions:

1. To what extent do you consider yourself a spiritual person?
2. To what extent do you consider yourself a religious person?

Table 5. Summary statistics and distribituon of firms tendency of religion focus in managing individuals

	Not applicable. There is no tendency at all (0)		Low tendency (1)		Moderate tendency (2)		High tendency (3)		Summary Statistics	
	N	%	N	%	N	%	N	%	Mean	SD
Recruitment is managed with no religion focus, i.e. same management for different religion	12	26.1%	5	10.9%	7	15.2%	22	47.8%	1.85	1.282
Training is managed with no religion focus, i.e. same management for different religion	9	19.6%	8	17.4%	6	13.0%	23	50.0%	1.93	1.218
Salary and pay is provided with no religion focus, i.e. same packages for different religion	10	21.7%	7	15.2%	6	13.0%	23	50.0%	1.91	1.244
Performance appraisal is measured and managed with no religion focus, i.e. same management for different religion	9	19.6%	7	15.2%	5	10.9%	25	54.3%	2.00	1.229
Motivation is provided with no religion focus, i.e. same management for different religion	11	23.9%	6	13.0%	8	17.4%	21	45.7%	1.85	1.247
Work relationship is with no religion focus, i.e. same for different religion	11	23.9%	6	13.0%	9	19.6%	20	43.5%	1.83	1.235

SD: standard deviation

3. How important would you say your religion is in your own life?
4. Life after death

The second factor was labeled 'believes of religion' which consists of the following questions:

1. How important is God in your life?
2. God
3. Heaven
4. Hell

Principal Component Analysis found that the 6 items of Managing Individuals were extracted into only one factor (unidimensional).

Kolmogorov-Smirnov normality test

Kolmogorov-Smirnov normality test found that religion values indicators and managing individuals were not normally distributed at 1% significance level since the p-value was less than 0.01.

Thus, parametric tests which assumes normality cannot be performed unless the above variables are transformed. Moreover, non-parametric tests which do not assume normality can be performed.

5.7 NATIONALITY EFFECT

Mann-Whitney test which is a non-parametric test was performed to confirm any statistically significant effect due to nationality is found on the religion values indicators or managing individuals. There was no statistically significant effect due to nationality found since p-value was greater than 0.05 with all variables except for religion values indictor 'behavior-based religion' where there was a statistically significant effect found due to nationality (Mann-Whitney U test statistic = 94.000, p-value = 0.044*). The box plot (Figure 6) shows this statistically significant effect due to nationality visually.

Figure 6. Box plot of behavior based religion by nationality

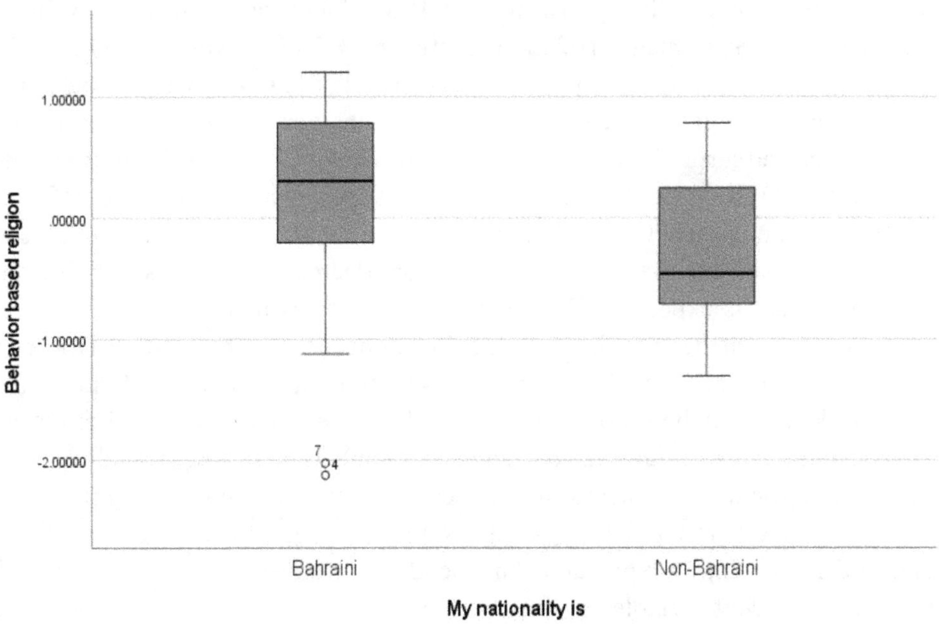

The mean and median values were computed (Table 6) to explain the nationality effect. Non-Bahrainis had negative mean and median values when compared to Bahrainis. This indicates that Non-Bahrainis had on average lower levels of behavior based religion when compared to Bahrainis.

Table 6, Summary statistics for behavior based religion by nationality

	My nationality is			
	Bahraini		Non-Bahraini	
	Mean	Median	Mean	Median
Behavior based religion	.09	.31	-.36	-.46

5.8 Religion Values Indicator Effect on Managing Individuals

Pairwise Correlation was performed to assess the correlation between every pair of the following variables of interest: managing individuals, religion values indicators, selected firm characteristics variables and selected individual characteristics variables.

Spearman correlation test shows that there was no statistically significant correlation found between behavior-based religion and believes of religion being the two factors of religion values indicators with managing individuals (Table 7).

In addition, managing individuals was found to have no statistically significant correlation with the selected firm characteristics or individual characteristics variables except for one statistically significant correlation found between behavior-based religion and age (Spearman correlation coefficient = .297*, p-value = 0.045) at 5% significance level. There was a positive weak correlation found between behavior-based religion and age. So, as age increases, the behavior-based religion increases.

Moreover, and surprisingly, there was a strong negative correlation found between behavior-based religion and believes of religion (Spearman correlation coefficient = -.703*, p-value = 0.000) at 1% significance level. Accordingly, as 'believes of religion' increases, the 'behavior-based religion' decreases. This is surprising and opposite to what is expected. The logical expectation is that if there would be a correlation between the two religion values indicators it would be positive. However, it was found to be negative which is the opposite. It might be that an individual may have high level of 'believes of religion', yet the same individual does not behave based on religion for any reason. And hence, implementing, practicing and behaving based on religion does not necessarily reflect and coin believes of religion.

Regression was used to investigate any statistically significant effect of religion values indicator being an explanatory/independent variable on managing individuals being the dependent variable.

For all sample respondents, religion values indicators were found to have no statistically significant effect on managing individuals. Then the sample was split by various firm characteristics and individual characteristics variables and regression analysis was run accordingly.

Table 7. Spearman correlation matrix

		Managing Individuals	Behavior based religion	Believes of religion
Managing Individuals	Spearman Correlation Coefficient	1.000	.107	-.146
	p-value	.	.478	.332
Behavior based religion	Spearman Correlation Coefficient	.107	1.000	-.703**
	p-value	.478	.	.000
Believes of religion	Spearman Correlation Coefficient	-.146	-.703**	1.000
	p-value	.332	.000	.
Firm size	Spearman Correlation Coefficient	.013	-.085	.291
	p-value	.930	.574	.050
Diversity in workforce	Spearman Correlation Coefficient	.080	-.178	.109
	p-value	.597	.236	.471
Diversity in management	Spearman Correlation Coefficient	-.083	-.218	.137
	p-value	.582	.145	.364
Years since existence	Spearman Correlation Coefficient	-.024	-.044	.160
	p-value	.874	.774	.288
My age	Spearman Correlation Coefficient	.172	.297*	-.184
	p-value	.252	.045	.220
My highest education degree attained	Spearman Correlation Coefficient	.003	.164	.034
	p-value	.984	.276	.824

* Significant at 5% (p-value < 0.05); ** significant at 1% (p-value < 0.01)
Source: authors

There was no statistically significant effect of religion values indicators found in all firm characteristics and individual characteristics variables except for nationality.

When the sample was split by nationality (Bahrainis versus Non-Bahrainis), there was no statistically significant effect of religion values indicators found on managing individuals for Bahrainis, however, there was a statistically significant effect of the religion values indicator that is ‘behavior-based religion’ (regression coefficient $\beta = -.604^{**}$, p-value = 0.008) on work relationship, at 1% significance level. This regression model (for non-Bahrainis alone) was adequate (F-value = 17.693**, p-value = 0.008). The R square was equal to .780 indicating that 78% of the variability in the dependent variable work relationship is explained by the behavior-based religion explanatory/independent variable.

Therefore, there was a statistically significant negative effect of behavior-based religion on managing individuals in the work relationship dimension only. The regression coefficient can be interpreted as a percentage of change. Thus, as the individual's behavior-based religion level increases by one unit, it is expected that on average, the work relationship being the managing individual dependent variable would drop by 60.4%.

It seems that being working in a country that is not your country of origin, and when the behavior-based religion level increases, the work relationship dimension of managing individual is influenced. This finding supports partially the main research hypothesis that stated a statistically significant effect of religion values indicator on managing individuals being moderated by individual characteristic (which is nationality).

Table 8 summarizes the final empirical evidence revealed based on the various analysis for each hypothesis tested.

Table 8. Summary of the decision regarding the research hypothesis

Research Hypothesis	Decision
H_{r1}: religion values are a statistically significant explanatory variable of managing individuals	Null hypothesis was not rejected. Thus, research hypothesis was not concluded.
H_{r2}: firm characteristics moderate the relationship between religion values and managing individuals	Null hypothesis was not rejected. Thus, research hypothesis was not concluded for all hypothesized moderators except for non-Bahrainis (nationality) which the statistical evidence supported the research hypothesis at 1% significance level.
H_{r3}: personal characteristics moderate the relationship between religion values and managing individuals	Null hypothesis was not rejected. Thus, research hypothesis was not concluded.

Here we discuss further several key findings found. Tracey et al (2014) mentioned that "there is a great value in connecting organizational research with a deeper appreciation and concern for religion". However, in this research there was no statistically significant correlation found between the religion values indicators and managing individual variables. This is a statistical finding. It might not necessarily mean that there is no role of religion when managing individuals. Also, having no correlation between the individual religion values indicators and the firm's tendency of religion focus representing the organizational behavior with regard to managing individuals in terms of recruitment, training, salary and pay, performance appraisal, motivation and work relationship is in-line with the overall culture of tolerance and coexistence in Bahrain. It is also in line with Bahrain Labor Law articles related to religion and women being a dimension of culture.

There was a negative correlation found between the two religion values indicators: 'behavior-based religion' and 'believes of religion'. This might be in-line with the American moral and social philosopher Eric Hoofer views summarized by his book titled 'The True Believer'.

Non-Bahrainis working in Bahrain were found to perceive a statistically significant effect of 'behavior-based religion' and firm's tendency to manage work relationships with religion focus. While Bahrainis working in Bahrain did not perceive such statistically significant influence. This might be due to the non-Bahrainis being more open to speak out with regard to a sensitive topic. This finding from one hand can be viewed a positive aspect were the employees who are having high level of 'behavior-based religion' are receiving different work relationship that is considering their religion value. But the same finding might indicate a negative aspect where the non-Bahrainis who have such high level of 'behavior-based religion' receiving different work relationship from those who have no or lower levels of 'behavior-based religion'. This negative aspect might also indicate how complicated and sensitive is the topic research as it deals with religion.

6 STUDY IMPLICATIONS

This section presents the conclusions revealed, followed by the implications and recommendations derived from the main findings and conclusions.

6.1 CONCLUSIONS

The main conclusions of this research are:

1. Religion values indicators are formed of two underlying extracted factors, we referred to them as 'behavior-based religion' and 'believe of religion'.
2. Nationality was found to have a statistically significant effect on 'behavior-based religion' only, where Bahraini respondents had on average higher levels when compared to non-Bahraini respondents. Other firm characteristics or individual characteristics were not found to have a statistically significant effect.

3. Surprisingly, there was a strong negative correlation found between 'behavior-based religion' and 'believes of religion'. Accordingly, as believes of religion increases, the behavior-based religion decreases. It might be that an individual may have high level of 'believes of religion', yet, the same individual does not behave based on religion for any reason. This is similar to the well know expression in law: de facto de jure.
4. There was no statistically significant correlation found between both factors of religion values indicators on all six managing individuals variables.
5. All individual characteristics were found to have no moderator effect on the relation between religion values indicators and managing individual variables except for nationality and work relationship variables of the managing individual variables, where for non-Bahraini respondents there was a negative effect of 'behavior-based religion' and work relationship tendency to be with no religion focus. Therefore, the third hypothesis was not rejected except for nationality.

6.2 RECOMMENDATIONS

(Mazur, 2021) stated that "Companies operating in a religiously diversified environment face, therefore, a unique opportunity of building organizational culture supportive of those differences. Not only by acknowledging them but demonstrating more social skills and emotional skills as openness, acceptance, respect, and inclusivity."

Derived from the reviewed literature and the study finding, the following recommendations were proposed.

1. Organizations and Managers must increase their understanding of how religion can influence and affect people's behavior and intentions in the workplace. Organizations can increase tolerance among employees by creating diverse teams within their organizations.
2. Human Resources Managers can increase awareness among employees and stakeholders to strengthen, respect and value those differences to help drive an organizations' business results by:
    a. Providing religion and spirituality education and
    b. Ongoing religious diversity training that will help drive employee engagement and create a more motivating work environment
3. Religious and spirituality diversity should not be just about policies and procedures. Organizations mut put it into practice with the ability to recognize, embrace and function in a religious and spiritually diverse working environment which is critical for employees' motivation and Business Continuity.

While there were statistically significant insights found based on analyzing the sample gathered, it is highly recommended to achieve a larger sample of 300 minimum in order to confirm these insights, with higher power. The insights found would be considered initial and subject to change.

Human Resources Managers can conduct similar frequent surveys on religion and culture as diversity management tool for business sustainability. It is highly recommended that HR management teams in both private and public sectors in the Kingdom of Bahrain be informed of the findings and insights of this chapter. The HR management teams are also recommended to take care more of non-Bahraini workers while managing to assure that their religion values that was found to be influencing their work relationships with superiors, peers and subordinates such as they are not harmed.

6.3 CHAPTER SUMMARY

With reference to (Mazur, 2021), it must be acknowledged "that religion is a source of values and norms and in this sense has a culture-forming nature, becoming one of the pillars of organizational culture".

Investigating religion role on organizational behavior in Bahraini organization was a challenge since it is considered a sensitive topic or even a taboo. This chapter explored the case of Bahrain. Other countries can be investigated with a similar approach. This chapter confirmed known norms in Bahrain that there is no influence between religion values indicators and the perception of managing individuals in the following HR functions: Recruitment, Training, Salary and Pay, Performance Appraisal and Motivation. Furthermore, this chapter recognized on area where religion values indicators influenced managing individuals work relationships.

This study has faced several limitations with regard to the topic which affected the data collection as number of respondents, honesty in answering the survey question and even more surprisingly in some managers refusing to participate in interview. This agrees with several research in self reposting studies especially with regard to sensitive topics; in a study conducted by Hayes (2015), The discussion highlighted the salience of socio-cultural factors in various research and implied that, "due to societal values, using self-reporting surveys to identify patterns in institutional practice may result in overrated self-evaluations" rather than the reality.

With reference to the relevant literature, it has been highlighted that there are insufficient studies in the specific research area of religion which has been largely excluded from some scholarly journals.

In this regard, there is clearly an opportunity for researchers to fill this academic and research gap and guide managers and decision makers in managing individuals in diverse environments.

6.4 THE WAY FORWARD

In such sensitive topics with considerable limitations, future researchers should exercise caution when generalizing results and take individual circumstances and experiences into consideration when making decisions based on this research or conducting similar research. The following are suggested areas for future research:

1. Future researchers are highly recommended to further examine two distinctive factors among the religion values indicators being referred to as 'behavior-based religion' and 'believe of religion'
2. More Research can be done using the World Values Survey in relation with religion and culture in Bahrain.
3. To conduct In-depth experts interviews with managers and business owners.
4. It would be interesting to make a narrative of organization dynamics of Bahrainis versus non-Bahrainis in organizations.
5. To perform a Study on diverse women and religiosity in organizations.
6. To conduct a comparative analysis between different firm sizes and different sectors. And this requires,
7. To collect a larger and more diverse sample size.

In general, we would like to find more research aiming to understand the different ways that business owners, managers, individuals, and institutions use religion and spirituality to engage, cope with, or to face the daily challenges in the workplace.

And we would like to end the chapter with a Quote after The Messenger of God, Prophet Mohamed, may God's prayers and peace be upon him, said (***RELIGION IS THE TRANSACTION AND BEHAVIOR***), and a quote is commonly stated, ***"Do not talk to me much about religion, but let me see religion in your behavior, morals and dealings."***

قال رسول الله عليه الصلاة والسلام (الدين المعاملة)، وكما قيل لا تحدثني كثيرا عن الدين ولكن دعني أرى الدين في سلوكك و أخلاقك و تعاملاتك

REFERENCES

Adawiyah, W. R., & Pramuka, B. A. (2017). Scaling the notion of Islamic spirituality in the Workplace. *Journal of Management Development, 36*(7), 877–898. doi:10.1108/JMD-11-2014-0153

Alkhatib, A. J., & Arnout, B. A. (2019). Is religion the missing part in leadership and organization Citizenship Behavior Theories? *Proceedings of DIALOGO-CONF 2019*. 10.18638/dialogo.2019.6.1.10

Askeland, G. A., & Døhlie, E. (2013). Contextualizing International Social Work: Religion as a relevant factor. *International Social Work, 58*(2), 261–269. doi:10.1177/0020872813482958

Bechert, I., & Quandt, M. (2013). *Issp Data Report: Religious Attitudes and Religious Change*. GESIS - Leibniz Institute for the Social Sciences.

CIA World Factbook. (n.d.). *Bahrain*. https://www.cia.gov/the-world-factbook/countries/bahrain/

Definitions, Compliance Manual Section 12. (n.d.). *The U.S. Equal Employment Opportunity Commission*. Retrieved May 2021, from www.eeoc.gov /policy/docs/religion.html#_Toc203359487

Etherington, M. (2019). Religion as a Workplace Issue: A Narrative Inquiry of Two People—One Muslim and the Other Christian. *SAGE Open, 9*(3). doi:10.1177/2158244019862729

Frunza, S. (2017). Ethical leadership, religion and personal development in the context of global crisis. *Journal for the Study of Religions and Ideologies, 16*(46), 3–16. http://jsri.ro/ojs/index.php/jsri/article/view/827

Hastings, R. R. (2021). *HR seeks balance in handling religion in the workplace*. SHRM. Retrieved July, 2021, from https://www.shrm.org/hr-today/news/hr-news/pages/handlingreligioninworkplace.aspx

Hayes, A. L. (2015). The role of cultural contexts in research design decisions. *SAGE Open, 5*(2). doi:10.1177/2158244015583336

Jonathan, W. P. G., Ong, K. L., & Hairon, S. (2009). A cross-cultural investigation of teachers' and reporting officers' self-ratings on teaching and leadership skills across Singapore and Bahrain. *International Journal of Educational Research, 48*(4), 258–273. doi:10.1016/j.ijer.2009.12.001

Julian Casablancas Quotes. (n.d.). *BrainyQuote.com*. Retrieved September, 2021, from BrainyQuote.com Web site: https://www.brainyquote.com/quotes/julian_casablancas_404685

Kingdom of Bahrain's National Portal. (n.d.). Retrieved May 2021, from https://www.bahrain.bh/new/en/home_en.html

Krause, N., & Ironson, G. (2019). Religious involvement, God images, and life satisfaction. *Mental Health, Religion & Culture*, *22*(1), 41–55. doi:10.1080/13674676.2019.1586860

Liu, C. H., & Robertson, P. J. (2011). Spirituality in the workplace: Theory and measurement. *Journal of Management Inquiry*, *20*(1), 35–50. doi:10.1177/1056492610374648

LMRA Expat Management System (EMS). (n.d.). http://blmi.lmra.bh/2021/03/data/ems/Table_07a.xlsx

Love, P., & Talbot, D. (1999). Defining spiritual development: A missing consideration for student affairs. *NASPA Journal*, *37*(1). Advance online publication. doi:10.2202/0027-6014.1097

Marques, J., Dhiman, S., & King, R. (2005). Spirituality in the workplace: Developing an integral model and a comprehensive definition. *The Journal of American Academy of Business, Cambridge*, *7*, 81–91.

Mazur, B. (2021). Organizational culture under religious influence. *A Closer Look at Organizational Culture in Action*. doi:10.5772/intechopen.90898

Phipps, K. A. (2012). Spirituality and strategic leadership: The influence of spiritual beliefs on strategic decision making. *Journal of Business Ethics*, *106*(2), 177–189. doi:10.100710551-011-0988-5

Society of Human Resources Management. (2008). *Global diversity and inclusion*. Retrieved May 2021, from https://www.shrm.org/hr-today/trends-and-forecasting/research-and-surveys/Documents/09-Diversity_and_Inclusion_Report.pdf

Spencer, M. (2012). *What is spirituality? A personal exploration*. Retrieved from https://www.rcpsych.ac.uk/docs/defaultsource/members/sigs/spiritualityspsig/what-is-spirituality-maya-spencerx.pdf?sfvrsn=f28df052_2

Tracey, P., Phillips, N., & Lounsbury, M. (2014). Taking religion seriously in the study of organizations. In Religion and Organization Theory (Vol. 41). Emerald Group Publishing Limited. doi:10.1108/S0733-558X20140000041009

United States Bureau of Democracy. (n.d.). *Human Rights and Labor. Bahrain: International Religious Freedom Report 2020*. https://bh.usembassy.gov/wp-content/uploads/sites/141/240282-BAHRAIN-2020-INTERNATIONAL-RELIGIOUS-FREEDOM-REPORT.pdf Retrieved in June 2021

U.S. Department of Labor. (n.d.). https://www.dol.gov/agencies/oasam/civil-rights-center/internal/policies/religious-discrimination-accommodation

U.S. Equal Employment Opportunity Commission. Title VII of the Civil Rights Act of 1964. Retrieved August 1, 2021, from https://www.eeoc.gov/statutes/title-vii-civil-rights-act-1964

Worden, S. (2003). The role of religious and nationalist ethics in strategic leadership: The case of J.N. Tata. *Journal of Business Ethics*, *47*(2), 147–164. doi:10.1023/A:1026050230808

Worden, S. (2005). Religion in strategic leadership: A positivistic, normative/theological, and strategic analysis. *Journal of Business Ethics*, *57*(3), 221–239. doi:10.100710551-004-6943-y

World Values Survey. (n.d.). https://www.worldvaluessurvey.org/WVSContents.jsp?CMSID=Findings

Ysseldyk, R., Matheson, K., & Anisman, H. (2010). Religiosity as identity: Toward an understanding of religion from a social identity perspective. *Personality and Social Psychology Review*, *14*(1), 60–71. doi:10.1177/1088868309349693 PMID:20089847

Zinnbauer, B. J., Pargament, K. I., & Scott, A. B. (1999). The emerging meanings of religiousness and spirituality: Problems and prospects. *Journal of Personality*, *67*(6), 889–919. doi:10.1111/1467-6494.00077

Chapter 6
Spirituality and the Negotiating Ability of Leaders

Sana Shabir
Central University of Kashmir, India

Abdul Gani
Central University of Kashmir, India

ABSTRACT

Since the early 1980s researchers have shown increased interest in integrating spirituality and leadership. Spirituality has emerged as a discrete construct underlying the essence of effective leadership, and the negotiating ability has been regarded as one of its core descriptors. The study, on which the present chapter is based, attempts to ascertain the relationship between spirituality and leaders' negotiating ability. The sample for this study consisted of 450 leaders and 904 subordinates working across different service and manufacturing sectors in India. With the help of a mixed-method research design, data was gathered employing several tools. Leaders' spirituality has been measured through MacDonald's spirituality inventory and their negotiating ability through Rai's model. The study reveals that leaders' negotiating ability is a function of spirituality, and a proper understanding of spirituality improves negotiating abilities of leaders. It offers workable suggestions and outlines the implications of the results for policy and practice.

INTRODUCTION

Present-day organizations represent globalized marketplaces that have witnessed the financial crisis, credit crunches, business scandals, mass layoffs, and economic shocks.

DOI: 10.4018/978-1-7998-9319-6.ch006

These together have led to increasing discontent with leadership in organizations that have continued to symbolize monetary success as a major forecaster of true leadership effectiveness, failing to recognize that organizational success does not solely depend on the production of goods and services in hyper-competitive business environments like that of today's (Bondoc, 2016; Padayachee, 2010). The stew of pressure from the employees, communities, and other key stakeholders who perceive success on broader terms calls for a change in outlook, from giving undue weightage to monetary success alone to a holistic perspective, that integrates economic and non-economic factors (Bondoc, 2016). As such, with time, leadership traits such as spirituality, compassion, and respect, integrating certain qualities into an individual's work, family, and relationships, have begun to gain attention. Spirituality has emerged in the literature as a discrete construct underlying the essence of effective leadership.

Many employees consider religion and spirituality as core domains of their lives (Hicks, 2003). A growing number of workers opt for non-work activities such as wellness programs, counseling, self-reflection, meditation, and religious and spiritual practices to do away with the anxiety, insecurity, and stress (Cartwright & Cooper, 1997). This along with some major corporate scandals, market crashes, global shocks, and unethical practices call for far-reaching initiatives to be taken up related to the social and ethical performance of organizations (Frederick, 2006).

A review of the leadership literature suggests that the spiritual and religious dimensions of leadership have only recently entered the leadership discourse. The new evidence on integration of spirituality and leadership at the workplace has brought positive changes in the relationship of leaders with their followers and has increased their effectiveness. There is evidence that organizational interventions in the form of workplace spirituality programs lead to positive outcomes like enhanced job satisfaction, reduced absenteeism, lesser attrition, less deviant behaviour, and more commitment towards the organization. When employees perceive their organization as being spiritual, they tend to be more ethical, have less fear, and are more creative. Spirituality when incorporated at the workplace is now thought to be a source of potential competitive advantage.

Workplace spirituality is about the dyadic relationship between leaders and the led, involving an understanding of each other as spiritual beings and having a sense of purpose that provides meaning. It is about peoples' experience of a sense of belonging and mutual connectedness with their workplace community. It is premised on the fact that people have both an inner and outer life and that the happy and satisfying inner life can have a positive impact on their outer life that in turn can have beneficial consequences for employee well-being, corporate responsibility, and sustainability, as well as financial performance. Integration of spirituality with leadership has given rise to the new paradigm of spiritual leadership. Spiritual leadership strives to create a vision through which the followers and leaders experience meaning and establish a culture based on spiritual values such as altruistic love, appreciation, genuine care, and concern, etc.

Since the 1980s researchers have shown increased interest in the integration of spirituality, faith, and leadership. Such integration, in practice, could also provide a way to activate beliefs and values for enhancing the moral and spiritual maturity of the leaders and the led. However, considering its significance, spirituality that acts as a powerful binding force in the lives of employees still does not find a significant place in most of the contemporary management and scientific literature and professional practice (Giacalone et al., 2005). Taken together, spirituality is one of the emerging fields that need to be studied further in detail. What separates effective leaders from non-effective ones can provide a useful ground to understand the role of spirituality in influencing a leader's effectiveness. The main functional dimensions of effective leadership, reflected in the existing literature, include leader-member exchange, communication effectiveness, conflict management styles, ethical decision-making, and negotiating ability. Therefore, it would be interesting to see how spirituality influences these dimensions of effective leadership.

To contribute to such a growing body of research, the macro study, on a part of which the present chapter is based, attempts to ascertain the relationship between spirituality and leadership effectiveness, with special reference to leaders' negotiating ability. It explores various antecedents of spirituality and leaders' negotiating ability and determines the nature of relationship between spirituality and negotiating ability of leaders. The remainder of this chapter reviews the available literature on the subject and identifies the gaps in the existing literature for developing a research framework for the study at hand. The next part of the chapter examines the links between spirituality and negotiating ability of leaders. The last section highlights the main conclusions of the study, offers workable suggestions for improving the impact of spirituality on negotiating ability of leaders, and outlines the implications of the study results for policy and practice. The section also highlights the limitations of the present research and identifies the future research agenda in the area.

Review of Literature and Hypothesis Formulation

There has been a substantial increase in spirituality research over the last decade (Liu & Robertson, 2011), and the literature on spirituality is spread across various fields of study including psychology, human resources, business studies, and communication. Spirituality, as a distinct concept, has gained tremendous popularity in literature and has been studied in association with various organizational variables like organizational commitment (Djafri & Noordin, 2017), social responsibility performance (Barron & Chou, 2017), strategic leadership (Phipps, 2012), ethics (McLaughlin, 2005), job satisfaction (Lazar, 2010), quality of life (Baker, 2003), religiousness and career adaptability (Duffy & Blustein, 2005), work attitude (Choerudin, 2014), and organizational performance (Karakas, 2010). Overall, spirituality has been seen as a precursor to fostering a positive impact in the organizational context (Bondoc, 2016).

Spirituality is predicted as a measure of how an individual deals with his/her existential direction, external social incentives or disincentives, and the degree of consciousness and compassion with everything beyond his/her self. It is generally associated with the meaningfulness of the work, feeling connected to the community, and the ability to express the feelings and work independently in a way that is believed to be correct (Wulandari, 2014). It reflects the utmost manifestation of a personal responsibility towards the individual and the collective reality entailing one's personal, work, and societal life that goes beyond 'self-gratification'. On promoting workplace spirituality, the positive work culture in the organization gets cultivated and that helps leaders to be more effective. Accordingly, in such an organization, flexible humanistic policies and practices form a basic part of the day-to-day operations (Boorom, 2009). This in turn has been linked to numerous positive outcomes such as enhanced employee commitment, team effectiveness and productivity, reduced absenteeism and turnover, and improved human health and psychological wellbeing (Daniel, 2010).

The rapid global transformations are changing the broader organizational outlook from being traditional to modern-day learning organizations. In such organizations, leadership effectiveness cannot exist in isolation. Essentially, leadership is not solely represented by authority, control, and power, but is the embodiment of compassion, empathy, inspiration, emotional bond, authenticity, spiritual values, and its appendages. Such an outlook has been corroborated by theoretical and empirical research in the field of leadership (Krishnakumar et al., 2015).

Earlier spirituality did not find explicitly a place in the leadership development process (Houston, 2014). Spirituality and leadership effectiveness has been in discord for many years with one being considered as an abstruse domain of mixed emotions and ideas; and the other as a realistic area of scientific inquisition rendering spirituality as more of a philosophy and leadership more of a science (Reave, 2005). It is because the scientific approaches that got developed over some time were easily applicable to leadership than spirituality that lacked scientific inquisition. Studies based on spirituality and leadership were short of the consensus on definitions, assumptions, theories, and clarity about the scope of the area with regards to contextual factors and its coverage. The previous research has been confined in its applicability to various workplace contexts and falls short of comprehending the degree and how spirituality integrates and manifests itself in the augmentation of leadership effectiveness. Newer models and patterns have been taking place in spirituality and leadership studies (Bindlish et al., 2012). Nevertheless, their linkage has of late sparked the interest among researchers, practitioners, academicians, and theorists (Elias et al., 2018; Houston, 2014). Scholars have examined this agenda from time to time and their connection is being studied in the fields of management, psychology, organizational science, and other related disciplines (Small, 2020). In ascertaining this linkage, studies have come up with mixed results (Hinds, 2005).

Many researchers have put forward spirituality as a concept that lies at the core of leadership effectiveness (Fry, 2005; Mitroff & Denton, 1999). Various emergent studies have illustrated an association between spiritual values and practices and leadership effectiveness (Sweeney & Fry, 2012). Spirituality aptly characterizes the motivation, heart, and mind of effective leadership (Saini & Burton, 2020). Effective leadership is a multi-disciplinary approach that not only encompasses disciplines such as sociology, psychology, and technology but embraces spirituality as well. It offers a deeper understanding of a leader's spiritual self along with the subordinates and the other key stakeholders (Burke, 2006). Leaders have now begun to incorporate spirituality into their work ushering the desirable changes in their relationships and their effectiveness (Neal, 2001).

Although there are various approaches to leadership, the spiritual leadership of late has kindled the interests of many leadership researchers (Bauman, 2013). Spiritual leadership has been studied in the purview of the doctrine based on different religious beliefs, such as Christian leadership, Vedic, and/or Islamic leadership (Aslan & Korkut, 2015). Spiritual leadership is an indwelling leadership approach that aims to establish and sustain meaningful relationships among leaders and employees. It relates more to a secular view as religion is not the main consideration, however, it emphasizes the virtues and moral values. Virtues such as ethics, values, honesty, and integrity that were earlier dormant in the organizational context have now gained attention in recent years (Brown & Trevino, 2006). It is believed that leaders who imbibe these will be more effective (Yukl, 2012). Spirituality and leadership association has become more prominent and a topic of discussion today more than ever before (Houston, 2014). Research on spirituality attributes and practices has been found to have an association with effective leadership at the global level (Den Hartog et al., 1999). Elaborating upon any leadership theory would not be possible without giving preeminence to spirituality (Bindlish et al., 2012). Numerous pieces of evidence based on effective leadership indicate that the relationship between spirituality and leadership is fundamental in nature (Boorom, 2009; Sanders III et al., 2003).

Leadership effectiveness can be measured by several ways considering the leader-subordinate perspectives, such as, actions of a leader for his/her followers and other organizational stakeholders that incorporate leader's ability to act innovatively and progress and retain the higher position in an organization, his/her growth along with the overall group, follower's satisfaction with the leader, level of motivation and commitment to adhere to and fulfill group objectives, developmental aspect of the followers (Yukl, 2006). The attributes of a leader including emotional maturity, stress tolerance, integrity, and energy level also play a significant role in determining leadership effectiveness. Moreover, the leader's technical, administrative, conceptual, and interpersonal skills affect their orientation. The key personality traits of effective leaders have been enlisted as tolerance for frustration, self-awareness, honesty, integrity, emotional stability, dominance, enthusiasm, assertiveness, extraversion, self-confidence, and objectivity. Meanwhile, task-related personality traits incorporate courage, empathy, initiative, resilience, internal locus of control, and flexibility, and adaptability. Leadership effectiveness depends on organizational culture, strategy, team dynamics, and leadership problem-situation (Yammarino, 2000).

At the core of the spirituality and leadership association lie the recognition that every individual has an inner voice which is the core element of one's integrity and this inner voice becomes the source of effectiveness while taking some important work and non-work decisions (Levy, 2000). Spirituality enhances leadership effectiveness by having a considerable effect on subordinates, facilitating attainment of goals, and integrating behavior, thereby, giving a direction to sustainable organizational leadership (Reave, 2005). Researchers also agree on a fact that the leaders who pursue spirituality in terms of their work-related tasks tend to be more effective (Fry & Cohen, 2009). Spiritual leadership is indispensable means of transforming the organization into a learning organization with continued success (Fry, 2003). Kriger and Seng (2005) assert that spirituality (in form of inner leadings) influences the leaders' values and attitudes, which in turn moderates the relationship between leaders' vision and leaders' behavior. This leads to subordinates' commitment to the organizational vision and goals. Together, these factors affect leadership effectiveness that is measured by the level of profit, employees' satisfaction, organizational good, and adherence to vision and values.

Spiritual leadership may be viewed as a positive consequence of consistent employee movement that calls for respect, appreciation, empowerment, and the ability to utilize the skills and contribute to the organizational goals (Aslan & Korkut, 2015). Practices based on spiritual leadership enhance the individual performance by reinforcing desirable values and behaviors among the followers such as respect for others, fair treatment, care and concern, recognition, and responsive listening (Reave 2005). Spirituality has also been associated with human behavior, creativity, and performance (Harlos, 2000). Apart from fostering spiritual survival and consciousness, spiritual leadership has other potential outcomes, such as organizational commitment, well-being, employee innovative behavior, job performance, job involvement, and job satisfaction (Murrell-Jones, 2012; Zhang & Yang, 2020). In addition to that, spiritual leadership has positive effects on organizational citizenship behaviors, along with the concern for the peers and coworkers and the dutifulness towards the organization (Chen & Yang, 2012). Spiritual leadership can uplift the spiritual well-being of individuals that paves a way to physical well-being and good health (Fry et al., 2006) that in turn alleviates the stress and improves interpersonal and emotional coping capabilities (Heintzman & Mannell, 2003). At a higher level, it creates conformity across different organizational levels leading to leadership effectiveness and increased productivity (Ali & Zaky, 2018).

While attempting to integrate spirituality and leadership, researchers have found spirituality and effective leadership are interrelated concepts (Macon, 2014; Mark et al., 2012). Combining the two terms implies that spiritual leadership is based on making individuals understand their inner selves and fostering a sense of meaning and significance among them. Spirituality provides an outlook of leadership in a way that brings together the behavior and dispositional character of individuals, leaders' influence on followers, and the attainments of goals (Reave, 2005). Spirituality can be prevalent in any organization, but when it comes to exhibiting effective leadership, it calls for the demonstration of spiritual values, beliefs, and practices on the part of the leader. The spiritual perspective of leaders helps them think about human needs and aspirations in a better way and instills a vision and inspiration among them (Hoyle, 2002).

Many leadership effectiveness attributes have been identified and brought together by previous research studies. These attributes include leader-member exchange (LMX), communication effectiveness (CE), ethical decision-making (EDM), conflict management style (CMS), and negotiation ability (NA). To date not much empirical research has been conducted on negotiating ability of leaders as a component of leadership effectiveness, though an active phase in negotiation has begun in the past few decades. Ranging from socio-psychological studies of the 1960s and 1970s that focused on individual differences of negotiators and situational patterns during negotiations to the behavioral decision-making perspective that evolved during the 1980s and 1990s, researchers, academicians, and practitioners have started to explore perspectives leading to actionable knowledge. Later in the 1990s, studies solely based on behavioral decisions faced criticisms; therefore, attempts were made again to encompass social dimensions into the process of negotiation. Individually none of these perspectives could fully explain the negotiation process and its outcomes. As such, an integrated approach was established. Having social and cognitive dimensions in negotiation studies broadened the scope of negotiation research. This way a broader theoretical negotiation framework was created and it led to a better understanding of the negotiation process while effectively combating the issues associated with negotiation (Ma, 2005). Thereafter, negotiation research gained momentum and is still in the phase of growth across various spectrums.

Negotiation is a dynamic social process in which two or more interdependent parties allocate and share resources, set priorities and come to conclusions, make mutually acceptable decisions, and/or resolve conflicts (Brett, 2014). It is a pervasive act where mixed motives are to be realized as such it involves cooperation as well as competition (Walton & McKersie, 1991). Herein, an attempt is made to arrive at an agreement that is acceptable to all the parties involved while advancing and safeguarding their concerns and interests (Brett et al., 2017). At the heart of the negotiation lies a conflict, but the other basic features of negotiation include the parties involved in the negotiation, their interests, the process itself, and the outcomes (Thompson & Hastie, 1990). Parties to negotiation partake to attain outcomes that benefit individuals as well as the organization. In case negotiators fail to resolve any deadlock, it gives rise to negative outcomes (Cotter & Henley, 2017). The process of negotiation reflects the interactions or activities that take place before the negotiation outcome. The negotiation outcome is the result of the bargaining situation (Thompson, 1990).

Negotiation theory highlights two types of strategies: distributive strategy and integrative strategy (Walton & McKersie, 1991). In a distributive strategy, the negotiator's focus is on self and claims values for self only whereas, in integrative strategy, value is created for both the self and the other as the goal is broader (Brett et al., 2017). While the distributive approach of negotiation is competitive, the integrative framework is designated by cooperative mechanisms. Based on their negotiation outcomes, distributive negotiation-based outcomes are impasse, and win-lose and integrative negotiation-based outcomes are suboptimum and optimum. The win-lose outcome generates lower profits and impasse yields no profits. The suboptimum and optimum integrative outcomes are associated with higher profits. These authors further assert that integrative orientation is preferred over distributive orientation due to greater profit and quality linked to it (Cotter & Henley, 2017).

Broadly, negotiation encompasses negotiating ability, negotiating style, and negotiating strategy (Kumar et al., 2009). Negotiating ability is considered to be a knack of an individual to resolve any conflict through negotiation and effectively maneuver the disputes. It is a characteristic that is not inherited necessarily but could be developed with time through training (Rai, 2013). Negotiation ability is measured through artfulness, diplomacy, detachedness, fair-mindedness, and sagacity (Rai, 2007). While artfulness represents the sharpness of a negotiator in dispute handling mechanisms, diplomacy outstretches tactics used by the negotiator. Detachedness demonstrates the rationality of negotiators, and fair-mindedness represents an equitable and selfless attitude. Sagacity denotes prudence and good judgment (Rai, 2013). These dimensions have a huge impact on the outcomes of negotiations and how the negotiation process is performed (Stoshikj, 2014).

In the process of negotiation, negotiators need to be cautious as they choose the strategies and tactics to get the work done (Tasa & Bell, 2017). Positive results can be attained only when a proper negotiating strategy is in place, an appropriate negotiating style is implemented and the right kind of negotiating ability is displayed.

Much of the focus has so far been on the strategic and style part of negotiations and less emphasis has been laid on negotiating ability of the leaders. The research literature that focuses on the spirituality and negotiation ability of leaders across multi-sector organizations in India is particularly limited.

Based on the available research and practice it is assumed that spiritual leadership would augment the leaders' negotiating ability by reinforcing desirable values and behaviors among the leaders and enhancing leaders' influence on followers by assuring them fair treatment and concern, recognition, and responsive listening; which would facilitate the attainment of goals acceptable to all the stakeholders while advancing and safeguarding their concerns and interests.

Therefore, it is hypothesized that:

H_1: There is a significant relationship between Spirituality and Negotiating Ability of Leaders.

MATERIAL AND METHOD

This write-up is based on a major study aimed at exploring the relationship between spirituality and leadership effectiveness; with negotiating ability as one of the major dimensions of leadership effectiveness. After allowing an attrition rate of five percent, the effective sample for this study consisted of 450 leaders and over 904 subordinates working across different service and manufacturing sectors in India, belonging to diverse socio-demographic groups and categories and chosen through multi-stage sampling techniques. For every respondent, an interview was conducted simultaneously to ensure that the quantitative information furnished aligns with the perceptions of the respondents. This has helped to endorse inferential statistics. The data were collected using multiple sources of evidence, thereby increasing the reliability and validity of the data collected.

Starting with exploratory research, the study follows the descriptive design and testing of the hypothesis. The descriptive design has been employed to describe various aspects of survey participants. The hypothesis-testing research design has been used to test the hypotheses of causal relationships between variables. Quantitative approach to research has been adopted in the study which assisted in testing hypotheses and determining the reliability and validity of measures.

The study uses two different sets of questionnaires; for leaders and subordinates. Respondents were asked to indicate their conformity with the questions asked on a five-point Likert-Scale ranging from strongly disagree (1) to strongly agree (5). Missing value analysis shows none of the missing values are present. Outlier identification has been done by z-score calculation. All the Z-scores values lie within the threshold value of ± .. Skewness and kurtosis estimates are indicative of non-normality of data not being an issue in this study since all the values on given items are within the acceptable range of < ± .3 and < ± .0 respectively.

For the assessment of spirituality MacDonald's (2000) five-dimensional Expressions of Spirituality Inventory (ESI) has been adapted. Its five dimensions are Cognitive Orientation towards Spirituality (COS), Experiential/Phenomenological Dimension (EPD), Existential Well-Being (EWB), Paranormal Beliefs (PAR), and Religiousness (REL).To examine negotiating ability, Rai's (2013) scale has been adapted as it has come up with acceptable psychometric properties and is very much applicable to industry, practitioners, and academia. The dimensions of the scale are artfulness, diplomacy, detachedness, fair-mindedness, and sagacity.

The questionnaires with some minor modifications have been refined and validated through EFA and CFA. In some cases, online questionnaires, prepared as Google forms, have been administered. Of all the questionnaires administered, the surveys with unengaged responses, missing data, outliers, acquiescence bias, and non-returnability left a total of forty-one questionnaires non-workable for the data analysis. Consequently, these inutile questionnaires have been removed from the supplementary questionnaires, thereby, ensuring the attainment of a reasonable sample size.

Before the main data collection, a preliminary study on 78 leaders and 159 subordinates was conducted to pretest the actual instrument of data collection, which reveals that all the scores across the given survey items fall within the threshold values. This process furnishes 104 items, with no item being deleted at this stage. Subsequently, this data has been subjected to further purification by conducting an exploratory factor analysis and confirmatory factor analysis. The overall reliability of the main variables of the study reveals that reliability scores are well above the minimum threshold of 0.7 for spirituality as well as the negotiation ability dimension of leadership effectiveness.

EFA has been employed on five dimensions of spirituality, each with six items that are a part of the original scale. Kaiser-Meyer-Olkin Measure of Sampling Adequacy (KMO) is higher than the threshold value of 0.50. The approximate Chi-Square is 4005.199 with 435 degrees of freedom which is significant at 0.05 level ($p < 0.05$). The value of the reliability coefficient is 0.901. Thus, the factor analysis is considered appropriate for further analysis. All the item communalities are within the acceptable range. Over 70 percent of the total variance is represented by the given factor matrix, thus implying that derived factors explain a significant level of variance. All the five factors are to be extracted ideally because these factors have an Eigenvalue greater than one and all the items are sufficiently representative of the given factors because all the items have fairly high loading (> 0.5) on their evaluative factors.

The five factors extracted through EFA are correlated with each other in a single measurement model for spirituality, as illustrated in Fig 1. The model outlines thirty items and five latent variables. Every construct has a minimum of three items and all items load on their relevant constructs. These items are hypothesized as being reflective. Fit statistics suggest that the goodness and badness indices are met by the given model ($\chi 2/df$ = 1.459, GFI = 0.814, CFI = 0.953, RMR = 0.066 and

Figure 1. Measurement Model of Spirituality

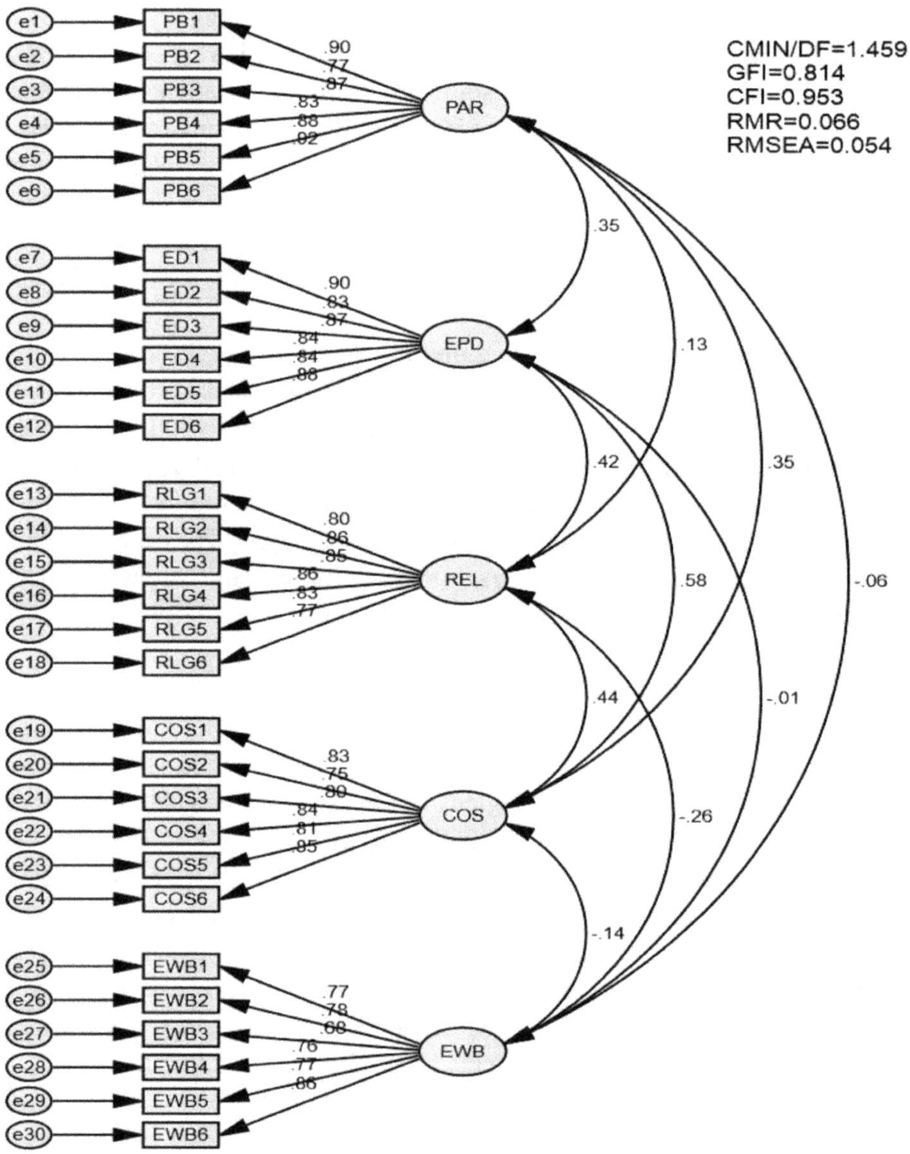

RMSEA = 0.054). As such, it points to a reasonably good model fit. Construct validity has been ensured by examining convergent as well as discriminant validity. The standardized loadings are above 0.5 thresholds. The AVE estimates exceed 0.5 and the reliability estimates are all greater than the 0.7 value. Therefore, all the thirty items are retained as adequate evidence of convergent validity is demonstrated.

EFA has been conducted separately for the dimensions of negotiation ability that constitute artfulness, diplomacy, detachedness, fair-mindedness, and sagacity. KMO value of 0.962 for negotiation ability indicates enough appropriateness of factor analysis along with Bartlett's test of sphericity ($\chi^2 = 5187.764$, df = 561, $p < 0.05$) that approves of further analysis. Cronbach's alpha of 0.976 for negotiation

Figure 2. Measurement Model of Negotiation Ability

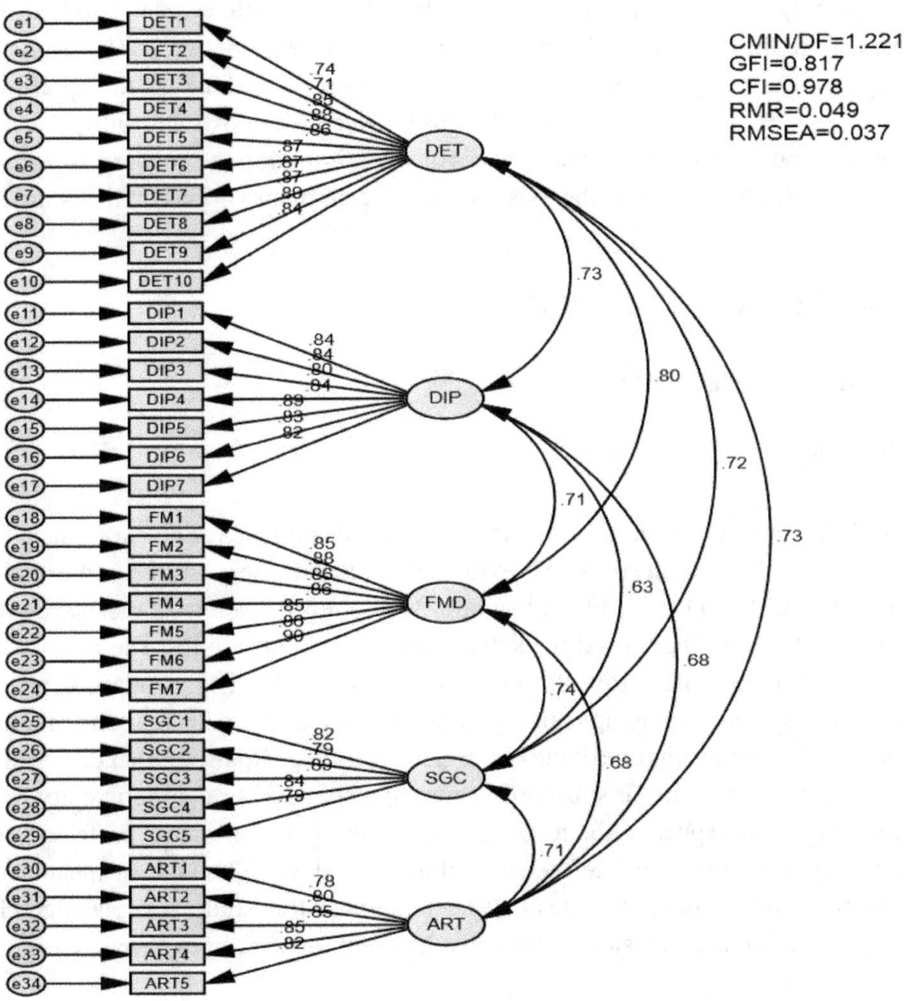

ability supports its overall reliability. Therefore, data statistics permit carrying out the subsequent analysis. The communalities estimation reveals that all values lie within the acceptable range and as such these items have adequate explanation power to be retained for further analysis. Based on the factor extraction, five factors have been obtained and these account for 71.46 percent of the variance. The Eigenvalue greater than one approves inclusion of five factors. Therefore, five factors have been considered for the subsequent analysis. The pattern matrix contains the highest loading of each item on their respective factors.

Specification of measurement model has allowed factors to correlate with each other. The items have loaded on their respective factors and each factor has a minimum of three items associated with it. The model (refer to Fig. 2) presents five latent variables with thirty-four reflective items.

Diagnostic measures of CFA (See Table 1) suggest that model fits the data reasonably ($\chi 2/df = 1.221$, GFI = 0.817, CFI = 0.978, RMR = 0.049 and RMSEA = 0.037). All the standardized item loadings of the given model exceed 0.5 and AVE estimates are also higher than the suggested minimum value of 0.5 and the square root of each AVE is greater than the correlations between the constructs with reflective items. Composite reliability values go beyond 0.7, implying the convergent validity of the model. This confirms the existence of discriminant validity in this study.

RESULTS AND DISCUSSION

Descriptive Statistics

Spirituality

Table 2 illustrates the mean and standard deviation values of the variables of spirituality considered in the present study. It is evident that religiousness has the highest mean score (M = 3.91, S.D = 0.739) and paranormal beliefs has a lowest mean score (M = 2.64, S.D = 0.928) amongst the sub-dimensions of spirituality. The mean score of spirituality computed from its sub-dimensions is 3.41. The standard deviation of constructs representing spirituality is below 1 or close to 1. Respondents thus consider religiousness as one of the key dimensions of spirituality. Other dimensions are also quite important for spirituality, but the respondents relate religiosity more to their spiritual aspects. About 28 percent of the partakers have professed that spirituality and religiosity are the same things for them. The highest mean score for overall religiousness indicates that leaders under this study acknowledge God is responsible for their existence and consider them to be inclined towards religion.

Table 1. Standardized Factor Loadings, AVE & Reliability Estimates

	ART	DIP	DET	FMD	SGC
ART1	0.78				
ART2	0.80				
ART3	0.85				
ART4	0.85				
ART5	0.82				
DIP1		0.84			
DIP2		0.84			
DIP3		0.80			
DIP4		0.84			
DIP5		0.89			
DIP6		0.83			
DIP7		0.82			
DET1			0.74		
DET2			0.71		
DET3			0.85		
DET4			0.88		
DET5			0.86		
DET6			0.87		
DET7			0.87		
DET8			0.97		
DET9			0.80		
DET10			0.84		
FM1				0.85	
FM2				0.88	
FM3				0.86	
FM4				0.86	
FM5				0.85	
FM6				0.86	
FM7				0.90	
SGC1					0.82
SGC2					0.79
SGC3					0.89
SGC4					0.84
SGC5					0.79
AVE	0.672	0.700	0.702	0.749	0.685
Construct Reliability	0.911	0.942	0.959	0.954	0.916

The statistics further indicate that existential well-being (M = 3.86, S.D = 0.787) does play a vital role in spirituality. Survey participants have deliberated on their competence to deal positively with the challenges of life. In a broader perspective, respondents opine that happiness, comfort with oneself, and doing things right without feeling tense and strained are significantly important for individuals' spiritual well-being. This advancement in mean scores is endorsed by the results of MacDonald et al (2015). The cognitive orientation towards spirituality (M = 3.64, S.D = 0.826) that is based on the inclination towards understanding spirituality and implementing it in personal life also carries a lot of significance for the spiritual domain. The higher COS scores mean that the respondents show greater levels of agreement with statements that spirituality is real, important, and given consideration in day-to-day living. They believe cognitive orientation towards spirituality is vital for human existence.

Respondents have varying opinions regarding the experiential or phenomenological dimension of spirituality. Since it includes such experiences that are mystical and transcendental, so it differs from person to person. The respondents agree that EPD is important for spirituality, albeit not overwhelmingly. It signifies that although partakers have had experiences wherein they felt profoundly connected to the spiritual aspects of things, yet they do not make tall claims of going beyond space and time. People who have not had such experiences may still be spiritual to some extent. Paranormal belief is somewhat related to spiritualism. It is a conviction that individuals have in uncommon phenomena: black magic, ghosts, psychokinesis, and the like. Data shows that partakers fairly believe in such happenings. However, they do not associate only these parameters with gauging spirituality. These results are supported by the findings of MacDonald et al. (2015), who reported cognitive orientation towards spirituality, existential well-being, and religiousness with higher mean scores than experiential/phenomenological dimension and paranormal beliefs.

Over 77 percent of participants indicated that they engage in some form of public religious activity at least once a month. For private religious activities, 91.1 percent of the respondents reported engaging in such activities at least once a month. In addition, when asked to rate the degree to which they considered themselves to be religious people, 86.6 percent of the sample responded as being "sort of", "pretty" or "very" religious while only 2.4 percent of the respondents indicated that they were "not at all" religious. While the largest group (71.8 percent) of respondents recognize religiosity and spirituality as different concepts, but 28.2 percent of them perceive religiosity and spirituality as the same. While evaluating the sources and extent to which these have influenced the understanding of religion and/or spirituality among the participants, it can be noted that parents are the greatest source of influence for 36.2 percent of the respondents. About 27 percent of the respondents express a good deal of influence from the religious figure/institution.

The highest percentage (39.7 percent) of respondents has revealed that neither does the employment setting (e.g. organization, institution, and business) support their spirituality satisfactorily, nor does it provide extensive spiritual support to its other employees (37.2 percent). Being in a leadership position, more than half (55 percent) of the respondents argue that they strive hard to support the subordinates' spirituality. Further examination of the data highlights that for 38 percent of the respondents, spirituality has a fair amount of influence on the completion of job functions, while a similar percentage (32.5 percent) reveals that spirituality exerts a fair amount of impact on how they relate to the subordinates. Just over half of the participants (57 percent) acknowledge that spirituality makes them better and effective leaders. In line with this, 53.8 percent of survey participants endorse spirituality as a facilitator of job effectiveness among the subordinates.

Not only do the leaders' perspectives authenticate the importance of spirituality in this study, but their subordinates' responses also corroborate these themes. Their views encapsulate the spiritual dimensions, policies, and strategies that leaders use to achieve effectiveness in their leadership paradigm. It further makes the infusion of spirituality into leadership an utmost necessity to make strides in leadership efforts and organizational outcomes.

Negotiating Ability

The overall mean of negotiating ability is 3.60, and the standard deviation is below 1 for all the sub-dimensions (Table 2). While evaluating the negotiation ability, the employees understudy consent to sagacity as a significant component of negotiating ability (M = 3.72, S.D = 0.840). They reveal that leaders seek out self-control, integrity, and prudence in their decisions and actions. Being communicative with the subordinates and, at the same time, upholding personal integrity has been seen as a salient feature of a sagacious leader. Such a leader has the elements of a positive attitude, unwavering virtues, and proactive behavior. A large number of respondents agree that artfulness is a minor factor that determines the negotiating ability of a leader (M = 3.45, S.D = 0.841). They emphasize that efficiency in dispute handling can be achieved if a leader can build and manage relationships, conduct negotiations, give due weightage to the issues at hand, and uses his/her wisdom to set things right. This shrewdness and calculatedness augment the negotiating ability, which in turn helps to reinforce the leadership effectiveness.

Detachedness (M = 3.69, S.D = 0.787) has also been given preference in evaluating negotiating ability of leaders. Their responses reflect that leaders who possess detached attributes can think and decide rationally. Subordinates understudy regard their leaders as rational thinkers who do not correlate their judgment with their desires, and this considerably helps in nurturing the leadership effectiveness. On this continuum, fair-mindedness (M = 3.58, S.D = 0.895) has been given the next preference as the respondents see their leaders as selfless and just in approach. Fair-minded leaders provide equal status to all subordinates irrespective of their rank or position. Such leaders consider all the parties to the dispute and ensure their participation while discussing the dispute. They can work with others and generate mutual trust. These leaders are expected to be reasonable, kind-hearted, and selfless.

A large number of respondents identify diplomacy as a key factor of negotiating ability. Respondents affirm that effective diplomatic leaders have the acumen of listening and understanding the views of others. They can generate meaningful conclusions, persuade others, and, at the same time, they have enhanced self-consciousness. Therefore, to advance leadership effectiveness, leaders need to be creative and sensitive in outlook and do not have to be solely dependent on personal charm to deal with the problems. Thus, leaders work tactfully and are shrewd in outlook when it comes to conciliation and handling disputes effectively. These statistics are in partial congruence with Rai's (2013) measurement of negotiating ability, where fair-mindedness scored the highest mean score and artfulness the lowest.

Table 2. Descriptive Analysis of Construct Variables

Construct Variables	Mean	Std. Deviation
	Spirituality	
COS	3.64	0.826
EPD	3.01	1.055
EWB	3.86	0.787
PAR	2.64	0.928
REL	3.91	0.739
Overall	**3.41**	**0.977**
Negotiating Ability		
ART	3.45	0.841
DIP	3.48	0.836
DET	3.69	0.787
FM	3.58	0.895
SGC	3.72	0.840
Overall	**3.60**	**0.778**

Spirituality and Negotiating Ability Relationship

The structural model findings indicate that spirituality has a significant positive impact on leadership effectiveness with a standardized regression weight of 0.35 and a critical ratio of 8.843 significant at 0.05. The R-square statistic shows that spirituality explains 13 percent of the variance in leadership effectiveness. It is an indication that spirituality is a predictor of leadership effectiveness.

The magnitude and significance of the loading estimates indicate that all five sub-dimensions of spirituality and all the five sub-dimensions of negotiating ability are relevant in predicting their respective constructs (refer to Table 3). In the case of spirituality, cognitive orientation towards spirituality has the maximum contribution with the highest loading, and in the case of negotiating ability, fair-mindedness and artfulness contribute the maximum with the highest loadings. It can also be clearly articulated that the negotiating ability (M = 3.60, S.D = 0.778) of a leader influences leadership effectiveness. Results show that leaders do possess a knack for mediation, bargaining, and mutual problem-solving.

Based on the results obtained, hypothesis $H_{1,}$ which states that the relationship between Spirituality and Negotiating Ability of leaders is significant, has been supported, thereby endorsing the importance of spirituality in enhancing negotiating ability dimension of leadership effectiveness. Consistent with the findings of Rai

Table 3. Structural Model Coefficients

Particulars	Std. Estimate	Std. Error	Critical Ratio	P-value
Determinants of Spirituality				
COS SPIRITUALITY	.945	.093	16.302	***
EPD SPIRITUALITY	.747	.103	16.233	***
EWB SPIRITUALITY	.460	.064	12.671	***
PAR SPIRITUALITY	.621	.092	10.240	***
REL SPIRITUALITY	.724	.350	6.669	***
Determinants of Negotiating Ability				
ART NA	.967	.045	25.815	***
DIP NA	.955	.045	23.853	***
DET NA	.946	.050	17.688	***
FMD NA	.977	.045	27.380	***
SGT NA	.966	.039	23.966	***
Determinant of Leadership Effectiveness				
NA LEFF	.966	.052	21.296	***

(2013), negotiating ability thus can be assumed as a significant trait of leaders regardless of their work domain.

CONCLUSION, SUGGESTIONS, AND IMPLICATIONS

The results reveal that spirituality and negotiating ability of leadership effectiveness share a significant positive relationship. The findings provide evidence that improving the core areas of spirituality can improve negotiating ability of leadership. The hypothesis of this study that spirituality could have a positive relationship with leaders' negotiating ability is supported by the data. It indicates the possibility that being spiritually active leads to negotiating ability of leaders.

The study emphasizes that leaders should act as moderators in connecting their spirituality with the employees' tasks, duties, and overall welfare. As effective moderators, leaders ought to be creative in their leadership approaches by externalizing the values, attitudes, behaviors, and responsibilities. This makes a huge difference towards the work and non-work realms of organizational members and enables them to experience a sense of belongingness and fetch a meaning and purpose in their lives (bin Abdullah et al., 2013).

The study results have illustrated religiousness, existential well-being, cognitive orientation towards spirituality, experiential/phenomenological dimension, and paranormal beliefs as important dimensions of leaders' spirituality. For leadership effectiveness, negotiating ability has been regarded as one of the core descriptors. It has been observed that the majority of the leaders understudy attend religious services frequently, and with increasing age, their exposure to spirituality and/or religion has developed further. Religion is seen as an outer expression of an individual's faith and belief, whereas spirituality is about unearthing the inner self.

The leaders under study have indicated that negotiating ability is a significant predictor of leadership effectiveness. These help them manage the subordinates and interact with the peer groups, deal with conflicts, instruct and direct the group members, build relationships, and make ethical decisions. Being pervasive constructs, a greater understanding of spirituality and negotiating ability, and how they correlate is believed to increase the welfare of the employees, organization, community, and the environment. It signifies the theoretical underpinnings of spirituality and negotiating ability is highly connected to practical life activities.

Spiritual leadership should be set up as an organizational requirement by making it a part of competency model building, performance management, quality management system, and management cadre evaluation. Preparation and professional development programs must be introduced in an institutionalized or formal way that helps training the leaders and subordinates through self-awareness, contemplation, and reflection. While conducting developmental workshops and training, a proper course on spirituality and leadership must be optionally offered that provides opportunities for delving into spirituality and leadership concerns.

Practicing spirituality should not remain confined to top-level managers. It needs to be embedded in organizational vision, mission, goals, values, and culture to reap its benefits across the organizational setup. Organizations' spiritual philosophy and guiding principles should be candidly disseminated through policies, procedures, and practices to make it evident that they prioritize and value spirituality at all levels. Mentoring and support from superiors, subordinates, and peers appreciably influence one's spirituality and leadership effectiveness. Organizations need to own up that spirituality is a pervasive concept that facilitates day-to-day functioning. Therefore, researchers need to work more in this field of inquiry and develop a robust and unified leadership effectiveness framework. At the individual and community level, such policies and practices need to be formulated and disseminated that make members aware, tolerant, and respectful towards the needs; faiths, beliefs, and emotions of others.

The findings of the current study indicate that they cannot assume that spirituality exists at workplaces that are correlated to nobility-based professions e.g. healthcare and education. It calls for assessing the true spiritual atmosphere in the organizations, regardless of the sector to which they belong. It needs to be realized that a particular sector or profession cannot be representative of spirituality, but it is the people and their way of working that makes the real difference. Therefore, proper assessment tools need to be identified and put in place to provide space for narration and engagement of spiritual experiences and determine the spiritual climate of the workplaces.

Leaders to be effective need to be aware of the existence of spiritual diversity and spiritual maturity and that their development takes place in stages. It requires proper understanding, evaluation, and implementation techniques to assist leaders in working with individuals with differing requirements. Leaders ought to create, promote, and support spiritual opportunities within as well as outside the organizations. These might include visits to spiritual institutions, spiritual training and development programs, spirituality-based workshops and seminars, and workplace ministries, etc. Leaders need to ensure that apart from being spiritually active themselves, they recruit and retain workers who are spiritually mature so that the individuals' and organizational values and goals go in the same direction (Banke et al., 2005). This would bring down the negative consequences and foster more positivity across the organizational platform.

The present study strives to establish a better understanding of the role that spirituality plays in guiding leadership effectiveness. Apart from the research domain, the employers, employees, and other stakeholders, and their recognition for morally upright leaders add to the significance of conducting this research. The importance of this study lies in the fact that its findings espouse spiritually informed leadership, and give way to robust and resilient leadership practices (Richardson, 2009). The findings of this research demonstrate that a proper spirituality orientation improves negotiating abilities of leadership. The present study also creates a new understanding and broadens the scope of literature in the areas of spirituality and leaders' negotiating abilities across various employment sectors.

LIMITATIONS AND FUTURE RESEARCH

The existing work that links spirituality to leadership is subjective and theory-driven, and the studies that show the relation between these two constructs have suggested that due to the generalizability issues, because of small sample sizes, weak correlations, and nature of research, further research is needed to substantiate it. Moreover, discrepancies existing in the literature that show no relationship between spirituality and leaders' negotiating ability, and being in its early stage of development makes this area of research more interesting. Therefore, empirical investigations would expand the body of knowledge by providing a glimpse of the correlation between spirituality and leaders' negotiating ability. Recognizing a linkage between spirituality and negotiating ability dimension of leadership effectiveness will aid leaders to go for self-discovery, inner motivation, and reflective inquisition. Leaders would be able to develop quality relationships, be more communicative, manage conflicts, take professional decisions, negotiate well, and create improved organizational culture (Macon Sr, 2014).

This study needs to be replicated with a broader section of partakers from different geographical contexts to add to the generalizability of the findings and with a greater exploration placed on different research instruments and mixed methodologies. Researchers also need to explore and test other predictor and dependent variables with longitudinal research design. Examining the role of religion in relation to spirituality along with comparative analysis based on demographic variations, generational differences, spiritual versus non-spiritual organizational setups, etc is a fruitful area of future research. The study strongly recommends retesting the proposed conceptual framework to endorse the study results. As a result of the paucity of studies based on spirituality and leaders' negotiating ability, examination of their linkage and how other variables influence their relationship continues to be of interest in empirical research. Sectoral distinction, generational gaps, leader – non-leader perception divergence, spiritual versus non-spiritual leadership, spiritually accommodating as opposed to non-accommodating organizational cultures, and demographic differences are some facets that call for additional research to be embarked on in this relatively new field of research.

REFERENCES

Ali, Z., & Zaky, M. (2018). Spiritual values and spiritual practices: Interactive effects on leadership effectiveness. *ETIKONOMI, 17*(1), 123–134. doi:10.15408/etk.v17i1.6497

Aslan, M., & Korkut, A. (2015). Spiritual leadership in primary schools in Turkey. *Journal of Educational and Social Research, 5*(2), 123–123. doi:10.5901/jesr.2015.v5n2p123

Baker, D. C. (2003). Studies of the inner life: The impact of spirituality on quality of life. *Quality of Life Research: An International Journal of Quality of Life Aspects of Treatment, Care and Rehabilitation, 12*(1), 51–57. doi:10.1023/A:1023573421158 PMID:12803311

Banke, S., Maldonado, N., Lacey, C. H., & Thompson, S. (2005). *The Role of Spirituality in Christian School Leadership: A Qualitative Study*. Online Submission.

Barron, K., & Chou, S. Y. (2017). Spirituality and social responsibility performance: The perspectives of religiously and non-religiously affiliated individuals. *Journal of Global Responsibility, 8*(1), 63–82. doi:10.1108/JGR-07-2016-0020

Bauman, D. C. (2013). Leadership and the three faces of integrity. *The Leadership Quarterly, 24*(3), 414–426. doi:10.1016/j.leaqua.2013.01.005

bin Abdullah, A. G. K., bt Ismail, A., & bin Mydin, A. (2013). The Moderating Effects of School Principals' Leadership Practices on the Workplace Spirituality and Leadership Effectiveness Relationship. *International Journal for Cross-Disciplinary Subjects in Education, 4*(4), 1318-1323.

Bindlish, P., Dutt, P., & Pardasani, R. (2012). From growing convergence of spirituality and leadership towards a unified leadership theory. *Journal of Spirituality, Leadership and Management, 6*(1), 3-23.

Bondoc, E. J. (2016). *A qualitative study of spiritual leadership in the workplace* (Doctoral dissertation). Northcentral University.

Boorom, R. (2009). *Spiritual leadership: A study of the relationship between spiritual leadership theory and transformational leadership* (Doctoral Dissertation). Available from ProQuest Dissertations and Theses database. (UMI No. 3377759).

Brett, J. M. (2014). *Negotiating globally: How to negotiate deals, resolve disputes, and make decisions across cultural boundaries* (3rd ed.). Jossey- Bass.

Brett, J. M., Gunia, B. C., & Teucher, B. M. (2017). Culture and negotiation strategy: A framework for future research. *The Academy of Management Perspectives, 31*(4), 288–308.

Brown, M. E., & Trevino, L. K. (2006). Ethical leadership: A review and future directions. *The Leadership Quarterly*, *17*(6), 595–616.

Burke, R. (2006). Leadership and spirituality. *Foresight*, *8*(6), 14–25.

Cartwright, S., & Cooper, C. L. (1997). *Managing workplace stress* (Vol. 1). Sage.

Chen, C. Y., & Yang, C. F. (2012). The impact of spiritual leadership on organizational citizenship behavior: A multi-sample analysis. *Journal of Business Ethics, 105*(1), 107–114.

Choerudin, A. (2014). The Relationship Between Spirituality and Work Attitude: A Empirical Study. *International Journal of Management Research and Reviews, 4*(4), 455.

Cotter, M. J., & Henley, J. A. (2017). Gender Contrasts in Negotiation Impasse Rates. *Management, 12*(1).

Daniel, J. L. (2010). The effect of workplace spirituality on team effectiveness. *Journal of Management Development*, *29*(5), 442–456.

Den Hartog, D. N., House, R. J., Hanges, P. J., Ruiz-Quintanilla, S. A., Dorfman, P. W., Abdalla, I. A., ... Zhou, J. (1999). Culture specific and cross-culturally generalizable implicit leadership theories: Are attributes of charismatic/transformational leadership universally endorsed? *The Leadership Quarterly*, *10*(2), 219–256.

Djafri, F., & Noordin, K. (2017). The impact of workplace spirituality on organizational commitment: A case study of Takaful agents in Malaysia. *Humanomics*, *33*(3), 384–396.

Duffy, R. D., & Blustein, D. L. (2005). The relationship between spirituality, religiousness, and career adaptability. *Journal of Vocational Behavior*, *67*(3), 429–440.

Elias, S., Cole, B., & Wilson-Jones, L. (2018). Leadership and spirituality: Conceptualization, definition and future directions in higher education. *Journal of Research Initiatives*, *3*(3), 3.

Frederick, W. C. (2006). *Corporation, be good! The story of corporate social responsibility*. Dog Ear Publishing.

Fry, L. W. (2003). Toward a theory of spiritual leadership. *The Leadership Quarterly*, *14*(6), 693–727.

Fry, L. W. (2005). Toward a theory of ethical and spiritual well-being and corporate social responsibility through spiritual leadership. In *Positive psychology in business ethics and corporate responsibility*. Academic Press.

Fry, L. W., & Cohen, M. P. (2009). Spiritual leadership as a paradigm for organizational transformation and recovery from extended work hours cultures. *Journal of Business Ethics*, *84*(2), 265–278.

Fry, L. W., Matherly, L. L., & Vitucci, S. (2006). Spiritual leadership theory as a source for future theory, research, and recovery from workaholism. *Research companion to working time and work addiction*, 330.

Giacalone, R., Jurkiewicz, C., & Fry, L. (2005). From advocacy to science. *Psychology of Religion and Spirituality*, 515–528.

Harlos, K. P. (2000). Toward a spiritual pedagogy: Meaning, practice, and applications in management education. *Journal of Management Education*, *24*(5), 612–627.

Heintzman, P., & Mannell, R. C. (2003). Spiritual functions of leisure and spiritual well-being: Coping with time pressure. *Leisure Sciences*, *25*(2-3), 207–230.

Hicks, D. A. (2003). *Religion and the workplace: Pluralism, spirituality, leadership*. Cambridge University Press.

Hinds, R. S. (2005). Consideration of the relationship between spiritual well-being and transformational leadership. *The Journal of Applied Management and Entrepreneurship*, *10*(2), 124.

Houston, G. G. (2014). *Spirituality and leadership: Integrating spirituality as a developmental approach of improving overall leader effectiveness* (Doctoral dissertation). Antioch University.

Hoyle, J. R. (2002). The highest form of leadership. *School Administrator*, *59*(8), 18–21.

Karakas, F. (2010). Spirituality and performance in organizations: A literature review. *Journal of Business Ethics*, *94*(1), 89–106.

Kriger, M., & Seng, Y. (2005). Leadership with inner meaning: A contingency theory of leadership based on the worldviews of five religions. *The Leadership Quarterly*, *16*(5), 771–806.

Krishnakumar, S., Houghton, J. D., Neck, C. P., & Ellison, C. N. (2015). The —good|| and the —bad|| of spiritual leadership. *Journal of Management, Spirituality & Religion*, *12*(1), 17–37.

Kumar, M., Rai, H., & Pati, S. P. (2009). An exploratory study on negotiating styles: Development of a measure. *Vikalpa, 34*(4), 37–50.

Lazar, A. (2010). Spirituality and job satisfaction among female Jewish Israeli hospital nurses. *Journal of Advanced Nursing, 66*(2), 334–344.

Levy, R. B. (2000). My experience as participant in the course on spirituality for executive leadership. *Journal of Management Inquiry, 9*(2), 129–131.

Liu, C. H., & Robertson, P. J. (2011). Spirituality in the workplace: Theory and measurement. *Journal of Management Inquiry, 20*(1), 35–50.

Ma, Z. (2005). *All negotiations are not perceived equal: the impact of culture and personality on cognitions, behaviors, and outcomes* (Doctoral dissertation). McGill University.

MacDonald, D. A. (2000). *The Expressions of Spirituality Inventory: Test development, validation and scoring information.* Unpublished test manual.

MacDonald, D. A., Friedman, H. L., Brewczynski, J., Holland, D., Salagame, K. K. K., Mohan, K. K., ... Cheong, H. W. (2015). Spirituality as a scientific construct: Testing its universality across cultures and languages. *PLoS One, 10*(3), e0117701.

Macon, G. K. Sr. (2014). *School leaders and spirituality: Perspectives of spirituality and spirituality's influence on principals in public schools in southeastern Louisiana.* Southeastern Louisiana University.

Mark, G. T., Wheeler, C. A., & Hodgson, M. N. (2012). Leader spirituality and leader virtues as predictors of effective leadership. *Journal of Spirituality, Leadership and Management, 6*(1), 35–47.

McLaughlin, C. (2005). Spirituality and ethics in business. *European Business Review, 17*(1).

Mitroff, I. I., & Denton, E. A. (1999). *A spiritual audit of corporate America: A hard look at spirituality, religion, and values in the workplace.* Jossey-Bass.

Murrell-Jones, M. (2012). A spiritually based leadership approach in the retail environment to assist with the challenges of employee morale and retention. *Journal of Business and Retail Management Research, 7*(1), 1–11.

Neal, J. A. (2001). Leadership and spirituality in the workplace. *Leadership theory, application, skill development*, 464-473.

Padayachee, N. K. D. (2010). *The application and relevance of spiritual leadership in the JSE top 40 companies* (Doctoral dissertation). University of Pretoria.

Phipps, K. A. (2012). Spirituality and strategic leadership: The influence of spiritual beliefs on strategic decision making. *Journal of Business Ethics, 106*(2), 177–189.

Rai, H. (2007). Dispute Handling Capability: Morphology and Modalities—Development of a Model. *Management and Labour Studies, 32*(2), 183–202.

Rai, H. (2013). The measurement of negotiating ability: Evidence from India. *Global Journal of Business Research, 7*(4), 109–125.

Reave, L. (2005). Spiritual values and practices related to leadership effectiveness. *The Leadership Quarterly, 16*(5), 655–687.

Richardson, T. N. (2009). *The impact of spirituality on the leadership practices of African American women college presidents* (Doctoral dissertation). The George Washington University.

Saini, K. M., & Burton, O. (2020). Mindfulness and spirituality: an enhanced leadership perspective. In *New Horizons in Positive Leadership and Change* (pp. 229–248). Springer.

Sanders, J. E., Hopkins, W. E., & Geroy, G. D. (2003). From transactional to transcendental: Toward an integrated theory of leadership. *Journal of Leadership & Organizational Studies, 9*(4), 21–31.

Small, E. (2020). How successful African-American male leaders in predominately White Organizations integrate spirituality with leadership practice. *Journal of Management, Spirituality & Religion, 17*(2), 184–208.

Stoshikj, M. (2014). Integrative and distributive negotiations and negotiation behavior. *Journal of Service Science Research, 6*(1), 29–69.

Sweeney, P. J., & Fry, L. W. (2012). Character development through spiritual leadership. *Consulting Psychology Journal, 64*(2), 89.

Tasa, K., & Bell, C. M. (2017). Effects of implicit negotiation beliefs and moral disengagement on negotiator attitudes and deceptive behavior. *Journal of Business Ethics, 142*(1), 169–183.

Thompson, L. (1990). Negotiation behavior and outcomes: Empirical evidence and theoretical issues. *Psychological Bulletin, 108*(3), 515.

Thompson, L., & Hastie, R. (1990). Judgment tasks and biases in negotiation. In B. H. Sheppard, M. H. Bazerman, & R. J. Lewicki (Eds.), *Research in negotiation in organizations* (Vol. 2, pp. 31–54). JAI Press.

Walton, R. E., & McKersie, R. B. (1991). *A behavioral theory of labor negotiations: An analysis of a social interaction system*. Cornell University Press.

Wulandari, F. (2014). Spirituality in workplace, individual spirituality and work behaviour: The study of higher education in Indonesia. *Individual Spirituality and Work Behaviour: The Study of Higher Education in Indonesia*.

Yammarino, F. J. (2000). Leadership skills: Introduction and overview. *The Leadership Quarterly*, *11*(1).

Yukl, G. (2012). Effective leadership behavior: What we know and what questions need more attention. *The Academy of Management Perspectives*, *26*(4), 66–85.

Yukl, G. A. (2006). *Leadership in organizations* (6th ed.). Pearson Prentice Hall.

Zhang, Y., & Yang, F. (2020). How and when spiritual leadership enhances employee innovative behavior. *Personnel Review*.

KEY TERMS AND DEFINITIONS

Leader-Member Exchange: It reflects the relationship of a leader with each subordinate that is guided strictly by the employment norms or is set apart by mutual compassion, trust, respect, affection, and shared influence.

Leadership: It is a collaborative endeavor of mindful behavior, actions, and spiritual orientation that inspires, unites, and empowers the individuals, fosters positive changes and developments, transforms workplaces, and improves the quality of life while working towards the achievement of mutual goals and aspirations.

Leadership Effectiveness: Leadership effectiveness is an ability to develop a clear and compelling vision, communicating that vision with clarity to the employee groups and teams in different positions, engaging in productive and ethical exchange with internal and external stakeholders to negotiate and resolve conflicts for delivering on the vision.

Negotiating Ability: It demonstrates a set of strengths required to understand and resolve the various forms of conflict and disputes through effective negotiation and dispute handling mechanisms.

Religiosity: Human functioning that is comprised of non-ordinary experiences which alter one's sense of self and relationship to others and the world as well as the beliefs, attitudes, behaviors, and lifestyle practices that are associated with such experiences.

Religiousness: It explains beliefs and behaviors associated with devout religious adherence and highlights the intrinsic ideas, values, attitudes, behaviors, and practices that are religious-oriented.

Spiritual Leader: Spiritual leader is the one who not only holds firmly to spiritual beliefs but manifests such views in their leadership behaviors and practices by integrating spirituality with the leadership in the workplace. Such a leader consciously takes care of both the Creator and the created.

Spiritual Leadership: It comprises the values, attitudes, and behaviors necessary to intrinsically motivate one's self and satisfy fundamental needs for spiritual well-being through calling and membership.

Spirituality: Spirituality for this study is a complex domain of human functioning that is comprised of non-ordinary experiences which alter one's sense of self and relationship to others and the world as well as the beliefs, attitudes, behaviors, and lifestyle practices that are associated with such experiences.

Chapter 7
Religion in the Workplace:
The Case of Bahraini Banks

Asma Ayari
https://orcid.org/0000-0002-2134-0624
University of Bahrain, Bahrain

ABSTRACT

This chapter is an exploratory study that explores the issues of the religious fact in Bahraini banks. The chapter will produce an understanding of this phenomenon, the different religious forms it takes, and its impact on the management of organizational functioning in Bahraini banks. First, a questionnaire will be distributed among 125 employees and managers working in Bahraini banks. The questionnaire will report the workplace religious positions and manifestations perceived by the employees. It will also say what religious facts and managerial solutions based on religion employees observe in the workplace. Then, semi-direct interviews conducted with 15 managers will help explore the challenges and issues related to religious practices. Finally, the data collected will be analyzed based on themes developed from the literature review. The results will show how religious values impact Bahraini bank management practices and functioning.

INTRODUCTION

Historically, organizations were inspired mainly by religion (Izak, 2009). What about today? Does religion remain a source of guidance and inspiration for the Organizations? The presence of religious actualities in business is becoming more and more significant. This phenomenon particularly reveals developments in society in general and can have real impacts on labor relations and the company's

DOI: 10.4018/978-1-7998-9319-6.ch007

performance (Cantone & Wiener, 2017). However, the religious issue at work is a sensitive subject. The religious fact poses, nowadays, multiple legal questions to companies (Gracia-Zamor, 2003). Whether employees at work must respect religious freedom, it may sometimes seem necessary to restrict the actions. Employers and human resources managers can find themselves helpless by the demands of some employees regarding their religious practice. Managers are increasingly called upon to manage the difficulties for companies to understand this phenomenon and integrate it into management (Wallace & al., 2014). In addition, religious issues are considered delicate situations, leading to negative consequences for organizations and potential losses of performance and motivation among employees (Topno & Syngkon, 2019; Sharma & Singh, 2020). However, unfortunately, few HR Managers are trained in these issues. Even, few types of research were done in this geographic era kingdom of Bahrain and the middle east.

Religion is one of the Arab culture's most significant and distinctive features. Many scientists identified religion as a critical variable influencing most aspects of Arab cultures (Shahin & Wright, 2004; Kalliny & Gentry, 2007). Islam is the most critical force in shaping culture in Islamic countries, particularly in Arab countries, including the Arabic language, traditions, and social life, which are all rooted in Islam and considered a whole way of life (Kavoossi, 2000). Weir (1998) stressed the distinctive characteristics of Arab culture as a fourth paradigm and the three most common paradigms such as American, EU, and Japanese cultural paradigms (Weir, 1998). In his cultural studies, Greet Hofstede (1991) referenced seven Arab countries as the "Arab group." He characterized those Arab groups as having high collectivism, considerable power distance, relatively strong uncertainty avoidance, moderate Masculinity/Femininity, and high collectivism. Sidani & Thornberry (2010) elaborated that Arab culture is adherent to religion and is characterized by familism, where the loyalty of individuals is to their families at the first place and then to the following social level that individuals belong to as their religious sect, tribe, or to the extended family. This characteristic supports Hofstede's (1991) finding of a significant power distance in Arab countries. Arabs are more traditional, past-oriented, unique, and stated that there are cultural variations, even within one country. As a result, Arabs represent a significant cultural group that is relatively neglected in cultural studies or has seldom been addressed adequately in the literature (San Martin et al., 2018).

Indeed, a company has an economic purpose, but it is also a place of socialization, discussions, interactions, even sometimes confrontation since the employee is also an individual with its history, convictions, culture, beliefs, or non-belief. From this point of view, we observe that the company's actors are more frequently than before confronted with the expression of religious convictions. Moreover, tensions associated with the emergence of xenophobia induced by the outward manifestation of religious views and behaviors have evolved in greater diversity in organizations (Cantone & Wiener, 2017). Religious conflicts in the workplace have been documented in many organizations, and these include opposing perspectives toward religious principles and their legitimacy in the workplace (Cornelius & al., 2001). Similarly, and from a perspective that combines sociology of public action and work, there would be room to consider professionalization in religious fact management.

1. LITERATURE REVIEW: THE RELIGIOUS FACTS IN THE ORGANIZATION

Religion is a new issue that affects both private business circles and those of government administrations or personnel. The religious question at work is a delicate one, and companies face a slew of legal challenges due to religious beliefs. The fact that religion exists at work, in the firm, is not trivial, and management's consideration of it is complex, mainly because it is polymorphic and hence difficult to explain (San Martin et al., 2018; Topno & Syngkon, 2019). Three significant instances of the study done in Management Sciences on the relationship between the organization, its management, and religion emerge. Themes include religious discourse on work and its organization, as well as corporate governance, religion as a source of inspiration for entrepreneurship (Audretsch & al., 2007; Duchon & Plowman, 2005; Topno & Syngkon, 2019), and religious facts in business and their impact on the operation of companies and management (Garcia-Zamor, 2003; Sharma & Singh, 2020).

Indeed, expressions of religious identification, such as requesting leave for religious celebrations, wearing a veil, a kippah, a crucifix, or employees who pray during their break, are becoming more widespread in the workplace (Topno & Syngkon, 2019). In most cases, the confessional display does not impair the company's ability to perform appropriately. However, the proportion of conflictual scenarios is gradually increasing, and a slight majority of circumstances now necessitate managerial intervention to address conflicts or reach a compromise (San Martin et al., 2018). The conflict surrounding religion at work and its management could be analyzed individually. Whether or not religious freedom should be honored by employees at work, limiting their events at times may be necessary (Sharma & Singh, 2020). However, while consulting actions on religious facts are emerging, we are witnessing the establishment of training in the fight against radicalization, in the management of religious fact, and on an unprecedented scale, at the initiative of public authorities (San Martin et al., 2018).

The evocation of religious tensions in the workplace should not prohibit researchers from investigating scenarios in which religion is likely to be considered a resource or a tool for work. This could be viewed from several perspectives: on the one hand, through how a religious ethos can influence the relationship to work; on the other hand, through how a religious ethos can influence the relationship to work (Weir, 1998). On the other hand, managers might consider how organizations can be led to use religion as a vector of social peace and a tool of governmentality. It can also be investigated how religion is used as a resource to prevent excesses or combat radicalization (Gracia-Zamor, 2003).

While several studies have objectified religious discrimination in employment, what methods can Bahraini managers use to reconcile religious commitments and professional norms that are a priori incompatible with these obligations?

2. METHODOLOGY OF RESEARCH

The main objective of this study is to investigate how religion impacts Bahraini bank's management practices and functioning. Therefore, a questionnaire survey was carried out between July and September 2021. It consisted of administering an online questionnaire with a sample of approximately 160 executives and managers operating in Bahrain. This quantitative part of the work was supplemented by field surveys involving qualitative methods and based on semi-directive interviews with 15 managers working in Bahraini banks. One hundred sixty complete questionnaires were collected and, after the deletion of non-actionable questionnaires, 125 were taken into account in the study. The analytical sample was made up of 55% men and 45% women (Figure 1). Seventy-seven percent of survey respondents are in charge

Figure 1. Repartition by gender

of a team of 2 to 45 individuals. The remaining 23% have executive status but do not have managerial responsibilities. The influence of the sample's features such as gender, religious affiliation, the function performed, degree of belief and practice, etc., has been rigorously investigated and taken into account in the analysis of the findings, particularly with the use of regularly used tests.

The questionnaire is organized and written in such a way that data may be collected to analyse:

- the types and significance of the religious facts;
- the styles of behavior used by practicing employees to display their religiosity;
- its impact on professional relationships among colleagues, as well as in the context of hierarchical and management relationships;
- Its impact on organizational functioning and executive action (work situations, management situations).

The 15 interviews were carried out between the end of July and the mid of September 2021. A considerable portion of interviews was recorded (with the consent of those present), leading to transcription and content analysis. These interviews lasted 20 minutes to an hour. A confidentiality commitment has been given, and the quotations included in this research are limited to a few lines. This will help to illustrate a point without allowing the person or organization to be identified.

3. ANALYSIS AND DISCUSSION

3.1. Religious Fact Inventory in Bahraini Banks

Based on 125 employees and managers working in Bahraini Islamic banks, the most common religion is Islam (present in 77% of the situations observed). Catholicism is present in 10% of situations, Hinduism with 3%, Buddhism worship in 2%, and others with 3% observed situations. In situations where these religions are present, Islam and Catholicism are most often the only visible religions.

The presence of religious facts in Bahraini banks and companies, in general, has asserted itself for a long time. Since Bahrain opened up to the international labor market, employees from different countries, nationalities and religiously appealed religions began to be part of the working group in Bahraini companies. Thus, 67% of the sample mentioned religious facts or symbols in their workplace compared to 28% who do not see religious observance (Figure 3).

Figure 2. % of situations concerned by each religion

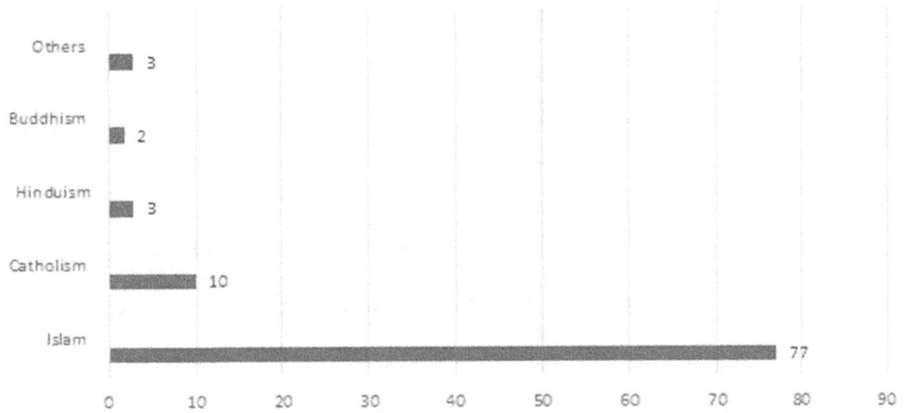

Figure 3. Do you mention any religious facts or symbols in your workplace?

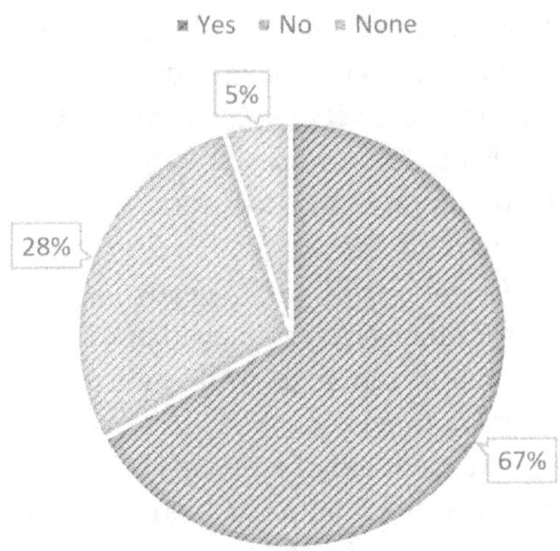

The wearing of religious symbols is the most frequent fact. Prayer, especially during breaks, is shared by the different cults, as religious objects in the workspace (Figure 4). As for Muslim facts, they have two characteristics of their own. The first is their greater diversity. The second is the presence of specific facts, particularly those relating to attitude towards women (refusal to work with women, to shake their hands, or to work under the orders of a woman).

Figure 4. What religious facts/symbols did you observe in your workplace?

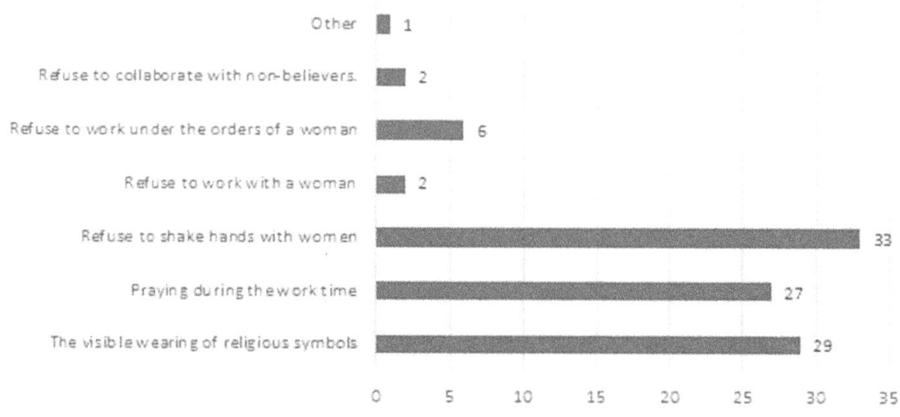

The refusal to shake hands with women, the visible wearing of religious signs, and the prayer during work time represent most of the facts identified in the workplace. However, do not forget that the survey is carried out in a Muslim country. These first three types of facts do not impact the organization of work and the employees and organization performance. The majority (14/15) of the interviewees mentioned that these facts do not have an impact on the work: "*as long as it remains discreet and the work is done, there is nothing to say*"; "*asking for permission to pry in the mosque, what matters is the work, I said yes when possible, and otherwise, I said no*".

This is not the case for other types of facts that our study identifies as being present in workspaces, such as refuse to work with women (2%) and under the orders of women (6%) and non-believers (2%). A minority (5/15) of interviewees advanced how some less frequent religious events but which intrinsically question the organization of work and its functioning such as relations between colleagues, the refusal to work with women or people who are not co-religionists, are not accepted: "refusing to work with someone is no, whatever or the reason", "*I have nothing against religion. I let him do his prayers in the dressing room, and it does not bother me. But refusing to work with a woman, it is out of the question*". These types of facts call for a specific managerial action that, a priori, calls more to disciplinary actions.

3.2. Religion and Social Relationships at Work

Based on the study results, the impact of the religious relationships between colleagues is not perceived as unfavourable by more than three-quarters of respondents in this investigation (figure 5). It also has a relatively limited impact on the relationship between supervisors and their subordinates, making it more difficult for just over a third of respondents to manage. On the other hand, it remains a delicate subject to address for 64% of the sample (figure 6), and that it is best to avoid for 52% of them (figure 7).

Figure 5. The religious fact has a negative impact on relationships between colleagues

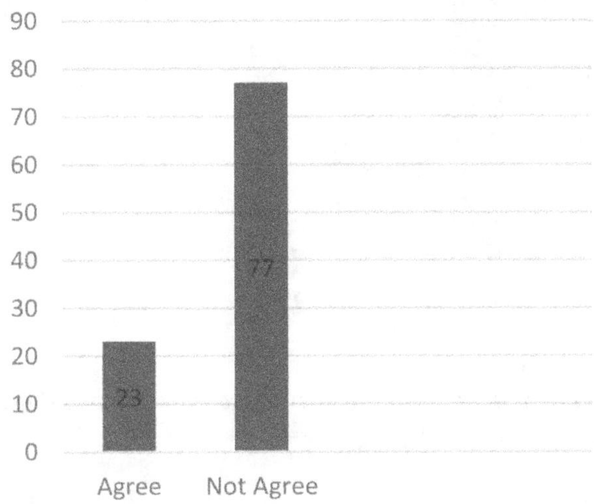

Figure 6. The religious fact makes the relations with my subordinates more difficult to manage

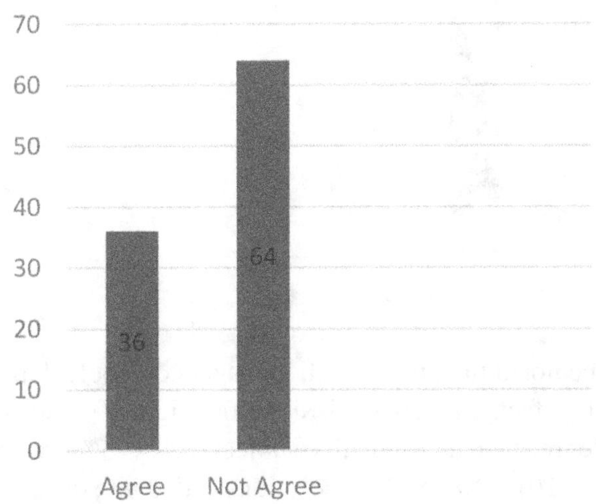

Figure 7. Religion is a subject of discussion to avoid between Colleagues

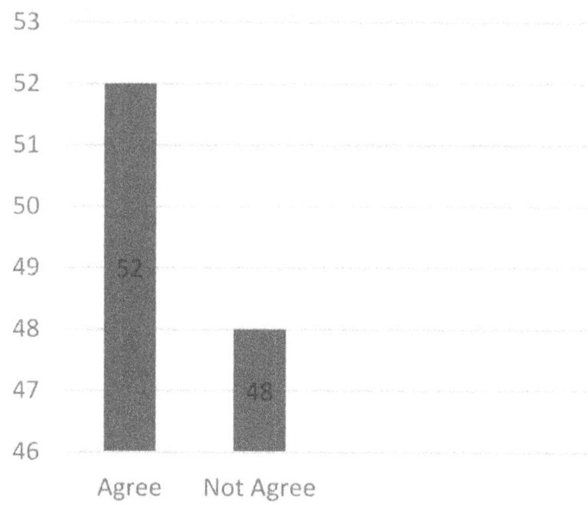

Figure 8. Religion is a subject more sensitive discussion to be addressed than others between colleagues

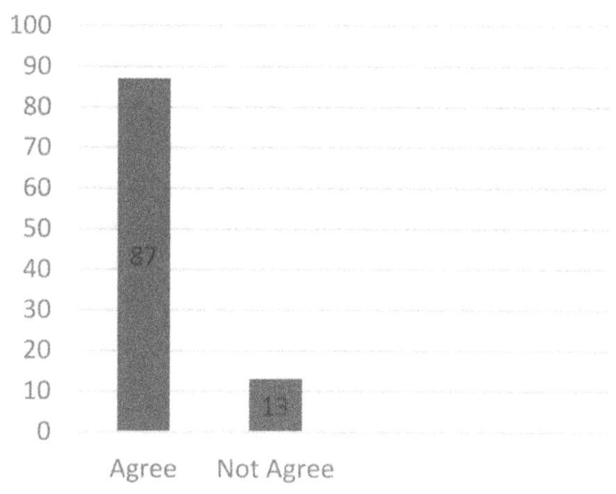

It should also be noted that, in general, managers do not feel in difficulty by the presence of religious facts in their work situation (figure 9). However, 87% of the employees consider religion as a sensitive subject. Few (13%) feel overwhelmed by this question (figure 10), 19% see their decisions called into question (figure 11), or 17% feel particular difficulties related to the presence of the fact religious (figure 12).

Figure 9. The religious fact makes my managerial activity more complex

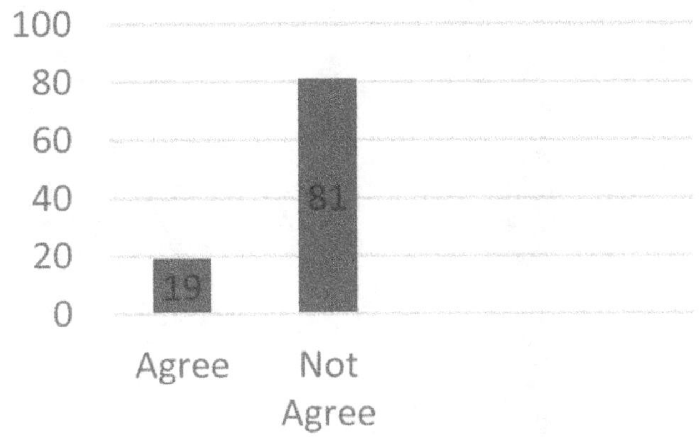

Figure 10. I often feel overwhelmed by the religious fact

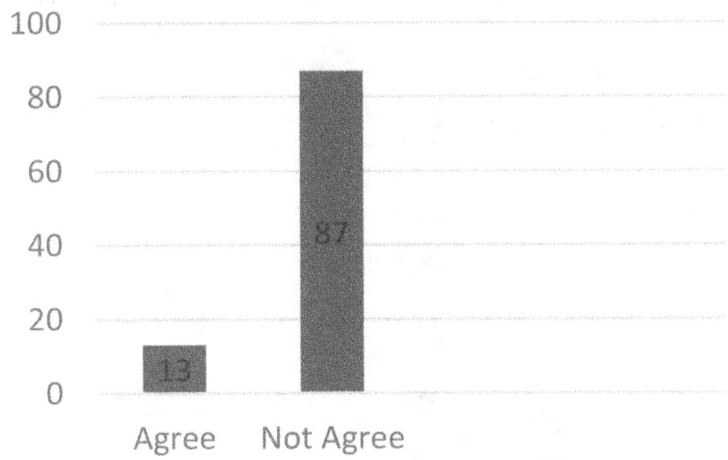

On these issues, when the employee is confronted with problematic situations, as shown in the graph below (figure 13), the employee tends to manage them alone as a priority. When asking for help, employees first contact the hierarchy and then the HR department, more rarely to the legal department of the company, colleagues, or employee representatives.

Figure 11. I do not feel any particular difficulties faced with situations marked by the religious fact

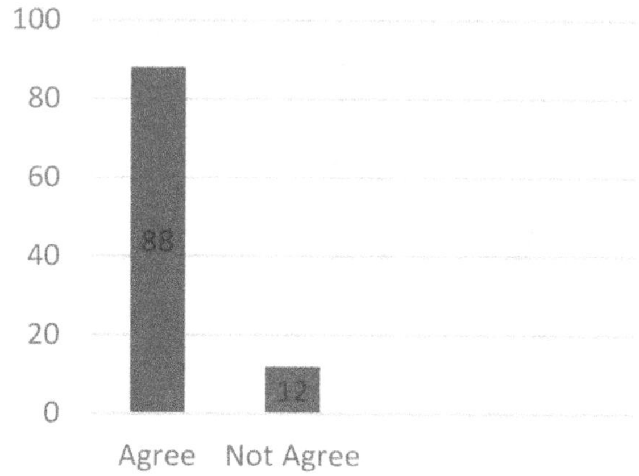

Figure 12. My decisions regarding the religious fact are well accepted

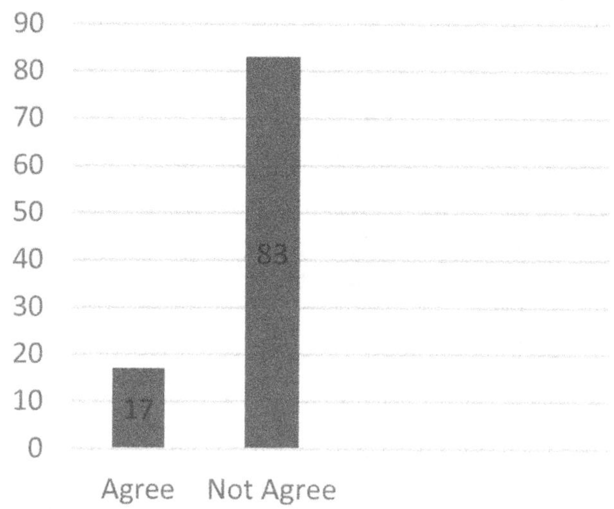

Figure 13. In the most problematic situations, have you asked for support?

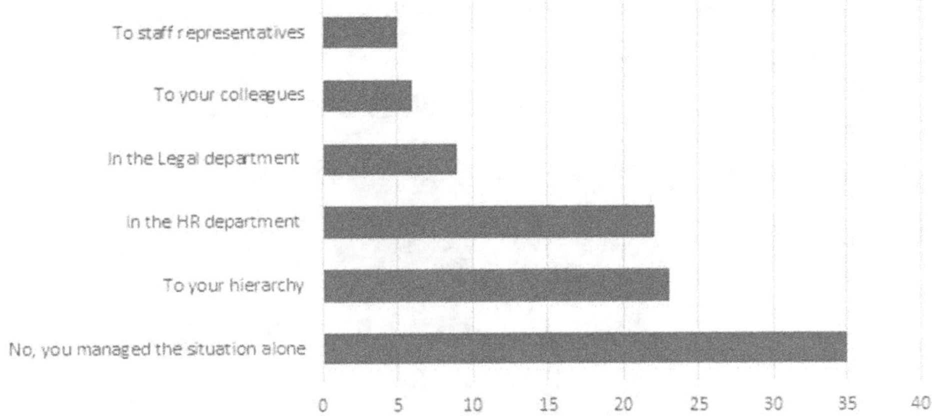

3.3. Religion and Employees' Performance: Does the Spiritual Reality Interfere with Organizational Functioning?

In 66% of instances marked by a regular or occasional religious fact, the graph displays the frequencies of the adverse effects of religion (figure 14). The application of the hygiene laws is considered, security is taken into account, the task is performed correctly, and the company is operating correctly or connections with clients or associates. It appears for the following variables:

- On the one hand, those religious facts do not, or seldom have a negative impact, in the majority of cases;
- On the other hand, these adverse religious factual effects are prevalent for a minority of scenarios that account for 9% to 28% of the total, according to the indicators.

Three levels of dysfunction: strong, moderate, and low, were identified. The results are presented in the graph below (figure 15). They show that, in 62% of situations, dysfunctions related to religious facts are low. In 24% of situations, these dysfunctions are moderate, and they are only strong in 14% of situations.

Based on the results, three levels of dysfunction link to religious situations, such as the frequency of tensions and conflicts, the impact on relationships between colleagues and on relationships with customers, and the impact on the proper completion of the work. This degree of dysfunction and the frequencies of negative impacts of the religious fact presented above are significantly related to the level of religious density of work situations. Situations marked by high density include two-thirds

Figure 14. Frequency of negative impacts of religion

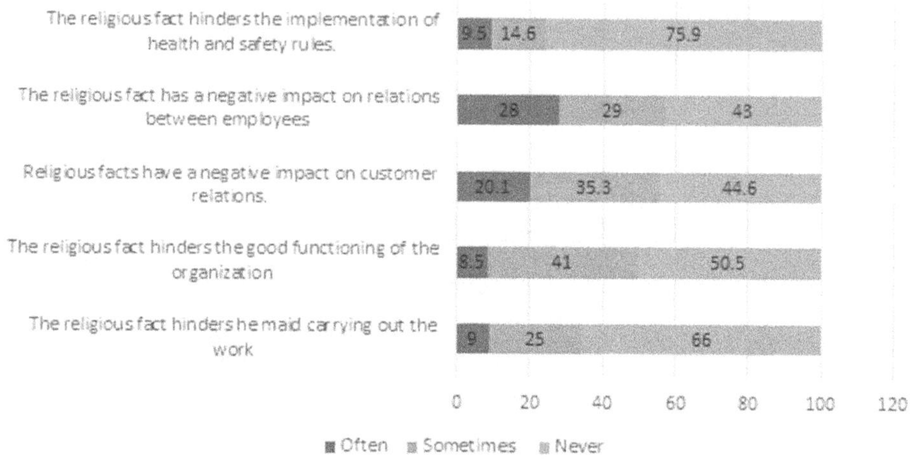

Figure 15. Degree of dysfunction in marked situationsoccasionally or regularly by the religious fact

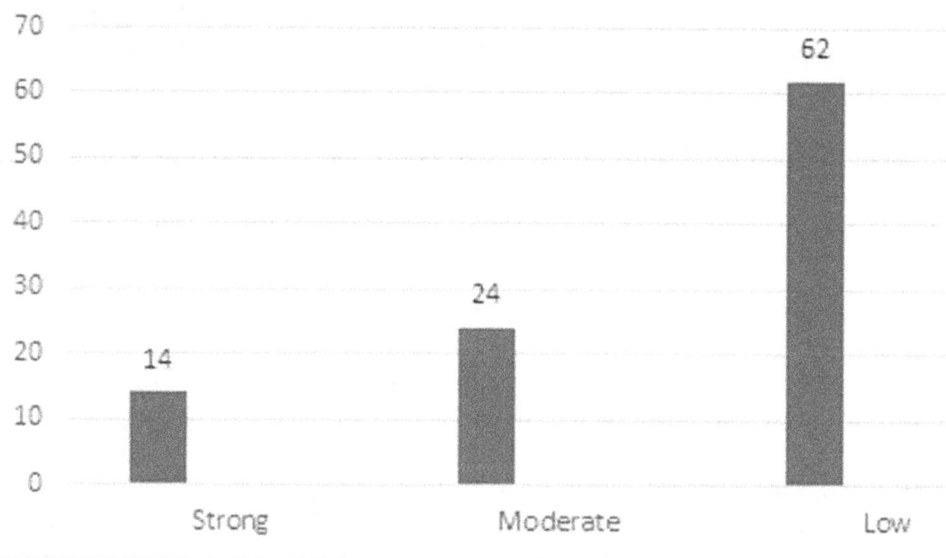

of situations marked by significant dysfunctions. Thus when the religious fact is present in a marked way and significantly influences work situations, dysfunctions are mostly strong management of the religious effect.

This study investigates the diversity of the religious facts on the performance of the employees working in Bahraini Islamic banks. The results show a different religious situation that hurts the function of the organization. However, what consideration of religion do Bahraini Islamic banks take to manage teams and work?

3.4. Management of the religious effect

Based on the respondents, they want that the organization considers and implement rules regarding what the employee can do and can not do regarding their religion but at the same time consider that the company can send a message to employees who believe on the occasion of a religious holiday and that the break time can be used to pray (figure 16). On the other hand, they object to the possibility of refusing to perform tasks or work with another person for religious reasons.

Figure 16. What can or cannot be done?

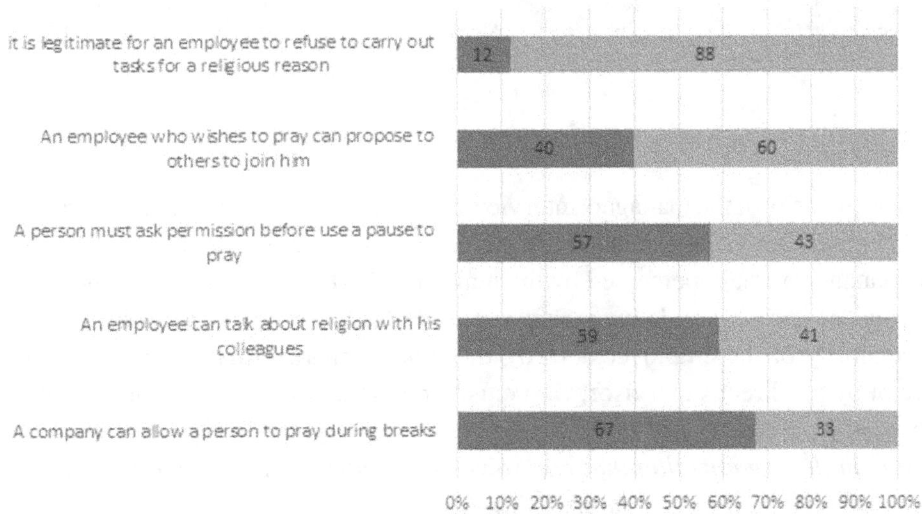

For a vast majority of respondents (9/10), "*the company must frame the expression of religiosity at work, particularly by taking an official position and by including specific requirements in the rules of procedure*". On the other hand, they are also mostly opposed to the condition of a place reserved for religious practice, denominational menus, or taking religious calendars at the management level. On this last point, they are in favor of adaptation pragmatic on a case-by-case basis.

Figure 17. What institutionalization of the religious fact?

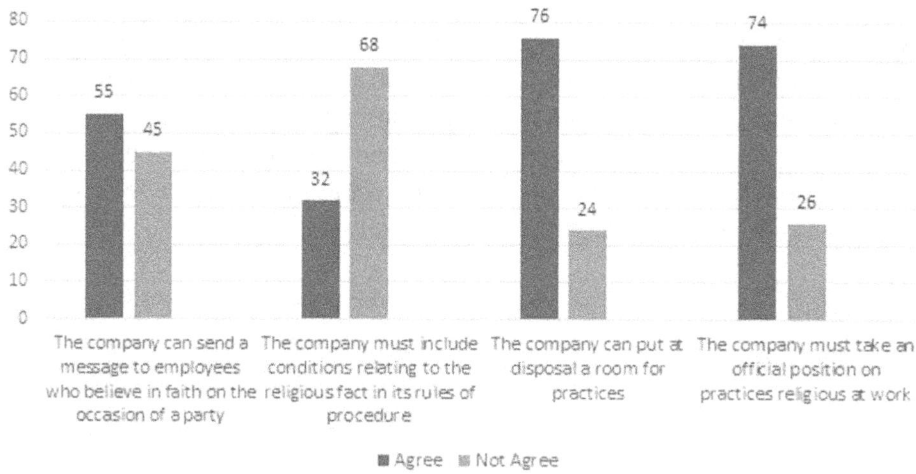

The majority of the managers interviewed (9/10) say they do not generally consider the religious dimension when it comes to managing employees and teams. However, the managers remain perceived by the majority (8/10) of interviewed employees as playing "*the primary role in the management of religious facts at work*". Thus, for the majority of the employees (7/10), these problematic situations must be taken care of by the direct supervisor, who must remain the prime contractor: "*if delicate situations*" or "*situations of blockages and conflicts appear,*" managers are "*the only person in the organization that can solve the problem*"; "*the search for solutions, even if it can rely on its hierarchy of available services*".

The managers must be at "*the heart of taking into account the religious fact when necessary*" for the majority (9/10) of the interviewees. Nevertheless, it must benefit from the support of the substantive services of its company (Human Resources and the legal department in particular) and its hierarchy (figure 18). A problem that may arise here is the distance to the field and the knowledge of the central services. The latter is, in effect, sometimes little informed and aware of the reality of certain situations encountered by the local management.

Figure 18. What process for managing situations related to the religious fact?

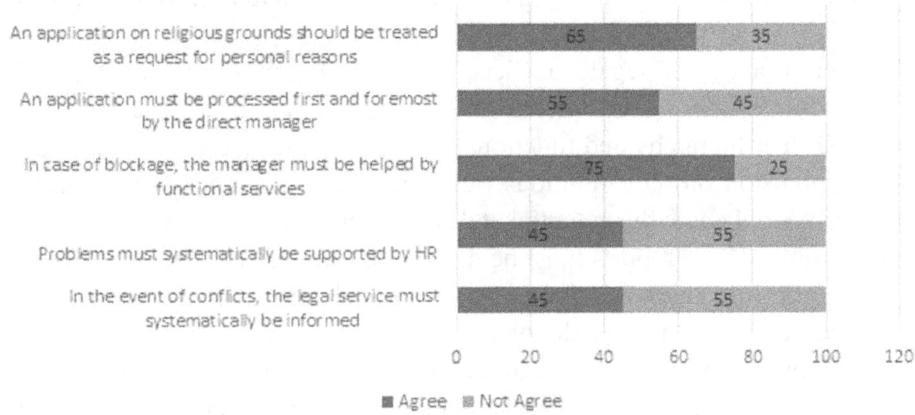

4. Recommendations: Social dialogue and Religious Beliefs at Work

Even if the spiritual reality subtly presents itself, it can have real-world consequences for employees' working conditions. It is also likely to have for the majority of the respondents (9/10) a significant impact on "*the company's operations, relationships with stakeholders, image, and place in its surroundings*". Therefore, businesses concerned with religion at work must give their employees and management a framework that allows them to comprehend the company's policy properly. The latter must be developed following the legal framework, but it cannot be confined to a resumption that is identical to it. It must also be "*the product of the company's decisions about diversity and social and societal responsibility*" for the majority of the respondents (7/10).

The corporation must consider its position between the logic of religious tolerance and inclusion. In either scenario, it must also consider limitations and concrete modalities. A participative method including internal and maybe external stakeholders of the company might help to clarify the guideline. It must, however, be above all a company's decision and thus carried out by its leaders. Furthermore, it must be accomplished by include components relevant to religious fact management in the norms of the procedure. The stakes are high:

- establish a national law that specifies, for both employees and management, what is and is not feasible in terms of the expression of religiosity and managerial action;

- give managers legitimacy to constrain the expression of religiosity at work within the limits of what is planned, allowing them to objectify their action;

In circumstances of legal conflicts, norms and procedures are required to justify binding actions against practitioners. Employees must also have the option of entering their hierarchy and functional services to seek aid in circumstances of undue compulsion on their religious freedom, stigmatization, or discrimination. They must be told about the potential and accompanied in this effort to the greatest extent possible. These reports must be dealt with methodically and factually once more. The priority means of action remain communication with the actors involved and viable solutions through dialogue. Employees must, however, rely on the company's protection in the event of a blockage or uncomfortable circumstance. This option must be available to both practicing employees and those who believe they are being discriminated against or stigmatized. This issue of prejudice must be closely monitored throughout the recruitment, as it mainly affects candidates of the Muslim faith. Here, systematic information and preventative activity are required.

Then, the demands of certain employees over their religious practice might disarm employers and human resource managers. Employers must clearly define human Resources policies, and they may include provisions in the rules of procedure for the establishment of the principle of neutrality. Of course, they must treat all employees fairly and refrain from promoting any specific faith. It is advised to plan, for example, an awareness campaign for managers or Human Resource Managers, mainly using religious management manuals.

Finally, a case of difficult situations must be dealt with systematically. In the event of behavior that breaches respect for people, their freedom, and the regulations established to maintain the efficient running of the organization, the corporation must be allowed to impose severe disciplinary measures on employees or management. Unacceptable behavior must be addressed as such, rather than waiting for it to be repeated.

CONCLUSION

The work situation is marked by religious facts and behaviors spotted in most Bahraini banks. It is most often the wearing of visible religious symbols, praying during work, or the refusal to shake hands with a woman. More rarely, behaviors have also been identified that call into question professional relationships (e.g., refusal to work with non-believers) or hostile behavior towards women (e.g., refusal to work with a woman or under her orders). These are also the cases of stigmatization and discrimination that concern practitioners of all religions. However, it should be emphasized that the most frequent religious fact is invisible; most practitioners, regardless of their religion, do not show their religiosity at work. The management function appears to be critical in demining religious fact situations that could be troublesome in the workplace. However, where the action of a group of practicing employees, for whom faith takes precedence over professional activity, strives to resist, more or less forcefully, in management, the latter fails. However, the reluctance to initiate a discussion might lead to stifling or even (very) problematic situations. In these cases, the manager must enlist the help of the company's hierarchy and functional services.

REFERENCES

Audretsch, D. B., Bonte, W., & Tamvada, J. P. (2007). Religion and entrepreneurship. SSRN *Electronic Journal*, 1-29. doi:10.2139/ssrn.1025968

Ayoun, B., Rowe, L., & Yassine, F. (2014). Is workplace spirituality associated with business ethics? *International Journal of Contemporary Hospitality Management, 27*(5), 938-957.

Bruce, S. (Ed.). (1992). *Religion and modernization. Sociologists and historians debate the secularization thesis.* Clarendon Press.

Cantone, J. A., & Wiener, R. L. (2017). Religion at work: Evaluating hostile work environment religious discrimination claims. *Psychology, Public Policy, and Law, 23*(3), 351–366. doi:10.1037/law0000132

Carswell, P., & Rolland, D. (2004). The role of religion in entrepreneurship participation and perception. *International Journal of Entrepreneurships and Small Business, 3*(4), 280–286.

Casanova, J. (1994). *Public religions in the modern world.* The University of Chicago Press. doi:10.7208/chicago/9780226190204.001.0001

Cavanagh, G., Hanson, B., Hanson, K., & Hinojoso, J. (2001). Toward a Spirituality for the Contemporary Organization: Implications for Work, Family and Society. In *Organizational behavior: Essential tenets for a new millennium.* South-Western College Publishing.

Cavanagh, G., Hanson, B., Hanson, K., & Hinojoso, J. (2001). Toward a Spirituality for the Contemporary Organization: Implications for Work, Family and Society. In *Organizational behavior: Essential tenets for a new millennium.* South-Western College Publishing.

Cornelius, N., Gooch, L., & Todd, S. (2001). Managing Difference Fairly: An Integrated "Partnership" Approach. In M. Noon & E. Ogbonna (Eds.), *Equality, Diversity and Disadvantage in Employment.* Palgrave Macmillan. doi:10.1057/9780333977880_3

Cui, J., Jo, H., Na, H., & Velasquez, M. (2015). Workforce Diversity and Religiosity. *Journal of Business Ethics, 128*(4), 743–767. doi:10.100710551-013-1984-8

Cutting, M., & Walsh, M. (2008). Religiosity Scales: What Are We Measuring in Whom? *Archive of Psychology of Religion, Volume, 30*(1), 137–154. doi:10.1163/157361208X317006

Davie, G. (1990). Believing without belonging: Is this the future of religion in Britain? *Social Compass*, *37*(4), 455–469. doi:10.1177/003776890037004004

Davie, G. H. (2002). *Europe: The exceptional case. Parameters of faith in the modern world*. Darton, Longman and Todd Ltd.

DeKlerk, J. J. (2005). Sprituality, Meaning in Life and Work WeUness: A Research Agenda. *The International Journal of Organizational Analysis*, *13*(1), 64–88. doi:10.1108/eb028998

Duchon, D., & Plowman, D. A. (2005). Nurturing the spirit at work: Impact on work unit performance. *The Leadership Quarterly*, *16*, 807–833.

Duffy, R. D. (2006). Spirituality, religion, and career development: Current status and future directions. *The Career Development Quarterly*, *55*, 52–63.

Fry, L. W. (2005). Toward a theory of ethical and spiritual well-being, and corporate social responsibility through spiritual leadership. Academic Press.

Garcia-Zamor, J. C. (2003). Workplace Spirituality and Organizational Performance. *Public Administration Review*, *63*(3), 355–363. doi:10.1111/1540-6210.00295

Glasner, P. (1977). *The sociology of secularisation. A critique of a concept*. Routledge & Kegan Paul.

Glock C. Y. (1962). On the study of religious commitment. *Religious Education, 57*, S98-S110.

Hofstede, G. (1991). *Cultures and Organizations: Software of the Mind*. McGraw-Hill.

Izak, M. (2009). Spirituality in organization: A dubious idea (?): Historically oriented sensemaking in spiritually imbued organizations. *Tamara*, *8*(1/2), 73–88.

Kalliny, M., & Gentry, L. (2007). Cultural values reflected in Arab and American Television Advertising. *Journal of Current Issues and Research in Advertising*, *29*(1), 15–32. doi:10.1080/10641734.2007.10505205

Kalliny, M., & Gentry, L. (2007). Cultural Values Reflected in Arab and American Television Advertising. *Journal of Current Issues and Research in Advertising*, *29*(1), 15–32. doi:10.1080/10641734.2007.10505205

Kavoossi, M. (2000). *The Globalization of Business and the Middle East: Opportunities and constraints*. Quorum Books.

McGhee, P., & Grant, P. (2008). Spirituality and ethical behavior in the workplace: Wishful thinking or authentic reality. *Electronic Journal of Business Ethics and Organization Studies, 13*(2), 61–69.

San Martin, A., Sinaceur, M., Madi, A., Tompson, S., Maddux, W.-W., & Kitayama, S. (2018). Self-assertive interdependence in Arab culture. *Nature Human Behaviour, 2*(11), 830–837. doi:10.103841562-018-0435-z PMID:31558808

Shahin, A. I., & Wright, P. W. (2004). Leadership in the context of culture: An Egyptian perspective. *Leadership and Organization Development Journal, 25*(6), 499–511. doi:10.1108/01437730410556743

Sharma, N., & Singh, R. K. (2020). Workplace spirituality and organizational effectiveness: Exploration of relationship and moderators. *Journal of Management, Spirituality & Religion, 18*(1), 15–34. doi:10.1080/14766086.2020.1829011

Topno, B., & Syngkon, R. A. J. (2019). The influence of religion on entrepreneurship: A study on tribal Christian entrepreneurs in Assam. *International Journal of Business and Management Invention, 8*(5), 1–7.

Wallace, M., Bradley, R.E., & Wright, A.H. (2014, Mar.). Religious affiliation and hiring discrimination in the American South: A Field Experiment. *Social Currents*.

Weir, C. (1998). Fiji and Fijians: Two Modes of missionary Discourse. *The Journal of Religious History, 22*(2), 152–167. doi:10.1111/1467-9809.00056

Chapter 8
Confluence of Workplace Spirituality and Leadership

Abdul Gani
Central University of Kashmir, India

Sana Shabir
Central University of Kashmir, India

ABSTRACT

Recent interest in the subject of workplace spirituality and leadership emphasizes the integrative potential of spirituality in the workplace as a means of increasing cohesiveness and leadership effectiveness. Relatively little attention has, so far, been devoted to how spirituality could act as a force of developing leadership effectiveness within organizations. Since workplace spirituality and leadership together are in a developing phase of postmodern discourse, the bridge between the two needs to be narrowed down by identifying the reasons for the evident disconnection between workplace outcomes and leadership spirituality and probing possible moderators and mediators of this relationship. The chapter encapsulates the existing research evidence on spirituality and leadership effectiveness to identify the future research agenda in the area. The review reveals that workplace spirituality and leadership share a significant positive relationship and that improving the core areas of spirituality can improve various dimensions of leadership.

INTRODUCTION

While spirituality is an emerging concept, leadership has been put through cyclical empirical research, focusing on traits, behaviors, styles, power, and situations. In

DOI: 10.4018/978-1-7998-9319-6.ch008

the earlier phases of leadership development, spirituality was distinguished as too ambiguous and personal to be regarded as a vital factor of leadership (Tomlinson, 2013). There existed very little research to empirically support the contribution of spiritual elements to leadership effectiveness (Dougherty, 2011). However, as leadership theory and practice progressed through different phases of the business environment, new research themes surfaced that gave due consideration to the spiritual dimension of the workforce and viewed leadership as the materialized dimension of a leader's spirituality (Fairholm, 1998). The present era of research marks the beginning of exploring the qualities of spiritual leadership and its association with numerous organizational outcomes (Giacalone et al., 2005; Malone & Fry, 2003; Townsend & Wichern, 1984). Since leaders tend to influence their followers, for this reason, leaders need to gain knowledge of their values, beliefs, strengths, and shortcomings which may otherwise act as a barrier to leadership (Macon Sr, 2014; Sorvaag, 2007). In this way, spiritual behavior among the individuals along with their leadership practices becomes much more evident, thereby making spiritually attuned practices flourish.

Although spirituality, through such research streams, has been linked to a fundamental characteristic of being human, it shows the integration of spirituality into the leadership research agenda through various dimensions remains yet to be explored fully (Padayachee, 2010). In essence, research is needed to analyze the relationship between spirituality and leadership effectiveness and whether spirituality plays any significant role in upholding effectiveness in leadership roles and practices. Building on the research on these primary constructs, the present study strives to understand better the role that spirituality plays in guiding leadership effectiveness. Apart from the research domain, the employers, employees, and other stakeholders and their recognition for morally upright leaders add to the significance of conducting this research. The importance of this study lies in the fact that its findings espouse spiritually informed leadership and give way to robust and resilient leadership practices (Richardson, 2009). It signals the value of consciousness and the ways to find meaning and purpose in life. Moreover, it relates this perspective to gaining inner peace, tranquility, confidence, and perseverance during times of stress, chaos, and organizational dysfunction pertinent to leadership (Ruiz, 2005).

Though many studies assert a strong connection between spirituality and leadership, others treat both individualized concepts (Dent et al., 2005). It is because of the inconsistency and inadequate consideration for the measurement and analysis concerning spirituality and leadership. This lack of consistency has been attributed to the concept and measurement being different and the presence of uncontrolled variables (if any) that are likely to affect this relation (Ali & Zaky, 2018). As such, gaining a broader understanding of how they correlate may help amplify the individuals' general welfare, workplace, and society. Therefore, scrutinizing the relation of workplace spirituality and leadership further still needs consideration. Accordingly, the present chapter seeks to examine specific links between them.

The existing research evidence on the relationship between workplace spirituality and leadership in organizations has been critically reviewed in this chapter to identify the gaps in the existing research that need to be filled up in future research on the subject. The study results provide insights and much-needed information concerning the implications of workplace spirituality and leadership for leaders, organizations, policymakers, practitioners, and researchers. It paves the way for spirituality to be a part of the leadership process alongside traditional leadership behaviors, skills, and experiences. With this, leaders can cultivate changes that impact individuals, groups, organizations, and ultimately society at large. Further, the study attempts to delve more into spirituality-based studies and learn how it influences the day-to-day activities of individuals, it would help leaders and subordinates to relate and discuss spirituality in the workplace context. Furnishing information on how effective leaders integrate spirituality into their professional lives demystifies the notion of spirituality being an abstract construct (Richardson, 2009). The present chapter acts as a springboard to provide further evidence on the subject.

Spirituality in Leadership

Spirituality has been overlooked in studies of leadership (Korac-Kakabadse et al., 2002). Both spirituality and leadership theories have been seen as separate fields of study. Due to the prevalence of apparent conceptual differences between spirituality and leadership, the development of spiritual leadership theory is still in its infancy (Sharma, 2010). Spiritual leadership later did form a part of military, academia, public, and private organizational studies and has revealed positive results. But the leaders could not subsume it wholly, instead fixated on conventional leadership practices (Latham, 2013; Sweeney & Fry, 2012). They somewhat could not recognize that organizational success did not solely rely on producing goods and services (Latham, 2014; Vasconcelos, 2011). As such, the non-financial and human dimensions of effective leadership remained largely ignored (Geh, 2014; Marques et al., 2011).

At the very outset, spirituality became associated with leadership by the work of Fairholm (1996), who highlighted the importance and role of spirituality in the workplace (Bertram, 2007). Gradually, also with the increase in complexities of the advanced marketplace, spirituality and its essence in a leader's life gained attention considerably, and that has been indicated in the popular works of Bolman and Deal (2001), Biberman and Whitty (2000), Korac-Kakabadse et al. (2002), Mitroff and Denton (1999), and Reave (2005). This major transformation that took place in many organizations led to the spirituality movement. The "spirituality movement" marked a beginning of spiritual aspects within the organizations that earlier were guided by set rules and regulations only. But with the influx of the "spirituality movement", focus got shifted to meaning, purpose, and a sense of community (Ashmos & Duchon, 2000). It embodies a quest for meaning, simplicity, connection to something higher (Oldenburg & Bandsuch, 1997). Individually, the concept of leadership through the domain of authority, traits, behavior, and the given situation has been studied widely. Of late, it has kindled an interest to understand how leadership and spirituality are integrated and how spirituality influences leaders and their followers.

While attempting to integrate spirituality and leadership, researchers have found spirituality and effective leadership are interrelated concepts (Macon Sr, 2014; Mark et al., 2012; Reave, 2005). Combining the two terms implies that spiritual leadership is based on making individuals understand their inner selves and fostering a sense of meaning and significance among them. Spirituality provides an outlook of leadership in a way that brings together the behavior and dispositional character of individuals, leaders' influence on followers, and the attainments of goals (Reave, 2005). This new paradigm about leadership implies that the leader's prime duty is to direct the employees and organizational activities in a manner where everyone's spiritual values are congruent with the work values (Fairholm, 1997). Spiritual leadership is considered a well-sorted and more inclusive form of leadership (Blanchard, 1999). Morris (1997) argues that a leader to be effective needs to value and nurture various aspects of the spiritual dimension. Fry (2003) defines spiritual leadership as the composition of values, beliefs, attitudes, and behaviors that necessitate motivating oneself and others to ensure spiritual endurance that can be achieved by creating a vision and proper social and organizational culture. With spiritual leadership in place, some new themes have emerged like interconnectedness (Dein, 2005), spirit and soul (Conger, 1994), altruistic love (Fry, 2003), purpose and meaning (Wong & Fry, 2013), inner life (Roof, 2001), management values (Pfeffer, 2003), spiritual diversity (Vu & Gill, 2019), and spiritual consciousness (Mayer, 2000). This form of leadership rebuffs the earlier models of human leadership, prioritizing values such as self-interest (Korac-Kakabadse et al., 2002).

Spirituality can be prevalent in any organization, but when it comes to exhibiting effective leadership, it calls for the demonstration of spiritual values, beliefs, and practices on the part of the leader. The spiritual perspective of leaders helps them think about human needs and aspirations in a better way and instills a vision and inspiration among them (Dantley, 2005; Hoyle, 2002). The theory of spiritual leadership fosters a holistic approach to leadership that fundamentally combines and strengthens the basic spheres of human life, such as the mind, body, spirit, and heart. It highlights the importance of interdependence among humanistic, spiritual, and natural realms (Reave, 2005). Spiritual leadership attempts to be an exemplar addressing various facets of leadership in the form of ethical leadership, profitability, employee well-being, sustainability, and social responsibility (Fry &

Slocum, 2008; Padayachee, 2010). Moreover, it stresses the constant efforts taken up to do anything in one"s control to ease the suffering of others (Vu & Gill, 2019). Spiritual leaders, from time to time, have stumped for integration of spirituality and business so at to fulfill the needs and aspirations of employees and organizations for long-term success by creating such a work environment where people get a sense of purpose, connectedness, and recognition (Bondoc, 2016; Fry & Cohen, 2009; Sweeney & Fry, 2012).

Leadership effectiveness is not to be necessarily appended to moral righteousness all the time because effective leaders can advance some appalling outcomes. As a matter of fact, leadership tends to bring about positive as well as negative consequences. Seemingly, effective leadership may prove to be contributing factor in enhancing social good but may also lead to social disaster. Practicing such leadership may demean others for personal gain. However, the leaders are not solely responsible for counterproductive actions and behaviors. Sometimes, it is due to the followers that negative repercussions arise for the leader. For example, the followers at times may glorify, enact or try to get on the good side of a leader, thereby depriving leaders of getting unbigoted responses or thinking on different lines of working (Washbush & Clements, 1999). It simply cripples down the very essence of effective leadership. Many research studies linked ineffective leadership to poor quality of processes and systems, but ineffectiveness in leadership is not necessarily due to poor organizational systems and processes (Latham, 2013).

Present-day organizations do not look for monetary benefits only but give due emphasis to spiritual orientation, spiritual well-being, and satisfaction of the individuals (Fairholm, 1996; Fox, 1994; Neal, 1997). There is no place for inflexible delineation between the work and non-work realms, where one thinks of spirituality as a part of the personal domain and leadership as a professional aspect (Scott, 1994). The presence of such a demarcation might otherwise dilute the essence of leadership as being holistic (Bhindi & Duignan, 1997). Essentially, true leadership is about enthusing in people's liveliness, spiritedness, care and concern, and awareness about the higher purpose of life. On these parameters, a good leader tries to bring out the best in his/her subordinates because the best is connected to one"s higher self (Hawley, 1993). Spirituality inherent in leadership can lead to positive outcomes such as increased job satisfaction, morale, commitment, and work quality, reduced absenteeism and turnover, enhanced corporate responsibility and sustainability, greater well-being and life satisfaction, and improved overall productivity (Fairholm, 1996; Fry, 2005b; Sweeney & Fry, 2012). Besides, employees who happen to work for spiritual organizations tend to be more confident, happy, creative, motivated, and ethical. In this way, the key stakeholders, i.e., the spiritual leaders, experience meaning, purpose, and interconnectedness in their lives, realize their potential, make a difference, and feel accepted, understood, valued, and appreciated (Fry, 2005b; Fry

& Cohen, 2009). Through the spiritual journey of a leader, the active spiritual well-being of an overall organization can be sustained. If spirituality gets neglected in the organizations, it may lead to a lack of motivation, morale, meaning, and enthusiasm to accomplish the tasks (Kriger & Seng, 2005). Thus, having spirituality ingrained in the leadership is an ever-emergent conceptualization in research.

Spiritual Leadership Frameworks

Individuals have a unique set of beliefs, values, attitudes, and the spirit they come with to their organization and constantly strive to experience a sense of transcendence and interconnectedness in their work. Like any other primary need, such as emotional, physical, and mental needs, people strive for their spiritual needs (Duchon & Plowman, 2005). Such needs can be met at the individual, group, and organizational levels. However, if the spiritual needs are met at the organizational level through spiritual leadership, the more positive outcomes get manifested. For example, employees as entrants to the organization are supported by providing altruistic love that in the long run gets displayed in the attempts by the followers towards the achievement of common organizational goals (Fry & Whittington, 2005). Spiritual leadership typically demonstrates a context that goes beyond workplace spirituality (Fry, 2008).

The source of spiritual leadership lies in one's inner life, moral sense, principles, and conscience. Through spiritual leadership, people envision and practice such positive experiences as it involves inspiring and encouraging the workers through such a vision and culture that is fundamentally based on altruistic values. Creating a transcendent vision (calling) helps individuals experience a meaningful life, whereas setting up a social/organizational culture (membership) makes them feel understood, respected, cared for, and appreciated. Spiritual leadership considers the stakeholder approach with various internal and external stakeholders (e.g., employees, shareholders, customers, suppliers, government, etc.) having a rightful concern in the organization's activities and outcomes (Freeman, 2010; Jones et al., 2007). The process of stakeholder effectiveness, which happens to be an elementary aspect of the spiritual leadership, relies on "appreciative inquiry" that primarily identifies and attends to the issues of the key stakeholders, exploring and rectifying what and why certain things go well and why not the others, and how the success can be percolated through the organization (Malone & Fry, 2003).

Spiritual leadership simply adduces that the trust and hope exhibited by the followers in their organization's vision set them going in a positive direction, whereby the positive forces incite the efforts and dedication through intrinsic desire and motivation. Precisely, those who practice spiritual leadership demonstrate higher life satisfaction and share more cordial bonds, which help to foster "the sense that life is purposeful and meaningful, the capacity to effectively manage one's surrounding world, the ability to follow inner convictions, and a sense of continuing growth and self-realization." Consequently, it enriches the spiritual well-being of the leader as well as the followers and has implications for the larger community (Fry & Matherly, 2006; Fry et al., 2005). In the context of the spiritual leadership framework, Korac-Kakabadse et al. (2002) propose the elements of spiritual leadership that include: forming mutual values, establishing a vision, sharing meaning, enabling, influence and control, instinct, service, and transformation.

Approaches to Spiritual Leadership

Since the inception of "spiritual leadership" as a concept, many researchers have developed arguments and assumptions by which spirituality can affect leadership. However, Fry (2003, 2005b) has presented the most exhaustive effort at developing a theory of spiritual leadership (Krishnakumar et al., 2015). Spiritual Leadership Theory (Fry, 2003) is a fundamental theory based on the organizational transformations incorporating the vision, faith, hope, and altruistic love that aim to establish "an intrinsically motivated, learning organization" (Fry & Matherly, 2006). It represents a new integrated form of leadership coupled with some value-based theories such as ethical leadership, authentic leadership, and ecological leadership (Krishnakumar et al., 2015). The rationale behind spiritual leadership is to cultivate the vision-value equivalence and systematic transformation across the different organizational levels that eventually promote higher levels of positive organizational outcomes. This shift from the traditional bureaucratic setup to the present-day learning organization is much required to respond to the prevailing dynamic global environment (Fry et al., 2005).

Fry (2003) classified the causal model of spiritual leadership along the three distinct lines (a) leader ideals, attitudes, and behaviors; (b) follower requirements for spiritual endurance; and (c) organizational results. The recent developments in the pursuit of workplace spirituality, spiritual leadership, and positive psychology led Fry (2005a) to supplement the spiritual leadership theory by incorporating the concepts of positive human health, ethical and psychological well-being, and life satisfaction (Fry & Matherly, 2006) that is attained by a nexus of values, attitudes, and behavior of individual with that of the universal system (Cashman, 1998; Fry, 2003; Fry & Whittington, 2005). Further, Fry (2003) contends that spiritual leadership theory takes on board the contemporary leadership theories and is also less confusing and conceptually more distinctive with theoretical simplicity. Thereafter, a revised causal model of spiritual leadership (see Fig. 1) was developed by Fry (2008). It considers inner life or spiritual practice as the source of spiritual leadership, and it generates hope/faith in a vision of providing service to others and the values of altruistic love. This hope/faith in the organizational vision drives positive expectations that kindle effort through intrinsic motivation. Consequently, the intrinsic motivation cycle represented by hope/faith (effort), vision (performance), and altruistic love (reward) enhance spiritual well-being (i.e., calling and membership) and the individual and organizational outcomes (e.g., organizational commitment and productivity, financial performance, employee life satisfaction, and corporate social responsibility).

SLT embraces an interactional approach that leads to a sense of empowerment among the different levels of employees (Khani et al., 2013; Krishnakumar et al., 2015). It has been validated across the different organizations as a causal model demonstrating the positive results for employees as well as employers in the form of organizational commitment, intrinsic motivation, sales and growth, employee satisfaction and well being, productivity, sustainable performance, and competitive advantage (Chen et al., 2012; Fry & Matherly, 2006; Fry & Slocum, 2008; Fry et al., 2005; Mitroff & Denton, 1999).

Figure 1. Revised Causal Model of Spiritual Leadership (Fry, 2008, p. 112).

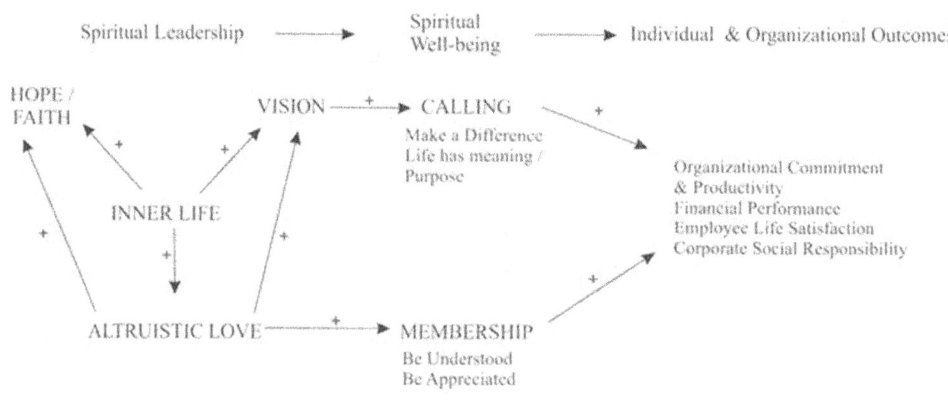

Spiritual leadership theory has received considerable recognition from theorists, researchers, and practitioners as it acts as the facilitator of the various dimensions of leadership across academia and practice by integrating the already established theories with the newly found assumptions, theories, and principles. It also circumvents the major drawbacks linked to the faulty enumeration of the measurement model (Fry et al., 2005). However, less empirical work has been done concerning the construct validity of the spiritual leadership causal model (Boorom, 2009). Various other approaches have been considered from time to time to study spiritual leadership regarding spiritual values and practices. For example, Sanders III et al. (2003) propose a model that relates the hierarchical levels of spirituality with structural levels of leadership accomplishments. The three hierarchical levels of leadership accomplishment are transactional, transformational, and transcendental. These have been postulated in congruence with three dimensions of spirituality: awareness, moral character, and belief. Further, these three theories of leadership presented in the model are connected along common continua that involve locus of control, effectiveness, and spirituality.

Reave (2005) focuses on the character and integrity of a leader. Likewise, there exist numerous traditional approaches to leadership that ascribe different terms to tap the essence of this concept. For example, in transformational leadership theory, character and integrity get evinced in the form of "idealized influence" that ingrains ethical behavior. In line with this is Benefiel's (2005) approach to spirituality in leadership that takes care of individual and organizational levels of spiritual transformation and suggests that spiritual development is concurrently a continuous and discontinuous process. It encompasses five stages: Awakening, Transition, Recovery, Dark Night, and Dawn. Awakening is the stage characterized by becoming spiritually aware, embracing spiritual practices, and undertaking associations with others on a spiritual pursuit. The transitional phase is embarked upon by questioning the followed spiritual path due to dissatisfaction with the spiritual practices and a sense of seclusion and confusion. In the stage of recovery, one tries to explore new ways of relating to the Divine Power through personal rejuvenation and endurance of new spiritual practices. It promotes awareness of daily sacredness and becomes a source of renewed joy. Followed by the night, spiritual practices no more yield desirable changes. Thus, spiritual progression comes to a halt, landing individuals into a deep abyss. But as the journey progresses, the dawn emerges, and it sets the peaceful congruence of individuals not just with the self but with the universe and the transcendent power. Therefore, it marks a new beginning of a higher good.

Another way forward is the "spiritual contingency model of spiritual leadership", which specifies basic spiritual leadership characteristics, such as interconnectedness, faith, and charisma, as antecedents to workplace outcomes. It highlights four key spiritual contingency factors (self-importance, drive to lead, organizational support, and integrity) acting as moderators of spiritual leadership (Krishnakumar et al., 2015). Besides, the influx of spiritual beliefs may influence the leadership in the following ways – firstly, it can expedite leader's focus on connectedness that highlights all people are interrelated in one way or the other (Tanyi, 2002); secondly, with existential faith, spiritual leaders will have a sense of humility, integrity, and concern for others, thereby, making leader more ethical; and lastly, by being charismatic, spiritual leaders can inspire and influence others (Krishnakumar et al., 2015). Resonating with the evolving frameworks of spiritual leadership, Sharma (2010) developed a conceptual model of spiritual leadership illustrating values and attributes (truthfulness, personality, integrity, concern, conscience, and humility) of a leader coupled with the practice of self-discipline, minimalism, individualized consideration, community service, and openness to faith. These, in accord with each other, lead to personal, organizational, and social outcomes. Furthermore, research has associated successful leadership with the idealized influence of the values and attributes of leader and practices and their quest for altruistic and transcendental goals. Accordingly, altruistic and transcendental goals and idealized influence have been taken as moderators in this framework of spiritual leadership.

Using a case study method, Doherty (2011) explored the relationship between spirituality and leadership among college students and developed a conceptual framework for spiritual leadership. Spirituality reflected an effect on leadership in the form of motivation, leadership values, justice, relationships, and community. In her study's conceptual framework, Doherty formulated six spheres of influence: purpose, relationship, ethics, service, spirit, and "an all-encompassing motivation for leadership: love" (p. 4). Geaney (2012) developed Spirituality Leadership Competency Model based on the leadership research and her work and experiences as a business executive. This model outlines the leaders' competencies and behaviors that positively impact the followers and bring about a sustainable change in the global community. It has been classified into the inner self, connection, role modeling, interactive trust, letting go, foresight, and successful business impact factors, reflecting the leaders'' desirable characteristics. However, there are some innate contradictions in putting together a leadership spirituality competency model with the conceptualization that business leadership's only responsibility is stockholder valuation.

The negative consequences associated with the various popular leadership approaches have been recognized in the spiritual leadership literature. Spirituality may be used as a tactic to pursue the organizational goals rather than the individual needs on a priority basis (Krishnakumar et al., 2015; Lips-Wiersma & Nilakant, 2008). It may give rise to inequity, division, and disbelief (Cavanagh & Bandsuch, 2002). As such, spiritual values and beliefs need to be identified and dealt with prudently without their becoming contemptuous agents for profit maximization (Vu & Gill, 2019). Another risk associated with incorporating a spiritual perspective into organizations is proselytism, through which individual's belief system and spiritual views tend to get influenced and using such tactics weakens the organizational support system (Karakas, 2010). It leaves employees in a dissatisfied and frustrated state because of being constrained, threatened and alienated and not respected for their diverse thought processes (Brown, 2003). Some employees also perceive holding spiritual conversations in organizations as an intrusion into their personal space and even view spirituality as too confidential to be discussed (Mirvis, 1997; Cavanagh, 1999).

In theory, research, and practice, legitimacy is yet another issue of spirituality (Karakas, 2010). In scientific research and practice, spirituality is not well-grounded (Giacalone et al., 2005). Nonetheless, spirituality is believed to be the most vital pursuit for organizations to pursue, and no organization can survive without spirituality being in place (Ali & Zaky, 2018). Therefore, spirituality remains largely a contested notion that needs further reformulation as it poses a great challenge to practice spirituality in the organizational context without inflicting one"s own religious beliefs and thoughts on others (Holland et al., 2016) while ensuring neither excessive sentimentalism nor exploitation gets cultivated (Vu & Gill, 2019).

Synthesis of the Literature

Table No. 1 summarizes major research studies that have focused on spirituality and leadership effectiveness. As outlined in the table, most research studies have made it evident that a positive relationship exists between spirituality and leadership effectiveness, implying thereby that as leaders introduce spirituality within the organizational day-to-day routine work, it enhances their effectiveness by producing positive outcomes.

Summary and Implications

Examination of the related literature has brought forth the antecedents of spirituality and leadership in organizations. While exploring leadership effectiveness, prior empirical investigations have overlooked many key components. Based on a theory, such components imply that leadership must manifest the shared values and norms of the organizations and communities to which leaders belong and are authorized to lead (Magnusen, 2002). Since different studies have come up with other conceptual frameworks and models, this write-up endeavored to amalgamate the core attributes of leadership effectiveness and proved that all these components are significant predictors of leadership effectiveness. The results reveal that spirituality and leadership effectiveness share a significant positive relationship. Further, the findings provide evidence that improving the core areas of spirituality can improve various dimensions of leadership. It clarifies why spirituality needs to be incorporated as an approach to abet leadership effectiveness.

With the rise in competition, complexities, and changes, the literature suggests that spirituality within the workplace is a recurring phenomenon that has demonstrated a renewed interest over the past decade (e.g., DuFour, 2004; Giacalone et al., 2005; Karakas, 2006). Accordingly, organizations need to consider this paradigm shift and integrate high-minded humanistic and spiritual values to let the individuals grow and prosper. It obligates unwavering efforts on the part of leaders and subordinates to reflect on the ways of embodying spirituality, creativity, motivation, understanding, reflection, and consideration into work (Karakas, 2010).

Table 1. Major Research Studies

Study	Purpose	Participants	Design/ Analysis	Outcomes
Walling (1994)	To explore the common boundaries between spirituality & leadership.	10 participants.	Qualitative interview methodology.	A significant association exists between individual's spiritual journey & leadership experiences.
Santerre (1997)	To study the relationship between spirituality & educational leadership.	6 educational leaders.	Open-ended interviews.	Findings unravel that spirituality influences leadership practice.
Delbecq (1999)	To study how spirituality affects business leadership.	N/A	Theme-based.	Spirituality positively transforms leadership.
Jones-Johnson (2001)	To evaluate the relationship between spirituality & selected leadership practices of female educational administrators.	63 female administrators.	Survey-based.	A positive association between spirituality & selected leadership practices has been reported.
Strack (2001)	To assess the link between spirituality & effective leadership practices among the healthcare managers.	319 healthcare managers.	Survey-based.	Results reveal a moderate positive correlation between spirituality & leadership.
Atlas (2002)	To evaluate spirituality's role in the work of African-American women principals in urban schools.	6 participants.	Qualitative methodology.	Respondents recognized a power outside themselves, referred to God by different names, believed that Higher Power guided them in every aspect of their life, had the conviction that God responds to the prayers directly & they practiced spirituality in numerous ways.
Korac-Kakabadse et al.(2002)	To review leadership praxis from different prisms of spirituality.	N/A	Review-based.	Findings endorse the linkage between spirituality & leadership.
Magnusen (2002)	To study the traits of effective leaders & the budding discernment about the importance of spirituality in leadership endeavors.	N/A	Review-based.	Findings emphasize the significance of spirituality towards leadership.
Strack et al. (2002)	To examine whether the healthcare leaders' spirituality affects leadership effectiveness.	N/A	Review-based.	Results reveal a strong link between spirituality & leadership effectiveness.
Miller (2003)	To identify how public school principals describe their spirituality & the practices by which those principals perceive that they demonstrate their spirituality in their leadership roles.	4 principals.	Mixed methods: Interview & survey.	Principals relate their spirituality mostly with idealism, altruism, relationships & a sense of mission. Nurturing relationships, engaging in self-reflection & sharing a sense of mission have been specified as examples of how spirituality affected their leadership.
Stiernberg (2003)	To assess the relationship between spirituality & five specific leadership practices of female K-12 administrators.	68 participants.	Survey-based.	A positive significant connection exists between spirituality & the given leadership practices.
Geaney (2004)	To assess how leaders actualize spirituality in their leadership practices.	11 participants.	Semi-structured interviews & a survey.	Leaders consider spirituality as a component of their leadership perspectives & envision spirituality as a basis for leadership practices.
Lyon (2004)	To investigate whether & in what ways spirituality is an aspect of leadership amongst the effective principals & whether employees were responsive to such leadership.	2 principals.	Qualitative: Case Study (interviews, questionnaires, document analysis, & on-site observations).	Principals lead from a well-developed set of principles, love & care for their employees, promote professional mastery & accomplishment enthusiastically & have designed their schools so that employees can learn & grow & then champion their achievements
Twymon (2004)	To determine the association between spirituality & leadership practices & establish what, if any, differences exist in the ratings of spirituality & the ratings of leadership practices.	78 respondents.	Survey-based.	A significant linkage between spirituality & leadership practices exists for female superintendents, and a statistically significant association between spirituality and the leadership practice was revealed for male superintendents.

continued on following page

Table 1. Continued

Study	Purpose	Participants	Design/ Analysis	Outcomes
Banke et al. (2005)	To examine the Christian school leaders' spiritual experiences.	12 Christian school leaders.	Qualitative: In-depth, open-ended interviews.	Spiritual leadership is an innate progression; spiritual leaders exhibit personal development, mobilize opportunities, & make personal & spiritual growth favorable in the school community & the leaders ensure their institution is spiritually and academically exceptional.
Dent et al. (2005)	To determine ways of distinguishing workplace spirituality, discover the link between spirituality & leadership, & ascertain dimensions & circumstances for facilitating spiritual leadership theory.	N/A	Review-based.	Results highlight that the majority of the researchers tie spirituality to religion and vice versa & a link exists between spirituality & productivity.
Meyer (2005)	To investigate the relationship between spiritual attitudes & transformational leaders, spirituality & demographic variables & assess its impact on transformational leadership.	105 principals.	Quantitative: Surveys.	The results of the study highlight that there is a significant relationship between transformational leadership, spiritual transcendence, & gender.
Reave (2005)	To review research to see what has spirituality to do with leadership effectiveness?	N/A	Review-based.	There is a steadiness between spiritual values & practices & effective leadership.
Shields (2005)	To connect spirituality with educational leadership.	N/A	Discourse-based.	Results highlight the importance of inspiring spiritual practices, acknowledging one's spirituality, opening to the spirituality of others & leading the communities based on truth.
Burke (2006)	To assess if effective leadership can be ascertained & can impel a spiritual connectedness between governments, organizations & society.	N/A	Review-based.	Findings show that spirituality is an important dimension of effective leadership.
Bertram (2007)	To explore the relationship between spirituality & the ability to cope, analyze the function that gender plays in determining any differences in the ability of an individual to cope as an educational leader.	65 executive leaders from the public education sector.	Quantitative: Surveys.	Results reveal no relationship between interpersonal conflict at work & spiritual well-being, no differences in these measures based on gender but a significant association between the capability to cope with stress & spirituality.
Bonner III (2007)	To examine how commonly are leadership Theories X (coercive), Y (humanistic), & Z (spiritual) put to use amongst the public school principals.	12 principals.	Quantitative approach.	X leaders do not almost exist. Y leaders do not compulsorily indicate reform, whereas Z leaders who are in the higher stages of moral & spiritual development have more bend towards reasoning & modifying the status quo in public education.
Ellison (2007)	To explore how African American higher education leaders define their pathways, struggles & successes in attaining & maintaining their positions.	5 participants.	Qualitative approach.	Results signify that respondents linked their spirituality to leadership practices.
Harris (2007)	To identify leaders recognized for being spiritual whose leadership practices/ experiences at the workplace signify emerging exemplar of spiritual leadership.	10 participants.	Qualitative Phenomenology.	Results reveal that educational success is measured not only in terms of hard data (e.g. test scores), but soft data (e.g., trust, respect, values, & service) is equally important.

continued on following page

Table 1. Continued

Study	Purpose	Participants	Design/ Analysis	Outcomes
Sorvaag (2007)	To examine the spiritual attitudes of K-12 public school principals, investigate whether spiritual transcendence orientation varies with the level of educational institute, age & gender& extend support for preparing the future educational leaders.	210 principals.	Quantitative: Survey.	Results show a disparity in spiritual transcendence orientation between elementary & secondary public school principals & between women & men in these roles. No significant difference has been observed amongst age categories in the K-12 public school principals.
Boorom (2009)	To examine the association between variables of spiritual leadership theory & transformational leadership behaviors, and spiritual leadership and leadership effectiveness.	500 participants	Survey method.	Leadership effectiveness vastly links to all SLT leader behaviors and spiritual leadership mediates the relationship of transformational leadership behaviors & leadership effectiveness.
Perkins et al. (2009)	To explore the relationship between educational leaders' spirituality & leadership practices.	71 school principals.	Quantitative: Survey research.	Findings endorse that a statistically significant relationship between spirituality & leadership practices does exist.
Ramirez (2009)	To discover spirituality's role in the work patterns of public school principals.	4 public school principals.	Qualitative: interviews, focus groups & documents	Results show that for the respondents positive influence on the elements of their early lives shaped the definition of spirituality.
Richardson (2009)	To investigate the influence of spirituality on leadership practices.	4 African American women college presidents	Multiple case-study approaches.	Spirituality has a significant impact on the practices of leadership.
Musick (2010)	To examine public school principals in challenging settings & develop a related theory/outline elucidating the role of spirituality in school leaders' professional lives.	12 principals.	Grounded theory methodology.	Those School leaders can be considered as spiritual leaders who advance through various platforms as their career stabilizes & grows. They later tend to become connectors & deal with leadership challenges that influence students' lives & aids in principals' professional lives.
Doherty (2011)	To investigate the bond between spirituality & leadership in college students.	Students, faculty & staff.	Case-study method.	Results show a moderate correlation between spirituality & leadership.
Dougherty (2011)	To examine the relation between spirituality, spiritual intelligence & leadership practices amongst student leaders in the BYU-Idaho Student Activities Program.	150 student leaders.	Survey-based.	Findings reveal that numerous measures of spirituality and spiritual intelligence significantly predict the leadership practices.
Fernando (2011)	To study the link between spirituality & leadership in the workplace.	N/A	Review-based.	A positive association between spirituality & leadership based on extensive review exists.
Freeman (2011)	To study spirituality & its effect on servant leadership formation & effectiveness.	N/A	Concept driven.	Findings indicate spiritual practices moderate the spiritual beliefs & leadership effectiveness.
Anderton (2012)	To establish whether a relationship exists between managers' declared leadership style & their perceived workplace spirituality.	401 managers.	Quantitative: Survey.	A statistically significant relationship does exist between declared leadership style & perceived workplace spirituality.
Bindlish et al. (2012)	To examine spirituality & leadership association.	N/A	Concept driven.	The study emphasizes the linkage between spirituality & leadership & calls for developing a unified model based on leadership with spirituality at its core.
Mark et al. (2012)	To examine spirituality & virtues of a leader as predictors of effective leadership.	143 leaders.	Questionnaire-based.	A leader's spiritual well-being influences how virtuously & actively followers, colleagues, & supervisors rate the leaders.

continued on following page

Table 1. Continued

Study	Purpose	Participants	Design/ Analysis	Outcomes
Hermans & Koerts (2013)	To study spirituality, leadership, & their relationship and examine 'discernment' as the link between spirituality & leadership.	97 principals.	Questionnaire-based.	Results identify trustworthy-guiding leadership, leadership based on empowerment, & autocratic leadership to which school leaders could relate.
Riera (2013)	To know how spirituality influences the leadership practices of senior student affairs administrators.	14 senior student affairs administrators.	Grounded theory methodology	The intersection of leadership & spirituality indicates a seamless connection between leadership & spirituality.
Sexton (2013)	To examine how managers incorporate spirituality into their practices & how these practices have impacted their careers.	6 mid-level management leaders.	Qualitative study: face-to-face interviews.	Participants incorporate spirituality into their leadership & witness positive outcomes, such as the positive impact on their careers.
Houston (2014)	To explore the relationship between spirituality & leadership effectiveness.	875 participants	Survey method.	Findings indicate that spirituality has a positive relationship with leadership effectiveness.
Macon Sr (2014)	To examine the role of spirituality in the lives of principals & whether spirituality helps in fulfilling the duties & responsibilities of a leader.	81 school principals.	Sequential triangulation mixed-method research design.	Results show that spirituality positively influences the role of principals as school leaders.
Zandi et al. (2015)	To examine the connection between spirituality & a leader's effectiveness.	278 companies.	Survey design.	The results reveal that the leaders' level of spirituality influences the leaders' effectiveness.
Bondoc (2016)	To analyze if the inadequacy of spiritual leadership leads to a disparity between employee & organizational needs.	10 front-line supervisors.	Qualitative case study.	Spirituality positively influences the workplace leadership. However, the absence of spiritual leadership leads to inconsistency between organizational and employee needs.
Dhiman (2017)	To highlight the significance of spirituality in the workplace & the role it plays in leading organizations.	N/A	Book chapter.	Any problem, be it at the organizational or societal level, could be solved at the basic level of the human spirit.
Ali & Zaky (2018)	To assess the interactive impact on leadership effectiveness created by spiritual values & practices.	227 respondents.	Survey design.	Results reveal the positive influence of spiritual values & spiritual practices on leadership effectiveness.
Nolan-Arañez & Ludvik (2018)	To look at the perspectives of student leaders' on how leadership development activities affected their spirituality.	10 students.	Qualitative case study design.	Results show a positive association between leadership development activities & programs & the spirituality of students' leaders.
Riasudeen & Singh (2020)	To study the mediating role of workplace spirituality in linkages between leadership effectiveness & psychological well-being.	630 employees.	Cross-sectional & non-experimental	The findings validate a significant relationship of leadership effectiveness & psychological well-being with workplace spirituality.
Komives et al. (2020)	To examine the connection between spirituality & leadership in higher education.	N/A	Book chapter.	A positive association between spirituality & leadership has been found out.
Sligh & Talbot (2020).	To highlight intersections of spirituality & leadership.	N/A	Book chapter.	Findings emphasize on bringing together both spirituality & leadership to receive productive outcomes.
Small (2020)	To study the leadership experiences among senior African-American men & how do they integrate spirituality with leadership.	5 senior officers.	Semi-structured, & face-to-face interviews	The study points to the successful integration of spirituality & leadership practice among African-American male leaders.
Steenkamp (2020)	To provide a theological conceptualization to leadership.	N/A	Concept driven.	The study highlights the evidence on the importance of spirituality in leadership.
Ulluwishewa et al. (2020)	To study spirituality, success & happiness & their implications for leaders.	N/A	Book chapter.	Having spirituality ingrained into leadership & business helps to gain monetary & non-monetary benefits.

continued on following page

Table 1. Continued

Study	Purpose	Participants	Design/ Analysis	Outcomes
Ribeiro et al. (2021)	To know how leadership & workplace spirituality could ensure nurses' well-being & quality of care in health care system.	N/A	Reflective-theme based.	Literature supports an association amongst spiritual leadership, workplace spirituality, & subjective well-being.
Widodo & Suryosukmono (2021)	To evaluate the relationship between spiritual leadership & spirituality in the organization towards self-transcendence & meaningful work.	150 respondents.	Survey design.	Spiritual leadership & workplace spirituality affects meaningful work, & share a positive impact on self-transcendence, which shares a significant relationship with meaningful work.

Different models and theories on spiritual leadership have led to ambiguity and divergence of perspectives in the research community (Abdullah et al., 2009). Since spirituality and leadership together are in a developing phase of postmodern discourse, the bridge between the two needs to be narrowed down by conducting more research and theory development. Moreover, elementary studies done so far have focused on the "what" and "why" of spiritual leadership, but how organizations can support spirituality and leadership needs to be addressed. This gains credibility as the theoretical and practical aspects of it are put together. Therefore, the value of theory lies in the practical implementation of spiritual leadership (Padayachee, 2010).

The earlier organizational studies have ignored the spiritual dimension of human beings, which implies disregarding the fundamental nature of being a human. Thus, it is the responsibility of contemporary leaders to explore and understand spirituality, know all are its features and make out how it finds expression in the workplace context because workplaces that are amenable to spirituality are more productive than workplaces where spirituality is overlooked (Duchon & Plowman, 2005). In this context, leadership is associated with the values and beliefs of the organizational members and community with which it resonates. However, bringing effectiveness through leadership largely depends on the leader's attributes. Prior empirical investigations into this aspect have overlooked the key characteristics of what constitutes an effective leader. Even after having evolved through several decades of research, a redefinition of effective leadership is yet to find its place in the global research arena (Magnusen, 2002). Therefore, researchers need to work more in this field of inquiry and develop a robust and unified leadership effectiveness framework.

Considering its relevance in the present-day context, spiritual leadership is to be introduced across the different walks of life in practical ways. It calls for introducing appropriate channels and mediums that bring about coordination and stability amongst the spiritual institutions, workplaces, and communities. Additionally, more cross-sectional dissemination about spirituality as a connector and not a separator in the course of organizational practices need to be in place. Policymakers and practitioners interested in spirituality and leadership effectiveness should not presume a person's personality as a separate characteristic from what a person does or how he/she behaves in public. Therefore, to improve organizational outcomes and have a positive societal impact, collaborating with community organizations may prove beneficial by offering more practical modes of working and additional support and resources (Jones, 2010).

Based on the information yielded in this review, leaders may enhance their leadership perspectives to embrace spirituality. For that, leaders can practice self-awareness and reflect upon their ways of seeing spirituality, what it means to them, and how they can implement it in their daily errands (Ramirez, 2009). They may generate value-based statements that get manifested in the organization's mission, vision, and objectives. Such core values may then be related to the expressions of spirituality. Likewise, leaders can talk about the spiritual context with the employees, trustees, vendors, customers, and communities. They can lay down the organizational chart as an informative illustration of values, ethics, and behaviors that give life to the fundamentals of their spiritual perspectives (Miller & Miller, 2002). Further, leaders have choices when it comes to demonstrating spirituality through leadership. They may want to practice spiritual leadership by considering social justice, human dignity, utilitarianism, altruistic love, stewardship, morality, benevolence, community development, and the like. Since this study has captured different life stages and sources of influence of spirituality, as such identification and development of beliefs, attitudes, and personalities through a proper analysis of life-shaping factors, school/college experiences, family structure, workplace dynamics, and the role of influential people could help in discovering "what, how, when" aspects of spiritual development. All this may help leaders to understand and work on different facets of spiritual upliftment.

It is imperative for leaders to identify with and reflect on how the intersection of spirituality and leadership acts as a valuable tool for enhancing self-awareness and being cognizant of how to influence others in the right direction. Socialization is another important factor that needs the attention of organizational leaders. By far, spirituality has remained dormant and not openly spoken about in relation to leadership (Riera, 2013). Yet, it affects the very essence of multiculturalism, particularly in today's dynamic global economy (Nash & Scott, 2009). Encouraging spiritual conversations and socializing with spiritually active people, institutions, and surroundings need to be undertaken. In this regard, shaping the work environment has been seen as an appropriate measure to promote spiritual growth. For example, prayer, contemplation, and mediation tools available to employees could draw their attention to their spiritual centering and development (Riera, 2013). The same could be made part of spiritual mentoring, preferred organizational governance policies, and other leadership practices to place the organization at a higher spiritual level, achieve employee development, and strengthen leadership effectiveness.

REFERENCES

Abdullah, A. G. K., Alzaidiyeen, N. J., & Aldarabah, I. T. (2009). Workplace spirituality and leadership effectiveness among educational managers in Malaysia. *European Journal of Soil Science*, *10*(2), 304–316.

Ali, Z., & Zaky, M. (2018). Spiritual values and spiritual practices: Interactive effects on leadership effectiveness. *ETIKONOMI*, *17*(1), 123–134. doi:10.15408/etk.v17i1.6497

Anderton, R. V. (2012). *The relationship between leadership styles and perceived workplace spirituality* (Doctoral dissertation). Capella University.

Ashmos, D. P., & Duchon, D. (2000). Spirituality at work: A conceptualization and measure. *Journal of Management Inquiry*, *9*(2), 134–145. doi:10.1177/105649260092008

Atlas, B. L. H. (2002). *The role of spirituality in the work of African-American women principals in urban schools*. The University of Wisconsin-Madison.

Banke, S., Maldonado, N., Lacey, C. H., & Thompson, S. (2005). *The Role of Spirituality in Christian School Leadership: A Qualitative Study*. Online Submission.

Benefiel, M. (2005). The second half of the journey: Spiritual leadership for organizational transformation. *The Leadership Quarterly*, *16*(5), 723–747. doi:10.1016/j.leaqua.2005.07.005

Bertram, B. (2007). *Reflective Analysis of the Role Spirituality Plays in Educational Leaders' Coping Successes with a Focus on Gender Divergence*. Academic Press.

Bhindi, N., & Duignan, P. (1997). Leadership for a new century: Authenticity, intentionality, spirituality and sensibility. *Educational Management & Administration, 25*(2), 117-132.

Biberman, J., & Whitty, M. D. (2000). *Work and spirit: A reader of new spiritual paradigms for organizations*. University of Scranton.

Bindlish, P., Dutt, P., & Pardasani, R. (2012). From growing convergence of spirituality and leadership towards a unified leadership theory. *Journal of Spirituality, Leadership and Management, 6*(1), 3-23.

Blanchard, K. (1999). *The heart of a leader: Insights on the art of influence*. Honor Books.

Bolman, L. G., & Deal, T. E. (2001). *Leading with soul: An uncommon journey of spirit, New & rev*. Jossey-Bass.

Bondoc, E. J. (2016). *A qualitative study of spiritual leadership in the workplace* (Doctoral dissertation). Northcentral University.

Bonner III, C. E. (2007). *From coercive to spiritual: What style of leadership is prevalent in k–12 public schools?* Academic Press.

Boorom, R. (2009). *Spiritual leadership: A study of the relationship between spiritual leadership theory and transformational leadership* (Doctoral Dissertation). Available from ProQuest Dissertations and Theses database. (UMI No. 3377759).

Burke, R. (2006). Leadership and spirituality. *Foresight*, *8*(6), 14–25. doi:10.1108/14636680610712504

Cashman, K. (1998). *Leadership from the inside out: Seven pathways to mastery*. Executive Excellence.

Chen, C. Y., Yang, C. Y., & Li, C. I. (2012). Spiritual Leadership, Follower Mediators, and Organizational Outcomes: Evidence From Three Industries Across Two Major Chinese Societies 1. *Journal of Applied Social Psychology*, *42*(4), 890–938. doi:10.1111/j.1559-1816.2011.00834.x

Conger, J. A. (1994). *Spirit at work: Discovering the spirituality in leadership*. Jossey-Bass.

Dantley, M. E. (2005). The power of critical spirituality to act and to reform. *Journal of School Leadership*, *15*(5), 500–518. doi:10.1177/105268460501500502

Dein, S. (2005). Spirituality, psychiatry and participation: A cultural analysis. *Transcultural Psychiatry*, *42*(4), 526–544. doi:10.1177/1363461505058909 PMID:16570516

Delbecq, A. L. (1999). Christian spirituality and contemporary business leadership. *Journal of Organizational Change Management*, *12*(4), 345–349. doi:10.1108/09534819910282180

Dent, E. B., Higgins, M. E., & Wharff, D. M. (2005). Spirituality and leadership: An empirical review of definitions, distinctions, and embedded assumptions. *The Leadership Quarterly*, *16*(5), 625–653. doi:10.1016/j.leaqua.2005.07.002

Dhiman, S. (2017). Leadership and spirituality. In *Leadership today* (pp. 139–160). Springer. doi:10.1007/978-3-319-31036-7_8

Doherty, E. P. (2011). *Leading with love: the confluence of spirituality and leadership in college students* (Doctoral Dissertation). Loyola University Chicago, Chicago, IL.

Dougherty, T. J. (2011). *The relationship between spirituality, spiritual intelligence, and leadership practices in student leaders in the BYU-Idaho student activities program*. Idaho State University.

Duchon, D., & Plowman, D. A. (2005). Nurturing the spirit at work: Impact on work unit performance. *The Leadership Quarterly, 16*(5), 807–833. doi:10.1016/j.leaqua.2005.07.008

DuFour, R. (2004). Leadership is an affair of the heart. *The Learning Professional, 25*(1), 67.

Ellison, M. T. (2007). *A qualitative study investigating how spirituality impacts African American male leaders in higher education* (Doctoral dissertation). Roosevelt University.

Fairholm, G. W. (1996). Spiritual leadership: Fulfilling whole-self needs at work. *Leadership and Organization Development Journal, 17*(5), 11–17. doi:10.1108/01437739610127469

Fairholm, G. W. (1997). *Capturing the heart of leadership: Spirituality and community in the new American workplace*. Praeger Publishers.

Fairholm, G. W. (1998). *Perspectives on leadership: From the science of management to its spiritual heart*. Quorum Books.

Fernando, M. (2011). *Spirituality and leadership*. Academic Press.

Fox, M. (1994). *The reinvention of work: A new vision of livelihood for our time*. Harper.

Freeman, G. T. (2011). Spirituality and servant leadership: A conceptual model and research proposal. *Emerging Leadership Journeys, 4*(1), 120-140.

Freeman, R. E. (2010). *Strategic management: A stakeholder approach*. Cambridge University Press. doi:10.1017/CBO9781139192675

Fry, L. W. (2003). Toward a theory of spiritual leadership. *The Leadership Quarterly, 14*(6), 693–727. doi:10.1016/j.leaqua.2003.09.001

Fry, L. W. (2005a). Toward a theory of ethical and spiritual well-being and corporate social responsibility through spiritual leadership. In *Positive psychology in business ethics and corporate responsibility*. Academic Press.

Fry, L. W. (2005b). Editorial: Introduction to the leadership quarterly special issue: Toward a paradigm of spiritual leadership. *The Leadership Quarterly*, *16*(5), 619–622. doi:10.1016/j.leaqua.2005.07.001

Fry, L. W. (2008). Spiritual leadership: State-of-the-art and future directions for theory, research, and practice. In Spirituality in business (pp. 106-124). Palgrave Macmillan.

Fry, L. W., & Cohen, M. P. (2009). Spiritual leadership as a paradigm for organizational transformation and recovery from extended work hours cultures. *Journal of Business Ethics*, *84*(2), 265–278. doi:10.100710551-008-9695-2

Fry, L. W., & Matherly, L. L. (2006, August). Spiritual leadership and organizational performance: An exploratory study. *Annual Meeting of the Academy of Management*. http://www. tarleton. edu/~ fry/sltorgperf. pdf

Fry, L. W., & Slocum, J. W. Jr. (2008). Maximizing the triple bottom line through spiritual leadership. *Organizational Dynamics*, *37*(1), 86–96. doi:10.1016/j.orgdyn.2007.11.004

Fry, L. W., Vitucci, S., & Cedillo, M. (2005). Spiritual leadership and army transformation: Theory, measurement, and establishing a baseline. *The Leadership Quarterly*, *16*(5), 835–862. doi:10.1016/j.leaqua.2005.07.012

Fry, L. W., & Whittington, J. L. (2005). In search of authenticity: Spiritual leadership theory as a source for future theory, research, and practice on authentic leadership. *Authentic leadership theory and practice: Origins, effects and development, 3*, 183-200.

Geaney, M. M. (2004). *Spirituality and business transformation: Exploring spirituality with executive leaders* (Doctoral dissertation). Union Institute and University.

Geaney, M. M. (2012, June). A spirituality leadership competency model: What does it take to be a spiritual business leader. In *8th International Conference on Catholic Social Thought and Management Education*. University of Dayton.

Geh, E. Z. (2014). The organizational spiritual leadership of worlds. *Leadership and Organization Development Journal*.

Giacalone, R., Jurkiewicz, C., & Fry, L. (2005). From advocacy to science. *Psychology of Religion and Spirituality*, 515–528.

Harris, P. L. A. (2007). *School experiences of principals perceived as spiritual leaders and how they reflect the emerging paradigm of spiritual leadership*. Lamar University-Beaumont.

Hawley, J. (1993). *Reawakening the spirit in work: The power of dharmic management*. Berrett Koehler Publishers.

Hermans, C. A. M., & Koerts, E. (2013). Towards a model of influence of spirituality on leadership: Empirical research of school leaders on Catholic schools in the Netherlands. *Journal of Beliefs & Values*, *34*(2), 204–219. doi:10.1080/13617672.2013.801685

Houston, G. G. (2014). *Spirituality and leadership: Integrating spirituality as a developmental approach of improving overall leader effectiveness* (Doctoral dissertation). Antioch University.

Hoyle, J. R. (2002). The highest form of leadership. *School Administrator*, *59*(8), 18–21.

Jones, A. D. (2010). *Leadership and spirituality: The indivisible leadership of African American school administrators as pastors* (Doctoral thesis). Iowa State University.

Jones, T. M., Felps, W., & Bigley, G. A. (2007). Ethical theory and stakeholder related decisions: The role of stakeholder culture. *Academy of Management Review*, *32*(1), 137–155. doi:10.5465/amr.2007.23463924

Jones-Johnson, N. F. (2001). *The relationship between spirituality and leadership practices of female administrators in higher education* (Doctoral dissertation). Baylor University.

KarakasF. (2006). Towards a universal set of values bridging east and west: Global positive spirituality for world peace. Available at SSRN 976770.

Karakas, F. (2010). Spirituality and performance in organizations: A literature review. *Journal of Business Ethics*, *94*(1), 89–106. doi:10.100710551-009-0251-5

Khani, A., Darvish, H., Miandari, K., & Arani, H. (2013). The role of spiritual leadership on empowering employees: A case study of educational system. *Management Science Letters, 3*(3), 1013-1018.

Komives, S. R., Mackie, M. M., Shalka, T. R., & Smith, M. (2020). Spirituality and Leadership: Research Supports the Connection. *New Directions for Student Leadership*, *2020*(166), 135–157. doi:10.1002/yd.20388 PMID:32543039

Korac-Kakabadse, N., Kouzmin, A., & Kakabadse, A. (2002). Spirituality and leadership praxis. *Journal of Managerial Psychology, 17*(3), 165–182. doi:10.1108/02683940210423079

Kriger, M., & Seng, Y. (2005). Leadership with inner meaning: A contingency theory of leadership based on the worldviews of five religions. *The Leadership Quarterly, 16*(5), 771–806. doi:10.1016/j.leaqua.2005.07.007

Krishnakumar, S., Houghton, J. D., Neck, C. P., & Ellison, C. N. (2015). The "good" and the "bad" of spiritual leadership. *Journal of Management, Spirituality & Religion, 12*(1), 17–37. doi:10.1080/14766086.2014.886518

Latham, J. R. (2013). A framework for leading the transformation to performance excellence part I: CEO perspectives on forces, facilitators, and strategic leadership systems. *The Quality Management Journal, 20*(2), 12–33. doi:10.1080/10686967.2013.11918095

Latham, J. R. (2014). Leadership for quality and innovation: Challenges, theories, and a framework for future research. *The Quality Management Journal, 21*(1), 11–15. doi:10.1080/10686967.2014.11918372

Lyon, S. B. (2004). *Spirituality and public school leadership* (Doctoral dissertation). Saint Louis University.

Macon, G. K. Sr. (2014). *School leaders and spirituality: Perspectives of spirituality and spirituality's influence on principals in public schools in southeastern Louisiana.* Southeastern Louisiana University.

Magnusen, C. L. (2002). Spirituality and leadership effectiveness: Historical and philosophical trends. *Journal of Catholic Education, 6*(2), 251–258. doi:10.15365/joce.0602082013

Malone, P. F., & Fry, L. W. (2003). Transforming schools through spiritual leadership: A field experiment. *Annual Meeting of the Academy of Management.*

Mark, G. T., Wheeler, C. A., & Hodgson, M. N. (2012). Leader spirituality and leader virtues as predictors of effective leadership. *Journal of Spirituality, Leadership and Management, 6*(1), 35–47.

Marques, J., Dhiman, S., King, R., & Afshar, T. (2011). Toward greater spirituality in personal and professional life: The movement gains momentum during these challenging times. *Organization Development Journal, 29*(3), 67.

Mayer, J. D. (2000). Spiritual intelligence or spiritual consciousness? *The International Journal for the Psychology of Religion, 10*(1), 47–56. doi:10.1207/S15327582IJPR1001_5

Meyer, L. D. (2005). *The relationship between principals' spiritual attitudes and transformational leadership* (Doctoral thesis). University of New Orleans.

Miller, P. B. (2003). *An exploratory study of the ways principals perceive that their spirituality contributes to their leadership*. Academic Press.

Miller, W. C., & Miller, D. R. (2002). *Spirituality: The emerging context for business leadership*. Global Dharma Center.

Mitroff, I. I., & Denton, E. A. (1999). *A spiritual audit of corporate America: A hard look at spirituality, religion, and values in the workplace*. Jossey-Bass.

Morris, T. (1997). *If Aristotle ran General Motors: The new soul of business*. Henry Holt and Company.

Musick, K. (2010). *Spirituality and school leadership: A grounded theory study*. Academic Press.

Nash, R. J., & Scott, L. (2009). Spirituality, religious pluralism, and higher education leadership development. *Rethinking leadership in a complex, multicultural, and global environment: New concepts and models for higher education*, 131-150.

Neal, J. A. (1997). Spirituality in management education: A guide to resources. *Journal of Management Education, 21*(1), 121–139. doi:10.1177/105256299702100111

Nolan-Arañez, S. I., & Ludvik, M. B. (2018). Positing a framework for cultivating spirituality through public university leadership development. *Journal of Research in Innovative Teaching & Learning*.

Oldenburg, D., & Bandsuch, M. (1997, May 7). The spirit at work: Companies should nurture the soul if they want more from employees. *The Detroit News*.

Padayachee, N. K. D. (2010). *The application and relevance of spiritual leadership in the JSE top 40 companies* (Doctoral dissertation). University of Pretoria.

Perkins, G., Wellman, N., & Wellman, W. (2009). Educational leadership: The relationship between spirituality and leadership practices. *Academic Leadership: The Online Journal, 7*(1), 14.

Pfeffer, J. (2003). Business and the spirit. Handbook of workplace spirituality and organizational performance, 29-45.

Ramirez, L. R. (2009). *Spirituality in the Praxis of Educational Leadership: Four public school principals perspectives on leading through spirituality* (Doctoral dissertation). Texas Tech University.

Reave, L. (2005). Spiritual values and practices related to leadership effectiveness. *The Leadership Quarterly*, *16*(5), 655–687. doi:10.1016/j.leaqua.2005.07.003

Riasudeen, S., & Singh, P. (2020). Leadership Effectiveness and Psychological Wellbeing: The Role of Workplace Spirituality. *Journal of Human Values*.

Ribeiro, M., Caldeira, S., Nunes, E., & Vieira, M. (2021). A commentary on spiritual leadership and workplace spirituality in nursing management. *Journal of Nursing Management*, *29*(3), 602–605. doi:10.1111/jonm.13196 PMID:33107658

Richardson, T. N. (2009). *The impact of spirituality on the leadership practices of African American women college presidents* (Doctoral dissertation). The George Washington University.

Riera, J. L. (2013). *Walking the labyrinth: Examining the intersection of spirituality and leadership among senior student affairs administrators* (Doctoral dissertation). University of Maryland, College Park.

Roof, W. C. (2001). *Spiritual marketplace: Baby boomers and the remaking of American religion*. Princeton University Press. doi:10.1515/9781400823086

Ruiz, R. (2005). *Spiritual dimension in educational leadership*. The University of Texas-Pan American.

Sanders, J. E. III, Hopkins, W. E., & Geroy, G. D. (2003). From transactional to transcendental: Toward an integrated theory of leadership. *Journal of Leadership & Organizational Studies*, *9*(4), 21–31. doi:10.1177/107179190300900402

Santerre, B. G. (1997). *Numinous leadership: Stories of educational leaders integrating spirituality and practice*. Academic Press.

Scott, K. T. (1994). Leadership and spirituality: A quest for reconciliation. *Spirit at work: Discovering the spirituality in leadership*, 63-99.

Sexton, N. L. (2013). *The perceived impact of spirituality on the leadership and careers of mid-level leaders* (Doctoral dissertation). University of La Verne.

Sharma, R. R. (2010). Preventing corruption through spiritual leadership in organisations. *Organizational immunity to corruption: Building theoretical and research foundations*, 247-260.

Shields, C. M. (2005). Liberating discourses: Spirituality and educational leadership. *Journal of School Leadership*, *15*(6), 608–623. doi:10.1177/105268460501500601

Sligh, C. E., & Talbot, D. M. (2020). Recognizing the Inevitable Intersections of Spiritual and Leadership Development. *New Directions for Student Leadership*, *2020*(166), 33–44. doi:10.1002/yd.20381 PMID:32543035

Small, E. (2020). How successful African-American male leaders in predominately White Organizations integrate spirituality with leadership practice. *Journal of Management, Spirituality & Religion*, *17*(2), 184–208. doi:10.1080/14766086.2019.1697727

Sorvaag, S. H. (2007). *The spiritual orientation of K–12 public school principals*. Saint Mary's University of Minnesota.

Steenkamp, Y. (2020). Fides in parenthesis: A spirituality of leadership for a (post-) secular (ising) world. *Hervormde Teologiese Studies*, *76*(2), 1–8. doi:10.4102/hts.v76i2.5876

Stiernberg, P. W. (2003). *The relationship between spirituality and leadership practices of female administrators in K–12 schools*. Baylor University.

Strack, G., Fottler, M., Wheatley, M., & Sodomka, P. (2002). Spirituality and effective leadership in healthcare: Is there a connection? *Frontiers of Health Services Management*, *18*(4), 3–18. doi:10.1097/01974520-200204000-00002 PMID:12087690

Strack, J. G. (2001). *The relationship of healthcare managers' spirituality to their self-perceived effective leadership practices* (Doctoral dissertation). Medical University of South Carolina.

Sweeney, P. J., & Fry, L. W. (2012). Character development through spiritual leadership. *Consulting Psychology Journal*, *64*(2), 89–107. doi:10.1037/a0028966

Tanyi, R. A. (2002). Towards clarification of the meaning of spirituality. *Journal of Advanced Nursing*, *39*(5), 500–509. doi:10.1046/j.1365-2648.2002.02315.x PMID:12175360

Tomlinson, H. (Ed.). (2013). *Educational management: Major themes in education*. Routledge. doi:10.4324/9780203463383

Townsend, J. S. II, & Wichern, F. B. (1984). The development of the spiritual leadership qualities inventory. *Journal of Psychology and Theology*, *12*(4), 305–313. doi:10.1177/009164718401200406

Twymon, P. M. (2004). *The relationship between spirituality and leadership practices of public school superintendents in Texas* (Doctoral dissertation). Baylor University.

Ulluwishewa, R., Uthumange, A., & Weerakoon, R. (2020). Spirituality, Success, and Happiness: Implications for Leadership in Business. In *New Horizons in Positive Leadership and Change* (pp. 143–157). Springer. doi:10.1007/978-3-030-38129-5_8

Vasconcelos, A. F. (2011). Pursuing organizational spirituality: Some lessons from a financial services corporation. *Management & Marketing*, *6*(3), 365.

Vu, M. C., & Gill, R. (2019). Letting go of the raft||–the art of spiritual leadership in contemporary organizations from a Buddhist perspective using skilful means. *Leadership*, *15*(3), 360–380. doi:10.1177/1742715018761931

Walling, D. M. (1994). *Spirituality and leadership* (Doctoral dissertation). University of San Diego.

Widodo, S., & Suryosukmono, G. (2021). Spiritual leadership, workplace spirituality and their effects on meaningful work: Self-transcendence as mediator role. *Management Science Letters*, *11*(7), 2115–2126. doi:10.5267/j.msl.2021.2.016

Wong, P., & Fry, P. S. (2013). *The human quest for meaning*. Routledge. doi:10.4324/9780203146286

Zandi, G., Sulaiman, M., & Rashed, N. (2015). Spirituality and leaders effectiveness: An Islamic perspective. *Asian Economic and Financial Review*, *5*(1), 155–166. doi:10.18488/journal.aefr/2015.5.1/102.1.155.166

KEY TERMS AND DEFINITIONS

Confluence: Merging/flowing/coming together of people or things or events or issues and the change brought about by coming together of these factors or events. For this write-up, confluence is about the unique integration of workplace spirituality and leadership.

Leadership: A collaborative endeavor of mindful behavior, actions, and spiritual orientation that inspires, unites, and empowers the individuals, fosters positive changes and developments, transforms workplaces, and improves the quality of life while working towards the achievement of mutual goals and aspirations.

Leadership Effectiveness: Ability to develop a clear and compelling vision, communicating that vision with clarity to the employee groups and teams in different positions, engaging in productive and ethical exchange with internal and external stakeholders to negotiate and resolve conflicts for delivering on the vision.

Religiosity: Human functioning is comprised of non-ordinary experiences which alter one's sense of self and relationship to others and the world as well as the beliefs, attitudes, behaviors, and lifestyle practices that are associated with such experiences.

Spiritual Leader: A leader who consciously takes care of both the Creator and the created. One who holds firmly to spiritual beliefs and manifests such views in his/her leadership behaviors and practices by integrating spirituality with the leadership in the workplace.

Spirituality: A complex domain of human functioning that is comprised of non-ordinary experiences which alter one's sense of self and relationship to others and the world as well as the beliefs, attitudes, behaviors, and lifestyle practices that are associated with such experiences.

Workplace: A place where people work, such as an office or factory. A workplace can be outdoors among nature, inside an office, or a virtual one, allowing people to work remotely. Productive workplaces possess an efficient and positive work environment. Understanding what a workplace is and how to create a spiritually productive work environment are important for leadership effectiveness in organizations.

Chapter 9
Leadership Styles:
The Case of Islamic Banks

Ebtihaj Al-Aali
University of Bahrain, Bahrain

Ralla Alazali
University of Bahrain, Bahrain

ABSTRACT

This research investigates leadership styles. It is an endeavor to point out unique features of leadership in Islamic banks. The research employs qualitative research. Leaders participating in this research are chief executive officers from Islamic banks. Interview is the research method used. The research is argued to enhance the understanding of leadership in Islamic banks. The understanding can shed light on applications of leadership theories in different contexts than the Western contexts. The later contexts are the situations at which theories of leadership have been developed. The research aims to illustrate whether different contexts can initiate leadership to transform or not. This in turn can help to have a better knowledge concerning human behaviour in organizations. The issue of sources of power utilised by interviewees is scrutinised as well. This is to investigate compatibility between leadership styles and sources of power employed.

INTRODUCTION

Leadership is a key to the success of organizations. Theories of leadership are developed to help organizations achieve their goals. Internal Organizational contexts are major determinant of leadership styles followed. The external environment

DOI: 10.4018/978-1-7998-9319-6.ch009

referring to industries, competitors, employees and customers affect leadership styles exercised. This is to say that stakeholders reflected by internal and external environments have major impacts on shaping leadership styles applied. Theories of leadership however vary in relation to the degree of corresponding to the interests of stakeholders. This research attempts to comprehend unique features of leadership styles if any in Islamic banks. The research consists of five sections. The first section presents definition of leadership and the differences between management and leadership. The second section elaborates on sources of power employed by the leaders. The third then examines theories of leadership. Literature review of Islamic banks is examined in section four. Methodology employed in this research is discussed in section five. Analysis of information collected are presented and scrutinised in section six. The conclusion of this paper then is illustrated in the last section.

LEADERSHIP: DEFINITION AND DIFFERENCES BETWEEN LEADERSHIP AND MANAGEMENT

Leadership is a phenomenon founded firstly in sociology and political science. Leader as a term has been around since 1300s (Yukl, 1989, King, 1990). King (1990) states that the term leadership came to lime in 1700s. However researches on leadership started in 20th century. King (1990) adds that definitions of leadership are as many as researches conducted to study the issues of leaders and leadership. Each theory is based on a specific definition. This is to say that each theory examines leadership from different perspective. Tosti and Jackson (1999) mention that there are more than 350 definitions for the phenomenon of leadership. Such definitions have been examined for the last 75 years. Griffin and Moorhead (2014) and Certo and Certo (2019) state that leadership revolves around influencing employees in organisations. Such influence refers to the abilities of leaders to develop visions, design strategies, motivate employees and cope-up with changes.

The influence associated with being leaders reveals the differences between management and leadership. Management focuses on formal managerial functions. These functions are planning and decision making, organizing including organizational and job designs, directing efforts and organizations and controlling. Monitoring performance and customer orientation policy are the two major concerns for managers (Kinicki & Williams, 2020). Certo & Creto (2029) add that leadership and management can go wrong under certain conditions. Managers go wrong when they under value the importance of human resources. Leadership goes wrong when goals are over or under the capabilities of Organizations. Ebert & Griffin (2029) contend that organizations need both leaders and managers. Management is required to deal with complexity. This is to say that organizations need to plan and make decisions, organise, direct and control. Leadership is needed to cope up with changes.

Griffin and Moorhead (2014) illustrate that leadership can be defined from two perspectives. The first assumes that leaders possess unique traits differentiating them from non leaders. The second postulates that leadership utilises non coercive influence tactics.

SOURCES OF POWER

It is mentioned above that management deals with complexity while leadership cope up with changes. This section elaborates on definition of power and differences between management and leadership in relation to sources of power employed. Al A'ali & Alazali (2018) explain that power is displayed through a mechanism. This mechanism stems from individuals' property or granted by structure. French and Raven (1959) state that there are five sources of power. Raven (1983) adds the sixth source of power named information. The person who possesses power use these sources at different time to influence others. The influencer, having the power, employs some or all sources of power based on two issues. The first is related to attributes of the situation. The second is regarding the traits of influencers and individuals to be influenced. The sources of power are as follows:

Legitimate power: Yukel (1989) illustrates that organizational position is a primary source for influencer. Authority associated with the position leads influencers to have power over their subordinates. The later acceptance of authority lead them to comply. Ebert and Griffin (2019) explains that the greater dependency of influencers on this type of power the less they can be viewed as leaders.

Reward power: Omisore and Nweke (2014) state that reward power aims to increase and improve desirable outcomes. Al A'ali & Alazali (2018) mention that the person possessing reward power can give or withhold what employees desire. Ebert and Griffin (2019) argue that the situation at which reward power is employed decides whether the influencer, a person possessing the power, is viewed as a manager or a leader. If subordinates whom to be influenced desire formal rewards then the influencer is seen as a manager. Subordinates seeking informal rewards such as recognition, praise and gratitude view their influencers as leaders.

Coercive power: Failure to achieve the desirable outcomes leads subordinates to experience penalties (Bass, 1990) . Ebert and Griffin (2019) explicate the types of penalties. These penalties can be classified as emotional, physical or psychological. They add that the more influencers rely on coercive power the less they will thought of as leaders.

Referent power: This power is originated from charisma, expertise and attraction (Yukl, 1981). Al A'ali and Alazali (2018) add that inspirational appeal leading subordinates to comply willingly is a reflection of referent power. Ebert and Griffin (2019) expound that charisma is an intangible characteristic of a leader. This characteristic leads to enthusiasm and loyalty. Ebert and Griffin (2019) affirm that referent power is affiliated with leaders.

Expert power: This type of power stems from expertise and formal knowledge that an influencer possesses in relation to specific activities, functions and issues. Ebert and Griffin (2019) assert that the influencers have expertise power under two conditions. The first is related to the greater the degree of importance of expertise. The second is concerned with the number of of individuals possessing of such expertise. This means that that expertise power is important when less individuals possess. Managers and leaders might have expertise power.

Information power: Ravan (1993) adds the sixth type of power sources. This is called information source of power. This type focuses on acquisition of information about organizational internal processes and about organizations and their external environments. Holders of information power control flows of information and knowledge. These holders are organizational politicians. Raven (1993) states as well that there is no connection between information power and organizational hierarchy and it's related authority.

THEORIES OF LEADERSHIP: LITERATURE REVIEW

This section examines evolution of leadership theories. Leadership theories have been classified based on their focus over time. Such focuses vary leading to develop themes (Al A'ali, 2009, Ebert & Griffin, 2019, Creto & Creto, 2019, Kinicki & Williams, 2020). King (1990) however argues that theories of leadership have evolved based on eras. King asserts that eras overlap. This makes the chronological evolution of leadership theories not precise in reflecting focuses or themes of leadership theories. However, this paper employs the common perspective of discussing chronological evolution of leadership theories for two reasons. The first is that this research looks for leadership styles at the present time and not looking at the evolution. The second is that chronological evolution aim at simplifying the features of thoughts. Such evolution is not assumed to be fixed. Theories of leadership can be viewed from two different angels (Griffin and Moorhead, 2014). The first stands for the focus. This is to say whether theories are examining traits or behavior of leadership. The second angle then related to the assumptions underlying theories; universality or contingency. Universality indicates that theories are valid at all the time and to all individuals. Contingency means that leadership theories change based on certain situations and their connected factors.

Below the discussion of universal approaches for leadership theories. This implies the discussion of trait and behavioral theories. The section then examines the contingency theories of leadership. Finally the section ends by exploring new perspectives of leadership theories.

Universal theories of leadership:

Universality assumes that theories are valid to all individuals and applicable at all situations. The is the main charactçristic of leadership theories developed in the early of last century. This group of theories consists of two sub groups. The first is the trait approach. Theories of trait approach assert that leaders possess physical, mental and psychological traits. Such traits differentiate between leaders and non leaders individuals (Griffin & Moorhead, 2014; Creto & Creto, 2019). This approach is being evaluated against two factors. The first is that the relationship between traits and being a leader is not specified. The second is that the attribute of universality is not valid. Individuals and situations are on continuous movement (Al A'ali, 2009).

The second is the behavioral approach. This approach postulates that effective leaders exhibit behaviors that non effective and non leaders do not display. The Behavioral approach is reflected into two studies. The first study is Michigan. The study states that leaders exhibit one of two styles of behavior. Leaders are either focusing on job or on employees. These styles of behavior are called job-centered or employ-centered. The two styles can not be exhibited by the same leader. This study suggests that effective group performance is achieved through employee-centered approach (Griffin Moorhead, 2014).

The second study is Ohio studies which focuses on consideration and initiating behaviors (Hellriegel, Slocum, & Woodman, 2001). Consideration affirms that leaders are employees oriented. Leaders listen to their employees, existing reciprocal trust and respect. The behavior of consideration is effective with employees appreciating involvement and participation. Initiating behavior contends that leaders are job oriented. Initiating leaders prescribe roles for themselves and their employees. Initiating leaders specify organizational goals, provide direction and monitoring performance (kinicki & Williams, 2020). Initiating leadership is effective when employees rely on their leaders to provide them with information and instructions (Hellriegel, Slocum, & Woodman,2001). Leaders based on Ohio Studies, can exhibit consideration and initiating behaviours at the same time on scale from low to high. Initial findings state that effective leaders exhibit high on both styles of behaviors. This finding changed once conducting more studies. It is found that employees with initiating leadership behavior show high performance but lower level of satisfaction. Besides employees with consideration leadership illustrate lower performance but higher level of satisfaction (Griffin & Moorhead,2014). The Ohio studies is similar to Michigan for being based on universality. Individuals and situational differences are overlooked.

Contingency Theories of Leadership

Contingency theories of leadership differ from the universal ones. Contingency theories acknowledge situational and individuals differences. Fiedler theory is the only exception. Fiedler theory is named as well as the least preferred coworker. The theory states the leaders behavior is measured through questionnaires (Ebert & Griffin, 2019). The questionnaire consists of 16 items including positive traits and negative traits at different ends. Positive traits carry high marks and negative traits have low marks. The respondent who scores high reflects relationship motivation leader. This is similar to employees-centered leadership. The respondent who scores low stands for job-centered leadership. Fiedler assumes that it is hard to change the styles of leadership. He then elaborates on situational favorableness to leaders. Three factors exhibit situational favorableness; leader-member relations, task structure and position power. These factors lead to the development of eight situations (Creto & Creto, 2019). If mismatch occurs between leaders styles and situational favorableness, Fiedler suggests to change situational factors to create new match. This suggestion shows that leadership styles are not contingent. The assumption of stable leadership styles according to Fiedler over looks individuals differences. Validity of the method measuring leadership styles i.e the questionnaire, is questioned as well.

The remaining part of the section discusses situational theories that acknowledge individuals and situational differences. Theories frequently examined by literature are scrutinized (Ebert & Griffin, 2019; Kinicki& Williams, 2020). These theories are Path-Goal leadership model, The Vroom-Yetton-Jago Model, Transactional and transformational leadership styles, Strategic leadership, leader-member exchange model and life cycle theory.

Path-Goal leadership Model argues that leaders show employees the paths to achieve organizational goals. To assure the achievements of the goals leaders make available the rewards desirable by employee. They, leaders, illustrate clearly the link between rewards and goals achievements. The model after revision and testing expands leaders behavior from four to six styles. These are clarifying the goals and paths to achieve, to be achievement oriented, facilitator, being supportive, group and team facilitator, group decision-making, representing groups positively in front of external groups and adding value. These behaviors are to influence two groups of factors. The first group is related to employees characteristics. There are five characteristics related to employees; locus of control, experience, need for clarity of path-goal, needs for achievement and ability to accomplish the task. The second group is connected to environmental factors. These factors are groups dynamic and structure of the task. Leaders behaviors influence employees and environmental characteristics leading to certain consequences. These consequences reflect effectiveness of leadership. The consequences are related to employees motivation, performance and satisfaction, acceptance of leaders, performance of work-unit and facilitating interaction. The revision of path-goal theory accomplishes two objectives. The first is to enhance internal motivation of employees. The second is to promote shared leadership styles (Griffin & Moorhead, 2014; Kinicki & Williams, 2020).

The second situational theory is Vroom-Yetton-Jago Leadership Model. Creto & Creto (2019) explain that the model illustrates five decision making models employed by leaders. Each of these decision making model reflects leadership styles. The five models are based on interactions between eight situational factors. These factors are firstly concerned mainly with leaders' competency, information and necessity of communication. The second group of factors are affiliated with team competence, expertise and support and degree of commitment. The last factor reflects the importance of the decision. These factors are measured on scale from high to low. Each decision making model specifies the degree of empowerment and participation granted to employees. Yukl (1989) argues that this model is more capable than other theories to cope up with the situational factors. However, it still requires more examinations to gather information in order to differentiate between decision making styles (Al A'ali, 2009).

Transactional and transformational leadership styles are the third to discuss. Transactional leadership revolves around contingent rewards to which employees performance are linked to. Employees through such linkage are motivated and their efforts are directed to achieve organizational goals.This can promote the desirable transactions between leaders and employees (Kinicki & Williams, 2020; Jones & George, 2003). Transformational leadership is different from transactional leadership style. Hellriegel, Slocum & Woodman (2001) assert that transformational leadership includes future anticipation, communicating vision for employees to embrace, train future leaders, enhancing organizational learning through rewards. This asserts the importance of combining transactional leadership to use with transformational leadership styles. Kinicki & Williams (2020) argue that such combination lead to superior individuals and then organizational performance.

Strategic leadership is a relatively new leadership style as Ebert and Griffin states (2019). This style focuses on studying internal and external environments. The internal environment examines strengths, weaknesses, culture and history of the organization. The external environment scans current economic situations and current conditions of the organization and opportunities and threats. The analysis of internal and external environments enables the organization to evaluate present strategies and develop better ones for the future.

Finally this section elaborates on two additional contemporary models of leadership; Leader- Member Exchange model and the Life Cycle Theory. The Leader-Member Exchange Model postulates that a leader develops different relationship with each employees. This is unlike previous theories and models that assume such relationships to be stable. The leader divides employees into two categories. The first category is named as in-group. The relationships between employees and their leaders are characterized by trust, liking, respect and mutual fate. Members of In-group receive attention and privileges. Out-group category is the the second group. Members of this group receive less attention and less privileges for they are overseen by the leaders. This model is subjected to intensive researches (Kinicki & Williams, 2020). The last model to examine is the Life Cycle Theory. This theory affirms that leadership styles depend on stage of maturity of followers i.e., employees. The majority of followers refers to competence, interest in responsibility, experience and motivation. The maturity is measured on scale from low, moderate to high. Leadership behaviour changes based on that scale. If maturity is low leaders exhibit task behaviour. Once maturity increases different levels of relationship behaviour i.e., person behaviour are displayed. The theory is still to be investigated for validity (Griffin and Moorhead, (2014).

ISLAMIC BANKING: LITERATURE REVIEW

This section examines literature review in relation to Islamic banking. The historical evolution of Islamic banking in general is discussed first. This section then explores the introduction of Islamic banking in Bahrain. Finally, the section elaborates on Literature concerning leadership in Islamic banks.

Historical Evolution

Gait and Worthington (2007, 4) defined Islamic finance as "a financial service principally implemented to comply with the main tenets of Sharia (or Islamic law)." Accordingly, Islamic rules are what distinguish Islamic banks from conventional banks. Ethics, wealth distribution, social and economic justice are valuable in Islam (Thaib & Pa, 2014). Therefore, Islamic finance is unique compared to other financial systems. One of these unique features is known as profit-and-loss sharing (PLS) paradigm that include mudarabah (profit-sharing) and musyarakah (joint venture) (Chong & Liu, 2009). Furthermore, Thaib and Pa (2014) stated that money in Islamic finance is used as a tool instead of a goal. Ariff (1988) highlighted three distinguishing features of Islamic banking: no interest, multi-purpose, and equity oriented. He added that in comparison to conventional banks, Islamic banking is riskier.

Islam main sources of Shaira are the Holy Quran and Prophet Mohamed Hadith. Therefore, it can be argued that Islamic banking as a concept was existed since the start of Islam. Islamic banking is a phenomenon that started in Egypt in 1963 in which, it based on profit-sharing from trade and industry instead of paid interests (Ariff, 1988). Malaysia hosted another Islamic investment company almost at the same period (Hassan & Aliyu, 2018). Hassan and Aliyu added that the 70s was the golden age for Islamic banks where they emerged in several countries that include Saudi Arabia, the United Arab Emirates, Sudan, Philippines, and Jordan. Since then, Islamic banks are growing in number and value worldwide that led to the creation of "Islamic Indexes" by Dow jones in 1999 (Khan, 2010). Ariff (1988) stated that more Islamic banks existed in the Middle East. Khan noticed that major Western banks are having Islamic banking subsidiaries or providing Islamic products. Since their existence in the 60s, Islamic banks are developing and improving (Maharani, Surachman, Sumiati, & Sudiro, 2017).

It has been noticed that the studies of Islamic banking were using normative judgement, descriptive analysis, theoretical development, and country experiences evaluation (Hassan & Aliyu, 2018). Islamic banking literature started since the 40s of the last century and it was highlighting writers' point of view rather than solid information about Islamic bank system (Ariff, 1988). This is an approval that Islamic banking literature at the beginning was based on ideas rather than real practice. Ariff realized that Islamic banking empirical studies had increased recently.

Islamic Banking in Bahrain

The first Islamic bank in Bahrain is Bahrain Islamic Bank that was established in 1979 (Ariff, 1988; CBB, 2020). It is noted that Islamic banking assets in Bahrain are growing rapidly (Khan, 2010) from USD 24.9 billion in 2014 to USD 32.1 billion in December 2019 (CBB, 2020). From the 94 banks in the Kingdom of Bahrain, there are 20 Islamic banks (6 retail and 14 wholesale) (CBB, 2020). Bahrain is considered the East center of Islamic Banking in the world, this is due to the increased number of Islamic banks in the country (Bahrain an International Financial Centre, 1994). Bahrain is the "hub of Islamic Banking" as it is hosting the largest number of Islamic Financial Institutions in the region (Memon, 2007). One of the most important body is the Accounting & Auditing Organization for Islamic Financial Institutions "AAOIFI". AAOIFI was established in 1991 as an international Autonomous non-profit making corporate body (Accounting and Auditing Standards for Islamic Financial Institutions, 1996). According to a current report by Central Bank of Bahrain (CBB) the Islamic banking sector contributed by more than 15% of assets of the total bank sector (CBB, 2020). This indicates that Islamic banking in Bahrain is grown much faster than the country banking system assets (Hidayat & Abduh, 2012).

Leadership in Islamic Banking

Islamic society values the role of leaders because of their responsibility to direct people and influence them (within the Islamic borders) to achieve their goals (Aravik, Sulastyawati, & Yunus, 2020). Prophet Mohamed (peace be upon him) was the first leader in Islam. His extraordinary abilities to lead people is considered as a model of successful leader. Islamic leadership was mentioned in the Holy Quran and the Prophet Hadith.

Thaib and Pa (2014) stated that management is considered as a sacred task in Islam that include several strict requirements that include labor rights and accountability. Leaders' ability to motivate employees and communicate the organization's vision play an important role on organizational effectiveness in Islamic banking (Maharani, Surachman, Sumiati, & Sudiro, 2017). According to Aravik, Sulastyawati, and Yunus (2020) Islamic banks success is depending on leadership. Inspirational motivation achieved by good communication about goals and challenges and encouraging teamwork is key for this success (Maharani, Surachman, Sumiati, & Sudiro, 2017). Sustainability is one of the most important goals for Muslim leaders (Thaib & Pa, 2014). Additionally, Islamic bank leaders must be smart communicators, act as change agents, coach their employees, having a service vision, and charismatic spirit (Aravik, Sulastyawati, & Yunus, 2020).

Previous research examined different styles of leadership in Islamic banking and its impact on employees. For example, a study on Islamic banks in Pakistan found that there is relationship between paternalistic leadership and employees' turnover intention. The authors of the study found that authoritarianism had positive impact on turnover, whereas; morality and benevolence leadership had negative influence on employees' intention of turnover (Abbas, Habib, & Siddique, 2020). Other styles of leadership that include transformational and transactional were also investigated. A study conducted on employees in Islamic bank in Makassar City found that transformational leadership has a stronger impact on employees' organizational citizenship behavior than transactional leadership style (Muhdar & Rahma, 2015). In addition, Muhdar and Rahma (2015) found that organizational citizenship behavior is positively affected by charisma, inspirational motivation, intellectual stimulation, and individualized attention. It can be argued that organizational citizenship behavior is important element to achieve effectiveness in Islamic banking sector (Maharani, Surachman, Sumiati, & Sudiro, 2017).

In a comparative study between Islamic and conventional banks in Malaysia, it has been found that employees in Islamic banks are affected significantly by authentic leadership style (Ahamed, Hassan, & Hashim, 2013). In addition, a study investigated the employment of spiritual leadership in Islamic banks as a more appropriate leadership style (Egel & Fry, 2017). A recent study investigated the importance of strategic leadership in the UAE Islamic banking sector found that it is significantly affect employees' performance and increase their job satisfaction (Alyileili, 2020). He added that leaders in Emirates Islamic banks must encourage their employees to share their ideas and contribute effectively to making decisions related to workplace problems.

METHODOLOGY

The first Islamic bank in Bahrain was first established in 1979. In 2017, 26 Islamic banks were licensed to operate in Bahrain (Al-Sadah, 2005, Oxford Business Groups, 2021). Despite that Bahrain is being a leading hub for Islamic banking and finance, no research was conducted to study their unique leadership styles. This characterize the research at hand as being an exploratory in nature. This, according to Al-A'ali (2020) AlSaffar & Al-A'ali (2021), illustrates the suitability of employing qualitative methodology. Qualitative methodology does not assume objective reality as quantitative methodology postulates. Burrell & Morgan (1979) affirms that quantitative methodology is based on objectivity and positivism. Qualitative methodology examines primary information collected and secondary data to grasp reality from participants' points of view (Cooper and Schindler, 2008). Therefore, the contemporary focus of this research in general and the lack of similar previous studies on Bahrain justify the utilisation of qualitative methodology. Qualitative methodology scrutinizes Ideas, perceptions and words expressed by participants to apprehend the issues being investigated. This research utilizes In-depth interview as a research method to collect primary information. CEO of three Islamic banks were interviewed. The busy schedule of Chief executive officers in banks at one hand and the constrains caused by the COVID-19 situation on the other hand imposed restrictions on the empirical work desired. Open-ended interviews with the CEOs of Islamic banks were conducted online. Every interview lasted from 45 to one hour. The questions asked were as follows:

1. Definition of an Organisation as perceived by leaders in Islamic banks
2. Definition of leadership styles as being practiced in Islamic banks
3. How leadership in Islamic banking differs from leadership styles discussed by contemporary theories

4. what are the unique features of Islamic leadership and its impacts on operations in Islamic banks

ANALYSIS AND DISCUSSION OF INFORMATION COLLECTED:

This section presents the analysis and discussion of collected information for the above mentioned questions.

Analysis of Information Concerning the Question Number one in Respect to the Definition of an Organization

The three interviewees state that Organizational structure of Islamic banks in essence does not differ than non Islamic banks. However, every Islamic banks has a body named a Sharia committee or a council attached to the main organizational chart. Non Islamic bank do not have such board or committee. The committee or council, according to interviewees, scrutinise the adherence of products offered to Sharia's principles. This may explains the reasons for the a few number of researches studying the organizational structure of Islamic banks. The researches focus only on Shria council or committee attached to the structure. This reflects what Ariff (1988) mentions that literature on Islamic banks at the beginning was based on ideas.

One interviewee adds that competition has eroded many differences between products offered by Islamic and non Islamic banks. The erosion was a must in order to survive in an industry at its maturity stage of development. The same interviewee argues that such erosion as well requires leaders to promote a culture of openness, creativity and respect for human resource. This entails the structure to be more flexible. He mentions the issue of women as an example. The later according to him, should be treated equally to men. Equality in term of evaluation and promotion. This interviewee raises the issue of diversity among employees in Islamic banking. Non of the researches reviewed above refer to such issue.

In relation to structural changes, the second interviewee states that the organizational structure changes as a result of two factors. The first t factor is market changes. The second is changes in human resource. He adds that people retire making a path for new blood to join. However, this interviewee has not referred to products changes of Islamic banks. He as well has not mention the issue of women in Islamic banks.

The third interviewee elaborates more on operational differences between Islamic and non Islamic banks. He explains that accountancy standards in Islamic banks are sharia compliance. Profit and loans followed by conventional banks are not applied by Islamic banks. He affirms that all these differences are reflection of sharia council practices in the Islamic banks. This is similar to the explanation of

Chang & Liu (2009) mentioned above in relation to operational differences between Islamic and non Islamic banks.

The purpose of asking this question is to point out differences if any between structures of Islamic and non Islamic banks. The impacts of such differences on leadership styles then can be investigated in the following question; number two. The analysis of collected information displays that no organizational structure differences between Islamic and non Islamic banks.

Analysis and Discussion of Collected Information in Relation to Question Number Two Regarding Definition of Leadership

The second question studies the definition of leadership held by Chief executive officers in Islamic banks. The question attempts to explore the definitions of leadership as perceived by the high rank officers who are expertise in their fields. The three interviewees assure that the quintessence of leadership in Islamic banks are similar to those of non Islamic banks. Leadership according to the interviewees, is about developing a vision and making sure it is achieved. All interviewees add that the vision should consider the broader picture of the bank. The broader picture should scrutinise the changes of internal and external situations. This enable the banks to cope up with the surroundings. The cope up mechanism leads to success desired.

Two interviewees seem to illustrate the significance roles of leaders in shaping visions. The visions are developed by leaders themselves. This because they have the legitimate and expertise power. No reference was made to the roles of others in shaping the visions. These two sources of power are used by managers as mentioned above in the literature review.

Only one interviewee highlights the importance of the roles of leaders in shaping organizational cultures. The culture of non Islamic banks, as mentioned by this interviewee, are more open to external environment. He is the same interviewee explaining that non conventional banks have less restrictions on women. Islamic banks impose restrictions on women for example dress codes. This is based on the assumption that Islamic banks comply to Islamic values and ethics. This compliance may lead Islamic bank to allow less employees participation in the decision making processes. To this interviewee employees' participation in organisations is crucial to achieve organizational visions. Such participation can enhance performance and commitment. This may exhibit that this third Interviewee relies on referent power as a mechanism to influence his subordinates. The views of this interviewee support the argument of Alyileili (2020). The later asserts that leaders in Islamic banks should encourage employees to participate in decision making processes as mentioned above.

In conclusion no differences are seen between leadership in Islamic and non Islamic banks. However only one interviewee emphasises the roles of subordinates in decision making processes. This highlights the differences between sources of power used by the three interviewees.

Analysis and Discussion of Question Three Concerning how Leadership in Islamic Banks Differs from Contemporary Leadership Theories

All interviewees contend that leadership styles in Islamic banks are similar to those of non Islamic banks. interviewees emphasises the role of leaders in developing successful business strategies. This according to the interviewees is the essence of contemporary leadership theories. Though visions development is a major roles of leaders, according to interviewees, two of them have not refer to employees' participation in developing and implementing such visions. Only one Interviewee adds that people are willing to participate in decision making if they are allowed to do so. He, the interviewee, has formed weekly gathering. He named it in Arabic "Majles". In English means council or assembly. The "Majles" aims to achieve two targets for him as a CEO. The first is to question existing functional practices and eliminate hierarchical barriers to communication. Eliminating barriers enhances processes of group dynamic and improve quality of decisions made. Besides this helps to reward efficiency and eliminate inefficiency and dysfunctional practices. The second Is to transmit knowledge and expertise from one level in organisations to another. The transmission can achieve Successors plan. The interviewee claims that many banks do not have succession plan. These two targets aimed to be achieved by Majles are compatible to essences of transformational leadership. The two earlier interviewees acknowledge situational changes and the need to change the visions and get commitment of employees through rewards. However, these two interviewees undervalue the role of employees as stakeholders employees. Participation of employees to decision making is not highlighted by these two interviewees. This is due to their belief that practices, functions and activities are based on Shria compliance. The two interviewees, stated above, seem to follow strategic leadership style. This upholds the findings of the study conducted by Alyileili (2020) on Islamic banks in United Arab Emirates. The same study shows the importance of leadership to enhance employees' participation to decision making processes.

Analysis and Discussion of Information Collected of Question Four Regarding the Unique Features of Leadership Styles in Islamic Banks and its Impacts on Operations:

Two of the interviewees asserts that Islamic banks' main target is to serve shareholders interest. The target of Islamic banks therefore is similar to that of conventional banks. For these interviewees, leadership in Islamic banks does not differ than leadership in non Islamic banks. However, the interviewees state, that leadership in Islamic banks has to comply to principles obliged by the Sharia council or board in the bank. This is the reason for the claim of one of the interviewees that 95% of leadership activities in Islamic banks are identical with contemporary leadership theories. The two interviewees add that leadership is about developing a vision which is continuously evaluated. The evaluation is required as a result of changes in external and internal environments. Examining such information demonstrate two issues. The first is that these interviewees rely on legitimate and expertise sources of power to promote the visions and make decisions. This argument is based on their explanation that Sharia board or council decides the products offered and their marketing strategies as well as. The second is that the compliance to Sharia council or board rules out the participative roles of employees in organizations. Employees are not seen as stakeholders by these two interviewees. The interviewees through accentuating the role of leaders in developing and implementing the visions is argued to adopt strategic leadership style. This is supported by Alyileili (2020) findings in relation to importance of strategic leadership in Islamic banks.

The third interviewee affirms that leadership in Islamic banks differs from non Islamic banks, though it should not. He elucidates that leaders should focus on developing and promoting performance-enhancing cultures. Cultures, he adds, are not stable. They are on continuous evolution. He expounds that the changes of cultures can be seen through the new products introduced by Islamic banks. Some of these products are compatible to those of non Islamic banks. He emphasises the role of leaders in cultures evolution. He describes the cultural changes initiated by him in his banks. He mentions some of these changes. He narrates the mechanisms used to change culture in his organization. He states for example methods to open communication channels, easing dress codes for women and stressing the importance of training for successors. These mechanisms reflect features of transformational leadership which aims to deal with changes. The transformational leader employs referent power to achieve goals as stated above. These findings uphold earlier conclusion by Muhdar & Rahma (2015). They state that transformational leadership has stronger impact on organizational citizenship as a reflection of cultural values.

CONCLUSION

This research attempts to study the leadership styles in Islamic banks in Bahrain. Though the fist Islamic bank in Bahrain was established in 1979, no similar research has been conducted to comprehend the styles of Leadership in Islamic banks. The research is an endeavour to investigate whether the contemporary leadership theories can be the base for leadership in Islamic banks. The research explains the differences between leadership and management. It is stated that management deals with complexities and leadership copes up with changes. The research as well seeks to relate sources of power to the leadership styles followed in Islamic banks. There are six sources of power. These sources are legitimate, rewards, coercive, referent, expertise and information. The research illustrates that theories of leadership can be viewed from two different angles. The first is universality reflected in to traits and behavioural theories. The second is contingency stands for Fiedler Least preferred Coworker, path-Goal theory, Vroom, Yetton & Jago Model, Transactional and Transformational leaderships theories, Strategic leadership, Leader- member exchange model and life - Cycle theory. This research is based on qualitative methodology. The qualitative methodology examines opinions and ideas of participants in the research to grasp reality. The research is exploratory in nature for no previous similar researches have been conducted on Islamic banks in Bahrain. Three Chief Executive Officers for Islamic Banks contribute to this research. In-depth interview is the research method used to collect information. Four questions are examined. The first investigates the differences in relation to the definitions of organizations between Islamic and non Islamic banks. The second then attempts to study the definitions of leadership held by the interviewees. The third expounds the compatibility between leadership styles followed in Islamic banks and contemporary leadership theories. The last question explores the unique features of leadership applied in Islamic banks. Questions number two and four elaborate on sources of power used by participants in this research. In conclusion the findings reveal that the definitions of organizations and leadership are compatible to contemporary management theories. The exception is that Islamic has a sharia council or board which non Islamic banks do not have.

Two interviewees highlight the importance of compliance to principles obliged by sharia council. This accentuates the legitimate power and expertise power that these two leaders rely on. However, the two interviewees recognize that internal and external environments shape visions. Such visions are not fixed. This is similar to principles of strategic leadership model. The remaining interviewee states that products offered by Islamic banks these days are similar to those of non Islamic banks. This is a result of the sever competition in a maturing industry. The role of the leaders in Islamic banks have to promote performance- enhancement cultures.

These cultures acknowledge the importance of participation of employees to achieve organizational goals. This interviewee is argued to follow transformational leadership. He seems to rely on referent power as an influence mechanism.

FUTURE RESEARCH

The above conclusions display the need for conducting more future researches in relation to Islamic banks in Bahrain. The following are the issues to explore in order to develop a better understanding of functions, activities and processes of Islamic banks:

- Conducting more research to develop a better comprehension of leadership styles in Islamic banks
- Examining cultures of Islamic banks in order to grasp their impacts on human resources
- Investigating the issue of diversity and its impacts on organizational performance

REFERENCES

Abbas, M., Habib, H., & Siddique, A. (2020). Impact of Paternalistic Leadership on Turnover Intention: Evidence from the Islamic Banking Industry of Karachi, Pakistan. *Journal of Business and Management*, *2*(2), 167–176.

Ahamed, F., Hassan, A., & Hashim, J. (2013). Authentic leadership, trust, and employees' work engagement: A comparative study of Islamic and conventional banks in Malaysia. *Journal of Global Business Advancement*, *6*(2), 152–166. doi:10.1504/JGBA.2013.053568

Al A'ali, E. (2009). Women's leadership styles in Scientific Journal for business and finance in vol. 1. Tanta University Press.

Al-A'ali, E. (2020). The Role of Auditing Firms in Promoting Ethical Consumerism. In *Ethical Consumerism and Comparative Studies Across. Different Cultures* (pp. 39–52). IGI Global. doi:10.4018/978-1-7998-0272-3.ch004

Al A'ali, E., & Alazali, R. M. (2018). Gender Differences in relation to Organization Sources of power. In M. M. Al-shammari & H. Masri (Eds.), *Arab Women and their Evolving Roles in Global Business Landscape*. doi:10.4018/978-1-5225-3710-6.ch001

AlSaffar, G., & Al-A'ali, E. (2021). *Psychiatry in the Midst of the Pandemic: A Narrative Perspective in Global Perspectives on Change Management and leadership in the Post COVID-19 Era*. IGI Global. doi:10.4018/978-1-7998-6948-1.ch002

Alyileili, S. S. (2020). The impact of strategic leadership on achieving job satisfaction for employees in the UAE Islamic banking sector. *International Journal of Innovations in Engineering Research and Technology*, *7*(10), 117–124.

Aravik, H., Sulastyawati, D., & Yunus, N. R. (2020). Leadership concept at sharia bank. *Islamic Banking*, *5*(2), 21–31.

Ariff, M. (1988). Islamic Banking. *Asian-Pacific Economic Literature*, *2*(2), 46–62. doi:10.1111/j.1467-8411.1988.tb00200.x

Bahrain an International Financial Centre (5th ed.). (1994). BMA Publication.

Bass, B. M. (1990). *Bass and Stogdill's Handbook of leadership: Theory, research, and managerial applications*. The Free Press.

Burrell, G., & Morgan, G. (1979). *Sociological Paradigms and Organisational Analysis*. Heinemann Educational Books Ltd.

CBB. (2020). *Financial Stability Report*. Central Bank of Bahrain.

Certo, S. C., & Certo, S. T. (2019). Modern management: Concepts and skills (global edition). Pearson Education Limited.

Chong, B. S., & Liu, M.-H. (2009). Islamic banking: Interest-free or interest-based? *Pacific-Basin Finance Journal*, *17*(1), 125–144. doi:10.1016/j.pacfin.2007.12.003

Cooper, D. R., & Schindler, P. S. (2008). *Business Research Methods* (10th ed.). McGraw Hill.

Ebert, R. J., & Griffin, R. W. (2019). *Business essential* (12th ed.). Pearson.

Egel, E., & Fry, L. W. (2017). Spiritual Leadership as a Model for Islamic Leadership. *Public Integrity*, *19*(1), 77–95. doi:10.1080/10999922.2016.1200411

French, J. R. P., Jr., & Raven, B. (1959). The bases of social power. In Studies in social power (pp. 250-167). University of Michigan.

Gait, A. H., & Worthington, A. C. (2007). *A Primer on Islamic Finance: Definitions*. Sources, Principles and Methods.

Griffin, R. W. & Moorhead, G. (2014). *Organizational Behavior*. Cengage Learning.

Hassan, M. K., & Aliyu, S. (2018). A contemporary survey of islamic banking literature. *Journal of Financial Stability*, *34*(1), 12–43. doi:10.1016/j.jfs.2017.11.006

Hellriegel, D., Slocum, J. W., Jr., & Woodman, R. W. (2001). Organizational behavior (9th ed.). South-Western College Publishing.

Hidayat, S. E., & Abduh, M. (2012). Does Financial Crisis Give Impacts on Bahrain Islamic Banking Performance? A Panel Regression Analysis. *International Journal of Economics and Finance*, *4*(7), 79–87. doi:10.5539/ijef.v4n7p79

Jones, G. R., & Gerorge, J. M. (2003). *Contemporary Management* (3rd ed.). McGraw-Hill Irwin.

Khan, F. (2010). How 'Islamic' is Islamic Banking? *Journal of Economic Behavior & Organization*, *76*(3), 805–820. doi:10.1016/j.jebo.2010.09.015

King, A. S. (1990). *Evolution of Leadership Theory*. in https://journals.sagepub.com/doi/pdf/10.1177/0256090919900205

Kinicki, A., & Williams, B. K. (2020). Management (9th ed.). New York: McGraw-Hill Education.

Maharani, V., Surachman, S., & Sudiro, A. (2017). The Effect of Transformational Leadership on Organizational Citizenship Behavior Mediated by Job Satisfaction and Organizational Commitment (Study of Islamic Bank in Malang Raya). *International Journal of Economic Research*, *14*(3), 213–226.

Memon, N. A. (2007). Islamic Banking: Present and Future Challenges. *Journal of Management and Social Sciences*, *3*(1), 1–10.

Muhdar & Rahma. (2015). The influence of spiritual intelligence, leadership, and organizational culture on organizational citizenship behavior: A study to Islamic bank in Makassar City. *Al-Ulum, 15*(1), 135 - 156.

Omisore, B. O., & Nweke, A. N. (2014). The Influence of Power and Politics in Organizations. *International Journal of Academic Research in Business & Social Sciences*, *4*(7), 165–183. doi:10.6007/IJARBSS/v4-i7/997

Ravan, B. H. (1993). The bases of power: Origins and recent developments. *The Journal of Social Issues*, *49*(4), 227–251. doi:10.1111/j.1540-4560.1993.tb0119.x

Thaib, L., & Pa, B. C. (2014). Islamic business leadership modelling for sustainable development. *International Journal of Multidisciplinary Academic Research*, *2*(1), 25–32.

Tosti, D., & Jackson, S. F. (1999). Influencing others to Act. In *Handbook of Human Performance Technology*. International Society for Performance Improvement.

Yukl, G. A. (1989). Leadership in Organizations (2nd ed.). Prentice-Hall International.

Chapter 10
Student Character Building and Behaviour Through Islamic Value-Based Teaching:
A Reference to Islamic School Organizations in Malaysia

Ismail Hussein Amzat
https://orcid.org/0000-0001-9973-9646
International Islamic University Malaysia, Malaysia

Riyadotul Jannah Mahyutan
International Islamic University Malaysia, Malaysia

Selly Isnaini Agus Riyantowo
International Islamic University Malaysia, Malaysia

Wan Nurul Ain W. Omar
International Islamic University Malaysia, Malaysia

Alwi Lubis
International Islamic University Malaysia, Malaysia

ABSTRACT

This chapter used qualitative methods to collect data on the influence of Islamic values in teaching in building student character in Malaysia schools. The population consisted of different schoolteachers from Selangor and Kuala Lumpur. Online interview was used to explore those teachers' perceptions on the inculcation of Islamic values in teaching on student character building. Data were analysed using thematic analysis. From the reports, inculcation of Islamic values was found to help in building students' good character, but to make it happen, teachers are seen as role players and models. Additionally, environment, parents, and peer support also played big roles in the inculcation of Islamic values in students. Media is reported to be used wisely to help children such as showing children the programs that promote Islam and its beauties. As an implication and conclusion, for schools to have good

DOI: 10.4018/978-1-7998-9319-6.ch010

organizational behaviour, Islamic values must be inculcated in teaching to impact positively student behaviour and attitude while becoming good persons with Islamic adab and akhlaq.

INTRODUCTION

Education is a cumulative teaching and learning process to transfer and obtain knowledge. Education can indirectly influence and assist students in their efforts to improve their physical, moral, spiritual, cognitive, mental, and intellectual abilities, which can gradually empower these students to reach the highest level of quality (Amin-Mt and Mustaffa 2019). Islamic education plays an important factor in this transit. It is beneficial first to review the general meaning of education from Arabic terms. The word education is known as *tarbiyah* in Arabic. "*Ibn Mandhur* maintains in *Lisan Al-'Arab* that *tarbiyah* means "addition up, growth, nourishment, care, and preservation" (Mandhur, 2003, p. 83). Learning involves two things تعليم teaching and تربيّة educating. *Ta'lim* from the root علم (to know, to perceive, to learn) which means to transfer knowledge and *tarbiyah* from the root ربّ (to increase, to grow) bringing up, polishing the potential, implies a state of spiritual and ethical nurturing following the will of God.

According to Salleh (2009) and Yasin (2013), education is conceptualised can be categorised into three; *1) Al-tarbiyyah, 2) Al-ta'alim and 3) At-ta'adib. Al-tarbiyyah* emphasises on individual's physical and intellectual development, *Al-ta'alim* emphasises on conducting teaching and learning while *At-ta`adib* emphasises on good morals and ethical values cultivation. These concepts and definitions are used to elaborate on the centrality and the meaning of Islamic education. No doubt, Islamic education plays an important role in the lives of Muslims. This is due to the fact that, it is not acquiring or seeking for knowledge that is deemed important in Islam but it is how the knowledge is used to prepare for the hereafter. There is no separation between Islam and character as Islam laid high emphasis on good character. It is part and parcel of Muslim to apply ethics in their daily lives and activities. Ethics or character distinguishes one person from another and its part of human and its considered as a way of thinking and behaving that has to do with the individual, family, community, nation and state. (Asmara, Isbandiyah and Rahayu, 2020).

Furthermore, a good character of an individual is the ability of making decisions and ability of accepting of any outcomes of his or her decisions. Character building is an ongoing process which does not based on heredity, but through formal and informal education process. The main objectives of Islamic religious education are to infuse Islamic values in teaching for Muslim students. Teachers are expected to go beyond academics and inculcate *adab* (morality) into young children (Badrasawi,

2018). Hence, they play a big role in engaging students in learning as well as creating effective and attractive learning for students (Mazwati, Shakour, Lina, 2018). Furthermore, when it comes to religious education and moral, Islam has laid a strong emphasis on moral education due to its strong connection with the Islamic religion. Islamic teaching is full of guidance for man and a way to the perfection of belief and moral. Hence, as a guide, from the Islamic teaching, there are some theoretical and practical programs and training that can boost a man's morality as well as its community. Islamic teaching and infusing Islamic values in teaching have a big impact and positive influence on students' moral development and their community. Thus, it can be considered as a tool for the individual's character development and nurture minds as well as souls.

In Malaysia, moral development is highly emphasised and enshrined in the Malaysian National Philosophy of Education (NPE) goals. The NPE is considered as a foundation in building a united and progressive community and nation. *According to the Ministry of Education (2008), the NPE states that "Education in Malaysia is an ongoing effort towards further developing the potential of individuals in a holistic and integrated manner, to produce individuals who are intellectually, spiritually, emotionally and physically balanced and harmonious based on a firm belief in and devotion to Allah. Such an effort is designed to produce Malaysian citizens who are knowledgeable and competent, who possess high moral standards and who are responsible and capable of achieving a high level of personal well-being as well as being able to contribute to the betterment of the family, society and the nation at large" (World Data on Education, 2006, p. 1).*

To fulfil the above-mentioned national education goals, education quality should be improved, particularly in terms of moral education, and Islamic moral knowledge and the student's general knowledge should be balanced. Furthermore, education is the most significant undertaking in a nation's growth; if a nation's progress does not go with morals and ethics development, the development may be compromised. Education, or the educational system, should now strike a balance between science and faith. In today's world, the younger generation's immorality has fallen in most nations, and civilizations are currently facing a rise in drug and human abuse, rampant gun shooting and other human atrocities.

Educators and instructors have a critical role in this situation, particularly in schools, in assimilating Islamic teachings into the curriculum and assigning activities that would assist students in building their character. Character education is an endeavour to teach students so that they can make everyday, intelligent decisions and act morally, while also contributing positively to their surroundings and having a noble character.

Schools, together with family and society, play an important role in character development (Asmara, Isbandiyah, Rahayu, 2020). The lack of efficiency of Islamic

Education in schools may be ascribed to the absence of excellent character among children in a Muslim community. According to Hashim (2004), only around 7% of secondary school teaching times were allocated to Islamic Education. Furthermore, in Islam, teaching is more than merely conveying academic information in the classroom. Furthermore, it necessitates the application of this information both inside and outside the classroom, as well as the use of excellent behaviour (akhlq), a healthy lifestyle, moral values, strong faith, and a pleasant attitude in all dealings and relationships with people (Badrasawi, 2018). "The aim of education is character," Prayitno and Belferik (2011) wrote. As a result, all educational activities should lead to the development of character. According to Kemas, (2017), in Islamic education, the method used by the teacher should always refer to the formation of morals and noble personality of learners under the guidance of the Quran and Sunnah of Prophet Muhammad.

In light of this, the authors aim to examine, through an empirical method, the influence of Islamic education on overcoming the crisis of *akhlak* while improving students' character. The study observes the practice of Islamic Education in formal schools, especially in secondary schools. Islamic education has been taught as the basic subject for developing character in Malaysian schools. Therefore, this study sets out to achieve the following objectives:

1. This study attempts to examine teachers' using Islamic value-based teaching in in building students' character and the challenges faced in the process in Islamic secondary schools in Malaysia.
2. To explore the impact of Islamic value-based teaching and student character building as well as sense of school organizational positive behaviour among students in Islamic secondary schools in Malaysia.

For the methods, this study uses qualitative methods by interviewing teachers from an Islamic school in Malaysia. The data was analyzed using a thematic approach. The findings will shed light on the roles that the Islamic value-based teaching play in teaching, building and improving students' characters in schools.

LITERATURE REVIEW

Philosophy of Islamic Education

The philosophy of Islamic Education has also been officially formulated as follows:

Islamic Education is a continuous effort to deliver knowledge, skill and emotional experience based on al-Qur'an and al-Sunnah to build behaviour, skill, personality and a view of life as the servant of Allah, responsible for self-development, the community, the environment and the nation for the sake of prosperity and salvation in this world and the hereafter. (Kementerian Pendidikan Malaysia, 2002, as cited in Tamuri, 2007, p. 2).

This continuous attempt can be recently seen in the latest statement of the aim of Islamic education which focused on the aspiration to educate good Muslim students:

Islamic Education aims to produce Muslims who are knowledgeable, devoted, pious, well-mannered and who also have virtuous characteristics based on al-Qur'an and al-Sunnah to become the righteous servants and vicegerents of Allah and contribute to civilization of race and nation. (Kementerian Pendidikan Malaysia, 2002, as cited in Tamuri, 2007, p. 2).

Infusing of Values in Teaching Islamic Education (Sister Jannah)

Values are standards of behaviour, beauty, truth, justice and efficiency that bind human beings which should be carried out and also maintained (Hamid, 2016). In other words, the value is considered important and good if it is in line with the needs of a surrounding society. The purpose of education, either in its content or in its formulation, cannot possibly be established without a proper understanding and knowledge of values. Even Hamid also found that Islam sees the existence of absolute values and also intrinsic values that serve as the centre and mouth of all values whose values are *tawheed* (*uluhiyah* and *rububiyah*) which is the goal (*ghayah*) of all Muslim activities. Instrumental values are values that serve as tools and prerequisites to achieve monotheistic values in daily life. These instrumental values are faced by many people such as the values of trust, honesty, justice, humanity, patience, work ethic and discipline. For that reason, Islam emphasizes the need for these values to be instilled in a person as a path to the formation of a monotheistic personality.

Sarwan (2010) argues that in Islamic education there are educational values that are developed and have the characteristics and characteristics of the Islamic education system. This is also supported by Dauri (2009) who also stated that the values in Islamic education is a pattern or nature inherent in Islamic education which is a determination that consists of views, norms and rules that exist in Islamic education. Which is often associated with faith, sharia, worship and also morality. Therefore, Pratama & Zulhijra (2019) also said that educational institutions are not just trying to transform knowledge, but it is much more complex and more important than that. It is a place to transform the values contained in the teachings of Islam that forms students' personalities in line with those values. In other words, the values that already exist in Islamic education must be taught to all mankind, especially to those who are Muslims. Islam does not come from tradition or man-made religion, but from Allah (SWT) through His revelation, the relationship is regulated between human beings (Ali, 2011).

Inculcating Islamic education in learners is one of the efforts in the growth of their personalities both systematically and pragmatically. It guides them in living in accordance with Islamic teachings while pursuing happiness in this world and the hereafter (Achmad, 2004). This is because Islamic education is an activity and also efforts of action as well as guidance done consciously and deliberately. Thus, it is planned that lead to the formation of the child's personality in accordance with the norms and values that have been determined by each religious teaching (Mastuhu, 2008). Therefore, it can be concluded that Islamic education must be taught because human beings are unlikely to know by themselves how to perform worship such as *infaq* and others if not through the learning process.

In this case, teachers are acknowledged to have a tremendous influence, especially on students, whether the students at the Primary School or Secondary (Nordin, 2003). This is also supported by Thaha (2006), which is he stated that as a teacher or educator, there are responsibilities to be bearded in building and educating students in the implementation of their daily worship. Besides, there are several important aspects in shaping the values of Islamic education that should be noted and taught by a teacher, such as: (a) worship education; (b) principles of Islamic teachings and reading the Quran; (c) moral education and; (d) Islamic faith education.

The implementation of Islamic education also needs to be known and understood by students. In the process of value transformation, there is a process of developing all aspects of the human personality which includes knowledge, attitudes and values as well as skills (Sadulloh, 2009). The main purpose of Islamic education is to infusing religious values so that students can overcome personalities that deviate from religious values and also every student can overcome their own delinquency so that they always carve their daily behaviour with noble character.

Character Building and Character Education

Globalization and international relations have affected aspects of global economics, politics and trade. While from the socio-cultural aspect, globalization also affects the values of social solidarity such as individualistic, materialistic and hedonistic attitudes. These effects have an impact on Malaysia society in terms of character education, which has been seen as a process in developing and shaping one's character through education (Bakhary, 2019). In addition, the world of education today is facing an urgent demand to prepare and equip students with skills to compete and face the current changes and challenges. Therefore, in this case, education can be used as a means to formulate strategies and measures to address the challenges and also various issues, especially those related to character building.

Even Fatmah (2018) also argues that, character building is a very important thing because it is a manifestation of the government's efforts to nurture a young generation with character. But to realize this, support from all parties is needed, especially educational institutions. This is because education can be used as one of the right solutions to shape and foster the personality of students. The growth and development of good character education can be an encouragement to students so that they do positive things and have the right life goals.

Just like other qualities of self, the character does not develop or form by itself. However, the formation and development of character in each individual can be influenced by natural factors (nature) and also the influence of the surrounding community. As is known, the character is the values of human behaviour that are closely related to God Almighty, oneself, fellow human beings, the environment, and nationality which are manifested in thoughts, attitudes, words, feelings and also actions based on norms; religious norms, laws, manners, culture and customs (Suwartini, 2017). Meanwhile, according to Kuh and Umbach (2004) character is a window into the personality, a constellation of attitudes, ethical considerations, values and behavioural patterns that represent what people believe and value and also how they think about what they do.

In this case, Islamic education is very important in shaping the character of a student and this can be seen in the research conducted by Choli, (2019) in which he argues that Islamic education for students is felt to be very important, even more so in shaping and developing the character of the student. Which is with this Islamic education, it can direct humans to be more useful, civilized and dignified in carrying out life in accordance with Islamic teachings in order to produce humans with good characters. In fact, he also argues that if instilling Islamic education from an early age, it can indirectly prepare a generation of nation with character, future generations of nation who are able to lead the nation, have noble character and become a generation of knowledge as well as always with the fear of God Almighty.

Therefore, teachers play an important role in shaping the character of students and seeing as role models or examples by the students in terms of behaviour and dress code during the learning process (Ningsih, 2015). In addition, Ningsih also argues that if character formation is done continuously through the cultivation of good character and applied with actions taken by the school, then the personality of students can be formed with characters who are religious; honest; responsible; independent; love to read; caring and hardworking.

Islamic Values for Human Behavior Development in Organizations

The reality of human life is often filled with values. Which these Islamic values have their own role to develop the individual from a physical point of view as well as personality (Jodi, 2018). Islamic values based on Shuhari & Hamat, (2015) refer to the characteristics and also the noble qualities that must be possessed by every Muslim individual or better known by the term personality or morality. Because of that, these values are intertwined with each other and when practicing the values that have been outlined by the Shari'ah, a comprehensive adherence to them must be done without neglecting any of those values. In addition, Islamic values have been reported to play big roles in the development of human behaviour especially when religion is infused. But there are differences between Islamic and western worldviews in terms of human development. From the Islamic worldview, human behaviour development is not as same as what is found in Western psychology research. As indicated by Islam, the development of human behaviour doesn't simply come from the communication of the id, inner self and the super conscience as Freud hypothesizes. Whereas, Human development in Islam is a religious cycle embraced by a person to draw out the positive qualities in him (Abdullah et al., 2017).

Every Muslim must work hard to have a good nature (*fitrah*), this is because they believe that one day they will return to Allah (SWT) and take responsibility for all the deeds they have done while in this world. Not only that, Islamic psychology also emphasizes that every human being will face and experience stress, struggle, disappointment and even nervousness in their daily lives. For that reason, a person's behaviour will develop when he remains on the right path of Islamic demands and virtues (Abdullah et al., 2017). This is very different from Western psychology where in Islamic psychology and in the Qur'an, the Prophet Muhammad (SAW) is a good example and should be emulated when a person seeks guidance when the human being is in trouble or pleasure and makes the Prophet Muhammad (SAW) as examples in shaping healthy behaviours. In fact (Abdullah et al., 2017) also stated in his writing that the Prophet Muhammad (SAW) has a quality behaviour, character and personality that should be emulated by his people and this is also explained in the Qur'an and Hadith. In addition, values are an important paradigm in shaping human attitudes and also guiding human behaviour or actions where morality can be formed through values as well as ethics influenced by morality (Haron, et al., 2020).

Ethics according to Al-Qudsy (2010) is a set of values and morals that can be skilled in shaping the behaviour of individuals, organizations and their work which is if there is no ethics then something bad will happen such as scandals in the industrial and business sectors. The use of the term ethics is equated with morality, which has similarities in terms of objects, namely both discussing the good and bad of human behaviour. While in Arabic ethics is also known as morality which means character, behaviour, temperament and also character. It can be concluded that ethics in Islam are all actions that are born with the impulse of the soul in the form of good or bad deeds (Badroen, 2006). Therefore, the application of ethics in an organization must be based on the Qur'an and also the Sunnah which is the best application of the rules, norms, practices and principles that are highly emphasized in Islam. In addition, Shafique et al., (2015) also argue that the application of ethics in an organization can increase motivation, increase job satisfaction as well as the dedication and commitment to life, the workplace and the organization.

Rivai et al., (2012) stated that Islam has three pillars, namely *tawheed*, *shariah* and also *akhlaq* in which *tawheed* is a creation of the oneness of Allah (SWT), interconnectedness and integration. *Shariah* can also be seen as a code of ethics for Muslims, while *akhlaq* is also defined as the practice of morality, manners and virtues. According to Tafsir, (2006); Rafiki and Wahab, (2014) in their research, they found that the *tawheed* paradigm can be applied in an effort to achieve unity and solidarity within an organization, while *akhlaq* (ethics) can also be used in an effort to improve ethics among workers who are in an organization. In other words, Islamic values can be applied in an effort to increase unity, motivation, trust and also integration within an organization, be it in the education sector or the business sector.

METHODS

Research Design

The research aims to investigate the teachers' perception Islamic value-based teaching in school, to identify the challenges faced by teachers in the process of using this method in building students' character. This study is a qualitative study that uses phenomenology as a methodology to answer the research question. According to Mills and Birks (2014), this qualitative research study aims to study the phenomena that affect the realities of individual and group life in a particular cultural or social context. Furthermore, according to Corbin & Strauss (2015), while using qualitative research, researchers can connect directly with their participants and see the world from their point of view.

The Population and Sample Size of the Study

The population of this study were Islamic schools in Malaysia and the sample size consists of eight teachers who teach in selected Islamic schools, such as ADNI Islamic school, Integrated Holistic School in Subang Bestiary, SRAI Sungai Chinchin, Brainy

Bunch International Islamic Montessori Setapak, *Mahad Tahfiz Integrasi Madinatul Huffaz*, and Mahad *Tahfiz an-Nur Matan Puchong*. The reason for choosing these teachers from various Islamic schools is to see the difference in how teachers from each school apply Islamic values in their teaching and how they build the character of their students in their school organization.

Sampling

In this study, the researchers used the purposeful sampling technique due to the chosen sample of respondents in this study. Before conducting an interview, the first thing that the researchers did was to ask the willingness of the respondents whether they are willing to actively participate in this study. A total of eight participants were interviewed and three of them were male teachers while the others were female teachers. In addition, all of the teachers were teaching Islamic subjects in their respective schools.

Data Collection

This study required information on teacher using Islamic value-based teaching method in their teaching in building or improving student's character in some Islamic schools in Malaysia. In this research, participants were approached first, through messaging (*WhatsApp*) asking their permission and volunteerism before being interviewed. After the participants expressed their intent to take part in this study, the researchers sent consent forms and interview questions to all respondents by using the WhatsApp application and Gmail. The participants were asked six questions, "How do you define Islamic values and character building in education?", "How does Islamic value-based teaching help students in their character enhancement or building?", "What are the main character values that have been taught?", "From your view, how are your student characters nowadays?", "What do you think about the environment or support system as regards to the Islamic value-based in teaching students?" and "What are the methods used by teachers to have more effectiveness Islamic value-based teaching among students?". The participants were given a choice whether to answer all the questions by using the English language or Bahasa Melayu. As mentioned before, due to Covid-19, all these questions were answered by the participants by sending the answers through voice message (*WhatsApp*) and Gmail.

Data Analysis

In this study, several steps were taken by the researchers to analyse the data. The results of the interviews obtained were immediately transcribed into Microsoft

Word 2010. This transcript process continues until the authors are satisfied with the quality of the transcriptions. Out of seven respondents, four of them used *Bahasa Melayu* to answer all the questions, so the researchers need to translate them. The next steps were defined together with coding as a method of labelling, gathering and organizing the data and reporting pattern (themes). Finally, all the data collected from the instrument will be analysed in line with the objective of the study.

Ethical Issues

This section highlights the importance of problems regarding ethical issues and the challenges that accompany it in conducting this study. According to Locke, Silverman, & Spiraduso, (2009), researchers should take important steps to ensure the privacy and dignity of participants can be properly protected. Various ethics must be considered by researchers during the conduct of this study, namely:

a) Participants are informed that they have the right to withdraw from this research at any time without any penalty imposed. They were also told that they could answer questions at any time until the time set by the researchers.
b) The objectives of the study are clearly stated in writing.
c) Each participant is given a written consent form.
d) All data collection techniques and tasks are communicated in writing to all participants.
e) Participants were also given a written transcript and the results from the interpretation of the data.

However, to maintain a high level of anonymity, the researchers labelled all teachers as Participant 1, Participant 2, Participant 3, Participant 4, Participant 5, Participant 6, Participant 7 and Participant 8. In addition, the names of participant were also coded using numbers to represent each name of participants in analysing and presenting data. Hiding the names o participant in data is very useful for providing Anonymity (Creswell, 2002).

Validity and Reliability

In contrast to quantitative research, validity in qualitative research according to Golafshani, (2003) is the consistency and reliability of activities as well as events related to the phenomenon addressed by the research results studied in research. The interviews used in this study were structured-interviews where the researchers asked questions that fit the objectives of this study. No additional questions were asked. Therefore, the respondents should answer all the questions with the appropriate answers. Commonly identified validation techniques used in the study include data source triangulation to corroborate evidence, bracketing to clarify bias and member checking. Member checking, which is identified as the most critical validation technique, was conducted with participants to determine the credibility of the findings and interpretations (Silverman, 2013). After several questions, the researchers discussed among themselves to choose the appropriate questions that could answer all the research questions from this study. After consulting the experts for the validity of the interview question, six questions were selected and given to the respondents.

INTERVIEW REPORTS

After completing abstractions, the researchers explained the result, which is in this result. Four themes emerged based on the objective of this study, namely to investigate the teachers' perception about Islamic value-based teaching in school, to identify the challenges faced by the teachers in the process of using this method in the classroom to build or develop students' character.

Theme 1: Role Model for Islamic Value-Based Teaching application for Student Character Building

In this study, the researchers discovered the importance of using Islamic value-based teaching to encourage students to have good characters. If that person wants to be a good student, they need to follow what is already mentioned in Al-Quran and Hadith. As can be seen in surah *Al-Ahzab* verse 21 which mean: "Indeed in the Messenger of Allah is the best example for you (to follow) that is for those who hope (pleasure) of Allah and (glory of life) in the hereafter and people who remember Allah a lot ". It can be shown that our Prophet Muhammad SAW is the best example that we as Muslims need to follow His character and behaviour.

Sub-Theme 1: Prophet Muhammad SAW and Sahabah as a Role Model

Islamic values based on the *Al-Quran* and Hadith teach the real concept of human life. Making the Prophet a 'role model' is an obligation and religious requirement that needs to be done by us as Muslims especially to be good students and have a good character. It can be seen from all the transcribed information that almost all the participants agreed and stated that as a student they need to make *Rasulullah* SAW and *Sahabah* as role models in their life. **Participant 1** said:

"So the student can apply Prophet Muhammad SAW) life practice to be a good Muslim and to have a good character building."

Participant 2: *"... the teacher can share with students the story of the prophet PBUH and the story of his companions regarding their good behaviours which influence the students to develop their good manners and good behaviours."*

Participant 3: *"Rasulullah is the best role model to be followed by all Muslims"*

Participant 5: *"... we need to see the Islamic value that has been taught in Islam for example what has been done by the Rasulullah with the Sahabah."*

Participant 6: *"...Rasullah and sahabat are our kiblat or bench mark in Islamic values and character-building."*

Sub-theme 2: Teacher as a Role Model

It is known that students spend most of their day or time in school, and it cannot be denied that their teachers are responsible for nurturing Islamic values in their students and forming good personalities. Furthermore, despite being responsible for nurturing Islamic values and forming a good personality, students will make their teachers their role models in school. In other words, what has been done by the teachers will be followed by the students since they put teachers as their role model and it is proven when some participants said that:

Participant 1: *"The Muslim life practice of teachers in the school will affect student to be a good Muslim."*

Participant 2: *"The school teacher should follow the Islamic values and principles in their daily lives and when they stay in the school."*

Participant 5: *"... teachers' character (akhlaq) will be the mirror for the students. If the teachers are good, the students will be good as well and vice versa."*

Participant 6: *"Teachers as a role model in school. We start from ourselves to show how to have Islamic values. Because students nowadays especially, will compare what we say and what we did."*

Participant 8: *"Personally, I encourage my students to follow what I have done, such as, every day you have to read the Qur'an before going to bed, praying even though one verse a day. So I gave the values of a good manners education by showing my true nature so it was more respected."*

Theme 2: Environmental Support to Influence Students Character Building and Islamic Value-based teaching

The environment is really an important factor to build the character of students. There is a possibility that what has been taught or applied in school will be useless if the environment does not support what has been taught or applied in school. This is supported by **participant 2** when he said that:

"... the environment has a huge impact and contribution to teach students anything. So, the congenial Islamic value-based environment should be created for the students."

So it is important to have support from family, friends and also teachers to build the character of the student and Islamic value-based teaching methods to teach them. One of the participants says that:

"Islamic environment is among the effective ways for adding the Islamic value to students. They tend to follow people around them. As their time is longer at school, so, the responsibility of teachers and friends is higher as their support system..."

Sub-Theme 1: Family Support

It has been mentioned before that a teacher is the role model of the students in school. However, when the students are going back home the same role is taken over by the parents of the students as well as the other family members. Despite how hard-working a teacher add Islamic values in teaching among the students while at school, it will not be successful without any support from their families, especially from their parents. It is because at home their parents will be the ones who monitor their children. Moreover, it cannot be denied that parents are the reflection of their children and parents play a big role at home. When the parents of a student have high Islamic values and good character, the children might have the same value and character as well. It is also supported by the participants in their statements:

Participant 1: *"At home, parents also play a great role in adding Islamic values among students. This has been proven for many students in school. Parents that have high Islamic values have more high character building students."*

Participant 5: *"... it can be seen in the current world that we live in that if we see a student with a good akhlaq, we will look at their family. In psychology, it is mentioned that the problematic students come from the problematic family, the one that put aside the religious aspect. But when we see a student with a good akhlaq, it goes the opposite way."*

Parents also play an important role in supporting every single thing that has been done by the teacher in school such as when the teacher gives homework to their students that means the teacher wants to apply the value of *Amanah* among the children, so the parents must keep an eye on their children. For example, **participant 1 said:** *"Every day, teachers will give them homework as Amanah to be completed at home. They are thought to be responsible with the work given by the teacher."*

Participant 6: *"We teach the students to have a simple and balanced life. However, when they have parents or family who doesn't really apply that concept. Well, it can be said that the students won't apply it at home. Because there is no support from the family to do so."*

Participant 7: *"To be honest, the students' character will depend on how their family is. When the family or parents are educated and care for their children, most of the time the students will have good character."*

Sub-Theme 2: Teacher Support

Teachers, as students' parents in school, and despite being students' role models in school, also have a responsibility or part to support their students in school to influence character building as well as to apply Islamic value-based teaching in the classroom. Moreover, according to the participants, teachers' support towards their students may differ from one another.

Participant 5: *"... in Madrasah, teachers really emphasize on the purity of soul... teachers will ask the students to be khidmat, because being khidmat is one of the ways to teach the students for being used to apply the sifat mahmudah (Good character) in their daily activities... teachers have to do tazkiyatun nafs..."*

Participant 6: *"... because for us teachers, we try not to just deliver the knowledge and understanding but we really try to put the understanding and knowledge in their heart. So that their heart can decide what to do and what not"*

Sub-theme 3: Peers Support

After parents who are responsible for their children at home and teachers who are responsible for their students, peers' support is also taking a part as the students' support system matters. As has been said by **participant 4:** *"They tend to follow people around them. As their time is longer at school, so, the responsibility of teachers and friends is higher as their support system.*

Theme 3: Challenges Faced by Teacher in Applying Islamic Values

There are several challenges faced by these teachers when it comes to the Islamic value-based teaching application in shaping the character-building of students, the challenges are:

Sub-Theme 1: Social Media, Friend Economy Status and Family Lifestyle

Social media impacts students negatively and positively but here social media give a negative impact on the student's life and it is supported by participants 3 and 4 which is:

Participant 3: "*Social media, friend economy status and their family lifestyle really influence our new generation..."*

Participant 4: "*Students nowadays are too much exposed to social media. So, their characters are far from children of their age. Sometimes, they act like adults and become rude to people around them. It shows the negative impacts of overdose social media."*

Sub-Theme 2: Hardly to Accept Any Opinion

Some teachers said that they faced challenges to handle their students' character because students nowadays are hard to manage and it can be proven according to the statement by participant 3:

Participant 3: *"With the digital era, students nowadays seem to have their own perception and hardly accept opinions from others except their parents..."*

Sub-Theme 3: Discipline Problem

As a human being, a Muslim student can do things that are forbidden to be done such as bullying, imitation etc. and this is one of the problems faced by teachers of Islamic values in the lives of students because their moral character is very low and the teacher needs to fix it. The problems faced by these teachers are:

Participant 2: *"The terrible thing is that if any students deny helping anyone then he will be threatened by him. In another word, the moral and ethical characters of the Bangladeshi students are very low and strongly needed to be improved."*

Participant 8: *"But some of them have discipline problems such as the student should enter his shirt into clothes, but there are some students who do not put his shirt in, this is a kind of trend to show they are gangsters."*

Theme 4: Adding Islamic Values through Islamic Education Subject

As stated in National Education Philosophy which emphasizes the building of a balanced and harmonious character intellectually, spiritually, emotionally and physically, based on belief and submission to Allah, the subject of Islamic Education is an important medium to achieve this objective. This subject already consists of six major areas which are *Aqidah*, Qur'an, *Hadith*, *Ibadah*, *Sirah* and *Adab*. Therefore, the effective teaching and learning process requires the Islamic education teacher's role in applying methods and activities as a medium to facilitate students to receive, understand and implement the content of the lessons. These supports the view of teachers:

Participant 4: "*As teachers, we need to use a variety of methods to tackle the students. Among the effective ones is the implementation of class schedules that include everything that can change their attitude. For example, solat dhuha, recitation of mathurat and Yasin".*

Participant 2*: "Teaching methodology should be more focused on the moral values, that means teachers should teach students most of the subjects in western perspective as well as the Islamic perspective."*

Participant 7: *"... education directly, that is by using the instructions, guidance, advice, mention the benefits and dangers of something.*

From these findings, we can conclude that using Islamic value-based teaching in class and subjects does improve students' good character and their Islamic values. Besides, the participants believed that the more teachers use Islamic value-based in the classroom, the better student will be in terms of morals and discipline as well as improving school behaviour.

RECOMMENDATIONS FOR FUTURE RESEARCH

Based on the findings of this research, the researchers found some recommendations for future research which this study only investigated about eight teachers from selected Islamic schools. However, the researchers hope that future research will use national schools or even if possible uses universities to investigate how the teachers and also the lecturers apply Islamic value-based teaching method in the teaching process. Besides that, this research is done qualitatively. It is hoped that one day there will be similar research that uses quantitative as their method of study. This study is done during the Covid-19 pandemic and it is difficult for the researchers to have face-to-face interviews since the movement during this pandemic is limited, so the researchers only can interview the teachers by using *WhatsApp* and *Gmai*l applications. It cannot be denied that when online applications are used as a medium to interview participants, of course, some difficulties occur and sometimes the data we get is unsatisfactory. We hope that future researchers will use face-to-face interviews to get satisfactory answers.

CONCLUSION

This study aimed to explore how character could be built or developed by using Islamic value-based teaching as well as Islamic school organizational behaviour. The findings of this study have shown that Islamic value-based teaching for student character building was not an easy task. It's a collaborative effort that has to be done by teachers, parents, peers and also surrounding communities. Teachers as role models in the school, have the responsibility for the Islamic value-based teaching in building students' character in the school and parental support of its application at home. *Rasulullah* SAW, and *Sahabah* are seen as the main references in terms of the *adab* and *akhlaq* as well as to improve Islamic values in accordance with Quranic teaching. Aishah R.A. has been asked by *Sahabah* how is the *akhlaq* of

Prophet Muhammad SAW? She answered that, *(khuluqul Quran)* means that the prophet's *akhlaq* reflects the Quranic teaching. Therefore, to become a good Muslim who has good *adab* and *akhlaq*, it is essential to make *Rasulullah* a role model and the Quran as a reference. When all these are applied in Islamic schools, it doesn't only help in using Islamic value-based teaching to develop student character and behaviour, but it also helps school organizations to have a peaceful environment as well as an Islamic culture. Malaysia has a perfect example of the role that Islamic values play in building, the Malaysian educational philosophy emphasized spirituality to provide a balanced and harmonious character in students that will benefit the social and educational organization. Again, from the findings of this study, social media has been portrayed as a bad influence on student behaviour and teachers and parents have roles to play in ensuring there is a limitation in the access of students to gadgets and media. The time students spend with the media and gadgets can be replaced by *zikir* and recitation of the Qur'an. Even the same media can be used to promote Islamic values and divert students to Islamic activities and knowledge. This will make a big change in students' behaviour or attitude on the way or method that social media, gadget and digits should be used.

REFERENCES

Abdul-Razak, M. A. (2011). *Contribution of Iqbal's Dynamic Personality Theory to Islamic Psychology: A Contrasting Analysis with Freud and Selected Mainstream Western Psychology* (Doctoral dissertation). International Islamic University Malaysia.

Abdullah, A. H., Ismai, M. S., Othman, M. S., & Nasir, N. (2017). Islamic View on the Role of Social Environment in Shaping Human Behaviour. *International Journal of Academic Research in Business & Social Sciences*, *7*(7), 886–859. doi:10.6007/IJARBSS/v7-i7/3162

Achmad, P. (2004). *Metodologi Pendidikan Agama Islam*. Bina Ilmu.

Al-Qudsy, S.H.I. (2010). *Etika Penjawat Awam dari Perspektif Islam*. Kuala Lumpur: Dewan Bahasa dan Pustaka.

Ali, Z. (2011). *Pendidikan Agma Islam*. Bumi Aksara.

Amin-Mt, M. A., & Mustaffa, A. (2019). Teachers Perception in Inculcating Islamic Values in Secondary Schools. *International Journal on E-Learning*, *1*(2), 83–88.

Asmara, Y., Isbandiyah, I., & Rahayu, A. (2020). Integration of islamic teaching into curriculum as strengthening character education. *Prodising ISID*, (1), 175–184.

Badrasawi, K. J., Preece, A. S., Hashim, C. N., & Azizi, N. M. S. (2017). The concept of Murabbi in Muslim Education with reference to selected teaching methods of the Prophet Muhammad. *Al-Shajarah,* 327-357.

Badroen, F. (2006). *Etika Bisnis Dalam Islam*. Kencana Perdana Media Group.

Bakhary, N. (2019). *Pendidikan karakter: Persediaan Mendepani Cabaran Pelbagai Dimensi*. https://www.pendidik.com.my/2019/07/15/pendidikan-karakter-persediaan-mendepani-cabaran-pelbagai-dimensi/

Chang, L. H. (2010). An appraisal on the implementation of moral education for schools in Malaysia. *Proceedings of the 4th International Conference on Teacher Education*, 3–12.

Choli, I. (2019). *Pembentukan Karakter melalui Pendidikan Islam*. file:///C:/Users/ACER/Downloads/511-Article%20Text-269-1-10 20191106%20(2).pdf

Corbin, J., & Strauss, A. (2015). *Basics of Qualitative Research. Sage*.

Creswell, J. W. (2002). *Educational research: Planning, conducting and evaluating quantitative and qualitative research*. Pearson.

Creswell, J. W., & Poth, C. N. (2016). *Qualitative Inquiry and Research Design: Choosing Among Five Approaches. Sage*.

Dauri, R. (2009). *Islam dan Nilai*. Pustaka Felichia.

Fatmah, N. (2018). *Pembentukan Karakter dalam Pendidikan*. https://core.ac.uk/download/pdf/276532588.pdf

Golafshani, N. (2003). Understanding Reliability and Validity in Qualitative Research. *Qualitative Report*, *8*(4), 597–607.

Hamid, A. (2016). Metode Internalisasi Nilai-Nilai Akhlak Dalam Pembelajaran Pendidikan Agama Islam Di Smp Negeri 17 Kota Palu. *Jurnal Pendidikan Agama Islam – Ta'lim*, *14*(2), 195-206.

Hamimah, K. (2018). Nilai-Nilai Islam Dalam Program Pemulihan Dan Rawatan Dadah Di Pengasih. *Islamiyyat*, *40*(2), 141–149.

Haron, H., Jamil, N. N., & Ramli, N. M. (2020). Western and Islamic Values and Ethics: Are They Different? *Journal of Governance and Integrity*, *4*(1), 12–28. doi:10.15282/jgi.4.1.2020.5609

Hasrul, M., & Fauzi, M. (2015, February). Nilai-Nilai Penting Individu Muslim Menurut Al-Ghazali. *Jurnal Islam Dan Masyarakat Kontemporari*, *9*, 41–60.

Hunt, S. D., & Vitell, S. (1986). A general theory of marketing ethics. *Journal of Macromarketing*, *6*(1), 5–16. doi:10.1177/027614678600600103

Jodi, K. H. M. (2018). Nilai-nilai Islam dalam Program Pemulihan dan Rawatan Dadah di Pengasih. *International Journal of Islamic Studies*, *40*(2), 141–149.

Kemas, O. H. (2017). The Islamic Education Methods in Al-Quran. *Ta'dib. Journal of Islamic Education*, *22*(1), 48–57.

Kuh, G. D., & Umbach, P. D. (2004). College and character: Insights from the national survey of student engagement. *New Directions for Institutional Research*, *2004*(122), 37–54. doi:10.1002/ir.108

Lewis, M., & Ponzio, V. (2016). Character Education as the Primary Purpose of Schooling for the Future. Jurnal Peuradeun Ilmiah. *International Multidisciplinary Journal*, *4*(2), 137–146. doi:10.13140/RG.2.1.4076.2486

Locke, L. F., Silverman, S. J., & Spirduso, W. W. (2009). *Reading and understanding research*. SAGE.

Mandhur, I. (2003). *Lisan al-'Arab* [Language of the Arabs]. Dar 'Alam al-Kutub.

Mastuhu. (2008). *Sistem Pendidikan Nasional Visoner*. Jakarta: Lentera Hati.

Milal, A. D. U., Rohmah, Z., Kusumajanti, W., Basthomi, Y., Sholihah, D. N., & Susilowati, M. (2020). Integrating character education in the English teaching at Islamic Junior high schools in Indonesia. *TEFLIN Journal*, *31*(1), 88–107. doi:10.15639/teflinjournal.v31i1/88-107

Mills, J., & Birks, M. (2014). *Qualitative Methodology: A Practical Guide*. SAGE. doi:10.4135/9781473920163

Ningsih, T. (2019). Peran Pendidikan Islam dalam Membentuk Karakter Siswa di Era Revolusi Industri 4.0 Pada Madrasah Tsanawiyah Negeri 1 Banyumas. *Insania*, *24*(2), 220–231. Advance online publication. doi:10.24090/insania.v24i2.3049

Nordin, W. M. Z. B. M. (2003). Peranan Pendidikan Islam dalam Falsafah Pendidikan Negara. In Memahami isu-isu pendidikan Islam di Malaysia (pp. 15-30). Kuala Lumpur: IKIM.

Omar, M. N. (2010). *Falsafah Akhlak, Penerbit Universiti Kebangsaan Malaysia*. Penerbit Universiti Kebangsaan Malaysia.

Pratama, I. P., & Zulhijra. (2019). Reformasi Pendidikan Islam Indonesia. *Jurnal PAI Raden Fatah, 1*(1), 117-127.

Prayitno & Belferik, M. (2011). *Pendidikan Karakter dalam Pembangunan Bangsa.* Jakarta Grasindo.

Qoyyimah, U. (2016). Inculcating character education through EFL teaching in Indonesian state schools. *Pedagogies, 11*(2), 109–126. doi:10.1080/1554480X.2016.1165618

Rafiki, A., & Wahab, K. A. (2014). Islamic Values and Principles in the Organization: A Review of Literature. *Asian Social Science, 10*(9), 1–8. doi:10.5539/ass.v10n9p1

Rivai, V., & Mulyadi, D. (2012). *Kepemimpinan dan Perilaku Organisasi Edisi Ketiga.* Jakarta: PT. Rajagrafindo Persada.

Sadulloh, U. (2009). *Pengantar Filsafat Pendidikan.* Alfabeta.

Salleh, M. J. (2009). *The integrated Islamic education: Principles and need for thematic approaches.* Singapore: Singapore Islamic Education System Seminar.

Sarwan, A. (2010). *Ciri-Ciri Pendidikan Islam.* Rosda Karya.

Sattar, A., & Aftab, M. A. (2017). The role of Islamic education in the character building of school going children. *Education Research International, 6*(2), 28–34.

Shafique, M. N., Iqra. Ahmad, N., Khurshid, M., & Ahmad, H. (2015). Islamic Values & Principles in the Organization. *Arabian Journal of Business and Management Review, 5*(2), 14–21.

Shuhari, M.H., & Hamat, M.F. (2015). The Important Values of Muslim Individuals According Al-Ghazali. *Nilai-Nilai Penting Individu Muslim Menurut Al-Ghazali.* doi:10.37231/jimk.2015.9.0.82

Suwartini, S. (2017). Pendidikan Karakter dan Pembangunan Sumber Daya Manusia Keberlanjutan. *Jurnal Pendidikan ke-SD-an, 4*(1), 220-234.

Tafsir, A. (2006). *Filsafat Pendidikan Islam, Integrasi Jasmani, Rohani, dan Kalbu Memanusiakan Manusia.* Remaja Rosdakarya.

Tamuri, A. H. (2007). Islamic Education teachers' perceptions of the teaching of akhlāq in Malaysian secondary schools. *Journal of Moral Education, 36*(3), 371–386. doi:10.1080/03057240701553347

Thaha, M. C. (2006). *Kapita Selekta Pendidikan Islam.* Pustaka Pelajar.

World Data on Education. (2006). *Principles and general objectives of education.* Retrieved from http://www.ibe.unesco.org/fileadmin/user_upload/archive/Countries/WDE/2006/ASIA_and_the_PACIFIC/Malaysia/Malaysia.pdf

Yasin, R. F., & Jani, M. S. (2013). Islamic Education: Aim and main features. *International Journal of Education and Research*, *1*(10), 1–18.

Yusof, H., Mohd Noor, M. A., Abdul Jalil, N., Mansor, M., & Awang, M. (2018). Nurturing Moral Values in Primary School. *International Journal of Academic Research in Business & Social Sciences*, *8*(7), 1144–1156. doi:10.6007/IJARBSS/v8-i7/4562

Yusoff, W., Mazwati, W., Preece, A. S., & Hamzah, L. M. (2018). Students' Experiences in Teaching and Learning Islamic Education Using Philosophical Inquiry Method. *Journal of Education and Learning*, *12*(2), 266–274. doi:10.11591/edulearn.v12i2.9492

Compilation of References

Abbasi, A. S., Rehman, K. U., & Bibi, A. (2011). Islamic work ethics: How it affects business performance. *Actual Problems of Economics*, *12*, 312–322.

Abbas, M., Habib, H., & Siddique, A. (2020). Impact of Paternalistic Leadership on Turnover Intention: Evidence from the Islamic Banking Industry of Karachi, Pakistan. *Journal of Business and Management*, *2*(2), 167–176.

Abdel-Khalek, A. M. (2014). Religiosity, health and happiness: Significant relations in adolescents from Qatar. *The International Journal of Social Psychiatry*, *60*(7), 656–661. doi:10.1177/0020764013511792 PMID:24327187

Abdel-Khalek, A., & Lester, D. (2006). Optimism and Pessimism in Kuwaiti and American College Students. *The International Journal of Social Psychiatry*, *52*(2), 110–126. doi:10.1177/0020764006062092 PMID:16615244

Abdullah, A. G. K., Alzaidiyeen, N. J., & Aldarabah, I. T. (2009). Workplace spirituality and leadership effectiveness among educational managers in Malaysia. *European Journal of Soil Science*, *10*(2), 304–316.

Abdullah, A. H., Ismai, M. S., Othman, M. S., & Nasir, N. (2017). Islamic View on the Role of Social Environment in Shaping Human Behaviour. *International Journal of Academic Research in Business & Social Sciences*, *7*(7), 886–859. doi:10.6007/IJARBSS/v7-i7/3162

Abdul-Razak, M. A. (2011). *Contribution of Iqbal's Dynamic Personality Theory to Islamic Psychology: A Contrasting Analysis with Freud and Selected Mainstream Western Psychology* (Doctoral dissertation). International Islamic University Malaysia.

Achmad, P. (2004). *Metodologi Pendidikan Agama Islam*. Bina Ilmu.

Adams, J. S., Tashchian, A., & Shore, T. H. (2001). Codes of ethics as signals for ethical behavior. *Journal of Business Ethics*, *29*(3), 199–211. doi:10.1023/A:1026576421399

Adawiyah, W. R., & Pramuka, B. A. (2017). Scaling the notion of Islamic spirituality in the Workplace. *Journal of Management Development*, *36*(7), 877–898. doi:10.1108/JMD-11-2014-0153

Ahamed, F., Hassan, A., & Hashim, J. (2013). Authentic leadership, trust, and employees' work engagement: A comparative study of Islamic and conventional banks in Malaysia. *Journal of Global Business Advancement*, *6*(2), 152–166. doi:10.1504/JGBA.2013.053568

Ahmad, S., Islam, T., & Kaleem, A. (2021). Workplace bullying in Pakistan: Mapping the implications of social cynicism and the moderation of Islamic work ethic. In P. D'Cruz, E. Noronha, & A. Mendonca (Eds.), *Asian Perspectives on Workplace Bullying and Harassment*. Springer. doi:10.1007/978-981-16-2362-2_4

Ahmed, A., Arshad, M. A., Mahmood, A., & Barkat, W. (2021). The impact of spiritual values on employees loyalty: The moderating role of Islamic work ethic. *International Journal of Ethics and Systems*, *37*(3), 341–355. doi:10.1108/IJOES-09-2020-0147

Ajiferuke, M., & Boddewyn, J. (1970). "Culture" and other explanatory variables in comparative management studies. *Academy of Management Journal*, *13*(2), 153–163.

Aktan, C. (1999). *Ahlak ve ahlak felsefesi*. ARI Düşünce ve Toplumsal Gelişim Derneği Yayınları.

Al A'ali, E. (2009). Women's leadership styles in Scientific Journal for business and finance in vol. 1. Tanta University Press.

Al A'ali, E., & Alazali, R. M. (2018). Gender Differences in relation to Organization Sources of power. In M. M. Al-shammari & H. Masri (Eds.), *Arab Women and their Evolving Roles in Global Business Landscape*. doi:10.4018/978-1-5225-3710-6.ch001

Al-A'ali, E. (1991). *The phenomenon of women in Management: An alternative perspective and its implication in the case of Bahrain* (Unpublished PhD thesis). University of Lancaster.

Al-A'ali, E. (1993). Assumptions Concerning Sicial Sciences: A comparative Perspective. American Journal of Islamic Sciences, 10(4), 485-490.

Al-A'ali, E. (1999). Training in Organizations Training: An Enhancement View. In *1999 International Performance Improvement Conference and Exposition*. Omnipress.

Al-A'ali, E. (1995). *Organisational change: A transformational perspective. In 1st Annual Asian Academy of Management*. Creating Management Synergy in Asian Economies.

Al-A'ali, E. (1996). *Some Fundamentals features of Arabic-Islamic culture and it's possible contribution to world peace in Creative Peace Through Encounter of World Cultures* (H. Beck & G. Schmirber, Eds.). Sri Satguru Publications.

Al-A'ali, E. (2020). The Role of Auditing Firms in Promoting Ethical Consumerism. In *Ethical Consumerism and Comparative Studies Across. Different Cultures* (pp. 39–52). IGI Global. doi:10.4018/978-1-7998-0272-3.ch004

Ali, A. (1988). Scaling an Islamic work ethic. *The Journal of Social Psychology*, *128*(5), 575–583. doi:10.1080/00224545.1988.9922911

Ali, A. (1992). The Islamic work ethic in Arabia. *The Journal of Social Psychology, 126*(5), 507–519.

Ali, A., & Al-Owaiah, A. (2008). Islamic work ethic: A critical review. *Cross Cultural Management, 15*(1), 5–19. doi:10.1108/13527600810848791

Ali, A., & Azim, A. (1994). Islamic work ethic and organization in development. *Proceedings of 23rd International Congress of Applied Psychology.*

Ali, J. A. (2005). *Islamic perspectives on management and organization*. Edward Elgar Publishing. doi:10.1080/14766080509518602

Ali, Z. (2011). *Pendidikan Agma Islam*. Bumi Aksara.

Ali, Z., & Zaky, M. (2018). Spiritual values and spiritual practices: Interactive effects on leadership effectiveness. *ETIKONOMI, 17*(1), 123–134. doi:10.15408/etk.v17i1.6497

Alkhatib, A. J., & Arnout, B. A. (2019). Is religion the missing part in leadership and organization Citizenship Behavior Theories? *Proceedings of DIALOGO-CONF 2019*. 10.18638/dialogo.2019.6.1.10

Allen, B. P., & Potkay, C. R. (1981). On the arbitrary distinction between states and traits. *Journal of Personality and Social Psychology, 41*(5), 916–928. doi:10.1037/0022-3514.41.5.916

Al-Meraie, A. M. (1984). *Prisoners of Aristotle*. Epistemics Institute Press.

Al-Qudsy, S.H.I. (2010). *Etika Penjawat Awam dari Perspektif Islam*. Kuala Lumpur: Dewan Bahasa dan Pustaka.

AlSaffar, G., & Al-A'ali, E. (2021). *Psychiatry in the Midst of the Pandemic: A Narrative Perspective in Global Perspectives on Change Management and leadership in the Post COVID-19 Era*. IGI Global. doi:10.4018/978-1-7998-6948-1.ch002

Al-Shamali, A., Irani, Z., Haffar, M., Al-Shamali, S., & Al-Shamali, F. (2021). The influence of Islamic Work Ethic on employees' responses to change in Kuwaiti Islamic banks. *International Business Review, 30*(5), 1–11. doi:10.1016/j.ibusrev.2021.101817

Altaf, A., & Awan, M. A. (2011). Moderating affect of workplace spirituality on the relationship of job overload and job satisfaction. *Journal of Business Ethics, 104*(1), 93–99. doi:10.100710551-011-0891-0

Alyileili, S. S. (2020). The impact of strategic leadership on achieving job satisfaction for employees in the UAE Islamic banking sector. *International Journal of Innovations in Engineering Research and Technology, 7*(10), 117–124.

Amin-Mt, M. A., & Mustaffa, A. (2019). Teachers Perception in Inculcating Islamic Values in Secondary Schools. *International Journal on E-Learning, 1*(2), 83–88.

Anderton, R. V. (2012). *The relationship between leadership styles and perceived workplace spirituality* (Doctoral dissertation). Capella University.

Aravik, H., Sulastyawati, D., & Yunus, N. R. (2020). Leadership concept at sharia bank. *Islamic Banking*, *5*(2), 21–31.

Ariff, M. (1988). Islamic Banking. *Asian-Pacific Economic Literature*, *2*(2), 46–62. doi:10.1111/j.1467-8411.1988.tb00200.x

Aron, R. (2007). *Sosyolojik düşüncenin evreleri* (A. Korkmaz, Trans.). Kırmızı Yayınları. (Original work published 1967)

Arslan, M. (2001). The work ethic values of Protestant British, Catholic Irish and Muslim Turkish managers. *Journal of Business Ethics*, *31*(4), 321–339. doi:10.1023/A:1010787528465

Ashmos, D. P., & Duchon, D. (2000). Spirituality at work: A conceptualization and measure. *Journal of Management Inquiry*, *9*(2), 134–145. doi:10.1177/105649260092008

Askeland, G. A., & Døhlie, E. (2013). Contextualizing International Social Work: Religion as a relevant factor. *International Social Work*, *58*(2), 261–269. doi:10.1177/0020872813482958

Aslan, M., & Korkut, A. (2015). Spiritual leadership in primary schools in Turkey. *Journal of Educational and Social Research*, *5*(2), 123–123. doi:10.5901/jesr.2015.v5n2p123

Asmara, Y., Isbandiyah, I., & Rahayu, A. (2020). Integration of islamic teaching into curriculum as strengthening character education. *Prodising ISID*, (1), 175–184.

Atlas, B. L. H. (2002). *The role of spirituality in the work of African-American women principals in urban schools*. The University of Wisconsin-Madison.

Audretsch, D. B., Bonte, W., & Tamvada, J. P. (2007). Religion and entrepreneurship. SSRN *Electronic Journal*, 1-29. doi:10.2139/ssrn.1025968

Auper, S., & Houtman, D. (2006). Oriental religion in the secular west: Globalization, new age, and the reenchantment of the world. *Globalization and Social Change*, 82.

Avey, J. B., Luthans, F., & Jensen, S. (2009). Psychological capital: A positive resource for combating employee stress and turnover. *Human Resource Management*, *48*(5), 677–693. doi:10.1002/hrm.20294

Avey, J., Luthans, F., & Mhatre, K. (2008). A call for longitudinal research in positive organizational behavior. *Journal of Organizational Behavior*, *29*(5), 705–711. doi:10.1002/job.517

Avolio, B., & Gardner, W. (2005). Authentic leadership development: Getting to the root of positive forms of leadership. *The Leadership Quarterly*, *16*(3), 315–338. doi:10.1016/j.leaqua.2005.03.001

Ayoun, B., Rowe, L., & Yassine, F. (2014). Is workplace spirituality associated with business ethics? *International Journal of Contemporary Hospitality Management, 27*(5), 938-957.

Badrasawi, K. J., Preece, A. S., Hashim, C. N., & Azizi, N. M. S. (2017). The concept of Murabbi in Muslim Education with reference to selected teaching methods of the Prophet Muhammad. *Al-Shajarah,* 327-357.

Badroen, F. (2006). *Etika Bisnis Dalam Islam.* Kencana Perdana Media Group.

Bahrain an International Financial Centre (5th ed.). (1994). BMA Publication.

Bailey, C., Yeoman, R., Madden, A., Thompson, M., & Kerridge, G. (2019). A Review of the Empirical Literature on Meaningful Work: Progress and Research Agenda. *Human Resource Development Review, 18*(1), 83–113. doi:10.1177/1534484318804653

Baker, D. C. (2003). Studies of the inner life: The impact of spirituality on quality of life. *Quality of Life Research: An International Journal of Quality of Life Aspects of Treatment, Care and Rehabilitation, 12*(1), 51–57. doi:10.1023/A:1023573421158 PMID:12803311

Bakhary, N. (2019). *Pendidikan karakter: Persediaan Mendepani Cabaran Pelbagai Dimensi.* https://www.pendidik.com.my/2019/07/15/pendidikan-karakter-persediaan-mendepani-cabaran-pelbagai-dimensi/

Bakirov, R. (2005). *İşletmelerde iş ahlakı ve sosyal sorumluluk* (Unpublished master's thesis). Gazi University Institution of Social Sciences, Ankara, Turkey.

Bakke, D. W. (2005). Joy at Work: A Revolutionary Approach to Fun on the Job. Penguin Group Inc.

Bakker, A. (2011). An evidence-based model of work engagement. *Current Directions in Psychological Science, 20*(4), 265–269. doi:10.1177/0963721411414534

Baloğlu, N., & Karadağ, E. (2009). A theoretical analysis about spiritual leadership. *Kuram ve Uygulamada Eğitim Yönetimi, 58*, 165–190.

Baltaş, A. (2002). İş hayatı, sorumluluk ve ahlak. *Activeline, 23*.

Bandura, A. (1994). Self-efficacy. In V. S. Ramachaudran (Ed.), *Encyclopedia of human behavior* (Vol. 4, pp. 71–81). Academic Press.

Bandura, A. (1997). *Self-efficacy: The exercise of control.* Freeman.

Banke, S., Maldonado, N., Lacey, C. H., & Thompson, S. (2005). *The Role of Spirituality in Christian School Leadership: A Qualitative Study.* Online Submission.

Barron, K., & Chou, S. Y. (2017). Spirituality and social responsibility performance: The perspectives of religiously and non-religiously affiliated individuals. *Journal of Global Responsibility, 8*(1), 63–82. doi:10.1108/JGR-07-2016-0020

Bass, B. M. (1990). *Bass and Stogdill's Handbook of leadership: Theory, research, and managerial applications.* The Free Press.

Bauer, M. W. (2003). Classical content analysis: A review. In M. W. Bauer & G. Gaskell (Eds.), *Qualitative researching with text, image and sound.* Sage Publication.

Bauman, D. C. (2013). Leadership and the three faces of integrity. *The Leadership Quarterly, 24*(3), 414–426. doi:10.1016/j.leaqua.2013.01.005

Bayat, A. (1992). The work ethic in Islam: A comparison with protestantism. *The Islamic Quarterly*, *36*(1), 5–27.

Baykal, E., & Zehir, C. (2018). Mediating effect of psychological capital on the relationship between spiritual leadership and performance. *E+M. Ekonomie a Management*, *21*(3), 124–140. doi:10.15240/tul/001/2018-3-008

Bechert, I., & Quandt, M. (2013). *Issp Data Report: Religious Attitudes and Religious Change*. GESIS - Leibniz Institute for the Social Sciences.

Becker, B. E., & Huselid, M. A. (1999). Overview: Strategic human resource management in five leading firms. *Human Resource Management Journal*, *38*(4), 287–301. doi:10.1002/(SICI)1099-050X(199924)38:4<287::AID-HRM2>3.0.CO;2-L

Bektaş, Ç., & Köseoğlu, M. A. (2008). Business ethics and its prevalence process. *Suleyman Demirel University Journal of Faculty of Economics and Administrative Sciences*, *13*(1), 145–158.

Benefiel, M. (2005). The second half of the journey: Spiritual leadership for organizational transformation. *The Leadership Quarterly*, *16*(5), 723–747. doi:10.1016/j.leaqua.2005.07.005

Berg, J., Grant, A., & Johnson, V. (2010). When Callings Are Calling: Crafting Work and Leisure in Pursuit of Unanswered Occupational Callings. *Organization Science*, *21*(5), 973–994. doi:10.1287/orsc.1090.0497

Berkelaar, B. L., & Buzzanell, P. M. (2015). Bait and switch or double-edged sword? The (sometimes) failed promises of calling. *Human Relations*, *68*(1), 157–178. doi:10.1177/0018726714526265

Bertram, B. (2007). *Reflective Analysis of the Role Spirituality Plays in Educational Leaders' Coping Successes with a Focus on Gender Divergence*. Academic Press.

Bhindi, N., & Duignan, P. (1997). Leadership for a new century: Authenticity, intentionality, spirituality and sensibility. *Educational Management & Administration, 25*(2), 117-132.

Biberman, J., & Whitty, M. D. (2000). *Work and spirit: A reader of new spiritual paradigms for organizations*. University of Scranton.

bin Abdullah, A. G. K., bt Ismail, A., & bin Mydin, A. (2013). The Moderating Effects of School Principals' Leadership Practices on the Workplace Spirituality and Leadership Effectiveness Relationship. *International Journal for Cross-Disciplinary Subjects in Education, 4*(4), 1318-1323.

Bindlish, P., Dutt, P., & Pardasani, R. (2012). From growing convergence of spirituality and leadership towards a unified leadership theory. *Journal of Spirituality, Leadership and Management, 6*(1), 3-23.

Blanchard, K. (1999). *The heart of a leader: Insights on the art of influence*. Honor Books.

Blood, M. R. (1969). Work values and job satisfaction. *The Journal of Applied Psychology*, *53*(6), 456–459. doi:10.1037/h0028653

Boa, K. (2001). *Conformed to His image: Biblical and practical approaches to spiritual formation*. Zondervan.

Bodinson, G. W. (2005). Change healthcare organizations from good to great. *Quality Progress*, *38*(11), 22.

Bolman, L. G., & Deal, T. E. (2001). *Leading with soul: An uncommon journey of spirit, New & rev*. Jossey-Bass.

Bondoc, E. J. (2016). *A qualitative study of spiritual leadership in the workplace* (Doctoral dissertation). Northcentral University.

Bonner III, C. E. (2007). *From coercive to spiritual: What style of leadership is prevalent in k–12 public schools?* Academic Press.

Boorom, R. (2009). *Spiritual leadership: A study of the relationship between spiritual leadership theory and transformational leadership* (Doctoral Dissertation). Available from ProQuest Dissertations and Theses database. (UMI No. 3377759).

Borkowski, N. (2005). *Overview and History of Organizational Behavior.* In N. Borkowski (Ed.), *Organizational Behavior in Health Care* (pp. 3–13). Jones and Bartlett publishers.

Brett, J. M. (2014). *Negotiating globally: How to negotiate deals, resolve disputes, and make decisions across cultural boundaries* (3rd ed.). Jossey- Bass.

Brett, J. M., Gunia, B. C., & Teucher, B. M. (2017). Culture and negotiation strategy: A framework for future research. *The Academy of Management Perspectives*, *31*(4), 288–308.

Brown, M. E., & Trevino, L. K. (2006). Ethical leadership: A review and future directions. *The Leadership Quarterly*, *17*(6), 595–616.

Brown, R. B. (2003). Organizational spirituality: The sceptic's version. *Organization*, *10*(2), 393–400. doi:10.1177/1350508403010002013

Bruce, S. (Ed.). (1992). *Religion and modernization. Sociologists and historians debate the secularization thesis*. Clarendon Press.

Bryd, K., Hageman, A., & Isle, D. (2007). Intrinsic motivation and subjective well-being: The unique contribution of intrinsic religious motivation. *The International Journal for the Psychology of Religion*, *17*(2), 41–156. doi:10.1080/10508610701244155

Bryman, A. (Ed.). (2011). *The SAGE handbook of leadership*. Sage Publications.

Buckingham, M., & Clifton, D. (2001). *Now, discover your strengths*. The Free Press.

Buckingham, M., & Coffman, C. (1999). *First, break all the rules*. Simon & Schuster.

Bunderson, J. S., & Thompson, J. A. (2009). The call of the wild: Zookeepers, callings, and the dual edges of deeply meaningful work. *Administrative Science Quarterly*, *54*(1), 32–57. doi:10.2189/asqu.2009.54.1.32

Burke, R. (2006). Leadership and spirituality. *Foresight*, *8*(6), 14–25.

Burrell, G., & Morgan, G. (1979). *Sociological Paradigms and Organisational Analysis*. Heinemann Educational Books Ltd.

Büte, M. (2011). The relationship between the effects of nepotism on the employees and human resource practices: A research on Turkish public banks. *Ataturk University Journal of Social Sciences*, *15*(1), 383–404.

Byrne, P. P. (2012). *The relationship between religiosity, general self-efficacy and locus of control* (Diploma thesis). School of Arts, Dublin Business School.

Calvin, J. (1574). *Sermons of M. John Calvin upon the Epistle of Saint Paul to the Galatians*. Lucas Harison and George Bishop.

Cameron, K. S., & Ettington, D. R. (1988). The conceptual foundations of organizational culture. In J. Smart (Ed.), *Higher education handbook of theory and research* (pp. 356–396). Agathon Press.

Cameron, K. S., & Spreitzer, G. M. (Eds.). (2012). *The Oxford Handbook of Positive Organizational Scholarship*. Oxford University Press.

Cameron, K., Dutton, J., Quinn, R., & Wrzesniewski, A. (2003). *Developing a discipline of positive organizational scholarship. Positive Organizational Scholarship*. Berrett-Koehler.

Cantone, J. A., & Wiener, R. L. (2017). Religion at work: Evaluating hostile work environment religious discrimination claims. *Psychology, Public Policy, and Law*, *23*(3), 351–366. doi:10.1037/law0000132

Carswell, P., & Rolland, D. (2004). The role of religion in entrepreneurship participation and perception. *International Journal of Entrepreneurships and Small Business*, *3*(4), 280–286.

Cartwright, S., & Cooper, C. L. (1997). *Managing workplace stress* (Vol. 1). Sage.

Casanova, J. (1994). *Public religions in the modern world*. The University of Chicago Press. doi:10.7208/chicago/9780226190204.001.0001

Cash, K. C., Gray, G. R., & Rood, S. A. (2000). A Framework for Accommodating Religion and Spirituality in the Workplace [and Executive Commentary]. *The Academy of Management Executive*, 124-134.

Cashman, K. (1998). *Leadership from the inside out: Seven pathways to mastery*. Executive Excellence.

Cavanagh, G. F. (1999). Spirituality for managers: Context and critique. *Journal of Organizational Change Management*, *12*(3), 186–199. doi:10.1108/09534819910273793

Cavanagh, G., Hanson, B., Hanson, K., & Hinojoso, J. (2001). Toward a Spirituality for the Contemporary Organization: Implications for Work, Family and Society. In *Organizational behavior: Essential tenets for a new millennium*. South-Western College Publishing.

CBB. (2020). *Financial Stability Report*. Central Bank of Bahrain.

Çelik, S. (2010). The relationship of the application of business ethics with employee satisfaction. *Turkish Journal of Business Ethics*, *3*(5), 21–40.

Certo, S. C., & Certo, S. T. (2019). Modern management: Concepts and skills (global edition). Pearson Education Limited.

Chang, L. H. (2010). An appraisal on the implementation of moral education for schools in Malaysia. *Proceedings of the 4th International Conference on Teacher Education*, 3–12.

Chan-Serafin, S., Brief, A. P., & George, J. M. (2013). Perspective—How does religion matter and why? Religion and the organizational sciences. *Organization Science*, *24*(5), 1585–1600. doi:10.1287/orsc.1120.0797

Chanzanagh, H. E., & Akbernejad, M. (2011). The meaning and dimensions of Islamic work ethic: Initial validation of a multidimensional IWE in Iranian society. *Social and Behavioral Sciences*, *30*, 916–924. doi:10.1016/j.sbspro.2011.10.178

Chapra, M. (1992). *Islam and the economic challenge*. International Institute of Islamic Thought.

Chen, C. Y., & Yang, C. F. (2012). The impact of spiritual leadership on organizational citizenship behavior: A multi-sample analysis. *Journal of Business Ethics*, *105*(1), 107–114.

Chen, C. Y., Yang, C. Y., & Li, C. I. (2012). Spiritual Leadership, Follower Mediators, and Organizational Outcomes: Evidence From Three Industries Across Two Major Chinese Societies 1. *Journal of Applied Social Psychology*, *42*(4), 890–938. doi:10.1111/j.1559-1816.2011.00834.x

Cheung, F., Tang, C. S., & Tang, S. (2011). Psychological capital as a moderator between emotional labor, burnout, and job satisfaction among school teachers in China. *International Journal of Stress Management*, *18*(4), 348–371. doi:10.1037/a0025787

Choerudin, A. (2014). The Relationship Between Spirituality and Work Attitude: A Empirical Study. *International Journal of Management Research and Reviews*, *4*(4), 455.

Choli, I. (2019). *Pembentukan Karakter melalui Pendidikan Islam*. file:///C:/Users/ACER/Downloads/511-Article%20Text-269-1-10 20191106%20(2).pdf

Chong, B. S., & Liu, M.-H. (2009). Islamic banking: Interest-free or interest-based? *Pacific-Basin Finance Journal*, *17*(1), 125–144. doi:10.1016/j.pacfin.2007.12.003

Chowdhury, R. M., & Fernando, M. (2013). The role of spiritual well-being and materialism in determining consumers' ethical beliefs: An empirical study with Australian consumers. *Journal of Business Ethics*, *113*(1), 61–79. doi:10.100710551-012-1282-x

Chughtai, A. A., & Buckley, F. (2008). Work Engagement and its Relationship with State and Trait Trust: A Conceptual Analysis. *Journal of Behavioral and Applied Management*, *10*, 47. doi:10.21818/001c.17170

CIA World Factbook. (n.d.). *Bahrain*. https://www.cia.gov/the-world-factbook/countries/bahrain/

Ciulla, J. B. (2005). Integrating leadership with ethics: Is good leadership contrary to human nature. *Handbook on responsible leadership and governance in global business*, 159-179.

Cole, G. A. (1993). *Management Theory and Practice*. DP Publication Ltd.

Conger, J. A. (1994). *Spirit at work: Discovering the spirituality in leadership*. Jossey-Bass.

Conroy, S. J., & Emerson, T. L. (2004). Business ethics and religion: Religiosity as a predictor of ethical awareness among students. *Journal of Business Ethics*, *50*(4), 383–396. doi:10.1023/B:BUSI.0000025040.41263.09

Cooper, D. R., & Schindler, P. S. (2008). *Business Research Methods* (10th ed.). McGraw Hill.

Corbin, J., & Strauss, A. (2015). *Basics of Qualitative Research. Sage.*

Cornelius, N., Gooch, L., & Todd, S. (2001). Managing Difference Fairly: An Integrated "Partnership" Approach. In M. Noon & E. Ogbonna (Eds.), *Equality, Diversity and Disadvantage in Employment*. Palgrave Macmillan. doi:10.1057/9780333977880_3

Cotter, M. J., & Henley, J. A. (2017). Gender Contrasts in Negotiation Impasse Rates. *Management, 12*(1).

Cowton, C., & Crisp, R. (1998). *Business ethics: perspectives on the practice of theory*. Oxford University Press.

Creswell, J. W. (2002). *Educational research: Planning, conducting and evaluating quantitative and qualitative research*. Pearson.

Creswell, J. W., & Poth, C. N. (2016). *Qualitative Inquiry and Research Design: Choosing Among Five Approaches. Sage.*

Cui, J., Jo, H., Na, H., & Velasquez, M. (2015). Workforce Diversity and Religiosity. *Journal of Business Ethics, 128*(4), 743–767. doi:10.100710551-013-1984-8

Cullen, J. B., Parboteeah, K. P., & Victor, B. (2003). The effects of ethical climates on organizational commitment: A two-study analysis. *Journal of Business Ethics*, *46*(2), 127–141. doi:10.1023/A:1025089819456

Cutting, M., & Walsh, M. (2008). Religiosity Scales: What Are We Measuring in Whom? *Archive of Psychology of Religion, Volume, 30*(1), 137–154. doi:10.1163/157361208X317006

Daniel, J. L. (2010). The effect of workplace spirituality on team effectiveness. *Journal of Management Development, 29*(5), 442–456.

Dantley, M. E. (2005). The power of critical spirituality to act and to reform. *Journal of School Leadership*, *15*(5), 500–518. doi:10.1177/105268460501500502

Dauri, R. (2009). *Islam dan Nilai*. Pustaka Felichia.

Davie, G. (1990). Believing without belonging: Is this the future of religion in Britain? *Social Compass*, *37*(4), 455–469. doi:10.1177/003776890037004004

Davie, G. H. (2002). *Europe: The exceptional case. Parameters of faith in the modern world.* Darton, Longman and Todd Ltd.

Dawkins, S., Martin, A., Scott, J., & Sanderson, K. (2015). Advancing conceptualization and measurement of psychological capital as a collective construct. *Human Relations, 68*(6), 925–949. doi:10.1177/0018726714549645

Definitions, Compliance Manual Section 12. (n.d.). *The U.S. Equal Employment Opportunity Commission.* Retrieved May 2021, from www.eeoc.gov/policy/docs/religion.html#_Toc203359487

Dein, S. (2005). Spirituality, psychiatry and participation: A cultural analysis. *Transcultural Psychiatry, 42*(4), 526–544. doi:10.1177/1363461505058909 PMID:16570516

DeKlerk, J. J. (2005). Sprituality, Meaning in Life and Work WeUness: A Research Agenda. *The International Journal of Organizational Analysis, 13*(1), 64–88. doi:10.1108/eb028998

Delbecq, A. L. (1999). Christian spirituality and contemporary business leadership. *Journal of Organizational Change Management, 12*(4), 345–349. doi:10.1108/09534819910282180

Den Hartog, D. N., House, R. J., Hanges, P. J., Ruiz-Quintanilla, S. A., Dorfman, P. W., Abdalla, I. A., ... Zhou, J. (1999). Culture specific and cross-culturally generalizable implicit leadership theories: Are attributes of charismatic/transformational leadership universally endorsed? *The Leadership Quarterly, 10*(2), 219–256.

Dent, E. B., Higgins, M. E., & Wharff, D. M. (2005). Spirituality and leadership: An empirical review of definitions, distinctions, and embedded assumptions. *The Leadership Quarterly, 16*(5), 625–653. doi:10.1016/j.leaqua.2005.07.002

Dhiman, S. (2017). Leadership and spirituality. In *Leadership today* (pp. 139–160). Springer. doi:10.1007/978-3-319-31036-7_8

Diener, E. (2009). Subjective well-being. *The science of well-being*, 11-58.

Djafri, F., & Noordin, K. (2017). The impact of workplace spirituality on organizational commitment: A case study of Takaful agents in Malaysia. *Humanomics, 33*(3), 384–396.

Doherty, E. P. (2011). *Leading with love: the confluence of spirituality and leadership in college students* (Doctoral Dissertation). Loyola University Chicago, Chicago, IL.

Dökmen, G., & Yeşilyurt, Ş. (2015). Islamic finance system in the context of religion and economy: The comparison with today's fiscal system. In *International Congress on Islamic Economics and Finance* (pp. 331-347). Academic Press.

Donaldson, S., Dollwet, M., & Rao, M. (2014). Happiness, excellence, and optimal human functioning revisited: Examining the peer-reviewed literature linked to positive psychology. *The Journal of Positive Psychology, 10*(3), 185–195. doi:10.1080/17439760.2014.943801

Dougherty, T. J. (2011). *The relationship between spirituality, spiritual intelligence, and leadership practices in student leaders in the BYU-Idaho student activities program.* Idaho State University.

Downe, J., Cowell, R., & Morgan, K. (2016). What determines ethical behavior in public organizations: Is it rules or leadership? *Public Administration Review*, *76*(6), 898–909. doi:10.1111/puar.12562

Drucker, P. F. (1985). The discipline of innovation. *Harvard Business Review*, *63*(3), 67–72. PMID:10272260

Duchon, D., & Plowman, D. A. (2005). Nurturing the spirit at work: Impact on work unit performance. *The Leadership Quarterly*, *16*(5), 807–833. doi:10.1016/j.leaqua.2005.07.008

Duffy, R. D. (2006). Spirituality, religion, and career development: Current status and future directions. *The Career Development Quarterly*, *55*, 52–63.

Duffy, R. D., & Blustein, D. L. (2005). The relationship between spirituality, religiousness, and career adaptability. *Journal of Vocational Behavior*, *67*(3), 429–440.

Duffy, R. D., & Sedlacek, W. E. (2007). The presence of and search for a calling: Connections to career development. *Journal of Vocational Behavior*, *70*(3), 590–601. doi:10.1016/j.jvb.2007.03.007

Duffy, R., Allan, B., Autin, K., & Douglass, R. (2014). Living a Calling and Work Well-Being: A Longitudinal Study. *Journal of Counseling Psychology*, *61*(4), 605–615. doi:10.1037/cou0000042 PMID:25181588

DuFour, R. (2004). Leadership is an affair of the heart. *The Learning Professional*, *25*(1), 67.

Dugan, J. P., & Komives, S. R. (2011). Leadership theories. *The handbook for student leadership development*, 35-57.

Durmuş, Z. (2002). Kur'ân'a göre insanın ilişkilerinde sorumlu olduğu temel ahlâkî ilke: Ahde vefâ. *Dinbilimleri Akademik Araştırma Dergisi*, *2*(2), 77–95.

Düşmezkalender, E., Secilmis, C., & Yilmaz, V. (2020). The effect of Islamic work ethic on person-organization fit and workplace deviance in hotels. *International Journal of Islamic and Middle Eastern Finance and Management*, *14*(1), 164–182. doi:10.1108/IMEFM-05-2019-0198

Ebert, R. J., & Griffin, R. W. (2019). *Business essential* (12th ed.). Pearson.

Egel, E., & Fry, L. W. (2017). Spiritual Leadership as a Model for Islamic Leadership. *Public Integrity*, *19*(1), 77–95. doi:10.1080/10999922.2016.1200411

Elangovan, A. R., Pinder, C., & McLean, M. (2010). Callings and organizational behavior. *Journal of Vocational Behavior*, *76*(3), 428–440. doi:10.1016/j.jvb.2009.10.009

Elias, S., Cole, B., & Wilson-Jones, L. (2018). Leadership and spirituality: Conceptualization, definition and future directions in higher education. *Journal of Research Initiatives*, *3*(3), 3.

Ellison, M. T. (2007). *A qualitative study investigating how spirituality impacts African American male leaders in higher education* (Doctoral dissertation). Roosevelt University.

Emmons, R. A. (1999). Religion in the psychology of personality: An introduction. *Journal of Personality*, *67*(6), 874–888. doi:10.1111/1467-6494.00076

Epstein, E. M. (2002). Religion and business–the critical role of religious traditions in management education. *Journal of Business Ethics*, *38*(1), 91–96. doi:10.1023/A:1015712827640

Eren, S. S., & Hayatoğlu, Ö. (2011). The effect of ethical climate on salesperson's job attitudes, and job performance: An application in pharmaceutical sector. *ZKU Journal of Social Sciences*, *7*(14), 109–128.

Etherington, M. (2019). Religion as a Workplace Issue: A Narrative Inquiry of Two People—One Muslim and the Other Christian. *SAGE Open*, *9*(3). doi:10.1177/2158244019862729

Ethics Resource Center. (2005). *The 2005 National Business Ethics Survey*. Ethics Resource Center.

Fairholm, G. W. (1996). Spiritual leadership: Fulfilling whole-self needs at work. *Leadership and Organization Development Journal*, *17*(5), 11–17. doi:10.1108/01437739610127469

Fairholm, G. W. (1997). *Capturing the heart of leadership: Spirituality and community in the new American workplace*. Praeger Publishers.

Fairholm, G. W. (1998). *Perspectives on leadership: From the science of management to its spiritual heart*. Quorum Books.

Fairlie, P. (2011). Meaningful Work, Employee Engagement, and Other Key Employee Outcomes: Implications for Human Resource Development. *Advances in Developing Human Resources*, *13*(4), 508–525. doi:10.1177/1523422311431679

Fatima, S., Sharif, S., & Khalid, I. (2018). How does religiosity enhance psychological well-being? Roles of self-efficacy and perceived social support. *Psychology of Religion and Spirituality*, *10*(2), 119–127. doi:10.1037/rel0000168

Fatmah, N. (2018). *Pembentukan Karakter dalam Pendidikan*. https://core.ac.uk/download/pdf/276532588.pdf

Fawcett, S. E., Brau, J. C., Rhoads, G. K., Whitlark, D., & Fawcett, A. M. (2008). Spirituality and organizational culture: Cultivating the ABCs of an inspiring workplace. *International Journal of Public Administration*, *31*(4), 420–438. doi:10.1080/01900690701590819

Fernandez, J. A. (2004). The gentleman's code of Confucius: Leadership by values. *Organizational Dynamics*, *33*(1), 21–21. doi:10.1016/j.orgdyn.2003.11.007

Fernando, M. (2011). *Spirituality and leadership*. Academic Press.

Fernando, M., & Chowdhury, R. M. (2010). The relationship between spiritual well-being and ethical orientations in decision making: An empirical study with business executives in Australia. *Journal of Business Ethics*, *95*(2), 211–225. doi:10.100710551-009-0355-y

Ferrell, O. C., Linda, F., & Fraedrich, J. F. (2004). *Business ethics: Ethical decision making and cases*. South-Western Cengage Learning.

Forest, J., Mageau, G.A., Sarrazin, C., & Morin, E.M. (2011). "Work is my passion": The different affective, behavioural, and cognitive consequences of harmonious and obsessive passion toward work. *Canadian Journal of Administrative Sciences-revue Canadienne Des Sciences De L Administration, 28*, 27–40.

Fox, M. (1994). *The reinvention of work: A new vision of livelihood for our time*. Harper.

Fradelos, E. C., Latsou, D., Mitsi, D., Tsaras, K., Lekka, D., Lavdaniti, M., Tzavella, F., & Papathanasiou, I. V. (2018). Assessment of the relation between religiosity, mental health, and psychological resilience in breast cancer patients. *Contemporary Oncology (Poznan, Poland), 22*(3), 172–177. doi:10.5114/wo.2018.78947 PMID:30455589

Frederick, W. C. (2006). *Corporation, be good! The story of corporate social responsibility*. Dog Ear Publishing.

Freeman, G. T. (2011). Spirituality and servant leadership: A conceptual model and research proposal. *Emerging Leadership Journeys, 4*(1), 120-140.

Freeman, R. E. (2010). *Strategic management: A stakeholder approach*. Cambridge University Press. doi:10.1017/CBO9781139192675

French, J. R. P., Jr., & Raven, B. (1959). The bases of social power. In Studies in social power (pp. 250-167). University of Michigan.

Frunza, S. (2017). Ethical leadership, religion and personal development in the context of global crisis. *Journal for the Study of Religions and Ideologies, 16*(46), 3–16. http://jsri.ro/ojs/index.php/jsri/article/view/827

Fry, L. W. (2005). Toward a theory of ethical and spiritual well-being and corporate social responsibility through spiritual leadership. In *Positive psychology in business ethics and corporate responsibility*. Academic Press.

Fry, L. W. (2005). Toward a theory of ethical and spiritual well-being, and corporate social responsibility through spiritual leadership. Academic Press.

Fry, L. W. (2005a). Toward a theory of ethical and spiritual well-being and corporate social responsibility through spiritual leadership. In *Positive psychology in business ethics and corporate responsibility*. Academic Press.

Fry, L. W. (2008). Spiritual leadership: State-of-the-art and future directions for theory, research, and practice. In Spirituality in business (pp. 106-124). Palgrave Macmillan.

Fry, L. W., & Matherly, L. L. (2006, August). Spiritual leadership and organizational performance: An exploratory study. *Annual Meeting of the Academy of Management.* http://www. tarleton.edu/~ fry/sltorgperf. pdf

Fry, L. W., & Whittington, J. L. (2005). In search of authenticity: Spiritual leadership theory as a source for future theory, research, and practice on authentic leadership. *Authentic leadership theory and practice: Origins, effects and development, 3*, 183-200.

Fry, L. W., Matherly, L. L., & Vitucci, S. (2006). Spiritual leadership theory as a source for future theory, research, and recovery from workaholism. *Research companion to working time and work addiction*, 330.

Fry, L. W. (2003). Toward a theory of spiritual leadership. *The Leadership Quarterly*, *14*(6), 693–727. doi:10.1016/j.leaqua.2003.09.001

Fry, L. W. (2005). Introduction to the leadership quarterly special issue: Toward a paradigm of spiritual leadership. *The Leadership Quarterly*, *16*(5), 619–622. doi:10.1016/j.leaqua.2005.07.001

Fry, L. W., & Cohen, M. P. (2009). Spiritual leadership as a paradigm for organizational transformation and recovery from extended work hours cultures. *Journal of Business Ethics*, *84*(2), 265–278.

Fry, L. W., Hannah, S. T., Noel, M., & Walumbwa, F. O. (2011). Impact of spiritual leadership on unit performance. *The Leadership Quarterly*, *22*(2), 259–270. doi:10.1016/j.leaqua.2011.02.002

Fry, L. W., & Slocum, J. W. Jr. (2008). Maximizing the triple bottom line through spiritual leadership. *Organizational Dynamics*, *37*(1), 86–96. doi:10.1016/j.orgdyn.2007.11.004

Fry, L. W., Vitucci, S., & Cedillo, M. (2005). Spiritual leadership and army transformation: Theory, measurement, and establishing a baseline. *The Leadership Quarterly*, *16*(5), 835–862. doi:10.1016/j.leaqua.2005.07.012

Gait, A. H., & Worthington, A. C. (2007). *A Primer on Islamic Finance: Definitions*. Sources, Principles and Methods.

Garcia-Zamor, J. C. (2003). Workplace spirituality and organizational performance. *Public Administration Review*, *63*(3), 355–363. doi:10.1111/1540-6210.00295

Gardner, W. L., & Schermerhorn, J. R. Jr. (2004). Unleashing individual potential. *Organizational Dynamics*, *3*(33), 270–281. doi:10.1016/j.orgdyn.2004.06.004

Gardner, W., Cogliser, C., Davis, K., & Dickens, M. (2011). Authentic leadership: A review of the literature and research agenda. *The Leadership Quarterly*, *22*(6), 1120–1145. doi:10.1016/j.leaqua.2011.09.007

Geaney, M. M. (2004). *Spirituality and business transformation: Exploring spirituality with executive leaders* (Doctoral dissertation). Union Institute and University.

Geaney, M. M. (2012, June). A spirituality leadership competency model: What does it take to be a spiritual business leader. In *8th International Conference on Catholic Social Thought and Management Education*. University of Dayton.

Geh, E. Z. (2014). The organizational spiritual leadership of worlds. *Leadership and Organization Development Journal*.

Geldenhuys, M., Łaba, K., & Venter, C. M. (2014). Meaningful work, work engagement and organisational commitment. *SA Journal of Industrial Psychology*, *40*(1). Advance online publication. doi:10.4102ajip.v40i1.1098

Gellman, L. (2013). Investing as a religious practice. *The Wall Street Journal.*

Giacalone, R., Jurkiewicz, C., & Fry, L. (2005). From advocacy to science. *Psychology of Religion and Spirituality*, 515–528.

Gill, R. (2006). Theory and practice of leadership. *Sage (Atlanta, Ga.).*

Glasner, P. (1977). *The sociology of secularisation. A critique of a concept.* Routledge & Kegan Paul.

Glock C. Y. (1962). On the study of religious commitment. *Religious Education, 57*, S98-S110.

Goel, P., & Misra, R. (2020). It's not inter-religiosity but intra-religiosity that really matters in attitude towards business ethics: Evidence from India. *International Journal of Ethics and Systems*, *36*(2), 167–184. doi:10.1108/IJOES-10-2018-0153

Golafshani, N. (2003). Understanding Reliability and Validity in Qualitative Research. *Qualitative Report*, *8*(4), 597–607.

Golestanipour, M. (2016). Simple and multiple relationships between ethical leadership, transformational leadership and ethical climate and organizational spirituality among the employees of the Iran national steel industrial group. *Review of European Studies*, *8*(2), 183. doi:10.5539/res.v8n2p183

Görgens-Ekermans, G., & Herbert, M. (2013). Psychological capital: Internal and external validity of the Psychological Capital Questionnaire (PCQ-24) on a South African sample. *SA Journal of Industrial Psychology, 39*(2).

Grant, A. M., Christianson, M. K., & Price, R. H. (2007). Happiness, health, or relationships? Managerial practices and employee well-being tradeoffs. *The Academy of Management Perspectives*, *21*(3), 51–63. doi:10.5465/amp.2007.26421238

Greenberg, J. (1977). The Protestant work ethic and reactions to negative performance evaluations on a laboratory task. *The Journal of Applied Psychology*, *62*(6), 682–690. doi:10.1037/0021-9010.62.6.682

Griffin, R. W. & Moorhead, G. (2014). *Organizational Behavior.* Cengage Learning.

Gruman, J. A., & Saks, A. M. (2011). Performance management and employee engagement. *Human Resource Management Review*, *21*(2), 123–136. doi:10.1016/j.hrmr.2010.09.004

Gupta, M., & Mikkilineni, S. (2018). Spirituality and Employee Engagement at Work. In S. Dhiman, G. Roberts, & J. Crossman (Eds.), The Palgrave Handbook of Workplace Spirituality and Fulfillment. Academic Press.

Haj, J. (1986). *Nadhrayat Al-Mahraifah Fi Al-islam* [An Epistemological Theory in Islam]. Al-Alfaen Press.

Halbesleben, J. R. B., & Bowler, W. M. (2007). Emotional exhaustion and job performance: The mediating role of motivation. *The Journal of Applied Psychology*, *91*(1), 93–106. doi:10.1037/0021-9010.92.1.93 PMID:17227154

Haldorai, K., Kim, W. G., Chang, H. S., & Li, J. J. (2020). Workplace spirituality as a mediator between ethical climate and workplace deviant behavior. *International Journal of Hospitality Management*, *86*, 102372. doi:10.1016/j.ijhm.2019.102372

Hamid, A. (2016). Metode Internalisasi Nilai-Nilai Akhlak Dalam Pembelajaran Pendidikan Agama Islam Di Smp Negeri 17 Kota Palu. *Jurnal Pendidikan Agama Islam – Ta'lim*, *14*(2), 195-206.

Hamimah, K. (2018). Nilai-Nilai Islam Dalam Program Pemulihan Dan Rawatan Dadah Di Pengasih. *Islamiyyat*, *40*(2), 141–149.

Harlos, K. P. (2000). Toward a spiritual pedagogy: Meaning, practice, and applications in management education. *Journal of Management Education*, *24*(5), 612–627.

Haron, H., Jamil, N. N., & Ramli, N. M. (2020). Western and Islamic Values and Ethics: Are They Different? *Journal of Governance and Integrity*, *4*(1), 12–28. doi:10.15282/jgi.4.1.2020.5609

Harris, P. L. A. (2007). *School experiences of principals perceived as spiritual leaders and how they reflect the emerging paradigm of spiritual leadership*. Lamar University-Beaumont.

Harter, J. K., Schmidt, F. L., Asplund, J. W., Killham, E. A., & Agrawal, S. (2010). Causal Impact of Employee Work Perceptions on the Bottom Line of Organizations. *Perspectives on Psychological Science*, *5*(4), 378–389. doi:10.1177/1745691610374589 PMID:26162184

Harter, J. K., Schmidt, F. L., & Hayes, T. L. (2002). Business-unit-level relationship between employee satisfaction, employee engagement, and business outcomes: A meta-analysis. *The Journal of Applied Psychology*, *87*(2), 268–279. doi:10.1037/0021-9010.87.2.268 PMID:12002955

Hashemi, N., Marzban, M., Sebar, B., & Harris, N. (2020). Religious identity and psychological well-being among middle-eastern migrants in Australia: The mediating role of perceived social support, social connectedness, and perceived discrimination. *Psychology of Religion and Spirituality*, *12*(4), 475–486. doi:10.1037/rel0000287

Hasrul, M., & Fauzi, M. (2015, February). Nilai-Nilai Penting Individu Muslim Menurut Al-Ghazali. *Jurnal Islam Dan Masyarakat Kontemporari*, *9*, 41–60.

Hassan, M. K., & Aliyu, S. (2018). A contemporary survey of islamic banking literature. *Journal of Financial Stability*, *34*(1), 12–43. doi:10.1016/j.jfs.2017.11.006

Hastings, R. R. (2021). *HR seeks balance in handling religion in the workplace*. SHRM. Retrieved July, 2021, from https://www.shrm.org/hr-today/news/hr-news/pages/handlingreligioninworkplace.aspx

Hawley, J. (1993). *Reawakening the spirit in work: The power of dharmic management*. Berrett Koehler Publishers.

Hayati, K., & Caniago, I. (2012). Islamic work ethic: The role of intrinsic motivation, job satisfaction, organizational commitment and job performance. *Procedia: Social and Behavioral Sciences*, *65*(3), 1102–1106. doi:10.1016/j.sbspro.2014.05.148

Hayes, A. L. (2015). The role of cultural contexts in research design decisions. *SAGE Open*, *5*(2). doi:10.1177/2158244015583336

Heintzman, P., & Mannell, R. C. (2003). Spiritual functions of leisure and spiritual well-being: Coping with time pressure. *Leisure Sciences*, *25*(2-3), 207–230.

Héliot, Y. F., Gleibs, I. H., Coyle, A., Rousseau, D. M., & Rojon, C. (2020). Religious identity in the workplace: A systematic review, research agenda, and practical implications. *Human Resource Management*, *59*(2), 153–173. doi:10.1002/hrm.21983

Hellriegel, D., Slocum, J. W., Jr., & Woodman, R. W. (2001). Organizational behavior (9th ed.). South-Western College Publishing.

Hermans, C. A. M., & Koerts, E. (2013). Towards a model of influence of spirituality on leadership: Empirical research of school leaders on Catholic schools in the Netherlands. *Journal of Beliefs & Values*, *34*(2), 204–219. doi:10.1080/13617672.2013.801685

Hewlin, P. F., Karelaia, N., Kouchaki, M., & Sedikides, C. (2020). Authenticity at work: Its shapes, triggers, and consequences. *Organizational Behavior and Human Decision Processes*, *158*, 80–82. doi:10.1016/j.obhdp.2020.01.010

Hicks, D. A. (2002). Spiritual and religious diversity in the workplace. *The Leadership Quarterly*, *13*(4), 379–396. doi:10.1016/S1048-9843(02)00124-8

Hicks, D. A. (2003). *Religion and the workplace: Pluralism, spirituality, leadership*. Cambridge University Press. doi:10.1017/CBO9780511615474

Hidayat, S. E., & Abduh, M. (2012). Does Financial Crisis Give Impacts on Bahrain Islamic Banking Performance? A Panel Regression Analysis. *International Journal of Economics and Finance*, *4*(7), 79–87. doi:10.5539/ijef.v4n7p79

Hill, P. C., Pargament, K. I., Hood, R. W., McCullough, J. M. E., Swyers, J. P., Larson, D. B., & Zinnbauer, B. J. (2000). Conceptualizing religion and spirituality: Points of commonality, points of departure. *Journal for the Theory of Social Behaviour*, *30*(1), 51–77. doi:10.1111/1468-5914.00119

Hinds, R. S. (2005). Consideration of the relationship between spiritual well-being and transformational leadership. *The Journal of Applied Management and Entrepreneurship*, *10*(2), 124.

Hofstede, G. (1991). *Cultures and Organizations: Software of the Mind*. McGraw-Hill.

Ho, J. A. (2010). Ethical perception: Are differences between ethnic groups situation dependent? *Business Ethics (Oxford, England)*, *19*(2), 154–182. doi:10.1111/j.1467-8608.2010.01583.x

Homaei, R., Bozorgi, Z. D., Ghahfarokhi, M. S., & Hosseinpour, S. (2016). Relationship between Optimism, Religiosity and Self-Esteem with Marital Satisfaction and Life Satisfaction. *International Education Studies, 9*(6), 53–61. doi:10.5539/ies.v9n6p53

Hoole, C., & Bonnema, J. (2015). Work engagement and meaningful work across generational cohorts. *SA Journal of Human Resource Management, 13*(1). Advance online publication. doi:10.4102ajhrm.v13i1.681

Houston, G. G. (2014). *Spirituality and leadership: Integrating spirituality as a developmental approach of improving overall leader effectiveness* (Doctoral dissertation). Antioch University.

Hoyle, J. R. (2002). The highest form of leadership. *School Administrator, 59*(8), 18–21.

Hungelmann, J., Kenkel-Rossi, E., Klassen, L., & Stollenwerk, R. M. (1985). Spiritual well-being in older adults: Harmonious interconnectedness. *Journal of Religion and Health, 24*(2), 147–153. doi:10.1007/BF01532258 PMID:24306074

Hunter, I., Dika, B., & Banning, J. (2010). College students' perceptions of calling in work and life: A qualitative analysis. *Journal of Vocational Behavior, 76*(2), 178–186. doi:10.1016/j.jvb.2009.10.008

Hunt, S. D., & Vitell, S. (1986). A general theory of marketing ethics. *Journal of Macromarketing, 6*(1), 5–16. doi:10.1177/027614678600600103

Hwang, R., Ku, N., Mao, H., & Lo, S. (1996). Hope and related factors of breast cancer women. *Nurs Res (China), 4*(1), 35–46.

Ilies, T., Morgeson, F., & Nahrgang, J. (2005). Authentic leadership and eudaemonic well-being: Understanding leader–follower outcomes. *The Leadership Quarterly, 16*(3), 373–394. doi:10.1016/j.leaqua.2005.03.002

Ivancevich, J. M., Konopaske, R., & Matteson, M. T. (2014). *Organizational Behavior & Management*. McGraw-Hill Irwin.

Izak, M. (2009). Spirituality in organization: A dubious idea (?): Historically oriented sensemaking in spiritually imbued organizations. *Tamara, 8*(1/2), 73–88.

Jaques, E. (1976). *A general theory of bureaucracy*. Halsted Press.

Javanmard, G. (2013). Religious Beliefs and Resilience in Academic Students. *Procedia: Social and Behavioral Sciences, 84*, 744–748. doi:10.1016/j.sbspro.2013.06.638

Jodi, K. H. M. (2018). Nilai-nilai Islam dalam Program Pemulihan dan Rawatan Dadah di Pengasih. *International Journal of Islamic Studies, 40*(2), 141–149.

Johns, G. (2006). The essential impact of context on organizational behavior. *Academy of Management Review, 31*(2), 386–408.

Jonathan, W. P. G., Ong, K. L., & Hairon, S. (2009). A cross-cultural investigation of teachers' and reporting officers' self-ratings on teaching and leadership skills across Singapore and Bahrain. *International Journal of Educational Research*, *48*(4), 258–273. doi:10.1016/j.ijer.2009.12.001

Jones, A. D. (2010). *Leadership and spirituality: The indivisible leadership of African American school administrators as pastors* (Doctoral thesis). Iowa State University.

Jones, G. R., & Gerorge, J. M. (2003). *Contemporary Management* (3rd ed.). McGraw-Hill Irwin.

Jones-Johnson, N. F. (2001). *The relationship between spirituality and leadership practices of female administrators in higher education* (Doctoral dissertation). Baylor University.

Jones, T. M., Felps, W., & Bigley, G. A. (2007). Ethical theory and stakeholder related decisions: The role of stakeholder culture. *Academy of Management Review*, *32*(1), 137–155. doi:10.5465/amr.2007.23463924

Judge, T., Heller, D., & Mount, M. (2002). Five-factor model of personality and job satisfaction: A meta-analysis. *The Journal of Applied Psychology*, *87*(3), 530–541. doi:10.1037/0021-9010.87.3.530 PMID:12090610

Julian Casablancas Quotes. (n.d.). *BrainyQuote.com*. Retrieved September, 2021, from BrainyQuote.com Web site: https://www.brainyquote.com/quotes/julian_casablancas_404685

Kahn, W. (1990). Psychological Conditions of Personal Engagement and Disengagement at Work. *Academy of Management Journal*, *33*(4), 692–724.

Kalliny, M., & Gentry, L. (2007). Cultural values reflected in Arab and American Television Advertising. *Journal of Current Issues and Research in Advertising*, *29*(1), 15–32. doi:10.1080/10641734.2007.10505205

Karagül, M. (2012). Akhism and social capital context of the business ethic and production. *Akademik Bakış Dergisi*, *32*, 1–16.

KarakasF. (2006). Towards a universal set of values bridging east and west: Global positive spirituality for world peace. Available at SSRN 976770.

Karakas, F. (2010). Spirituality and performance in organizations: A literature review. *Journal of Business Ethics*, *94*(1), 89–106. doi:10.100710551-009-0251-5

Kassarjian, H. H. (1977). Content analysis in consumer research. *The Journal of Consumer Research*, *4*(1), 8–18. doi:10.1086/208674

Katz, D., & Kahn, R. L. (1978). *The social psychology of organizations* (Vol. 2). Wiley.

Kavoossi, M. (2000). *The Globalization of Business and the Middle East: Opportunities and constraints*. Quorum Books.

Kayadibi, F. (2007). The dinamic forces of development in Islam. *Darulfunun İlahiyat*, *15*, 1–24.

Kemas, O. H. (2017). The Islamic Education Methods in Al-Quran. *Ta'dib. Journal of Islamic Education, 22*(1), 48–57.

Kernis, M. H., & Goldman, B. M. (2006). A multicomponent conceptualization of authenticity: Theory and research. In M. P. Zanna (Ed.), Advances in experimental social psychology (Vol. 38, pp. 283–357). doi:10.1016/S0065-2601(06)38006-9

Keyes, C. L. M. (2002). The mental health continuum: From languishing to flourishing in life. *Journal of Health and Social Behavior, 43*(2), 207–222. doi:10.2307/3090197 PMID:12096700

Khalid, F., Mirza, S. S., Bin-Feng, C., & Saeed, N. (2020). Learning Engagements and the Role of Religion. *SAGE Open, 10*(1). Advance online publication. doi:10.1177/2158244019901256

Khan, F. (2010). How 'Islamic' is Islamic Banking? *Journal of Economic Behavior & Organization, 76*(3), 805–820. doi:10.1016/j.jebo.2010.09.015

Khani, A., Darvish, H., Miandari, K., & Arani, H. (2013). The role of spiritual leadership on empowering employees: A case study of educational system. *Management Science Letters, 3*(3), 1013-1018.

Khan, K., & Arshad, M. (2016). Impact of Islamic Work Ethics on employees' behavior: Case of Kabul based organizations, Afghanistan. *Abasyn Journal of Social Sciences, 9*(2), 366–375.

Kilmann, R. H., Saxton, M. J., & Serpa, R. (1985). *Gaining control of the corporate culture.* Jossey-Bass.

Kim, D., Fisher, D., & McCalman, D. (2009). Modernism, Christianity, and business ethics: A worldview perspective. *Journal of Business Ethics, 90*(1), 115–121. doi:10.100710551-009-0031-2

King, A. S. (1990). *Evolution of Leadership Theory.* in https://journals.sagepub.com/doi/pdf/10.1177/0256090919900205

Kingdom of Bahrain's National Portal. (n.d.). Retrieved May 2021, from https://www.bahrain.bh/new/en/home_en.html

King, S., & Nicol, D. M. (1999). Organizational enhancement through recognition of individual spirituality: Reflections of Jaques and Jung. *Journal of Organizational Change Management, 12*(3), 234–243. doi:10.1108/09534819910274026

King, W., & He, J. (2005). Understanding the role and methods of meta-analysis in IS research. *Communications of the Association for Information Systems, 16*, 665–686. doi:10.17705/1CAIS.01632

Kinicki, A., & Williams, B. K. (2020). Management (9th ed.). New York: McGraw-Hill Education.

Kitagava, J. (1985). *Comparative work ethics.* Library of Congress.

Kleinhandler, C. (2016). *Haredi Jewish start-up founder from Israel.* BBC Online. Retrieved from https://www.bbc.co.uk/news/magazine-37300929

Koburtay, T., & Alzoubi, A. (2021). The linkages between person-organization spirituality fit and workers' psychological well-being. *The Journal of Social Psychology*, *161*(1), 103–118. doi:10.1080/00224545.2020.1778618 PMID:32538323

Koburtay, T., & Syed, J. (2021). Do religion and spirituality matter for hotel workers' well-being and guests' happiness? An update of the Attraction-Selection-Attrition theory. *International Journal of Hospitality Management*, *95*, 102951. doi:10.1016/j.ijhm.2021.102951

Kolodinsky, R., Giacalone, R., & Jurkiewicz, C. (2008). Workplace Values and Outcomes: Exploring Personal, Organizational, and Interactive Workplace Spirituality. *Journal of Business Ethics*, *81*(2), 465–480. doi:10.100710551-007-9507-0

Komives, S. R., Mackie, M. M., Shalka, T. R., & Smith, M. (2020). Spirituality and Leadership: Research Supports the Connection. *New Directions for Student Leadership*, *2020*(166), 135–157. doi:10.1002/yd.20388 PMID:32543039

Konz, G. N., & Ryan, F. X. (1999). Maintaining an organizational spirituality: No easy task. *Journal of Organizational Change Management*, *12*(3), 200–210. doi:10.1108/09534819910273865

Korac-Kakabadse, N., Kouzmin, A., & Kakabadse, A. (2002). Spirituality and leadership praxis. *Journal of Managerial Psychology*, *17*(3), 165–182. doi:10.1108/02683940210423079

Kotter, J. P. (1996). Why transformation efforts fail. *Harvard Business Review*.

Kouzes, J. M., Posner, B. Z., & Maxwell, J. C. (2004). *Christian reflections on the leadership challenge*. Jossey-Bass.

Kram, K. E., Wasserman, I. C., & Yip, J. (2012). Metaphors of Identity and Professional Practice: Learning From the Scholar–Practitioner. *The Journal of Applied Behavioral Science*, *48*(3), 304–341. doi:10.1177/0021886312439097

Krause, N., & Ironson, G. (2019). Religious involvement, God images, and life satisfaction. *Mental Health, Religion & Culture*, *22*(1), 41–55. doi:10.1080/13674676.2019.1586860

Kriger, M., & Seng, Y. (2005). Leadership with inner meaning: A contingency theory of leadership based on the worldviews of five religions. *The Leadership Quarterly*, *16*(5), 771–806.

Krippendorff, K. (2004). Reliability in content analysis: Some common misconceptions and recommendations. *Human Communication Research*, *30*(3), 411–433. doi:10.1111/j.1468-2958.2004.tb00738.x

Krishnakumar, S., Houghton, J. D., Neck, C. P., & Ellison, C. N. (2015). The "good" and the "bad" of spiritual leadership. *Journal of Management, Spirituality & Religion*, *12*(1), 17–37. doi:10.1080/14766086.2014.886518

Krishnakumar, S., Houghton, J. D., Neck, C. P., & Ellison, C. N. (2015). The —good|| and the —bad|| of spiritual leadership. *Journal of Management, Spirituality & Religion*, *12*(1), 17–37.

Krishnakumar, S., & Neck, C. P. (2002). The "what", "why" and "how" of spirituality in the workplace. *Journal of Managerial Psychology, 17*(3), 153–164. doi:10.1108/02683940210423060

Kuh, G. D., & Umbach, P. D. (2004). College and character: Insights from the national survey of student engagement. *New Directions for Institutional Research, 2004*(122), 37–54. doi:10.1002/ir.108

Kumar, M., Rai, H., & Pati, S. P. (2009). An exploratory study on negotiating styles: Development of a measure. *Vikalpa, 34*(4), 37–50.

Kumar, N., & Rose, R. C. (2010). Examining the link between Islamic work ethic and innovation capability. *Journal of Management Development, 29*(1), 79–93. doi:10.1108/02621711011009081

Kurpis, L. V., Beqiri, M. S., & Helgeson, J. G. (2008). The effects of commitment to moral self-improvement and religiosity on ethics of business students. *Journal of Business Ethics, 80*(3), 447–463. doi:10.100710551-007-9430-4

Kurt, A. (2009). *İslam çalışma ahlakı*. Emin Yayınları.

Latham, J. R. (2013). A framework for leading the transformation to performance excellence part I: CEO perspectives on forces, facilitators, and strategic leadership systems. *The Quality Management Journal, 20*(2), 12–33. doi:10.1080/10686967.2013.11918095

Latham, J. R. (2014). Leadership for quality and innovation: Challenges, theories, and a framework for future research. *The Quality Management Journal, 21*(1), 11–15. doi:10.1080/10686967.2014.11918372

Lazar, A. (2010). Spirituality and job satisfaction among female Jewish Israeli hospital nurses. *Journal of Advanced Nursing, 66*(2), 334–344.

Lee, D. J., Sirgy, M. J., Efraty, D., & Siegel, P. (2003). A study of quality of work life, spiritual well-being, and life satisfaction. Handbook of workplace spirituality and organizational performance, 209-230.

Levy, R. B. (2000). My experience as participant in the course on spirituality for executive leadership. *Journal of Management Inquiry, 9*(2), 129–131.

Lewis, M., & Ponzio, V. (2016). Character Education as the Primary Purpose of Schooling for the Future. Jurnal Peuradeun Ilmiah. *International Multidisciplinary Journal, 4*(2), 137–146. doi:10.13140/RG.2.1.4076.2486

Lips-Wiersma, M., & Morrise, L. (2009). Discriminating between 'meaningful work' and the 'management of meaning. *Journal of Business Ethics, 88*(3), 491–511. doi:10.100710551-009-0118-9

Liu, C. H., & Robertson, P. J. (2011). Spirituality in the workplace: Theory and measurement. *Journal of Management Inquiry, 20*(1), 35–50. doi:10.1177/1056492610374648

LMRA Expat Management System (EMS). (n.d.). http://blmi.lmra.bh/2021/03/data/ems/Table_07a.xlsx

Locke, L. F., Silverman, S. J., & Spirduso, W. W. (2009). *Reading and understanding research.* SAGE.

Love, P., & Talbot, D. (1999). Defining spiritual development: A missing consideration for student affairs. *NASPA Journal, 37*(1). Advance online publication. doi:10.2202/0027-6014.1097

Lu, C. S., & Lin, C. C. (2014). The effects of ethical leadership and ethical climate on employee ethical behavior in the international port context. *Journal of Business Ethics, 124*(2), 209–223. doi:10.100710551-013-1868-y

Lundberg, C. C. (1988). Working with culture. *Journal of Organizational Change Management, 1*(2), 38–47. doi:10.1108/eb025598

Luria, G., & Yagil, D. (2008). Procedural justice, ethical climate and service outcomes in restaurants. *International Journal of Hospitality Management, 27*(2), 276–283. doi:10.1016/j.ijhm.2007.07.022

Luthans, F. (2002a). Positive organizational behavior: Developing and managing psychological strengths. *The Academy of Management Executive, 16*(1), 57–72. doi:10.5465/ame.2002.6640181

Luthans, F. (2002b). The need for and meaning of positive organizational behavior. *Journal of Organizational Behavior, 23*(6), 695–706. doi:10.1002/job.165

Luthans, F., & Avolio, B. (2009). The "point" of positive organizational behavior. *Journal of Organizational Behavior, 30*(2), 291–307. doi:10.1002/job.589

Luthans, F., Van Wyk, R., & Walumbwa, F. (2004). Recognition and development of hope for South African organizational leaders. *Leadership and Organization Development Journal, 25*(6), 512–527. doi:10.1108/01437730410556752

Luthans, F., & Youssef, C. M. (2007). Emerging positive organizational behavior. *Journal of Management, 33*(3), 321–349. doi:10.1177/0149206307300814

Luthans, F., Youssef, C. M., Sweetman, D. S., & Harms, P. D. (2013). Meeting the leadership challenge of employee well-being through relationship PsyCap and health PsyCap. *Journal of Leadership & Organizational Studies, 20*(1), 118–133. doi:10.1177/1548051812465893

Luthans, F., Youssef-Morgan, C. M., & Avolio, B. J. (2015). *Psychological Capital and Beyond.* Oxford University Press.

Lyon, S. B. (2004). *Spirituality and public school leadership* (Doctoral dissertation). Saint Louis University.

Ma, Z. (2005). *All negotiations are not perceived equal: the impact of culture and personality on cognitions, behaviors, and outcomes* (Doctoral dissertation). McGill University.

MacDonald, D. A. (2000). *The Expressions of Spirituality Inventory: Test development, validation and scoring information.* Unpublished test manual.

MacDonald, D. A., Friedman, H. L., Brewczynski, J., Holland, D., Salagame, K. K. K., Mohan, K. K., ... Cheong, H. W. (2015). Spirituality as a scientific construct: Testing its universality across cultures and languages. *PLoS One, 10*(3), e0117701.

Macey, W. H., & Schneider, B. (2008). The meaning of employee engagement. *Industrial and Organizational Psychology: Perspectives on Science and Practice, 1*(1), 3–30. doi:10.1111/j.1754-9434.2007.0002.x

Macon, G. K. Sr. (2014). *School leaders and spirituality: Perspectives of spirituality and spirituality's influence on principals in public schools in southeastern Louisiana*. Southeastern Louisiana University.

Magnusen, C. L. (2002). Spirituality and leadership effectiveness: Historical and philosophical trends. *Journal of Catholic Education, 6*(2), 251–258. doi:10.15365/joce.0602082013

Maharani, V., Surachman, S., & Sudiro, A. (2017). The Effect of Transformational Leadership on Organizational Citizenship Behavior Mediated by Job Satisfaction and Organizational Commitment (Study of Islamic Bank in Malang Raya). *International Journal of Economic Research, 14*(3), 213–226.

Mahgniya, M. J. (1982). *Ma'lam Al-Falsafa Al-Isslammiyyah [The major features of Islamic philosophy]*. Al-Hilal Library.

Malone, P. F., & Fry, L. W. (2003). *Transforming schools through spiritual leadership: A field experiment.* Academy of Management.

Malone, P. F., & Fry, L. W. (2003). Transforming schools through spiritual leadership: A field experiment. *Annual Meeting of the Academy of Management.*

Mandhur, I. (2003). *Lisan al-'Arab* [Language of the Arabs]. Dar 'Alam al-Kutub.

Mannan, M. A. (1986). *Islamic economics: Foundations of Islamic economics: Theory and practice*. Hodder and Stoughton.

Mark, G. T., Wheeler, C. A., & Hodgson, M. N. (2012). Leader spirituality and leader virtues as predictors of effective leadership. *Journal of Spirituality, Leadership and Management, 6*(1), 35–47.

Marques, J., Dhiman, S., & King, R. (2005). Spirituality in the workplace: Developing an integral model and a comprehensive definition. *The Journal of American Academy of Business, Cambridge, 7*, 81–91.

Marques, J., Dhiman, S., King, R., & Afshar, T. (2011). Toward greater spirituality in personal and professional life: The movement gains momentum during these challenging times. *Organization Development Journal, 29*(3), 67.

Marx, K., & Engels, F. (1992). *Alman İdeolojisi* (S. Belli, Trans.). Sol Yayınları. (Original work published 1932)

Masten, A. S., & Reed, M. G. (2002). Resilience in development. In C. R. Snyder & S. J. Lopez (Eds.), *Handbook of positive psychology* (pp. 74–80). Oxford University Press.

Mastuhu. (2008). *Sistem Pendidikan Nasional Visoner*. Jakarta: Lentera Hati.

Maurer, T. J., & Pierce, H. R. (1998). A comparison of Likert scale and traditional measures of self-efficacy. *The Journal of Applied Psychology*, *83*(2), 324–329. doi:10.1037/0021-9010.83.2.324

May, D. R., Gilson, R. L., & Harter, L. M. (2004). The Psychological Conditions of Meaningfulness, Safety and Availability and the Engagement of the Human Spirit at Work. *Journal of Occupational and Organizational Psychology*, *77*(1), 11–37. doi:10.1348/096317904322915892

Mayer, J. D. (2000). Spiritual intelligence or spiritual consciousness? *The International Journal for the Psychology of Religion*, *10*(1), 47–56. doi:10.1207/S15327582IJPR1001_5

Mazur, B. (2021). Organizational culture under religious influence. *A Closer Look at Organizational Culture in Action*. doi:10.5772/intechopen.90898

Mazur, B. (2015). Basic assumptions of organizational culture in religiously diverse environments. *International Journal of Contemporary Management*, *14*(3), 115–132.

McDaniel, S. W., & Burnett, J. J. (1990). Consumer religiosity and retail store evaluative criteria. *Journal of the Academy of Marketing Science*, *18*(2), 101–112. doi:10.1007/BF02726426

McEachern, A. (1984). *Organizational Illusions*. Shale Books.

McGhee, P., & Grant, P. (2008). Spirituality and ethical behavior in the workplace: Wishful thinking or authentic reality. *Electronic Journal of Business Ethics and Organization Studies*, *13*(2), 61–69.

McKee, A., & Morey, A. (2003). *Primal Leadership*. Macmillan Audio.

McLaughlin, C. (2005). Spirituality and ethics in business. *European Business Review*, *17*(1).

McNamara, T. (1998). Policy and social considerations in language assessment. *Annual Review of Applied Linguistics*, *18*, 304–319. doi:10.1017/S0267190500003603

McShane, S. L., & Von Glinow, M. A. (2010). *Organizational Behavior*. McGraw-Hill Irwin.

Memon, N. A. (2007). Islamic Banking: Present and Future Challenges. *Journal of Management and Social Sciences*, *3*(1), 1–10.

Merrens, M. R., & Garrett, J. B. (1975). The Protestant Ethic Scale as a predictor of repetitive work performance. *The Journal of Applied Psychology*, *60*(1), 125–127. doi:10.1037/h0076297 PMID:1110253

Meyer, L. D. (2005). *The relationship between principals' spiritual attitudes and transformational leadership* (Doctoral thesis). University of New Orleans.

Meyers, C. (2007). *Industrial psychology*. Garnsey Press.

Milal, A. D. U., Rohmah, Z., Kusumajanti, W., Basthomi, Y., Sholihah, D. N., & Susilowati, M. (2020). Integrating character education in the English teaching at Islamic Junior high schools in Indonesia. *TEFLIN Journal, 31*(1), 88–107. doi:10.15639/teflinjournal.v31i1/88-107

Miller, P. B. (2003). *An exploratory study of the ways principals perceive that their spirituality contributes to their leadership*. Academic Press.

Miller, A. (2008). A critique of positive psychology—Or 'the new science of happiness.'. *Journal of Philosophy of Education, 42*(3-4), 591–608. doi:10.1111/j.1467-9752.2008.00646.x

Miller, W. C., & Miller, D. R. (2002). *Spirituality: The emerging context for business leadership*. Global Dharma Center.

Milliman, J., Ferguson, J., Trickett, D., & Condemi, B. (1999). Spirit and community at Southwest Airlines. *Journal of Organizational Change Management, 12*(3), 221–233. doi:10.1108/09534819910273928

Mills, J., & Birks, M. (2014). *Qualitative Methodology: A Practical Guide*. SAGE. doi:10.4135/9781473920163

Mitroff, I. I., & Denton, E. A. (1999). *A spiritual audit of corporate America: A hard look at spirituality, religion, and values in the workplace*. Jossey-Bass.

Mitroff, I., & Denton, E. A. (1999). A Study of Spirituality in the Workplace. *Sloan Management Review, 40*, 83–92.

Momeni, K., & Shahbazi Rad, A. (2012). Relationship of spirituality, resiliency, and coping strategies with quality of life in university students. *Journal of Behavioral Science., 6*, 1–2.

Moorhead, G., & Griffin, R. S. (2011). Organizational Behavior (11th ed.). Academic Press.

Morris, T. (1997). *If Aristotle ran General Motors: The new soul of business*. Henry Holt and Company.

Muhdar & Rahma. (2015). The influence of spiritual intelligence, leadership, and organizational culture on organizational citizenship behavior: A study to Islamic bank in Makassar City. *Al-Ulum, 15*(1), 135 - 156.

Munn, S. L. (2013). Unveiling the Work–Life System: The Influence of Work–Life Balance on Meaningful Work. *Advances in Developing Human Resources, 15*(4), 401–417. doi:10.1177/1523422313498567

Murat, G., Dursun, S., & Şen, M. (2016). A view of industrial relations from Islamic perspective. *Ataturk University Journal of Economics & Administrative Sciences, 30*(5), 1031–1046.

Murrell-Jones, M. (2012). A spiritually based leadership approach in the retail environment to assist with the challenges of employee morale and retention. *Journal of Business and Retail Management Research, 7*(1), 1–11.

Musick, K. (2010). *Spirituality and school leadership: A grounded theory study*. Academic Press.

Nash, R. J., & Scott, L. (2009). Spirituality, religious pluralism, and higher education leadership development. *Rethinking leadership in a complex, multicultural, and global environment: New concepts and models for higher education*, 131-150.

Nasr, S. H. (1984). Islamic work ethics. *Hamdard Islamicus*, *7*(4), 25–35.

Nasr, S. H. (2009). Islamic work ethic. *Turkish Journal of Business Ethic*, *2*(3), 143–151.

Neal, J. A. (2001). Leadership and spirituality in the workplace. *Leadership theory, application, skill development*, 464-473.

Neal, A., & Griffin, M. A. (1999). Developing a model of individual performance for human resource management. *Asia Pacific Journal of Human Resources*, *37*(2), 44–59. doi:10.1177/103841119903700205

Neal, J. A. (1997). Spirituality in management education: A guide to resources. *Journal of Management Education*, *21*(1), 121–139. doi:10.1177/105256299702100111

Neo, J. L. (2018). Definitional imbroglios: A critique of the definition of religion and essential practice tests in religious freedom adjudication. *International Journal of Constitutional Law*, *16*(2), 574–595. doi:10.1093/icon/moy055

Newman, A., Herman, H. M., Schwarz, G., & Nielsen, I. (2018). The effects of employees' creative self-efficacy on innovative behavior: The role of entrepreneurial leadership. *Journal of Business Research*, *89*, 1–9. doi:10.1016/j.jbusres.2018.04.001

Nie, F. (2019). Religion and self-efficacy: A multilevel approach. *Mental Health, Religion & Culture*, *22*(3), 279–292. doi:10.1080/13674676.2019.1612337

Ningsih, T. (2019). Peran Pendidikan Islam dalam Membentuk Karakter Siswa di Era Revolusi Industri 4.0 Pada Madrasah Tsanawiyah Negeri 1 Banyumas. *Insania*, *24*(2), 220–231. Advance online publication. doi:10.24090/insania.v24i2.3049

Nolan-Arañez, S. I., & Ludvik, M. B. (2018). Positing a framework for cultivating spirituality through public university leadership development. *Journal of Research in Innovative Teaching & Learning*.

Nordin, W. M. Z. B. M. (2003). Peranan Pendidikan Islam dalam Falsafah Pendidikan Negara. In Memahami isu-isu pendidikan Islam di Malaysia (pp. 15-30). Kuala Lumpur: IKIM.

Norman, S., Avey, J., Nimnicht, J., & Pigeon, N. G. (2010). The interactive effects of psychological capital and organizational identity on employee citizenship and deviance behaviors. *Journal of Leadership & Organizational Studies*, *17*(4), 380–391. doi:10.1177/1548051809353764

Oates, K. L. M., Hall, M. E. L., & Anderson, T. L. (2005). Calling and conflict: A qualitative exploration of interrole conflict and the sanctification of work in Christian mothers in academia. *Journal of Psychology and Theology*, *33*(3), 210–223. doi:10.1177/009164710503300306

Oldenburg, D., & Bandsuch, M. (1997, May 7). The spirit at work: Companies should nurture the soul if they want more from employees. *The Detroit News*.

Omar, M. N. (2010). *Falsafah Akhlak, Penerbit Universiti Kebangsaan Malaysia*. Penerbit Universiti Kebangsaan Malaysia.

Omisore, B. O., & Nweke, A. N. (2014). The Influence of Power and Politics in Organizations. *International Journal of Academic Research in Business & Social Sciences*, *4*(7), 165–183. doi:10.6007/IJARBSS/v4-i7/997

Oruc, E., & Kutanis, O. (2015). The views of academic staff on psychological capital: A qualitative study in Turkey. *International Journal of Scientific Research and Innovative Technology*, *2*(5), 1–9.

Oumlil, A. B., & Balloun, J. L. (2009). Ethical decision-making differences between American and Moroccan managers. *Journal of Business Ethics*, *84*(4), 457–478. doi:10.100710551-008-9719-y

Ozer, D. J., & Benet-Martínez, V. (2006). Personality and the prediction of consequential outcomes. *Annual Review of Psychology*, *57*(1), 401–421. doi:10.1146/annurev.psych.57.102904.190127 PMID:16318601

Özgener, Ş. (2009). *İş ahlakının temelleri yönetsel bir yaklaşım* (2nd ed.). Nobel Yayınları.

Padayachee, N. K. D. (2010). *The application and relevance of spiritual leadership in the JSE top 40 companies* (Doctoral dissertation). University of Pretoria.

Pakdaman, M., & Balideh, M. (2020). The Study of the Effect of Psychological Capital and Spiritual Intelligence on the Performance of Individuals: A Review Study. *Archives of Pharmacy Practice (Mumbai)*, *11*(S1), 126–136.

Paloutzian, R. F. (1996). Understanding Religious Conversion (Book). *The International Journal for the Psychology of Religion*, *6*(3), 225–227. doi:10.120715327582ijpr0603_9

Parboteeah, K. P., Chen, H. C., Lin, Y. T., Chen, I. H., Lee, A. Y., & Chung, A. (2010). Establishing organizational ethical climates: How do managerial practices work? *Journal of Business Ethics*, *97*(4), 599–611. doi:10.100710551-010-0527-9

Parker, S. (1998). Enhancing role breadth self-efficacy: The roles of job enrichment and other organizational interventions. *The Journal of Applied Psychology*, *6*(6), 835–852. doi:10.1037/0021-9010.83.6.835 PMID:9885197

Paterson, T., Luthans, F., & Jeung, W. (2014). Thriving at work: Impact of psychological capital and supervisor support. *Journal of Organizational Behavior*, *35*(3), 434–446. doi:10.1002/job.1907

Peltonen, T. (2020). *16 The Role of Religion in Cross-Cultural Management: Three Perspectives*. The SAGE Handbook of Contemporary Cross-Cultural Management.

Perkins, G., Wellman, N., & Wellman, W. (2009). Educational leadership: The relationship between spirituality and leadership practices. *Academic Leadership: The Online Journal*, *7*(1), 14.

Perreault, W. D. Jr, & Leigh, L. E. (1989). Reliability of nominal data based on qualitative judgments. *JMR, Journal of Marketing Research, 26*(2), 135–148. doi:10.1177/002224378902600201

Petchsawang, P., & McLean, G. N. (2017). Workplace spirituality, mindfulness meditation, and work engagement. *Journal of Management, Spirituality & Religion, 14*(3), 216–244. doi:10.1080/14766086.2017.1291360

Peterson, C., & Seligman, M. E. P. (2004). *Character strengths and virtues: A classification and handbook.* New York: Oxford University Press.

Pew Research Center. (2015). *America's changing religious landscape*. Pew Research Publications.

Pfeffer, J. (2003). Business and the spirit. Handbook of workplace spirituality and organizational performance, 29-45.

Phau, I., & Kea, G. (2007). Attitudes of university students toward business ethics: A cross-national investigation of Australia, Singapore and Hong Kong. *Journal of Business Ethics, 72*(1), 61–75. doi:10.100710551-006-9156-8

Phipps, K. A. (2012). Spirituality and strategic leadership: The influence of spiritual beliefs on strategic decision making. *Journal of Business Ethics, 106*(2), 177–189. doi:10.100710551-011-0988-5

Pourghaznein, T., Hoshmand, P., Talasaz Firouzi, E., & Esmailli, H. (2003). The sources of inspiration and the level of hope among cancer patients. *Majallah-i Ravanpizishki va Ravanshinasi-i Balini-i Iran, 8*(4), 82–87.

Pratama, I. P., & Zulhijra. (2019). Reformasi Pendidikan Islam Indonesia. *Jurnal PAI Raden Fatah, 1*(1), 117-127.

Prayitno & Belferik, M. (2011). *Pendidikan Karakter dalam Pembangunan Bangsa*. Jakarta Grasindo.

Qasim, M., Irshad, M., Majeed, M., & Rizvi, S. T. H. (2021). Examining impact of Islamic work ethic on task performance: Mediating effect of psychological capital and a moderating role of ethical leadership. *Journal of Business Ethics*, 1–13. doi:10.100710551-021-04916-y

Qoyyimah, U. (2016). Inculcating character education through EFL teaching in Indonesian state schools. *Pedagogies, 11*(2), 109–126. doi:10.1080/1554480X.2016.1165618

Racelis, A. D. (2010). Relationship between employee perceptions of corporate ethics and organizational culture: An exploratory study. *Asia Pacific Management Review, 15*(2).

Rafiki, A., & Wahab, K. A. (2014). Islamic Values and Principles in the Organization: A Review of Literature. *Asian Social Science, 10*(9), 1–8. doi:10.5539/ass.v10n9p1

Rai, H. (2007). Dispute Handling Capability: Morphology and Modalities— Development of a Model. *Management and Labour Studies, 32*(2), 183–202.

Rai, H. (2013). The measurement of negotiating ability: Evidence from India. *Global Journal of Business Research*, *7*(4), 109–125.

Ramirez, L. R. (2009). *Spirituality in the Praxis of Educational Leadership: Four public school principals perspectives on leading through spirituality* (Doctoral dissertation). Texas Tech University.

Ravan, B. H. (1993). The bases of power: Origins and recent developments. *The Journal of Social Issues*, *49*(4), 227–251. doi:10.1111/j.1540-4560.1993.tb0119.x

Reave, L. (2005). Spiritual values and practices related to leadership effectiveness. *The Leadership Quarterly*, *16*(5), 655–687.

Renz, S. M., Carrington, J. M., & Badger, T. A. (2018). Two strategies for qualitative content analysis: An intramethod approach to triangulation. *Qualitative Health Research*, *28*(5), 824–831. doi:10.1177/1049732317753586 PMID:29424274

Riasudeen, S., & Singh, P. (2020). Leadership Effectiveness and Psychological Wellbeing: The Role of Workplace Spirituality. *Journal of Human Values*.

Ribeiro, M., Caldeira, S., Nunes, E., & Vieira, M. (2021). A commentary on spiritual leadership and workplace spirituality in nursing management. *Journal of Nursing Management*, *29*(3), 602–605. doi:10.1111/jonm.13196 PMID:33107658

Rice, G. (1999). Islamic ethics and the implications for business. *Journal of Business Ethics*, *18*(4), 345–358. doi:10.1023/A:1005711414306

Richardson, T. N. (2009). *The impact of spirituality on the leadership practices of African American women college presidents* (Doctoral dissertation). The George Washington University.

Richardson, G. (2002). The metatheory of resilience and resiliency. *Journal of Clinical Psychology*, *58*(3), 307–321. doi:10.1002/jclp.10020 PMID:11836712

Richardson, G., Neiger, B., Jensen, S., & Kumpfer, K. (1990). The resiliency model. *Health Education*, *21*(6), 33–39. doi:10.1080/00970050.1990.10614589

Riera, J. L. (2013). *Walking the labyrinth: Examining the intersection of spirituality and leadership among senior student affairs administrators* (Doctoral dissertation). University of Maryland, College Park.

Rivai, V., & Mulyadi, D. (2012). *Kepemimpinan dan Perilaku Organisasi Edisi Ketiga*. Jakarta: PT. Rajagrafindo Persada.

Roberts, S., Scherer, L., & Bowyer, C. (2011). Job Stress and Incivility: What Role Does Psychological Capital Play? *Journal of Leadership & Organizational Studies*, *18*(4), 449–458. doi:10.1177/1548051811409044

Rodrigues, H. P., & Harding, J. S. (2008). *Introduction to the Study of Religion*. Routledge. doi:10.4324/9780203891728

Rokhman, W. (2010). The effect of Islamic work ethics on work outcomes. *JBO - Electronic Journal of Business Ethics and Organization Studies, 15*(1), 21-27.

Roof, R. (2015). The association of individual spirituality on employee engagement: The Spirit at work. *Journal of Business Ethics, 130*(3), 585–599. doi:10.100710551-014-2246-0

Roof, W. C. (2001). *Spiritual marketplace: Baby boomers and the remaking of American religion.* Princeton University Press. doi:10.1515/9781400823086

Ruiz, R. (2005). *Spiritual dimension in educational leadership*. The University of Texas-Pan American.

Rust, R. T., & Cooil, B. (1994). Reliability measures for qualitative data: Theory and implications. *JMR, Journal of Marketing Research, 31*(1), 1–14. doi:10.1177/002224379403100101

Saban, D., Basalamah, S., Gani, A., & Rahman, Z. (2020). Impact of Islamic work ethics, competencies, compensation, work culture on job satisfaction and employee performance: The case of four star hotels. *European Journal of Business & Management Research, 5*(1), 1–8. doi:10.24018/ejbmr.2020.5.1.181

Sackmann, S. A. (1991). Uncovering culture in organizations. *The Journal of Applied Behavioral Science, 27*(3), 295–317. doi:10.1177/0021886391273005

Sadulloh, U. (2009). *Pengantar Filsafat Pendidikan*. Alfabeta.

Saeidi, M. S., Pour Ebrahim, T., Bagherian, F., & Mansour, L. (2010). The relationship between spirituality and resilience of families, the quality of communication in family mediation. *J Manag Syst, 2*, 63–79.

Saini, K. M., & Burton, O. (2020). Mindfulness and spirituality: an enhanced leadership perspective. In *New Horizons in Positive Leadership and Change* (pp. 229–248). Springer.

Saks, A. M. (2006). Antecedents and consequences of employee engagement. *Journal of Managerial Psychology, 21*(7), 600–619. doi:10.1108/02683940610690169

Salanova, M., Agut, S., & Peiró, J. M. (2005, November). Linking Organizational Resources and Work Engagement to Employee Performance and Customer Loyalty: The Mediation of Service Climate. *The Journal of Applied Psychology, 90*(6), 1217–1227. doi:10.1037/0021-9010.90.6.1217 PMID:16316275

Salleh, M. J. (2009). *The integrated Islamic education: Principles and need for thematic approaches.* Singapore: Singapore Islamic Education System Seminar.

San Martin, A., Sinaceur, M., Madi, A., Tompson, S., Maddux, W.-W., & Kitayama, S. (2018). Self-assertive interdependence in Arab culture. *Nature Human Behaviour, 2*(11), 830–837. doi:10.103841562-018-0435-z PMID:31558808

Sandelands, L. (2012). God we trust: A comparison of spiritualities at work. Academic Press.

Sandelands, L. E. (2003). The argument for God from organization studies. *Journal of Management Inquiry*, *12*(2), 168–177. doi:10.1177/1056492603012002008

Sanders, J. E., Hopkins, W. E., & Geroy, G. D. (2003). From transactional to transcendental: Toward an integrated theory of leadership. *Journal of Leadership & Organizational Studies*, *9*(4), 21–31.

Sanders, J. O. (1988). *Christian spiritual leadership*. Ae Chan Co.

Santerre, B. G. (1997). *Numinous leadership: Stories of educational leaders integrating spirituality and practice*. Academic Press.

Sarwan, A. (2010). *Ciri-Ciri Pendidikan Islam*. Rosda Karya.

Sattar, A., & Aftab, M. A. (2017). The role of Islamic education in the character building of school going children. *Education Research International*, *6*(2), 28–34.

Saylı, H., Ağca, V., Kızıldağ, D., & Yaşar Uğurlu, Ö. (2009). Ethics, corporate reputation and business performance relationships: A research in the first 500 big firms in Turkey. *Suleyman Demirel University The Journal of Faculty of Economics and Administrative Sciences*, *14*(2), 171–180.

Schaufeli, W. B., & Bakker, A. B. (2004). Job demands, job resources, and their relationship with burnout and engagement: A multi-sample study. *Journal of Organizational Behavior*, *25*(3), 293–437. doi:10.1002/job.248

Schaufeli, W. B., Bakker, A. B., & Salanova, M. (2006). The Measurement of Work Engagement With a Short Questionnaire: A Cross-National Study. *Educational and Psychological Measurement*, *66*(4), 701–716. doi:10.1177/0013164405282471

Schaufeli, W. B., Salanova, M., González-Romá, V., & Bakker, A. B. (2002). The measurement of engagement and burnout: A two sample confirmatory factor analytic approach. *Journal of Happiness Studies: An Interdisciplinary Forum on Subjective Well-Being*, *3*(1), 71–92. doi:10.1023/A:1015630930326

Schilderman, H. (2014). Religion as concept and measure. *Journal of Empirical Theology*, *27*(1), 1–16. doi:10.1163/15709256-12341298

Schneider, B. (1987). The people make the place. *Personnel Psychology*, *40*(3), 437–453. doi:10.1111/j.1744-6570.1987.tb00609.x

Schwepker, C. H. Jr. (2001). Ethical climate's relationship to job satisfaction: Organizational commitment and turnover intention in the sales force. *Journal of Business Research*, *54*(1), 39–52. doi:10.1016/S0148-2963(00)00125-9

Scott, K. T. (1994). Leadership and spirituality: A quest for reconciliation. *Spirit at work: Discovering the spirituality in leadership*, 63-99.

Seligman, M. E. P. (1999). *Seligman speech at Lincoln Summit*. Retrieved from https://www.sas.upenn.edu/psych/seligman/lincspeech.htm

Seligman, M. E. P., & Csikszentmihalyi, M. (2000). Positive psychology: An introduction. *The American Psychologist*, *55*(1), 5–14. doi:10.1037/0003-066X.55.1.5 PMID:11392865

Seligman, M. E. P., Steen, T., Park, N., & Person, C. (2005). Positive psychology progress: Empirical validation of interventions. *The American Psychologist*, *60*(5), 410–421. doi:10.1037/0003-066X.60.5.410 PMID:16045394

Şengül, F. N. (2017). *A study on Islamic work ethic and economy from sociology of religion* (Unpublished master's thesis). Yıldırım Beyazıt University, Ankara, Turkey.

Sexton, N. L. (2013). *The perceived impact of spirituality on the leadership and careers of mid-level leaders* (Doctoral dissertation). University of La Verne.

Shafique, M. N., Iqra. Ahmad, N., Khurshid, M., & Ahmad, H. (2015). Islamic Values & Principles in the Organization. *Arabian Journal of Business and Management Review*, *5*(2), 14–21.

Shahin, A. I., & Wright, P. W. (2004). Leadership in the context of culture: An Egyptian perspective. *Leadership and Organization Development Journal*, *25*(6), 499–511. doi:10.1108/01437730410556743

Sharma, R. R. (2010). Preventing corruption through spiritual leadership in organisations. *Organizational immunity to corruption: Building theoretical and research foundations*, 247-260.

Sharma, N., & Singh, R. K. (2020). Workplace spirituality and organizational effectiveness: Exploration of relationship and moderators. *Journal of Management, Spirituality & Religion*, *18*(1), 15–34. doi:10.1080/14766086.2020.1829011

Shields, C. M. (2005). Liberating discourses: Spirituality and educational leadership. *Journal of School Leadership*, *15*(6), 608–623. doi:10.1177/105268460501500601

Shuck, B., & Wollard, K. (2010). Employee engagement and HRD: A seminal review of the foundations. *Human Resource Development Review*, *9*(1), 89–110. doi:10.1177/1534484309353560

Shuhari, M.H., & Hamat, M.F. (2015). The Important Values of Muslim Individuals According Al-Ghazali. *Nilai-Nilai Penting Individu Muslim Menurut Al-Ghazali*. doi:10.37231/jimk.2015.9.0.82

Sligh, C. E., & Talbot, D. M. (2020). Recognizing the Inevitable Intersections of Spiritual and Leadership Development. *New Directions for Student Leadership*, *2020*(166), 33–44. doi:10.1002/yd.20381 PMID:32543035

Small, E. (2020). How successful African-American male leaders in predominately White Organizations integrate spirituality with leadership practice. *Journal of Management, Spirituality & Religion*, *17*(2), 184–208.

Smart, J. C., & Hamm, R. E. (1992). *Organizational Culture and Effectiveness in Two-Year Colleges.* AIR 1992 Annual Forum Paper.

Snyder, C. R., Irving, L. M., & Anderson, J. R. (1991). *Hope and health: Measuring the will and the way. In The handbook of social and clinical psychology: The health perspective*. Pergamon Press.

Snyder, C. R., & Lopez, S. J. (Eds.). (2009). *Handbook of positive psychology*. Oxford university press.

Snyder, C. R., Shorey, H. S., Cheavens, J., Pulvers, K. M., Adams, V. H., & Wiklund, C. (2002). Hope and academic success in college. *Journal of Educational Psychology, 94*(4), 820–826. doi:10.1037/0022-0663.94.4.820

Society for Human Resource Management. (2008). *Religion and Corporate Culture: Accommodating Religious Diversity in the Workplace*. SHRM.

Society of Human Resources Management. (2008). *Global diversity and inclusion.* Retrieved May 2021, from https://www.shrm.org/hr-today/trends-and-forecasting/research-and-surveys/Documents/09-Diversity_and_Inclusion_Report.pdf

Sorvaag, S. H. (2007). *The spiritual orientation of K–12 public school principals*. Saint Mary's University of Minnesota.

Spencer, M. (2012). *What is spirituality? A personal exploration.* Retrieved from https://www.rcpsych.ac.uk/docs/defaultsource/members/sigs/spiritualityspsig/what-is-spirituality-maya-spencerx.pdf?sfvrsn=f28df052_2

Spreitzer, G., Sutcliffe, K., Dutton, J., Sonenshein, S., & Grant, A. (2005). A Socially Embedded Model of Thriving at Work. *Organization Science, 16*(5), 537–549. doi:10.1287/orsc.1050.0153

Stajkovic, A. D., & Luthans, F. (1998). Self-Efficacy and Work-Related Performance: A Meta-Analysis. *Psychological Bulletin, 124*(2), 240–261. doi:10.1037/0033-2909.124.2.240

Steenkamp, Y. (2020). Fides in parenthesis: A spirituality of leadership for a (post-) secular (ising) world. *Hervormde Teologiese Studies, 76*(2), 1–8. doi:10.4102/hts.v76i2.5876

Steger, M. F., & Dik, B. J. (2009). If one is looking for meaning in life, does it help to find meaning at work? *Applied Psychology. Health and Well-Being, 1*(3), 303–320. doi:10.1111/j.1758-0854.2009.01018.x

Steger, M. F., Dik, B. J., & Duffy, R. D. (2012). Measuring Meaningful Work: The Work and Meaning Inventory (WAMI). *Journal of Career Assessment, 20*(3), 322–337. doi:10.1177/1069072711436160

Stemler, S. E. (2015). Content analysis. In R. Scott & S. Kosslyn (Eds.), *Emerging trends in the social and behavioral sciences*. John Wiley & Sons. doi:10.1002/9781118900772.etrds0053

Stiernberg, P. W. (2003). *The relationship between spirituality and leadership practices of female administrators in K–12 schools*. Baylor University.

Stoshikj, M. (2014). Integrative and distributive negotiations and negotiation behavior. *Journal of Service Science Research, 6*(1), 29–69.

Strack, J. G. (2001). *The relationship of healthcare managers' spirituality to their self-perceived effective leadership practices* (Doctoral dissertation). Medical University of South Carolina.

Strack, G., Fottler, M., Wheatley, M., & Sodomka, P. (2002). Spirituality and effective leadership in healthcare: Is there a connection? *Frontiers of Health Services Management, 18*(4), 3–18. doi:10.1097/01974520-200204000-00002 PMID:12087690

Suwartini, S. (2017). Pendidikan Karakter dan Pembangunan Sumber Daya Manusia Keberlanjutan. *Jurnal Pendidikan ke-SD-an, 4*(1), 220-234.

Sweeney, P. J., & Fry, L. W. (2012). Character development through spiritual leadership. *Consulting Psychology Journal, 64*(2), 89.

Syarif, A. H., Rahmawati, A., & Fasa, M. I. (2019). The effect of Islamic work ethic and productivity on work quality through the employee performance. *Review of Islamic Economics and Finance, 2*(2), 92–101. doi:10.17509/rief.v2i1.22375

Tabakoğlu, A. (1996). *İslâm ve ekonomik hayat*. Ankara, Turkey: Diyanet işleri Başkanlığı Yayınları.

Tabakoğlu, A. (2008). Ahilik ve iş ahlakı. İstanbul Ticaret Odası İGİAD İş Ahlakı Sempozyumu, 31, 37-52.

Tafsir, A. (2006). *Filsafat Pendidikan Islam, Integrasi Jasmani, Rohani, dan Kalbu Memanusiakan Manusia*. Remaja Rosdakarya.

Tamuri, A. H. (2007). Islamic Education teachers' perceptions of the teaching of akhlāq in Malaysian secondary schools. *Journal of Moral Education, 36*(3), 371–386. doi:10.1080/03057240701553347

Tanyi, R. A. (2002). Towards clarification of the meaning of spirituality. *Journal of Advanced Nursing, 39*(5), 500–509. doi:10.1046/j.1365-2648.2002.02315.x PMID:12175360

Tasa, K., & Bell, C. M. (2017). Effects of implicit negotiation beliefs and moral disengagement on negotiator attitudes and deceptive behavior. *Journal of Business Ethics, 142*(1), 169–183.

Terkel, S. (1972). *Working*. Avon Books.

Thaha, M. C. (2006). *Kapita Selekta Pendidikan Islam*. Pustaka Pelajar.

Thaib, L., & Pa, B. C. (2014). Islamic business leadership modelling for sustainable development. *International Journal of Multidisciplinary Academic Research, 2*(1), 25–32.

Thompson, L. (1990). Negotiation behavior and outcomes: Empirical evidence and theoretical issues. *Psychological Bulletin, 108*(3), 515.

Thompson, L., & Hastie, R. (1990). Judgment tasks and biases in negotiation. In B. H. Sheppard, M. H. Bazerman, & R. J. Lewicki (Eds.), *Research in negotiation in organizations* (Vol. 2, pp. 31–54). JAI Press.

Tomlinson, H. (Ed.). (2013). *Educational management: Major themes in education*. Routledge. doi:10.4324/9780203463383

Topno, B., & Syngkon, R. A. J. (2019). The influence of religion on entrepreneurship: A study on tribal Christian entrepreneurs in Assam. *International Journal of Business and Management Invention*, *8*(5), 1–7.

Tosti, D., & Jackson, S. F. (1999). Influencing others to Act. In *Handbook of Human Performance Technology*. International Society for Performance Improvement.

Townsend, J. S. II, & Wichern, F. B. (1984). The development of the spiritual leadership qualities inventory. *Journal of Psychology and Theology*, *12*(4), 305–313. doi:10.1177/009164718401200406

Townsend, P., & Gebhardt, J. E. (2008). Employee engagement—Completely. *Human Resource Management International Digest*, *16*(3), 22–24. doi:10.1108/09670730810869529

Tracey, P., Phillips, N., & Lounsbury, M. (2014). Taking religion seriously in the study of organizations. In Religion and Organization Theory (Vol. 41). Emerald Group Publishing Limited. doi:10.1108/S0733-558X20140000041009

Türkdoğan, O. (1996). *İslâm ekonomik sistemi ve Weberci görüşler*. Turan Yayıncılık.

Turner, P., & Turner, S. (2009). Triangulation in practice. *Virtual Reality (Waltham Cross)*, *13*(3), 171–181. doi:10.100710055-009-0117-2

Twymon, P. M. (2004). *The relationship between spirituality and leadership practices of public school superintendents in Texas* (Doctoral dissertation). Baylor University.

U.S. Department of Labor. (n.d.). https://www.dol.gov/agencies/oasam/civil-rights-center/internal/policies/religious-discrimination-accommodation

U.S. Equal Employment Opportunity Commission. Title VII of the Civil Rights Act of 1964. Retrieved August 1, 2021, from https://www.eeoc.gov/statutes/title-vii-civil-rights-act-1964

Ulluwishewa, R., Uthumange, A., & Weerakoon, R. (2020). Spirituality, Success, and Happiness: Implications for Leadership in Business. In *New Horizons in Positive Leadership and Change* (pp. 143–157). Springer. doi:10.1007/978-3-030-38129-5_8

United States Bureau of Democracy. (n.d.). *Human Rights and Labor. Bahrain: International Religious Freedom Report 2020*. https://bh.usembassy.gov/wp-content/uploads/sites/141/240282-BAHRAIN-2020-INTERNATIONAL-RELIGIOUS-FREEDOM-REPORT.pdf Retrieved in June 2021

Vallerand, R. J., & Houlfort, N. (2003). Passion at Work: Toward a New Conceptualization. In S. W. Gilliland, D. D. Steiner, & D. P. Skarlicki (Eds.), *Emerging Perspective on Values in Organizations* (pp. 175–204). Information Age Publishing.

Van Buren, H. J. III, Syed, J., & Mir, R. (2020). Religion as a macro social force affecting business: Concepts, questions, and future research. *Business & Society*, *59*(5), 799–822. doi:10.1177/0007650319845097

Van Zyl, L. E., Deacon, E., & Rothmann, S. (2010). Towards happiness: Experience of work-role fit, meaningfulness, and work engagement of industrial/organisational psychologists in South Africa. *SA Journal of Industrial Psychology*, *36*(1), 1–10. doi:10.4102ajip.v36i1.890

Vasconcelos, A. F. (2011). Pursuing organizational spirituality: Some lessons from a financial services corporation. *Management & Marketing*, *6*(3), 365.

Verschoor, C. C. (2006). Strong ethics is a critical quality of leadership. *Strategic Finance*, 19-21.

Victor, B., & Cullen, J. B. (1987). A theory and measure of ethical climate in organizations. *Research in Corporate Social Performance and Policy*, *9*, 51-71.

Vitell, S. J. (2009). The role of religiosity in business and consumer ethics: A review of the literature. *Journal of Business Ethics*, *90*(2), 155–167. doi:10.100710551-010-0382-8

Vu, M. C., & Gill, R. (2019). Letting go of the raft||–the art of spiritual leadership in contemporary organizations from a Buddhist perspective using skilful means. *Leadership*, *15*(3), 360–380. doi:10.1177/1742715018761931

Wallace, M., Bradley, R.E., & Wright, A.H. (2014, Mar.). Religious affiliation and hiring discrimination in the American South: A Field Experiment. *Social Currents*.

Walling, D. M. (1994). *Spirituality and leadership* (Doctoral dissertation). University of San Diego.

Walton, R. E., & McKersie, R. B. (1991). *A behavioral theory of labor negotiations: An analysis of a social interaction system*. Cornell University Press.

Ward, B. (2003). *The Desert Fathers: Sayings of the early Christian monks*. Penguin Books.

Warrick, D. D. (2017). What leaders need to know about organizational culture. *Business Horizons*, *60*(3), 395–404. doi:10.1016/j.bushor.2017.01.011

Warr, P. (1987). *Work, unemployment, and mental health*. Oxford University Press.

Watson, P., Morris, R., & Hood, R. Jr. (1988). Sin and self-functioning: II. Grace, guilt, and psychological adjustment. *Journal of Psychology and Theology*, *16*(3), 270–281. doi:10.1177/009164718801600306

Weaver, G. R., & Agle, B. R. (2002). Religiosity and ethical behavior in organizations: A symbolic interactionist perspective. *Academy of Management Review*, *27*(1), 77–97. doi:10.2307/4134370

Weeks, W. A., Loe, T. W., Chonko, L. B., & Wakefield, K. (2004). The effect of perceived ethical climate on the search for sales force excellence. *Journal of Personal Selling & Sales Management*, *24*(3), 199–214.

Weick, K. E. (2021). Perspective Construction in Organizational Behavior. *Annual Review of Organizational Psychology and Organizational Behavior, 4*, 1-17. Retrieved from https://www.annualreviews.org/doi/full/10.1146/annurev-orgpsych-032516-113043

Weir, C. (1998). Fiji and Fijians: Two Modes of missionary Discourse. *The Journal of Religious History*, *22*(2), 152–167. doi:10.1111/1467-9809.00056

White, M. D., & Marsh, E. E. (2006). Content analysis: A flexible methodology. *Library Trends*, *55*(1), 22–24. doi:10.1353/lib.2006.0053

Whyte, W. H. (1965). *The Organization Man*. Penguin Books Ltd.

Wibowo, G. (2017). Comparison of the Models of Organizational Behavior: A Review. *Management and Economics Research Journal, 2*, 32-40.

Wicks, A. (2014). Stakeholder theory and spirituality. *Journal of Management, Spirituality & Religion*, *11*(4), 294–306. doi:10.1080/14766086.2014.917984

Widodo, S., & Suryosukmono, G. (2021). Spiritual leadership, workplace spirituality and their effects on meaningful work: Self-transcendence as mediator role. *Management Science Letters*, *11*(7), 2115–2126. doi:10.5267/j.msl.2021.2.016

Wiebe, K. F., & Fleck, J. R. (1980). Personality correlates of intrinsic, extrinsic, and nonreligious orientations. *The Journal of Psychology*, *105*(2), 181–187. doi:10.1080/00223980.1980.9915149

Wilensky, H. L. (1960). Work, careers and social integration. *International Social Science Journal*, *12*(4), 543–560.

Wong, P., & Fry, P. S. (2013). *The human quest for meaning*. Routledge. doi:10.4324/9780203146286

Worden, S. (2003). The role of religious and nationalist ethics in strategic leadership: The case of J.N. Tata. *Journal of Business Ethics*, *47*(2), 147–164. doi:10.1023/A:1026050230808

Worden, S. (2005). Religion in Strategic Leadership: A Positivistic, Normative/Theological, and Strategic Analysis. *Journal of Business Ethics*, *57*(3), 221–239. doi:10.100710551-004-6943-y

World Data on Education. (2006). *Principles and general objectives of education*. Retrieved from http://www.ibe.unesco.org/fileadmin/user_upload/archive/Countries/WDE/2006/ASIA_and_the_PACIFIC/Malaysia/Malaysia.pdf

World Values Survey. (n.d.). https://www.worldvaluessurvey.org/WVSContents.jsp?CMSID=Findings

Wright, K. K. (2010). *An examination of the relationship between teacher efficacy and teacher religiosity* (Ph.D. Thesis). University of North Texas.

Wright, T. A. (2003). Positive organizational behavior: An idea whose time has truly come. *Journal of Organizational Behavior*, *24*(4), 437–442. doi:10.1002/job.197

Wrzesniewski, A., McCauley, C., Rozin, P., & Schwartz, B. (1997). Jobs, Careers, And Callings: People's Relations To Their Work. *Journal of Research in Personality*, *31*(1), 21–33. doi:10.1006/jrpe.1997.2162

Wulandari, F. (2014). Spirituality in workplace, individual spirituality and work behaviour: The study of higher education in Indonesia. *Individual Spirituality and Work Behaviour: The Study of Higher Education in Indonesia.*

Xanthopoulou, D., Bakker, A. B., & Fischbach, A. (2013). Work engagement among employees facing emotional demands: The role of personal resources. *Journal of Personnel Psychology, 12*(2), 74–84. doi:10.1027/1866-5888/a000085

Yammarino, F. J. (2000). Leadership skills: Introduction and overview. *The Leadership Quarterly, 11*(1).

Yasin, R. F., & Jani, M. S. (2013). Islamic Education: Aim and main features. *International Journal of Education and Research, 1*(10), 1–18.

Yıldırım, A., & Şimşek, H. (2003). *Sosyal bilimlerde nitel araştırma yöntemleri*. Seçkin Yayıncılık.

Yousef, D. A. (2000). Organizational commitment as a mediator of the relationship between Islamic work ethic and attitudes toward organizational change. *Human Relations, 53*(4), 513–537. doi:10.1177/0018726700534003

Yousef, D. A. (2001). Islamic work ethic – A moderator between organizational commitment and job satisfaction in a cross-cultural context. *Personnel Review, 30*(2), 152–169. doi:10.1108/00483480110380325

Youseff, C., & Luthans, F. (2007). Positive organizational behavior in the workplace: The impact of hope, optimism, and resilience. *Journal of Management, 33*(5), 774–800. doi:10.1177/0149206307305562

Ysseldyk, R., Matheson, K., & Anisman, H. (2010). Religiosity as identity: Toward an understanding of religion from a social identity perspective. *Personality and Social Psychology Review, 14*(1), 60–71. doi:10.1177/1088868309349693 PMID:20089847

Yukl, G. A. (1989). Leadership in Organizations (2nd ed.). Prentice-Hall International.

Yukl, G. (2012). Effective leadership behavior: What we know and what questions need more attention. *The Academy of Management Perspectives, 26*(4), 66–85.

Yukl, G. A. (2006). *Leadership in organizations* (6th ed.). Pearson Prentice Hall.

Yunan, W., Ahmad, A., & Omar, Z. (2017). The Experience of Workplace Spirituality: Do Age and Educational Attainment Matter? *International Journal of Academic Research in Business & Social Sciences, 7*(7), 61–69. doi:10.6007/IJARBSS/v7-i7/3078

Yusoff, W., Mazwati, W., Preece, A. S., & Hamzah, L. M. (2018). Students' Experiences in Teaching and Learning Islamic Education Using Philosophical Inquiry Method. *Journal of Education and Learning, 12*(2), 266–274. doi:10.11591/edulearn.v12i2.9492

Yusof, H., Mohd Noor, M. A., Abdul Jalil, N., Mansor, M., & Awang, M. (2018). Nurturing Moral Values in Primary School. *International Journal of Academic Research in Business & Social Sciences*, *8*(7), 1144–1156. doi:10.6007/IJARBSS/v8-i7/4562

Zaim, H. (2012). *İş hayatında erdemli insan*. Empati Matbaacılık.

Zandi, G., Sulaiman, M., & Rashed, N. (2015). Spirituality and leaders effectiveness: An Islamic perspective. *Asian Economic and Financial Review*, *5*(1), 155–166. doi:10.18488/journal.aefr/2015.5.1/102.1.155.166

Zellars, K. L., Perrewé, P. L., & Brees, J. R. (2010). The multiple roles of spirituality in occupational stress and well-being. In *Handbook of workplace spirituality and organizational performance* (pp. 243–256). Routledge.

Zhang, Y., & Yang, F. (2020). How and when spiritual leadership enhances employee innovative behavior. *Personnel Review*.

Zinnbauer, B. J., & Pargament, K. I. (2005). Religiousness and spirituality. Handbook of the psychology of religion and spirituality, 21-42.

Zinnbauer, B. J., Pargament, K. I., & Scott, A. B. (1999). The emerging meanings of religiousness and spirituality: Problems and prospects. *Journal of Personality*, *67*(6), 889–919. doi:10.1111/1467-6494.00077

Zohar, D. (1997). *Rewiring the Corporate Brain*. Bevrett-Koehler Publishing.

Related References

To continue our tradition of advancing information science and technology research, we have compiled a list of recommended IGI Global readings. These references will provide additional information and guidance to further enrich your knowledge and assist you with your own research and future publications.

Abtahi, M. S., Behboudi, L., & Hasanabad, H. M. (2017). Factors Affecting Internet Advertising Adoption in Ad Agencies. *International Journal of Innovation in the Digital Economy*, *8*(4), 18–29. doi:10.4018/IJIDE.2017100102

Agrawal, S. (2017). The Impact of Emerging Technologies and Social Media on Different Business(es): Marketing and Management. In O. Rishi & A. Sharma (Eds.), *Maximizing Business Performance and Efficiency Through Intelligent Systems* (pp. 37–49). Hershey, PA: IGI Global. doi:10.4018/978-1-5225-2234-8.ch002

Alnoukari, M., Razouk, R., & Hanano, A. (2016). BSC-SI: A Framework for Integrating Strategic Intelligence in Corporate Strategic Management. *International Journal of Social and Organizational Dynamics in IT*, *5*(2), 1–14. doi:10.4018/IJSODIT.2016070101

Alnoukari, M., Razouk, R., & Hanano, A. (2016). BSC-SI, A Framework for Integrating Strategic Intelligence in Corporate Strategic Management. *International Journal of Strategic Information Technology and Applications*, *7*(1), 32–44. doi:10.4018/IJSITA.2016010103

Altındağ, E. (2016). Current Approaches in Change Management. In A. Goksoy (Ed.), *Organizational Change Management Strategies in Modern Business* (pp. 24–51). Hershey, PA: IGI Global. doi:10.4018/978-1-4666-9533-7.ch002

Alvarez-Dionisi, L. E., Turner, R., & Mittra, M. (2016). Global Project Management Trends. *International Journal of Information Technology Project Management*, *7*(3), 54–73. doi:10.4018/IJITPM.2016070104

Anantharaman, R. N., Rajeswari, K. S., Angusamy, A., & Kuppusamy, J. (2017). Role of Self-Efficacy and Collective Efficacy as Moderators of Occupational Stress Among Software Development Professionals. *International Journal of Human Capital and Information Technology Professionals*, *8*(2), 45–58. doi:10.4018/IJHCITP.2017040103

Aninze, F., El-Gohary, H., & Hussain, J. (2018). The Role of Microfinance to Empower Women: The Case of Developing Countries. *International Journal of Customer Relationship Marketing and Management*, *9*(1), 54–78. doi:10.4018/IJCRMM.2018010104

Arsenijević, O. M., Orčić, D., & Kastratović, E. (2017). Development of an Optimization Tool for Intangibles in SMEs: A Case Study from Serbia with a Pilot Research in the Prestige by Milka Company. In M. Vemić (Ed.), *Optimal Management Strategies in Small and Medium Enterprises* (pp. 320–347). Hershey, PA: IGI Global. doi:10.4018/978-1-5225-1949-2.ch015

Aryanto, V. D., Wismantoro, Y., & Widyatmoko, K. (2018). Implementing Eco-Innovation by Utilizing the Internet to Enhance Firm's Marketing Performance: Study of Green Batik Small and Medium Enterprises in Indonesia. *International Journal of E-Business Research*, *14*(1), 21–36. doi:10.4018/IJEBR.2018010102

Atiku, S. O., & Fields, Z. (2017). Multicultural Orientations for 21st Century Global Leadership. In N. Baporikar (Ed.), *Management Education for Global Leadership* (pp. 28–51). Hershey, PA: IGI Global. doi:10.4018/978-1-5225-1013-0.ch002

Atiku, S. O., & Fields, Z. (2018). Organisational Learning Dimensions and Talent Retention Strategies for the Service Industries. In N. Baporikar (Ed.), *Global Practices in Knowledge Management for Societal and Organizational Development* (pp. 358–381). Hershey, PA: IGI Global. doi:10.4018/978-1-5225-3009-1.ch017

Ávila, L., & Teixeira, L. (2018). The Main Concepts Behind the Dematerialization of Business Processes. In M. Khosrow-Pour, D.B.A. (Ed.), Encyclopedia of Information Science and Technology, Fourth Edition (pp. 888-898). Hershey, PA: IGI Global. doi:10.4018/978-1-5225-2255-3.ch076

Bartens, Y., Chunpir, H. I., Schulte, F., & Voß, S. (2017). Business/IT Alignment in Two-Sided Markets: A COBIT 5 Analysis for Media Streaming Business Models. In S. De Haes & W. Van Grembergen (Eds.), *Strategic IT Governance and Alignment in Business Settings* (pp. 82–111). Hershey, PA: IGI Global. doi:10.4018/978-1-5225-0861-8.ch004

Bashayreh, A. M. (2018). Organizational Culture and Organizational Performance. In W. Lee & F. Sabetzadeh (Eds.), *Contemporary Knowledge and Systems Science* (pp. 50–69). Hershey, PA: IGI Global. doi:10.4018/978-1-5225-5655-8.ch003

Bedford, D. A. (2018). Sustainable Knowledge Management Strategies: Aligning Business Capabilities and Knowledge Management Goals. In N. Baporikar (Ed.), *Global Practices in Knowledge Management for Societal and Organizational Development* (pp. 46–73). Hershey, PA: IGI Global. doi:10.4018/978-1-5225-3009-1.ch003

Benmoussa, F., Nakara, W. A., & Jaouen, A. (2016). The Use of Social Media by SMEs in the Tourism Industry. In I. Lee (Ed.), *Encyclopedia of E-Commerce Development, Implementation, and Management* (pp. 2159–2170). Hershey, PA: IGI Global. doi:10.4018/978-1-4666-9787-4.ch155

Berger, R. (2016). Indigenous Management and Bottom of Pyramid Countries: The Role of National Institutions. In U. Aung & P. Ordoñez de Pablos (Eds.), *Managerial Strategies and Practice in the Asian Business Sector* (pp. 107–123). Hershey, PA: IGI Global. doi:10.4018/978-1-4666-9758-4.ch007

Bharwani, S., & Musunuri, D. (2018). Reflection as a Process From Theory to Practice. In M. Khosrow-Pour, D.B.A. (Ed.), Encyclopedia of Information Science and Technology, Fourth Edition (pp. 1529-1539). Hershey, PA: IGI Global. doi:10.4018/978-1-5225-2255-3.ch132

Bhatt, G. D., Wang, Z., & Rodger, J. A. (2017). Information Systems Capabilities and Their Effects on Competitive Advantages: A Study of Chinese Companies. *Information Resources Management Journal, 30*(3), 41–57. doi:10.4018/IRMJ.2017070103

Bhushan, M., & Yadav, A. (2017). Concept of Cloud Computing in ESB. In R. Bhadoria, N. Chaudhari, G. Tomar, & S. Singh (Eds.), *Exploring Enterprise Service Bus in the Service-Oriented Architecture Paradigm* (pp. 116–127). Hershey, PA: IGI Global. doi:10.4018/978-1-5225-2157-0.ch008

Bhushan, S. (2017). System Dynamics Base-Model of Humanitarian Supply Chain (HSCM) in Disaster Prone Eco-Communities of India: A Discussion on Simulation and Scenario Results. *International Journal of System Dynamics Applications, 6*(3), 20–37. doi:10.4018/IJSDA.2017070102

Biswas, A., & De, A. K. (2017). On Development of a Fuzzy Stochastic Programming Model with Its Application to Business Management. In S. Trivedi, S. Dey, A. Kumar, & T. Panda (Eds.), *Handbook of Research on Advanced Data Mining Techniques and Applications for Business Intelligence* (pp. 353–378). Hershey, PA: IGI Global. doi:10.4018/978-1-5225-2031-3.ch021

Bücker, J., & Ernste, K. (2018). Use of Brand Heroes in Strategic Reputation Management: The Case of Bacardi, Adidas, and Daimler. In A. Erdemir (Ed.), *Reputation Management Techniques in Public Relations* (pp. 126–150). Hershey, PA: IGI Global. doi:10.4018/978-1-5225-3619-2.ch007

Bureš, V. (2018). Industry 4.0 From the Systems Engineering Perspective: Alternative Holistic Framework Development. In R. Brunet-Thornton & F. Martinez (Eds.), *Analyzing the Impacts of Industry 4.0 in Modern Business Environments* (pp. 199–223). Hershey, PA: IGI Global. doi:10.4018/978-1-5225-3468-6.ch011

Buzady, Z. (2017). Resolving the Magic Cube of Effective Case Teaching: Benchmarking Case Teaching Practices in Emerging Markets – Insights from the Central European University Business School, Hungary. In D. Latusek (Ed.), *Case Studies as a Teaching Tool in Management Education* (pp. 79–103). Hershey, PA: IGI Global. doi:10.4018/978-1-5225-0770-3.ch005

Campatelli, G., Richter, A., & Stocker, A. (2016). Participative Knowledge Management to Empower Manufacturing Workers. *International Journal of Knowledge Management, 12*(4), 37–50. doi:10.4018/IJKM.2016100103

Căpusneanu, S., & Topor, D. I. (2018). Business Ethics and Cost Management in SMEs: Theories of Business Ethics and Cost Management Ethos. In I. Oncioiu (Ed.), *Ethics and Decision-Making for Sustainable Business Practices* (pp. 109–127). Hershey, PA: IGI Global. doi:10.4018/978-1-5225-3773-1.ch007

Carneiro, A. (2016). Maturity in Health Organization Information Systems: Metrics and Privacy Perspectives. *International Journal of Privacy and Health Information Management, 4*(2), 1–18. doi:10.4018/IJPHIM.2016070101

Chan, R. L., Mo, P. L., & Moon, K. K. (2018). Strategic and Tactical Measures in Managing Enterprise Risks: A Study of the Textile and Apparel Industry. In K. Strang, M. Korstanje, & N. Vajjhala (Eds.), *Research, Practices, and Innovations in Global Risk and Contingency Management* (pp. 1–19). Hershey, PA: IGI Global. doi:10.4018/978-1-5225-4754-9.ch001

Chandan, H. C. (2016). Motivations and Challenges of Female Entrepreneurship in Developed and Developing Economies. In N. Baporikar (Ed.), *Handbook of Research on Entrepreneurship in the Contemporary Knowledge-Based Global Economy* (pp. 260–286). Hershey, PA: IGI Global. doi:10.4018/978-1-4666-8798-1.ch012

Charlier, S. D., Burke-Smalley, L. A., & Fisher, S. L. (2018). Undergraduate Programs in the U.S: A Contextual and Content-Based Analysis. In J. Mendy (Ed.), *Teaching Human Resources and Organizational Behavior at the College Level* (pp. 26–57). Hershey, PA: IGI Global. doi:10.4018/978-1-5225-2820-3.ch002

Chaudhuri, S. (2016). Application of Web-Based Geographical Information System (GIS) in E-Business. In U. Panwar, R. Kumar, & N. Ray (Eds.), *Handbook of Research on Promotional Strategies and Consumer Influence in the Service Sector* (pp. 389–405). Hershey, PA: IGI Global. doi:10.4018/978-1-5225-0143-5.ch023

Choudhuri, P. S. (2016). An Empirical Study on the Quality of Services Offered by the Private Life Insurers in Burdwan. In U. Panwar, R. Kumar, & N. Ray (Eds.), *Handbook of Research on Promotional Strategies and Consumer Influence in the Service Sector* (pp. 31–55). Hershey, PA: IGI Global. doi:10.4018/978-1-5225-0143-5.ch002

Dahlberg, T., Kivijärvi, H., & Saarinen, T. (2017). IT Investment Consistency and Other Factors Influencing the Success of IT Performance. In S. De Haes & W. Van Grembergen (Eds.), *Strategic IT Governance and Alignment in Business Settings* (pp. 176–208). Hershey, PA: IGI Global. doi:10.4018/978-1-5225-0861-8.ch007

Damnjanović, A. M. (2017). Knowledge Management Optimization through IT and E-Business Utilization: A Qualitative Study on Serbian SMEs. In M. Vemić (Ed.), *Optimal Management Strategies in Small and Medium Enterprises* (pp. 249–267). Hershey, PA: IGI Global. doi:10.4018/978-1-5225-1949-2.ch012

Daneshpour, H. (2017). Integrating Sustainable Development into Project Portfolio Management through Application of Open Innovation. In M. Vemić (Ed.), *Optimal Management Strategies in Small and Medium Enterprises* (pp. 370–387). Hershey, PA: IGI Global. doi:10.4018/978-1-5225-1949-2.ch017

Daniel, A. D., & Reis de Castro, V. (2018). Entrepreneurship Education: How to Measure the Impact on Nascent Entrepreneurs. In A. Carrizo Moreira, J. Guilherme Leitão Dantas, & F. Manuel Valente (Eds.), *Nascent Entrepreneurship and Successful New Venture Creation* (pp. 85–110). Hershey, PA: IGI Global. doi:10.4018/978-1-5225-2936-1.ch004

David, F., van der Sijde, P., & van den Besselaar, P. (2016). Enterpreneurial Incentives, Obstacles, and Management in University-Business Co-Operation: The Case of Indonesia. In J. Saiz-Álvarez (Ed.), *Handbook of Research on Social Entrepreneurship and Solidarity Economics* (pp. 499–518). Hershey, PA: IGI Global. doi:10.4018/978-1-5225-0097-1.ch024

David, R., Swami, B. N., & Tangirala, S. (2018). Ethics Impact on Knowledge Management in Organizational Development: A Case Study. In N. Baporikar (Ed.), *Global Practices in Knowledge Management for Societal and Organizational Development* (pp. 19–45). Hershey, PA: IGI Global. doi:10.4018/978-1-5225-3009-1.ch002

Delias, P., & Lakiotaki, K. (2018). Discovering Process Horizontal Boundaries to Facilitate Process Comprehension. *International Journal of Operations Research and Information Systems*, *9*(2), 1–31. doi:10.4018/IJORIS.2018040101

Denholm, J., & Lee-Davies, L. (2018). Success Factors for Games in Business and Project Management. In *Enhancing Education and Training Initiatives Through Serious Games* (pp. 34–68). Hershey, PA: IGI Global. doi:10.4018/978-1-5225-3689-5.ch002

Deshpande, M. (2017). Best Practices in Management Institutions for Global Leadership: Policy Aspects. In N. Baporikar (Ed.), *Management Education for Global Leadership* (pp. 1–27). Hershey, PA: IGI Global. doi:10.4018/978-1-5225-1013-0.ch001

Deshpande, M. (2018). Policy Perspectives for SMEs Knowledge Management. In N. Baporikar (Ed.), *Knowledge Integration Strategies for Entrepreneurship and Sustainability* (pp. 23–46). Hershey, PA: IGI Global. doi:10.4018/978-1-5225-5115-7.ch002

Dezdar, S. (2017). ERP Implementation Projects in Asian Countries: A Comparative Study on Iran and China. *International Journal of Information Technology Project Management*, *8*(3), 52–68. doi:10.4018/IJITPM.2017070104

Domingos, D., Martinho, R., & Varajão, J. (2016). Controlled Flexibility in Healthcare Processes: A BPMN-Extension Approach. In M. Cruz-Cunha, I. Miranda, R. Martinho, & R. Rijo (Eds.), *Encyclopedia of E-Health and Telemedicine* (pp. 521–535). Hershey, PA: IGI Global. doi:10.4018/978-1-4666-9978-6.ch040

Domingos, D., Respício, A., & Martinho, R. (2017). Reliability of IoT-Aware BPMN Healthcare Processes. In C. Reis & M. Maximiano (Eds.), *Internet of Things and Advanced Application in Healthcare* (pp. 214–248). Hershey, PA: IGI Global. doi:10.4018/978-1-5225-1820-4.ch008

Dosumu, O., Hussain, J., & El-Gohary, H. (2017). An Exploratory Study of the Impact of Government Policies on the Development of Small and Medium Enterprises in Developing Countries: The Case of Nigeria. *International Journal of Customer Relationship Marketing and Management*, *8*(4), 51–62. doi:10.4018/IJCRMM.2017100104

Durst, S., Bruns, G., & Edvardsson, I. R. (2017). Retaining Knowledge in Smaller Building and Construction Firms. *International Journal of Knowledge and Systems Science*, *8*(3), 1–12. doi:10.4018/IJKSS.2017070101

Edvardsson, I. R., & Durst, S. (2017). Outsourcing, Knowledge, and Learning: A Critical Review. *International Journal of Knowledge-Based Organizations*, *7*(2), 13–26. doi:10.4018/IJKBO.2017040102

Edwards, J. S. (2018). Integrating Knowledge Management and Business Processes. In M. Khosrow-Pour, D.B.A. (Ed.), Encyclopedia of Information Science and Technology, Fourth Edition (pp. 5046-5055). Hershey, PA: IGI Global. doi:10.4018/978-1-5225-2255-3.ch437

Ejiogu, A. O. (2018). Economics of Farm Management. In *Agricultural Finance and Opportunities for Investment and Expansion* (pp. 56–72). Hershey, PA: IGI Global. doi:10.4018/978-1-5225-3059-6.ch003

Ekanem, I., & Abiade, G. E. (2018). Factors Influencing the Use of E-Commerce by Small Enterprises in Nigeria. *International Journal of ICT Research in Africa and the Middle East*, *7*(1), 37–53. doi:10.4018/IJICTRAME.2018010103

Ekanem, I., & Alrossais, L. A. (2017). Succession Challenges Facing Family Businesses in Saudi Arabia. In P. Zgheib (Ed.), *Entrepreneurship and Business Innovation in the Middle East* (pp. 122–146). Hershey, PA: IGI Global. doi:10.4018/978-1-5225-2066-5.ch007

El Faquih, L., & Fredj, M. (2017). Ontology-Based Framework for Quality in Configurable Process Models. *Journal of Electronic Commerce in Organizations*, *15*(2), 48–60. doi:10.4018/JECO.2017040104

El-Gohary, H., & El-Gohary, Z. (2016). An Attempt to Explore Electronic Marketing Adoption and Implementation Aspects in Developing Countries: The Case of Egypt. *International Journal of Customer Relationship Marketing and Management*, *7*(4), 1–26. doi:10.4018/IJCRMM.2016100101

Entico, G. J. (2016). Knowledge Management and the Medical Health Librarians: A Perception Study. In J. Yap, M. Perez, M. Ayson, & G. Entico (Eds.), *Special Library Administration, Standardization and Technological Integration* (pp. 52–77). Hershey, PA: IGI Global. doi:10.4018/978-1-4666-9542-9.ch003

Faisal, M. N., & Talib, F. (2017). Building Ambidextrous Supply Chains in SMEs: How to Tackle the Barriers? *International Journal of Information Systems and Supply Chain Management*, *10*(4), 80–100. doi:10.4018/IJISSCM.2017100105

Fernandes, T. M., Gomes, J., & Romão, M. (2017). Investments in E-Government: A Benefit Management Case Study. *International Journal of Electronic Government Research*, *13*(3), 1–17. doi:10.4018/IJEGR.2017070101

Fouda, F. A. (2016). A Suggested Curriculum in Career Education to Develop Business Secondary Schools Students' Career Knowledge Management Domains and Professional Thinking. *International Journal of Technology Diffusion*, *7*(2), 42–62. doi:10.4018/IJTD.2016040103

Gallardo-Vázquez, D., & Pajuelo-Moreno, M. L. (2016). How Spanish Universities are Promoting Entrepreneurship through Your Own Lines of Teaching and Research? In L. Carvalho (Ed.), *Handbook of Research on Entrepreneurial Success and its Impact on Regional Development* (pp. 431–454). Hershey, PA: IGI Global. doi:10.4018/978-1-4666-9567-2.ch019

Gao, S. S., Oreal, S., & Zhang, J. (2018). Contemporary Financial Risk Management Perceptions and Practices of Small-Sized Chinese Businesses. In I. Management Association (Ed.), Global Business Expansion: Concepts, Methodologies, Tools, and Applications (pp. 917-931). Hershey, PA: IGI Global. doi:10.4018/978-1-5225-5481-3.ch041

Garg, R., & Berning, S. C. (2017). Indigenous Chinese Management Philosophies: Key Concepts and Relevance for Modern Chinese Firms. In B. Christiansen & G. Koc (Eds.), *Transcontinental Strategies for Industrial Development and Economic Growth* (pp. 43–57). Hershey, PA: IGI Global. doi:10.4018/978-1-5225-2160-0.ch003

Gencer, Y. G. (2017). Supply Chain Management in Retailing Business. In U. Akkucuk (Ed.), *Ethics and Sustainability in Global Supply Chain Management* (pp. 197–210). Hershey, PA: IGI Global. doi:10.4018/978-1-5225-2036-8.ch011

Giacosa, E. (2016). Innovation in Luxury Fashion Businesses as a Means for the Regional Development. In L. Carvalho (Ed.), *Handbook of Research on Entrepreneurial Success and its Impact on Regional Development* (pp. 206–222). Hershey, PA: IGI Global. doi:10.4018/978-1-4666-9567-2.ch010

Giacosa, E. (2018). The Increasing of the Regional Development Thanks to the Luxury Business Innovation. In L. Carvalho (Ed.), *Handbook of Research on Entrepreneurial Ecosystems and Social Dynamics in a Globalized World* (pp. 260–273). Hershey, PA: IGI Global. doi:10.4018/978-1-5225-3525-6.ch011

Gianni, M., & Gotzamani, K. (2016). Integrated Management Systems and Information Management Systems: Common Threads. In P. Papajorgji, F. Pinet, A. Guimarães, & J. Papathanasiou (Eds.), *Automated Enterprise Systems for Maximizing Business Performance* (pp. 195–214). Hershey, PA: IGI Global. doi:10.4018/978-1-4666-8841-4.ch011

Gianni, M., Gotzamani, K., & Linden, I. (2016). How a BI-wise Responsible Integrated Management System May Support Food Traceability. *International Journal of Decision Support System Technology*, *8*(2), 1–17. doi:10.4018/IJDSST.2016040101

Glykas, M., & George, J. (2017). Quality and Process Management Systems in the UAE Maritime Industry. *International Journal of Productivity Management and Assessment Technologies*, *5*(1), 20–39. doi:10.4018/IJPMAT.2017010102

Glykas, M., Valiris, G., Kokkinaki, A., & Koutsoukou, Z. (2018). Banking Business Process Management Implementation. *International Journal of Productivity Management and Assessment Technologies*, *6*(1), 50–69. doi:10.4018/IJPMAT.2018010104

Gomes, J., & Romão, M. (2017). The Balanced Scorecard: Keeping Updated and Aligned with Today's Business Trends. *International Journal of Productivity Management and Assessment Technologies*, *5*(2), 1–15. doi:10.4018/IJPMAT.2017070101

Gomes, J., & Romão, M. (2017). Aligning Information Systems and Technology with Benefit Management and Balanced Scorecard. In S. De Haes & W. Van Grembergen (Eds.), *Strategic IT Governance and Alignment in Business Settings* (pp. 112–131). Hershey, PA: IGI Global. doi:10.4018/978-1-5225-0861-8.ch005

Grefen, P., & Turetken, O. (2017). Advanced Business Process Management in Networked E-Business Scenarios. *International Journal of E-Business Research*, *13*(4), 70–104. doi:10.4018/IJEBR.2017100105

Haider, A., & Saetang, S. (2017). Strategic IT Alignment in Service Sector. In S. Rozenes & Y. Cohen (Eds.), *Handbook of Research on Strategic Alliances and Value Co-Creation in the Service Industry* (pp. 231–258). Hershey, PA: IGI Global. doi:10.4018/978-1-5225-2084-9.ch012

Haider, A., & Tang, S. S. (2016). Maximising Value Through IT and Business Alignment: A Case of IT Governance Institutionalisation at a Thai Bank. *International Journal of Technology Diffusion*, *7*(3), 33–58. doi:10.4018/IJTD.2016070104

Hajilari, A. B., Ghadaksaz, M., & Fasghandis, G. S. (2017). Assessing Organizational Readiness for Implementing ERP System Using Fuzzy Expert System Approach. *International Journal of Enterprise Information Systems*, *13*(1), 67–85. doi:10.4018/IJEIS.2017010105

Haldorai, A., Ramu, A., & Murugan, S. (2018). Social Aware Cognitive Radio Networks: Effectiveness of Social Networks as a Strategic Tool for Organizational Business Management. In H. Bansal, G. Shrivastava, G. Nguyen, & L. Stanciu (Eds.), *Social Network Analytics for Contemporary Business Organizations* (pp. 188–202). Hershey, PA: IGI Global. doi:10.4018/978-1-5225-5097-6.ch010

Hall, O. P. Jr. (2017). Social Media Driven Management Education. *International Journal of Knowledge-Based Organizations*, *7*(2), 43–59. doi:10.4018/IJKBO.2017040104

Hanifah, H., Halim, H. A., Ahmad, N. H., & Vafaei-Zadeh, A. (2017). Innovation Culture as a Mediator Between Specific Human Capital and Innovation Performance Among Bumiputera SMEs in Malaysia. In N. Ahmad, T. Ramayah, H. Halim, & S. Rahman (Eds.), *Handbook of Research on Small and Medium Enterprises in Developing Countries* (pp. 261–279). Hershey, PA: IGI Global. doi:10.4018/978-1-5225-2165-5.ch012

Hartlieb, S., & Silvius, G. (2017). Handling Uncertainty in Project Management and Business Development: Similarities and Differences. In Y. Raydugin (Ed.), *Handbook of Research on Leveraging Risk and Uncertainties for Effective Project Management* (pp. 337–362). Hershey, PA: IGI Global. doi:10.4018/978-1-5225-1790-0.ch016

Hass, K. B. (2017). Living on the Edge: Managing Project Complexity. In Y. Raydugin (Ed.), *Handbook of Research on Leveraging Risk and Uncertainties for Effective Project Management* (pp. 177–201). Hershey, PA: IGI Global. doi:10.4018/978-1-5225-1790-0.ch009

Hassan, A., & Privitera, D. S. (2016). Google AdSense as a Mobile Technology in Education. In J. Holland (Ed.), *Wearable Technology and Mobile Innovations for Next-Generation Education* (pp. 200–223). Hershey, PA: IGI Global. doi:10.4018/978-1-5225-0069-8.ch011

Hassan, A., & Rahimi, R. (2016). Consuming "Innovation" in Tourism: Augmented Reality as an Innovation Tool in Digital Tourism Marketing. In N. Pappas & I. Bregoli (Eds.), *Global Dynamics in Travel, Tourism, and Hospitality* (pp. 130–147). Hershey, PA: IGI Global. doi:10.4018/978-1-5225-0201-2.ch008

Hawking, P., & Carmine Sellitto, C. (2017). Developing an Effective Strategy for Organizational Business Intelligence. In M. Tavana (Ed.), *Enterprise Information Systems and the Digitalization of Business Functions* (pp. 222–237). Hershey, PA: IGI Global. doi:10.4018/978-1-5225-2382-6.ch010

Hawking, P., & Sellitto, C. (2017). A Fast-Moving Consumer Goods Company and Business Intelligence Strategy Development. *International Journal of Enterprise Information Systems, 13*(2), 22–33. doi:10.4018/IJEIS.2017040102

Hawking, P., & Sellitto, C. (2017). Business Intelligence Strategy: Two Case Studies. *International Journal of Business Intelligence Research, 8*(2), 17–30. doi:10.4018/IJBIR.2017070102

Haynes, J. D., Arockiasamy, S., Al Rashdi, M., & Al Rashdi, S. (2016). Business and E Business Strategies for Coopetition and Thematic Management as a Sustained Basis for Ethics and Social Responsibility in Emerging Markets. In M. Al-Shammari & H. Masri (Eds.), *Ethical and Social Perspectives on Global Business Interaction in Emerging Markets* (pp. 25–39). Hershey, PA: IGI Global. doi:10.4018/978-1-4666-9864-2.ch002

Hee, W. J., Jalleh, G., Lai, H., & Lin, C. (2017). E-Commerce and IT Projects: Evaluation and Management Issues in Australian and Taiwanese Hospitals. *International Journal of Public Health Management and Ethics, 2*(1), 69–90. doi:10.4018/IJPHME.2017010104

Hernandez, A. A. (2018). Exploring the Factors to Green IT Adoption of SMEs in the Philippines. *Journal of Cases on Information Technology, 20*(2), 49–66. doi:10.4018/JCIT.2018040104

Hernandez, A. A., & Ona, S. E. (2016). Green IT Adoption: Lessons from the Philippines Business Process Outsourcing Industry. *International Journal of Social Ecology and Sustainable Development, 7*(1), 1–34. doi:10.4018/IJSESD.2016010101

Hollman, A., Bickford, S., & Hollman, T. (2017). Cyber InSecurity: A Post-Mortem Attempt to Assess Cyber Problems from IT and Business Management Perspectives. *Journal of Cases on Information Technology, 19*(3), 42–70. doi:10.4018/JCIT.2017070104

Igbinakhase, I. (2017). Responsible and Sustainable Management Practices in Developing and Developed Business Environments. In Z. Fields (Ed.), *Collective Creativity for Responsible and Sustainable Business Practice* (pp. 180–207). Hershey, PA: IGI Global. doi:10.4018/978-1-5225-1823-5.ch010

Ilahi, L., Ghannouchi, S. A., & Martinho, R. (2016). A Business Process Management Approach to Home Healthcare Processes: On the Gap between Intention and Reality. In M. Cruz-Cunha, I. Miranda, R. Martinho, & R. Rijo (Eds.), *Encyclopedia of E-Health and Telemedicine* (pp. 439–457). Hershey, PA: IGI Global. doi:10.4018/978-1-4666-9978-6.ch035

Iwata, J. J., & Hoskins, R. G. (2017). Managing Indigenous Knowledge in Tanzania: A Business Perspective. In P. Jain & N. Mnjama (Eds.), *Managing Knowledge Resources and Records in Modern Organizations* (pp. 198–214). Hershey, PA: IGI Global. doi:10.4018/978-1-5225-1965-2.ch012

Jabeen, F., Ahmad, S. Z., & Alkaabi, S. (2016). The Internationalization Decision-Making of United Arab Emirates Family Businesses. In N. Zakaria, A. Abdul-Talib, & N. Osman (Eds.), *Handbook of Research on Impacts of International Business and Political Affairs on the Global Economy* (pp. 1–22). Hershey, PA: IGI Global. doi:10.4018/978-1-4666-9806-2.ch001

Jain, P. (2017). Ethical and Legal Issues in Knowledge Management Life-Cycle in Business. In P. Jain & N. Mnjama (Eds.), *Managing Knowledge Resources and Records in Modern Organizations* (pp. 82–101). Hershey, PA: IGI Global. doi:10.4018/978-1-5225-1965-2.ch006

Jamali, D., Abdallah, H., & Matar, F. (2016). Opportunities and Challenges for CSR Mainstreaming in Business Schools. *International Journal of Technology and Educational Marketing*, *6*(2), 1–29. doi:10.4018/IJTEM.2016070101

James, S., & Hauli, E. (2017). Holistic Management Education at Tanzanian Rural Development Planning Institute. In N. Baporikar (Ed.), *Management Education for Global Leadership* (pp. 112–136). Hershey, PA: IGI Global. doi:10.4018/978-1-5225-1013-0.ch006

Janošková, M., Csikósová, A., & Čulková, K. (2018). Measurement of Company Performance as Part of Its Strategic Management. In R. Leon (Ed.), *Managerial Strategies for Business Sustainability During Turbulent Times* (pp. 309–335). Hershey, PA: IGI Global. doi:10.4018/978-1-5225-2716-9.ch017

Jean-Vasile, A., & Alecu, A. (2017). Theoretical and Practical Approaches in Understanding the Influences of Cost-Productivity-Profit Trinomial in Contemporary Enterprises. In A. Jean Vasile & D. Nicolò (Eds.), *Sustainable Entrepreneurship and Investments in the Green Economy* (pp. 28–62). Hershey, PA: IGI Global. doi:10.4018/978-1-5225-2075-7.ch002

Jha, D. G. (2016). Preparing for Information Technology Driven Changes. In S. Tiwari & L. Nafees (Eds.), *Innovative Management Education Pedagogies for Preparing Next-Generation Leaders* (pp. 258–274). Hershey, PA: IGI Global. doi:10.4018/978-1-4666-9691-4.ch015

Joia, L. A., & Correia, J. C. (2018). CIO Competencies From the IT Professional Perspective: Insights From Brazil. *Journal of Global Information Management*, *26*(2), 74–103. doi:10.4018/JGIM.2018040104

Juma, A., & Mzera, N. (2017). Knowledge Management and Records Management and Competitive Advantage in Business. In P. Jain & N. Mnjama (Eds.), *Managing Knowledge Resources and Records in Modern Organizations* (pp. 15–28). Hershey, PA: IGI Global. doi:10.4018/978-1-5225-1965-2.ch002

K., I., & A, V. (2018). Monitoring and Auditing in the Cloud. In K. Munir (Ed.), *Cloud Computing Technologies for Green Enterprises* (pp. 318-350). Hershey, PA: IGI Global. doi:10.4018/978-1-5225-3038-1.ch013

Kabra, G., Ghosh, V., & Ramesh, A. (2018). Enterprise Integrated Business Process Management and Business Intelligence Framework for Business Process Sustainability. In A. Paul, D. Bhattacharyya, & S. Anand (Eds.), *Green Initiatives for Business Sustainability and Value Creation* (pp. 228–238). Hershey, PA: IGI Global. doi:10.4018/978-1-5225-2662-9.ch010

Kaoud, M. (2017). Investigation of Customer Knowledge Management: A Case Study Research. *International Journal of Service Science, Management, Engineering, and Technology*, *8*(2), 12–22. doi:10.4018/IJSSMET.2017040102

Kara, M. E., & Fırat, S. Ü. (2016). Sustainability, Risk, and Business Intelligence in Supply Chains. In M. Erdoğdu, T. Arun, & I. Ahmad (Eds.), *Handbook of Research on Green Economic Development Initiatives and Strategies* (pp. 501–538). Hershey, PA: IGI Global. doi:10.4018/978-1-5225-0440-5.ch022

Katuu, S. (2018). A Comparative Assessment of Enterprise Content Management Maturity Models. In N. Gwangwava & M. Mutingi (Eds.), *E-Manufacturing and E-Service Strategies in Contemporary Organizations* (pp. 93–118). Hershey, PA: IGI Global. doi:10.4018/978-1-5225-3628-4.ch005

Khan, M. A. (2016). MNEs Management Strategies in Developing Countries: Establishing the Context. In M. Khan (Ed.), *Multinational Enterprise Management Strategies in Developing Countries* (pp. 1–33). Hershey, PA: IGI Global. doi:10.4018/978-1-5225-0276-0.ch001

Khan, M. A. (2016). Operational Approaches in Organizational Structure: A Case for MNEs in Developing Countries. In M. Khan (Ed.), *Multinational Enterprise Management Strategies in Developing Countries* (pp. 129–151). Hershey, PA: IGI Global. doi:10.4018/978-1-5225-0276-0.ch007

Kinnunen, S., Ylä-Kujala, A., Marttonen-Arola, S., Kärri, T., & Baglee, D. (2018). Internet of Things in Asset Management: Insights from Industrial Professionals and Academia. *International Journal of Service Science, Management, Engineering, and Technology*, *9*(2), 104–119. doi:10.4018/IJSSMET.2018040105

Klein, A. Z., Sabino de Freitas, A., Machado, L., Freitas, J. C. Jr, Graziola, P. G. Jr, & Schlemmer, E. (2017). Virtual Worlds Applications for Management Education. In L. Tomei (Ed.), *Exploring the New Era of Technology-Infused Education* (pp. 279–299). Hershey, PA: IGI Global. doi:10.4018/978-1-5225-1709-2.ch017

Kożuch, B., & Jabłoński, A. (2017). Adopting the Concept of Business Models in Public Management. In M. Lewandowski & B. Kożuch (Eds.), *Public Sector Entrepreneurship and the Integration of Innovative Business Models* (pp. 10–46). Hershey, PA: IGI Global. doi:10.4018/978-1-5225-2215-7.ch002

Kumar, J., Adhikary, A., & Jha, A. (2017). Small Active Investors' Perceptions and Preferences Towards Tax Saving Mutual Fund Schemes in Eastern India: An Empirical Note. *International Journal of Asian Business and Information Management, 8*(2), 35–45. doi:10.4018/IJABIM.2017040103

Lassoued, Y., Bouzguenda, L., & Mahmoud, T. (2016). Context-Aware Business Process Versions Management. *International Journal of e-Collaboration, 12*(3), 7–33. doi:10.4018/IJeC.2016070102

Lavassani, K. M., & Movahedi, B. (2017). Applications Driven Information Systems: Beyond Networks toward Business Ecosystems. *International Journal of Innovation in the Digital Economy, 8*(1), 61–75. doi:10.4018/IJIDE.2017010104

Lazzareschi, V. H., & Brito, M. S. (2017). Strategic Information Management: Proposal of Business Project Model. In G. Jamil, A. Soares, & C. Pessoa (Eds.), *Handbook of Research on Information Management for Effective Logistics and Supply Chains* (pp. 59–88). Hershey, PA: IGI Global. doi:10.4018/978-1-5225-0973-8.ch004

Lederer, M., Kurz, M., & Lazarov, P. (2017). Usage and Suitability of Methods for Strategic Business Process Initiatives: A Multi Case Study Research. *International Journal of Productivity Management and Assessment Technologies, 5*(1), 40–51. doi:10.4018/IJPMAT.2017010103

Lee, I. (2017). A Social Enterprise Business Model and a Case Study of Pacific Community Ventures (PCV). In V. Potocan, M. Üngan, & Z. Nedelko (Eds.), *Handbook of Research on Managerial Solutions in Non-Profit Organizations* (pp. 182–204). Hershey, PA: IGI Global. doi:10.4018/978-1-5225-0731-4.ch009

Lee, L. J., & Leu, J. (2016). Exploring the Effectiveness of IT Application and Value Method in the Innovation Performance of Enterprise. *International Journal of Enterprise Information Systems, 12*(2), 47–65. doi:10.4018/IJEIS.2016040104

Lee, Y. (2016). Alignment Effect of Entrepreneurial Orientation and Marketing Orientation on Firm Performance. *International Journal of Customer Relationship Marketing and Management, 7*(4), 58–69. doi:10.4018/IJCRMM.2016100104

Leon, L. A., Seal, K. C., Przasnyski, Z. H., & Wiedenman, I. (2017). Skills and Competencies Required for Jobs in Business Analytics: A Content Analysis of Job Advertisements Using Text Mining. *International Journal of Business Intelligence Research, 8*(1), 1–25. doi:10.4018/IJBIR.2017010101

Leu, J., Lee, L. J., & Krischke, A. (2016). Value Engineering-Based Method for Implementing the ISO14001 System in the Green Supply Chains. *International Journal of Strategic Decision Sciences, 7*(4), 1–20. doi:10.4018/IJSDS.2016100101

Levy, C. L., & Elias, N. I. (2017). SOHO Users' Perceptions of Reliability and Continuity of Cloud-Based Services. In M. Moore (Ed.), *Cybersecurity Breaches and Issues Surrounding Online Threat Protection* (pp. 248–287). Hershey, PA: IGI Global. doi:10.4018/978-1-5225-1941-6.ch011

Levy, M. (2018). Change Management Serving Knowledge Management and Organizational Development: Reflections and Review. In N. Baporikar (Ed.), *Global Practices in Knowledge Management for Societal and Organizational Development* (pp. 256–270). Hershey, PA: IGI Global. doi:10.4018/978-1-5225-3009-1.ch012

Lewandowski, M. (2017). Public Organizations and Business Model Innovation: The Role of Public Service Design. In M. Lewandowski & B. Kożuch (Eds.), *Public Sector Entrepreneurship and the Integration of Innovative Business Models* (pp. 47–72). Hershey, PA: IGI Global. doi:10.4018/978-1-5225-2215-7.ch003

Lhannaoui, H., Kabbaj, M. I., & Bakkoury, Z. (2017). A Survey of Risk-Aware Business Process Modelling. *International Journal of Risk and Contingency Management, 6*(3), 14–26. doi:10.4018/IJRCM.2017070102

Li, J., Sun, W., Jiang, W., Yang, H., & Zhang, L. (2017). How the Nature of Exogenous Shocks and Crises Impact Company Performance?: The Effects of Industry Characteristics. *International Journal of Risk and Contingency Management, 6*(4), 40–55. doi:10.4018/IJRCM.2017100103

Lu, C., & Liu, S. (2016). Cultural Tourism O2O Business Model Innovation-A Case Study of CTrip. *Journal of Electronic Commerce in Organizations, 14*(2), 16–31. doi:10.4018/JECO.2016040102

Machen, B., Hosseini, M. R., Wood, A., & Bakhshi, J. (2016). An Investigation into using SAP-PS as a Multidimensional Project Control System (MPCS). *International Journal of Enterprise Information Systems*, *12*(2), 66–81. doi:10.4018/IJEIS.2016040105

Malega, P. (2017). Small and Medium Enterprises in the Slovak Republic: Status and Competitiveness of SMEs in the Global Markets and Possibilities of Optimization. In M. Vemić (Ed.), *Optimal Management Strategies in Small and Medium Enterprises* (pp. 102–124). Hershey, PA: IGI Global. doi:10.4018/978-1-5225-1949-2.ch006

Malewska, K. M. (2017). Intuition in Decision-Making on the Example of a Non-Profit Organization. In V. Potocan, M. Üngan, & Z. Nedelko (Eds.), *Handbook of Research on Managerial Solutions in Non-Profit Organizations* (pp. 378–399). Hershey, PA: IGI Global. doi:10.4018/978-1-5225-0731-4.ch018

Maroofi, F. (2017). Entrepreneurial Orientation and Organizational Learning Ability Analysis for Innovation and Firm Performance. In N. Baporikar (Ed.), *Innovation and Shifting Perspectives in Management Education* (pp. 144–165). Hershey, PA: IGI Global. doi:10.4018/978-1-5225-1019-2.ch007

Martins, P. V., & Zacarias, M. (2017). A Web-based Tool for Business Process Improvement. *International Journal of Web Portals*, *9*(2), 68–84. doi:10.4018/IJWP.2017070104

Matthies, B., & Coners, A. (2017). Exploring the Conceptual Nature of e-Business Projects. *Journal of Electronic Commerce in Organizations*, *15*(3), 33–63. doi:10.4018/JECO.2017070103

McKee, J. (2018). Architecture as a Tool to Solve Business Planning Problems. In M. Khosrow-Pour, D.B.A. (Ed.), Encyclopedia of Information Science and Technology, Fourth Edition (pp. 573-586). Hershey, PA: IGI Global. doi:10.4018/978-1-5225-2255-3.ch050

McMurray, A. J., Cross, J., & Caponecchia, C. (2018). The Risk Management Profession in Australia: Business Continuity Plan Practices. In N. Bajgoric (Ed.), *Always-On Enterprise Information Systems for Modern Organizations* (pp. 112–129). Hershey, PA: IGI Global. doi:10.4018/978-1-5225-3704-5.ch006

Meddah, I. H., & Belkadi, K. (2018). Mining Patterns Using Business Process Management. In R. Hamou (Ed.), *Handbook of Research on Biomimicry in Information Retrieval and Knowledge Management* (pp. 78–89). Hershey, PA: IGI Global. doi:10.4018/978-1-5225-3004-6.ch005

Mendes, L. (2017). TQM and Knowledge Management: An Integrated Approach Towards Tacit Knowledge Management. In D. Jaziri-Bouagina & G. Jamil (Eds.), *Handbook of Research on Tacit Knowledge Management for Organizational Success* (pp. 236–263). Hershey, PA: IGI Global. doi:10.4018/978-1-5225-2394-9.ch009

Mnjama, N. M. (2017). Preservation of Recorded Information in Public and Private Sector Organizations. In P. Jain & N. Mnjama (Eds.), *Managing Knowledge Resources and Records in Modern Organizations* (pp. 149–167). Hershey, PA: IGI Global. doi:10.4018/978-1-5225-1965-2.ch009

Mokoqama, M., & Fields, Z. (2017). Principles of Responsible Management Education (PRME): Call for Responsible Management Education. In Z. Fields (Ed.), *Collective Creativity for Responsible and Sustainable Business Practice* (pp. 229–241). Hershey, PA: IGI Global. doi:10.4018/978-1-5225-1823-5.ch012

Muniapan, B. (2017). Philosophy and Management: The Relevance of Vedanta in Management. In P. Ordóñez de Pablos (Ed.), *Managerial Strategies and Solutions for Business Success in Asia* (pp. 124–139). Hershey, PA: IGI Global. doi:10.4018/978-1-5225-1886-0.ch007

Muniapan, B., Gregory, M. L., & Ling, L. A. (2016). Marketing Education in Sarawak: Looking at It from the Employers' Viewpoint. In B. Smith & A. Porath (Eds.), *Global Perspectives on Contemporary Marketing Education* (pp. 112–130). Hershey, PA: IGI Global. doi:10.4018/978-1-4666-9784-3.ch008

Murad, S. E., & Dowaji, S. (2017). Using Value-Based Approach for Managing Cloud-Based Services. In A. Turuk, B. Sahoo, & S. Addya (Eds.), *Resource Management and Efficiency in Cloud Computing Environments* (pp. 33–60). Hershey, PA: IGI Global. doi:10.4018/978-1-5225-1721-4.ch002

Mutahar, A. M., Daud, N. M., Thurasamy, R., Isaac, O., & Abdulsalam, R. (2018). The Mediating of Perceived Usefulness and Perceived Ease of Use: The Case of Mobile Banking in Yemen. *International Journal of Technology Diffusion*, *9*(2), 21–40. doi:10.4018/IJTD.2018040102

Naidoo, V. (2017). E-Learning and Management Education at African Universities. In N. Baporikar (Ed.), *Management Education for Global Leadership* (pp. 181–201). Hershey, PA: IGI Global. doi:10.4018/978-1-5225-1013-0.ch009

Naidoo, V., & Igbinakhase, I. (2018). Opportunities and Challenges of Knowledge Retention in SMEs. In N. Baporikar (Ed.), *Knowledge Integration Strategies for Entrepreneurship and Sustainability* (pp. 70–94). Hershey, PA: IGI Global. doi:10.4018/978-1-5225-5115-7.ch004

Nayak, S., & Prabhu, N. (2017). Paradigm Shift in Management Education: Need for a Cross Functional Perspective. In N. Baporikar (Ed.), *Management Education for Global Leadership* (pp. 241–255). Hershey, PA: IGI Global. doi:10.4018/978-1-5225-1013-0.ch012

Ndede-Amadi, A. A. (2016). Student Interest in the IS Specialization as Predictor of the Success Potential of New Information Systems Programmes within the Schools of Business in Kenyan Public Universities. *International Journal of Information Systems and Social Change, 7*(2), 63–79. doi:10.4018/IJISSC.2016040104

Nedelko, Z., & Potocan, V. (2016). Management Practices for Processes Optimization: Case of Slovenia. In G. Alor-Hernández, C. Sánchez-Ramírez, & J. García-Alcaraz (Eds.), *Handbook of Research on Managerial Strategies for Achieving Optimal Performance in Industrial Processes* (pp. 545–561). Hershey, PA: IGI Global. doi:10.4018/978-1-5225-0130-5.ch025

Nedelko, Z., & Potocan, V. (2017). Management Solutions in Non-Profit Organizations: Case of Slovenia. In V. Potocan, M. Üngan, & Z. Nedelko (Eds.), *Handbook of Research on Managerial Solutions in Non-Profit Organizations* (pp. 1–22). Hershey, PA: IGI Global. doi:10.4018/978-1-5225-0731-4.ch001

Nedelko, Z., & Potocan, V. (2017). Priority of Management Tools Utilization among Managers: International Comparison. In V. Wang (Ed.), *Encyclopedia of Strategic Leadership and Management* (pp. 1083–1094). Hershey, PA: IGI Global. doi:10.4018/978-1-5225-1049-9.ch075

Nedelko, Z., Raudeliūnienė, J., & Črešnar, R. (2018). Knowledge Dynamics in Supply Chain Management. In N. Baporikar (Ed.), *Knowledge Integration Strategies for Entrepreneurship and Sustainability* (pp. 150–166). Hershey, PA: IGI Global. doi:10.4018/978-1-5225-5115-7.ch008

Nguyen, H. T., & Hipsher, S. A. (2018). Innovation and Creativity Used by Private Sector Firms in a Resources-Constrained Environment. In S. Hipsher (Ed.), *Examining the Private Sector's Role in Wealth Creation and Poverty Reduction* (pp. 219–238). Hershey, PA: IGI Global. doi:10.4018/978-1-5225-3117-3.ch010

Nycz, M., & Półkowski, Z. (2016). Business Intelligence as a Modern IT Supporting Management of Local Government Units in Poland. *International Journal of Knowledge and Systems Science, 7*(4), 1–18. doi:10.4018/IJKSS.2016100101

Obaji, N. O., Senin, A. A., & Olugu, M. U. (2016). Supportive Government Policy as a Mechanism for Business Incubation Performance in Nigeria. *International Journal of Information Systems and Social Change, 7*(4), 52–66. doi:10.4018/IJISSC.2016100103

Obicci, P. A. (2017). Risk Sharing in a Partnership. In *Risk Management Strategies in Public-Private Partnerships* (pp. 115–152). Hershey, PA: IGI Global. doi:10.4018/978-1-5225-2503-5.ch004

Obidallah, W. J., & Raahemi, B. (2017). Managing Changes in Service Oriented Virtual Organizations: A Structural and Procedural Framework to Facilitate the Process of Change. *Journal of Electronic Commerce in Organizations, 15*(1), 59–83. doi:10.4018/JECO.2017010104

Ojasalo, J., & Ojasalo, K. (2016). Service Logic Business Model Canvas for Lean Development of SMEs and Start-Ups. In N. Baporikar (Ed.), *Handbook of Research on Entrepreneurship in the Contemporary Knowledge-Based Global Economy* (pp. 217–243). Hershey, PA: IGI Global. doi:10.4018/978-1-4666-8798-1.ch010

Ojo, O. (2017). Impact of Innovation on the Entrepreneurial Success in Selected Business Enterprises in South-West Nigeria. *International Journal of Innovation in the Digital Economy, 8*(2), 29–38. doi:10.4018/IJIDE.2017040103

Okdinawati, L., Simatupang, T. M., & Sunitiyoso, Y. (2017). Multi-Agent Reinforcement Learning for Value Co-Creation of Collaborative Transportation Management (CTM). *International Journal of Information Systems and Supply Chain Management, 10*(3), 84–95. doi:10.4018/IJISSCM.2017070105

Ortner, E., Mevius, M., Wiedmann, P., & Kurz, F. (2016). Design of Interactional Decision Support Applications for E-Participation in Smart Cities. *International Journal of Electronic Government Research, 12*(2), 18–38. doi:10.4018/IJEGR.2016040102

Pal, K. (2018). Building High Quality Big Data-Based Applications in Supply Chains. In A. Kumar & S. Saurav (Eds.), *Supply Chain Management Strategies and Risk Assessment in Retail Environments* (pp. 1–24). Hershey, PA: IGI Global. doi:10.4018/978-1-5225-3056-5.ch001

Palos-Sanchez, P. R., & Correia, M. B. (2018). Perspectives of the Adoption of Cloud Computing in the Tourism Sector. In J. Rodrigues, C. Ramos, P. Cardoso, & C. Henriques (Eds.), *Handbook of Research on Technological Developments for Cultural Heritage and eTourism Applications* (pp. 377–400). Hershey, PA: IGI Global. doi:10.4018/978-1-5225-2927-9.ch018

Parry, V. K., & Lind, M. L. (2016). Alignment of Business Strategy and Information Technology Considering Information Technology Governance, Project Portfolio Control, and Risk Management. *International Journal of Information Technology Project Management, 7*(4), 21–37. doi:10.4018/IJITPM.2016100102

Pashkova, N., Trujillo-Barrera, A., Apostolakis, G., Van Dijk, G., Drakos, P. D., & Baourakis, G. (2016). Business Management Models of Microfinance Institutions (MFIs) in Africa: A Study into Their Enabling Environments. *International Journal of Food and Beverage Manufacturing and Business Models, 1*(2), 63–82. doi:10.4018/IJFBMBM.2016070105

Patiño, B. E. (2017). New Generation Management by Convergence and Individual Identity: A Systemic and Human-Oriented Approach. In N. Baporikar (Ed.), *Innovation and Shifting Perspectives in Management Education* (pp. 119–143). Hershey, PA: IGI Global. doi:10.4018/978-1-5225-1019-2.ch006

Pawliczek, A., & Rössler, M. (2017). Knowledge of Management Tools and Systems in SMEs: Knowledge Transfer in Management. In A. Bencsik (Ed.), *Knowledge Management Initiatives and Strategies in Small and Medium Enterprises* (pp. 180–203). Hershey, PA: IGI Global. doi:10.4018/978-1-5225-1642-2.ch009

Pejic-Bach, M., Omazic, M. A., Aleksic, A., & Zoroja, J. (2018). Knowledge-Based Decision Making: A Multi-Case Analysis. In R. Leon (Ed.), *Managerial Strategies for Business Sustainability During Turbulent Times* (pp. 160–184). Hershey, PA: IGI Global. doi:10.4018/978-1-5225-2716-9.ch009

Perano, M., Hysa, X., & Calabrese, M. (2018). Strategic Planning, Cultural Context, and Business Continuity Management: Business Cases in the City of Shkoder. In A. Presenza & L. Sheehan (Eds.), *Geopolitics and Strategic Management in the Global Economy* (pp. 57–77). Hershey, PA: IGI Global. doi:10.4018/978-1-5225-2673-5.ch004

Pereira, R., Mira da Silva, M., & Lapão, L. V. (2017). IT Governance Maturity Patterns in Portuguese Healthcare. In S. De Haes & W. Van Grembergen (Eds.), *Strategic IT Governance and Alignment in Business Settings* (pp. 24–52). Hershey, PA: IGI Global. doi:10.4018/978-1-5225-0861-8.ch002

Perez-Uribe, R., & Ocampo-Guzman, D. (2016). Conflict within Colombian Family Owned SMEs: An Explosive Blend between Feelings and Business. In J. Saiz-Álvarez (Ed.), *Handbook of Research on Social Entrepreneurship and Solidarity Economics* (pp. 329–354). Hershey, PA: IGI Global. doi:10.4018/978-1-5225-0097-1.ch017

Pérez-Uribe, R. I., Torres, D. A., Jurado, S. P., & Prada, D. M. (2018). Cloud Tools for the Development of Project Management in SMEs. In R. Perez-Uribe, C. Salcedo-Perez, & D. Ocampo-Guzman (Eds.), *Handbook of Research on Intrapreneurship and Organizational Sustainability in SMEs* (pp. 95–120). Hershey, PA: IGI Global. doi:10.4018/978-1-5225-3543-0.ch005

Petrisor, I., & Cozmiuc, D. (2017). Global Supply Chain Management Organization at Siemens in the Advent of Industry 4.0. In L. Saglietto & C. Cezanne (Eds.), *Global Intermediation and Logistics Service Providers* (pp. 123–142). Hershey, PA: IGI Global. doi:10.4018/978-1-5225-2133-4.ch007

Pierce, J. M., Velliaris, D. M., & Edwards, J. (2017). A Living Case Study: A Journey Not a Destination. In N. Silton (Ed.), *Exploring the Benefits of Creativity in Education, Media, and the Arts* (pp. 158–178). Hershey, PA: IGI Global. doi:10.4018/978-1-5225-0504-4.ch008

Radosavljevic, M., & Andjelkovic, A. (2017). Multi-Criteria Decision Making Approach for Choosing Business Process for the Improvement: Upgrading of the Six Sigma Methodology. In J. Stanković, P. Delias, S. Marinković, & S. Rochhia (Eds.), *Tools and Techniques for Economic Decision Analysis* (pp. 225–247). Hershey, PA: IGI Global. doi:10.4018/978-1-5225-0959-2.ch011

Radovic, V. M. (2017). Corporate Sustainability and Responsibility and Disaster Risk Reduction: A Serbian Overview. In M. Camilleri (Ed.), *CSR 2.0 and the New Era of Corporate Citizenship* (pp. 147–164). Hershey, PA: IGI Global. doi:10.4018/978-1-5225-1842-6.ch008

Raghunath, K. M., Devi, S. L., & Patro, C. S. (2018). Impact of Risk Assessment Models on Risk Factors: A Holistic Outlook. In K. Strang, M. Korstanje, & N. Vajjhala (Eds.), *Research, Practices, and Innovations in Global Risk and Contingency Management* (pp. 134–153). Hershey, PA: IGI Global. doi:10.4018/978-1-5225-4754-9.ch008

Raman, A., & Goyal, D. P. (2017). Extending IMPLEMENT Framework for Enterprise Information Systems Implementation to Information System Innovation. In M. Tavana (Ed.), *Enterprise Information Systems and the Digitalization of Business Functions* (pp. 137–177). Hershey, PA: IGI Global. doi:10.4018/978-1-5225-2382-6.ch007

Rao, Y., & Zhang, Y. (2017). The Construction and Development of Academic Library Digital Special Subject Databases. In L. Ruan, Q. Zhu, & Y. Ye (Eds.), *Academic Library Development and Administration in China* (pp. 163–183). Hershey, PA: IGI Global. doi:10.4018/978-1-5225-0550-1.ch010

Ravasan, A. Z., Mohammadi, M. M., & Hamidi, H. (2018). An Investigation Into the Critical Success Factors of Implementing Information Technology Service Management Frameworks. In K. Jakobs (Ed.), *Corporate and Global Standardization Initiatives in Contemporary Society* (pp. 200–218). Hershey, PA: IGI Global. doi:10.4018/978-1-5225-5320-5.ch009

Renna, P., Izzo, C., & Romaniello, T. (2016). The Business Process Management Systems to Support Continuous Improvements. In W. Nuninger & J. Châtelet (Eds.), *Handbook of Research on Quality Assurance and Value Management in Higher Education* (pp. 237–256). Hershey, PA: IGI Global. doi:10.4018/978-1-5225-0024-7.ch009

Rezaie, S., Mirabedini, S. J., & Abtahi, A. (2018). Designing a Model for Implementation of Business Intelligence in the Banking Industry. *International Journal of Enterprise Information Systems, 14*(1), 77–103. doi:10.4018/IJEIS.2018010105

Riccò, R. (2016). Diversity Management: Bringing Equality, Equity, and Inclusion in the Workplace. In J. Prescott (Ed.), *Handbook of Research on Race, Gender, and the Fight for Equality* (pp. 335–359). Hershey, PA: IGI Global. doi:10.4018/978-1-5225-0047-6.ch015

Romano, L., Grimaldi, R., & Colasuonno, F. S. (2017). Demand Management as a Success Factor in Project Portfolio Management. In L. Romano (Ed.), *Project Portfolio Management Strategies for Effective Organizational Operations* (pp. 202–219). Hershey, PA: IGI Global. doi:10.4018/978-1-5225-2151-8.ch008

Rostek, K. B. (2016). Risk Management: Role and Importance in Business Organization. In D. Jakóbczak (Ed.), *Analyzing Risk through Probabilistic Modeling in Operations Research* (pp. 149–178). Hershey, PA: IGI Global. doi:10.4018/978-1-4666-9458-3.ch007

Rouhani, S., & Savoji, S. R. (2016). A Success Assessment Model for BI Tools Implementation: An Empirical Study of Banking Industry. *International Journal of Business Intelligence Research, 7*(1), 25–44. doi:10.4018/IJBIR.2016010103

Ruan, Z. (2016). A Corpus-Based Functional Analysis of Complex Nominal Groups in Written Business Discourse: The Case of "Business". *International Journal of Computer-Assisted Language Learning and Teaching, 6*(2), 74–90. doi:10.4018/IJCALLT.2016040105

Ruhi, U. (2018). Towards an Interdisciplinary Socio-Technical Definition of Virtual Communities. In M. Khosrow-Pour, D.B.A. (Ed.), Encyclopedia of Information Science and Technology, Fourth Edition (pp. 4278-4295). Hershey, PA: IGI Global. doi:10.4018/978-1-5225-2255-3.ch371

Ryan, J., Doster, B., Daily, S., & Lewis, C. (2016). A Case Study Perspective for Balanced Perioperative Workflow Achievement through Data-Driven Process Improvement. *International Journal of Healthcare Information Systems and Informatics, 11*(3), 19–41. doi:10.4018/IJHISI.2016070102

Safari, M. R., & Jiang, Q. (2018). The Theory and Practice of IT Governance Maturity and Strategies Alignment: Evidence From Banking Industry. *Journal of Global Information Management*, *26*(2), 127–146. doi:10.4018/JGIM.2018040106

Sahoo, J., Pati, B., & Mohanty, B. (2017). Knowledge Management as an Academic Discipline: An Assessment. In B. Gunjal (Ed.), *Managing Knowledge and Scholarly Assets in Academic Libraries* (pp. 99–126). Hershey, PA: IGI Global. doi:10.4018/978-1-5225-1741-2.ch005

Saini, D. (2017). Relevance of Teaching Values and Ethics in Management Education. In N. Baporikar (Ed.), *Management Education for Global Leadership* (pp. 90–111). Hershey, PA: IGI Global. doi:10.4018/978-1-5225-1013-0.ch005

Sambhanthan, A. (2017). Assessing and Benchmarking Sustainability in Organisations: An Integrated Conceptual Model. *International Journal of Systems and Service-Oriented Engineering*, *7*(4), 22–43. doi:10.4018/IJSSOE.2017100102

Sambhanthan, A., & Potdar, V. (2017). A Study of the Parameters Impacting Sustainability in Information Technology Organizations. *International Journal of Knowledge-Based Organizations*, *7*(3), 27–39. doi:10.4018/IJKBO.2017070103

Sánchez-Fernández, M. D., & Manríquez, M. R. (2018). The Entrepreneurial Spirit Based on Social Values: The Digital Generation. In P. Isaias & L. Carvalho (Eds.), *User Innovation and the Entrepreneurship Phenomenon in the Digital Economy* (pp. 173–193). Hershey, PA: IGI Global. doi:10.4018/978-1-5225-2826-5.ch009

Sanchez-Ruiz, L., & Blanco, B. (2017). Process Management for SMEs: Barriers, Enablers, and Benefits. In M. Vemić (Ed.), *Optimal Management Strategies in Small and Medium Enterprises* (pp. 293–319). Hershey, PA: IGI Global. doi:10.4018/978-1-5225-1949-2.ch014

Sanz, L. F., Gómez-Pérez, J., & Castillo-Martinez, A. (2018). Analysis of the European ICT Competence Frameworks. In V. Ahuja & S. Rathore (Eds.), *Multidisciplinary Perspectives on Human Capital and Information Technology Professionals* (pp. 225–245). Hershey, PA: IGI Global. doi:10.4018/978-1-5225-5297-0.ch012

Sarvepalli, A., & Godin, J. (2017). Business Process Management in the Classroom. *Journal of Cases on Information Technology*, *19*(2), 17–28. doi:10.4018/JCIT.2017040102

Satpathy, B., & Muniapan, B. (2016). Ancient Wisdom for Transformational Leadership and Its Insights from the Bhagavad-Gita. In U. Aung & P. Ordoñez de Pablos (Eds.), *Managerial Strategies and Practice in the Asian Business Sector* (pp. 1–10). Hershey, PA: IGI Global. doi:10.4018/978-1-4666-9758-4.ch001

Saygili, E. E., Ozturkoglu, Y., & Kocakulah, M. C. (2017). End Users' Perceptions of Critical Success Factors in ERP Applications. *International Journal of Enterprise Information Systems*, *13*(4), 58–75. doi:10.4018/IJEIS.2017100104

Saygili, E. E., & Saygili, A. T. (2017). Contemporary Issues in Enterprise Information Systems: A Critical Review of CSFs in ERP Implementations. In M. Tavana (Ed.), *Enterprise Information Systems and the Digitalization of Business Functions* (pp. 120–136). Hershey, PA: IGI Global. doi:10.4018/978-1-5225-2382-6.ch006

Seidenstricker, S., & Antonino, A. (2018). Business Model Innovation-Oriented Technology Management for Emergent Technologies. In M. Khosrow-Pour, D.B.A. (Ed.), Encyclopedia of Information Science and Technology, Fourth Edition (pp. 4560-4569). Hershey, PA: IGI Global. doi:10.4018/978-1-5225-2255-3.ch396

Senaratne, S., & Gunarathne, A. D. (2017). Excellence Perspective for Management Education from a Global Accountants' Hub in Asia. In N. Baporikar (Ed.), *Management Education for Global Leadership* (pp. 158–180). Hershey, PA: IGI Global. doi:10.4018/978-1-5225-1013-0.ch008

Sensuse, D. I., & Cahyaningsih, E. (2018). Knowledge Management Models: A Summative Review. *International Journal of Information Systems in the Service Sector*, *10*(1), 71–100. doi:10.4018/IJISSS.2018010105

Sensuse, D. I., Wibowo, W. C., & Cahyaningsih, E. (2016). Indonesian Government Knowledge Management Model: A Theoretical Model. *Information Resources Management Journal*, *29*(1), 91–108. doi:10.4018/irmj.2016010106

Seth, M., Goyal, D., & Kiran, R. (2017). Diminution of Impediments in Implementation of Supply Chain Management Information System for Enhancing its Effectiveness in Indian Automobile Industry. *Journal of Global Information Management*, *25*(3), 1–20. doi:10.4018/JGIM.2017070101

Seyal, A. H., & Rahman, M. N. (2017). Investigating Impact of Inter-Organizational Factors in Measuring ERP Systems Success: Bruneian Perspectives. In M. Tavana (Ed.), *Enterprise Information Systems and the Digitalization of Business Functions* (pp. 178–204). Hershey, PA: IGI Global. doi:10.4018/978-1-5225-2382-6.ch008

Shaikh, A. A., & Karjaluoto, H. (2016). On Some Misconceptions Concerning Digital Banking and Alternative Delivery Channels. *International Journal of E-Business Research*, *12*(3), 1–16. doi:10.4018/IJEBR.2016070101

Shams, S. M. (2016). Stakeholder Relationship Management in Online Business and Competitive Value Propositions: Evidence from the Sports Industry. *International Journal of Online Marketing*, *6*(2), 1–17. doi:10.4018/IJOM.2016040101

Shamsuzzoha, A. (2016). Management of Risk and Resilience within Collaborative Business Network. In R. Addo-Tenkorang, J. Kantola, P. Helo, & A. Shamsuzzoha (Eds.), *Supply Chain Strategies and the Engineer-to-Order Approach* (pp. 143–159). Hershey, PA: IGI Global. doi:10.4018/978-1-5225-0021-6.ch008

Shaqrah, A. A. (2018). Analyzing Business Intelligence Systems Based on 7s Model of McKinsey. *International Journal of Business Intelligence Research, 9*(1), 53–63. doi:10.4018/IJBIR.2018010104

Sharma, A. J. (2017). Enhancing Sustainability through Experiential Learning in Management Education. In N. Baporikar (Ed.), *Management Education for Global Leadership* (pp. 256–274). Hershey, PA: IGI Global. doi:10.4018/978-1-5225-1013-0.ch013

Shetty, K. P. (2017). Responsible Global Leadership: Ethical Challenges in Management Education. In N. Baporikar (Ed.), *Innovation and Shifting Perspectives in Management Education* (pp. 194–223). Hershey, PA: IGI Global. doi:10.4018/978-1-5225-1019-2.ch009

Sinthupundaja, J., & Kohda, Y. (2017). Effects of Corporate Social Responsibility and Creating Shared Value on Sustainability. *International Journal of Sustainable Entrepreneurship and Corporate Social Responsibility, 2*(1), 27–38. doi:10.4018/IJSECSR.2017010103

Škarica, I., & Hrgović, A. V. (2018). Implementation of Total Quality Management Principles in Public Health Institutes in the Republic of Croatia. *International Journal of Productivity Management and Assessment Technologies, 6*(1), 1–16. doi:10.4018/IJPMAT.2018010101

Smuts, H., Kotzé, P., Van der Merwe, A., & Loock, M. (2017). Framework for Managing Shared Knowledge in an Information Systems Outsourcing Context. *International Journal of Knowledge Management, 13*(4), 1–30. doi:10.4018/IJKM.2017100101

Soares, E. R., & Zaidan, F. H. (2016). Information Architecture and Business Modeling in Modern Organizations of Information Technology: Professional Career Plan in Organizations IT. In G. Jamil, J. Poças Rascão, F. Ribeiro, & A. Malheiro da Silva (Eds.), *Handbook of Research on Information Architecture and Management in Modern Organizations* (pp. 439–457). Hershey, PA: IGI Global. doi:10.4018/978-1-4666-8637-3.ch020

Sousa, M. J., Cruz, R., Dias, I., & Caracol, C. (2017). Information Management Systems in the Supply Chain. In G. Jamil, A. Soares, & C. Pessoa (Eds.), *Handbook of Research on Information Management for Effective Logistics and Supply Chains* (pp. 469–485). Hershey, PA: IGI Global. doi:10.4018/978-1-5225-0973-8.ch025

Spremic, M., Turulja, L., & Bajgoric, N. (2018). Two Approaches in Assessing Business Continuity Management Attitudes in the Organizational Context. In N. Bajgoric (Ed.), *Always-On Enterprise Information Systems for Modern Organizations* (pp. 159–183). Hershey, PA: IGI Global. doi:10.4018/978-1-5225-3704-5.ch008

Steenkamp, A. L. (2018). Some Insights in Computer Science and Information Technology. In *Examining the Changing Role of Supervision in Doctoral Research Projects: Emerging Research and Opportunities* (pp. 113–133). Hershey, PA: IGI Global. doi:10.4018/978-1-5225-2610-0.ch005

Studdard, N., Dawson, M., Burton, S. L., Jackson, N., Leonard, B., Quisenberry, W., & Rahim, E. (2016). Nurturing Social Entrepreneurship and Building Social Entrepreneurial Self-Efficacy: Focusing on Primary and Secondary Schooling to Develop Future Social Entrepreneurs. In Z. Fields (Ed.), *Incorporating Business Models and Strategies into Social Entrepreneurship* (pp. 154–175). Hershey, PA: IGI Global. doi:10.4018/978-1-4666-8748-6.ch010

Sun, Z. (2016). A Framework for Developing Management Intelligent Systems. *International Journal of Systems and Service-Oriented Engineering*, *6*(1), 37–53. doi:10.4018/IJSSOE.2016010103

Swami, B., & Mphele, G. T. (2016). Problems Preventing Growth of Small Entrepreneurs: A Case Study of a Few Small Entrepreneurs in Botswana Sub-Urban Areas. In N. Baporikar (Ed.), *Handbook of Research on Entrepreneurship in the Contemporary Knowledge-Based Global Economy* (pp. 479–508). Hershey, PA: IGI Global. doi:10.4018/978-1-4666-8798-1.ch020

Tabach, A., & Croteau, A. (2017). Configurations of Information Technology Governance Practices and Business Unit Performance. *International Journal of IT/Business Alignment and Governance*, *8*(2), 1–27. doi:10.4018/IJITBAG.2017070101

Talaue, G. M., & Iqbal, T. (2017). Assessment of e-Business Mode of Selected Private Universities in the Philippines and Pakistan. *International Journal of Online Marketing*, *7*(4), 63–77. doi:10.4018/IJOM.2017100105

Tam, G. C. (2017). Project Manager Sustainability Competence. In *Managerial Strategies and Green Solutions for Project Sustainability* (pp. 178–207). Hershey, PA: IGI Global. doi:10.4018/978-1-5225-2371-0.ch008

Tambo, T. (2018). Fashion Retail Innovation: About Context, Antecedents, and Outcome in Technological Change Projects. In I. Management Association (Ed.), Fashion and Textiles: Breakthroughs in Research and Practice (pp. 233-260). Hershey, PA: IGI Global. doi:10.4018/978-1-5225-3432-7.ch010

Tambo, T., & Mikkelsen, O. E. (2016). Fashion Supply Chain Optimization: Linking Make-to-Order Purchasing and B2B E-Commerce. In S. Joshi & R. Joshi (Eds.), *Designing and Implementing Global Supply Chain Management* (pp. 1–21). Hershey, PA: IGI Global. doi:10.4018/978-1-4666-9720-1.ch001

Tandon, K. (2016). Innovative Andragogy: The Paradigm Shift to Heutagogy. In S. Tiwari & L. Nafees (Eds.), *Innovative Management Education Pedagogies for Preparing Next-Generation Leaders* (pp. 238–257). Hershey, PA: IGI Global. doi:10.4018/978-1-4666-9691-4.ch014

Tantau, A. D., & Frăţilă, L. C. (2018). Information and Management System for Renewable Energy Business. In *Entrepreneurship and Business Development in the Renewable Energy Sector* (pp. 200–244). Hershey, PA: IGI Global. doi:10.4018/978-1-5225-3625-3.ch006

Teixeira, N., Pardal, P. N., & Rafael, B. G. (2018). Internationalization, Financial Performance, and Organizational Challenges: A Success Case in Portugal. In L. Carvalho (Ed.), *Handbook of Research on Entrepreneurial Ecosystems and Social Dynamics in a Globalized World* (pp. 379–423). Hershey, PA: IGI Global. doi:10.4018/978-1-5225-3525-6.ch017

Trad, A., & Kalpić, D. (2016). The E-Business Transformation Framework for E-Commerce Architecture-Modeling Projects. In I. Lee (Ed.), *Encyclopedia of E-Commerce Development, Implementation, and Management* (pp. 733–753). Hershey, PA: IGI Global. doi:10.4018/978-1-4666-9787-4.ch052

Trad, A., & Kalpić, D. (2016). The E-Business Transformation Framework for E-Commerce Control and Monitoring Pattern. In I. Lee (Ed.), *Encyclopedia of E-Commerce Development, Implementation, and Management* (pp. 754–777). Hershey, PA: IGI Global. doi:10.4018/978-1-4666-9787-4.ch053

Trad, A., & Kalpić, D. (2018). The Business Transformation Framework, Agile Project and Change Management. In M. Khosrow-Pour, D.B.A. (Ed.), Encyclopedia of Information Science and Technology, Fourth Edition (pp. 620-635). Hershey, PA: IGI Global. doi:10.4018/978-1-5225-2255-3.ch054

Trad, A., & Kalpić, D. (2018). The Business Transformation and Enterprise Architecture Framework: The Financial Engineering E-Risk Management and E-Law Integration. In B. Sergi, F. Fidanoski, M. Ziolo, & V. Naumovski (Eds.), *Regaining Global Stability After the Financial Crisis* (pp. 46–65). Hershey, PA: IGI Global. doi:10.4018/978-1-5225-4026-7.ch003

Turulja, L., & Bajgoric, N. (2018). Business Continuity and Information Systems: A Systematic Literature Review. In N. Bajgoric (Ed.), *Always-On Enterprise Information Systems for Modern Organizations* (pp. 60–87). Hershey, PA: IGI Global. doi:10.4018/978-1-5225-3704-5.ch004

van Wessel, R. M., de Vries, H. J., & Ribbers, P. M. (2016). Business Benefits through Company IT Standardization. In K. Jakobs (Ed.), *Effective Standardization Management in Corporate Settings* (pp. 34–53). Hershey, PA: IGI Global. doi:10.4018/978-1-4666-9737-9.ch003

Vargas-Hernández, J. G. (2017). Professional Integrity in Business Management Education. In N. Baporikar (Ed.), *Management Education for Global Leadership* (pp. 70–89). Hershey, PA: IGI Global. doi:10.4018/978-1-5225-1013-0.ch004

Vasista, T. G., & AlAbdullatif, A. M. (2017). Role of Electronic Customer Relationship Management in Demand Chain Management: A Predictive Analytic Approach. *International Journal of Information Systems and Supply Chain Management, 10*(1), 53–67. doi:10.4018/IJISSCM.2017010104

Vergidis, K. (2016). Rediscovering Business Processes: Definitions, Patterns, and Modelling Approaches. In P. Papajorgji, F. Pinet, A. Guimarães, & J. Papathanasiou (Eds.), *Automated Enterprise Systems for Maximizing Business Performance* (pp. 97–122). Hershey, PA: IGI Global. doi:10.4018/978-1-4666-8841-4.ch007

Vieru, D., & Bourdeau, S. (2017). Survival in the Digital Era: A Digital Competence-Based Multi-Case Study in the Canadian SME Clothing Industry. *International Journal of Social and Organizational Dynamics in IT, 6*(1), 17–34. doi:10.4018/IJSODIT.2017010102

Vijayan, G., & Kamarulzaman, N. H. (2017). An Introduction to Sustainable Supply Chain Management and Business Implications. In M. Khan, M. Hussain, & M. Ajmal (Eds.), *Green Supply Chain Management for Sustainable Business Practice* (pp. 27–50). Hershey, PA: IGI Global. doi:10.4018/978-1-5225-0635-5.ch002

Vlachvei, A., & Notta, O. (2017). Firm Competitiveness: Theories, Evidence, and Measurement. In A. Vlachvei, O. Notta, K. Karantininis, & N. Tsounis (Eds.), *Factors Affecting Firm Competitiveness and Performance in the Modern Business World* (pp. 1–42). Hershey, PA: IGI Global. doi:10.4018/978-1-5225-0843-4.ch001 von Rosing, M., Fullington, N., & Walker, J. (2016). Using the Business Ontology and Enterprise Standards to Transform Three Leading Organizations. *International Journal of Conceptual Structures and Smart Applications*, *4*(1), 71–99. doi:10.4018/IJCSSA.2016010104

von Rosing, M., & von Scheel, H. (2016). Using the Business Ontology to Develop Enterprise Standards. *International Journal of Conceptual Structures and Smart Applications*, *4*(1), 48–70. doi:10.4018/IJCSSA.2016010103

Walczak, S. (2016). Artificial Neural Networks and other AI Applications for Business Management Decision Support. *International Journal of Sociotechnology and Knowledge Development*, *8*(4), 1–20. doi:10.4018/IJSKD.2016100101

Wamba, S. F., Akter, S., Kang, H., Bhattacharya, M., & Upal, M. (2016). The Primer of Social Media Analytics. *Journal of Organizational and End User Computing*, *28*(2), 1–12. doi:10.4018/JOEUC.2016040101

Wang, C., Schofield, M., Li, X., & Ou, X. (2017). Do Chinese Students in Public and Private Higher Education Institutes Perform at Different Level in One of the Leadership Skills: Critical Thinking?: An Exploratory Comparison. In V. Wang (Ed.), *Encyclopedia of Strategic Leadership and Management* (pp. 160–181). Hershey, PA: IGI Global. doi:10.4018/978-1-5225-1049-9.ch013

Wang, F., Raisinghani, M. S., Mora, M., & Wang, X. (2016). Strategic E-Business Management through a Balanced Scored Card Approach. In I. Lee (Ed.), *Encyclopedia of E-Commerce Development, Implementation, and Management* (pp. 361–386). Hershey, PA: IGI Global. doi:10.4018/978-1-4666-9787-4.ch027

Wang, J. (2017). Multi-Agent based Production Management Decision System Modelling for the Textile Enterprise. *Journal of Global Information Management*, *25*(4), 1–15. doi:10.4018/JGIM.2017100101

Wiedemann, A., & Gewald, H. (2017). Examining Cross-Domain Alignment: The Correlation of Business Strategy, IT Management, and IT Business Value. *International Journal of IT/Business Alignment and Governance*, *8*(1), 17–31. doi:10.4018/IJITBAG.2017010102

Wolf, R., & Thiel, M. (2018). Advancing Global Business Ethics in China: Reducing Poverty Through Human and Social Welfare. In S. Hipsher (Ed.), *Examining the Private Sector's Role in Wealth Creation and Poverty Reduction* (pp. 67–84). Hershey, PA: IGI Global. doi:10.4018/978-1-5225-3117-3.ch004

Wu, J., Ding, F., Xu, M., Mo, Z., & Jin, A. (2016). Investigating the Determinants of Decision-Making on Adoption of Public Cloud Computing in E-government. *Journal of Global Information Management, 24*(3), 71–89. doi:10.4018/JGIM.2016070104

Xu, L., & de Vrieze, P. (2016). Building Situational Applications for Virtual Enterprises. In I. Lee (Ed.), *Encyclopedia of E-Commerce Development, Implementation, and Management* (pp. 715–724). Hershey, PA: IGI Global. doi:10.4018/978-1-4666-9787-4.ch050

Yablonsky, S. (2018). Innovation Platforms: Data and Analytics Platforms. In *Multi-Sided Platforms (MSPs) and Sharing Strategies in the Digital Economy: Emerging Research and Opportunities* (pp. 72–95). Hershey, PA: IGI Global. doi:10.4018/978-1-5225-5457-8.ch003

Yusoff, A., Ahmad, N. H., & Halim, H. A. (2017). Agropreneurship among Gen Y in Malaysia: The Role of Academic Institutions. In N. Ahmad, T. Ramayah, H. Halim, & S. Rahman (Eds.), *Handbook of Research on Small and Medium Enterprises in Developing Countries* (pp. 23–47). Hershey, PA: IGI Global. doi:10.4018/978-1-5225-2165-5.ch002

Zanin, F., Comuzzi, E., & Costantini, A. (2018). The Effect of Business Strategy and Stock Market Listing on the Use of Risk Assessment Tools. In *Management Control Systems in Complex Settings: Emerging Research and Opportunities* (pp. 145–168). Hershey, PA: IGI Global. doi:10.4018/978-1-5225-3987-2.ch007

Zgheib, P. W. (2017). Corporate Innovation and Intrapreneurship in the Middle East. In P. Zgheib (Ed.), *Entrepreneurship and Business Innovation in the Middle East* (pp. 37–56). Hershey, PA: IGI Global. doi:10.4018/978-1-5225-2066-5.ch003

About the Contributors

Ebtihaj Al-Aali is an associate professor. She worked for University of Bahrain. She holds a Ph.D. In Industrial psychology and industrial sociology from University of Lancaster in U.k. Her research interests are mainly women in management, Organizational Behavior, Organizational theory, Business Ethics, management change and Islamic philosophy. She published many articles in different journals. She as well co-edited two books published by IGI.

* * *

Fatema Alaali joined AUBH in September 2019, as Assistant Professor of Economics in the College of Business and Management. She teaches the Principles of Microeconomics and Principles of Macroeconomics courses, and serves as: the Chair of the University Curriculum Committee, a member of the Admission and Scholarship Committee, and a member of the Accreditation Committee. Prior to taking on the role at AUBH, Dr. Alaali joined Ahlia University, Bahrain, in 2015 as an Assistant Professor of Economics. During her teaching career, she has taught multiple levels of Economics courses such as: Principles of Microeconomics and Macroeconomics; Intermediate Microeconomics; International Economics; Industrial Organization; Econometrics; and Monetary and Financial Systems. Her experience extends to helping students explore and define their academic, career, and life goals, by serving as an academic advisor to a number of Economics and Finance undergraduate program students. In addition, she has supervised several undergraduate students in their final projects as well as MBA and Engineering Management students in their theses. Dr. Alaali gained the fellowship of the Higher Education Academy in the UK (FHEA) in December 2018, demonstrating her commitment to teaching, learning, and students. Her research interests include areas of applied economics and finance, while her recent research projects focus on energy prices and their impact on firm investment and assets. She is currently working on papers in the field of environmental economics. She completed her studies at the University of Bahrain and earned a Bachelor of Science in Chemical Engineering in 2004. She received her Ph.D. in Economics from the University of Sheffield, UK in 2015, where she worked as a teaching assistant while studying for her Ph.D.

Ismail Hussein Amzat obtained his Bachelor degree In Arabic Language and Literature from Al-Azhar University, Cairo Egypt, Master degree in Education on Educational Administration from International Islamic University Malaysia and Doctoral degree in Education on Educational Management, Planning and Policy from University Malaysia. He is currently an Associate Professor at International Islamic University Malaysia (IIUM) and previously worked as a senior visiting lecturer of Educational Management at the Universiti Utara Malaysia (UUM). He was also a visiting Assistant Professor at Sultan Qaboos University, Oman. He has published quite reasonable papers in many reputable journals indexed in Scopus and ISI on university management, school leadership, job satisfaction and decision-making. He is an editor of a book "Fast forwarding Higher Education Institutions for Global Challenges: Perspectives and Approaches" by Springer, 2016 and "Teacher Empowerment toward Professional Development & Practices: Perspectives across Borders" by Springer, 2017 and "Teacher Professional Knowledge and Development for Reflective & Inclusive Practices" by Routledge, 2017.

Asma Ayari is a Ph.D. holder in Management from IAE University de Lille, France; Assistant Professor at the University of Bahrain teaching management, organizational behavior, and HRM; and an MSc and MBA thesis supervisor and reviewer.

Riyadotul Jannah Binti Mahyutan was born in Medan, Indonesia, in 1991. In 1993, her parents moved to Malaysia and open their business there. She and her three brothers grow up there and at the age 19, she moved alone to Indonesia for further her study there. She received the Bachelor degree in Education of Office Administrasion from University of Negeri Medan, Indonesia in 2010 and come back to Malaysia for her Master Degree. After finish her degree in 2014, she teach English subject for the high schools and also private tuition in the evening until June 2017. She took her Master degree in Educational Management & Leadership from International Islamic University Malaysia, in 2017. She also worked as a teacher in the kindergarten during her Master degree. During her study and exactly in 2019, she worked with her professor, Associate Professor Ismail Hussein Amzat and also her friends that writing a book chapter which is the title "Professional Development & Training Needs for Administrator: A Case of Islamic University in Malaysia". At the same year, she also be an assistance for the same lecturer for his project which required her to go to several university in different state.

Nehal El Naggar is a Doctorate degree holder with 22 years of experience; she has been working as a Researcher, Academic Instructor, Advisor and a Business and Management Consultant. She has been teaching both the undergraduate and graduate students in various National and International Universities in Egypt and

Bahrain. She has been actively involved in assisting and supervising post graduate students both on the Masters and Doctorate levels. Dr.Nehal is one of the leading researchers in eGovernment, eGovernment Readiness and Employability in Egypt. Believing in people and developing human capital she specialized in Human Resource Management. Dr. Nehal has been guiding the students on startup and mentoring entrepreneurial projects where four of her teams won the 'Best Company Award' in the INJAZ Bahrain Young Entrepreneurship Company (YEC) Competition for two consecutive years (2017-2018), the INJAZ Al Arabs 'Best Product Award' in 2018 in Kuwait, the "Best Social Impact Award" YEC 2020" and the Best Company Award "YEC2021).

Abdul Gani has a rare blend of teaching, research, training and administrative experience of over three and a half decades at four world reputed Universities. He is presently serving the Central University of Kashmir (CUK) as Head, Department of Management Studies. Earlier, Prof Abdul Gani served as the founder Registrar, Dean of three Schools of Studies, Director (Admissions) and Director(R&D) at the Central University of Kashmir. Prior to joining CUK, Prof Gani served University of Kashmir in various c and managed the Regional capacities, Indira Gandhi National Open University (IGNOU) as founder Regional Director, as Professor and Head, Department of Business Administration, Arab Open University, Riyadh, Saudi Arabia . Prof Gani's earlier job offers include Associate Professor in Management at International Islamic University, Malaysia and Professor in the Faculty of Commerce and Management Studies at University of Kashmir. Prof Gani is the recipient of prestigious Fulbright Fellowship, Shastri –Indo Canadian Fellowship, UK OU International Fellowship and ICSSR Fellowship. Prof Gani has lectured in various institutions of international repute in Canada, France, Malaysia, Egypt, Kuwait and Bahrain. Prof Gani has authored two books, ten book chapters and contributed over 65 papers in journals at international level. Besides conducting training programmes and leading capacity development and trainer training programmes, he has attended many national and international conferences/workshops. A founder Editor of a refereed journal, Prof. Gani is on the editorial boards of eight international Journals and member of 15 professional bodies.

Hanan Naser holds a PhD in Economics from University of Sheffield, UK. She also honors Fellow and Senior Fellow Awards from the Higher Educational Academy (HEA), UK. Hanan is working as an Associate Professor in Business and Economics at the American University of Bahrain (AUBH), Bahrain. She is also the Programs Lead at the College of Business and Management at AUBH as well as a Chair of the Research Council. Before joining to AUBH, Hanan was an Assistant Professor in Business Studies and the Head of Research Council at Arab Open University (AOU), Bahrain, for three years. Her research expertise area is in the field of Business Management, Energy Economics, Stock Markets and Environmental Issues. Hanan is a co-founder of 'Bahrain Research Consortium (BRC)' (http://www.bahrainrc.org), which is a non- profit organization that aims at promoting and supporting research activities in the region for academics, entrepreneurs, and SMEs. She is a member of Bahrain Economist Society and Bahrain Statistical Society. She is an active research reviewer for number of international academic journals such as Energy, Energy Policy, Energy Economics, Empirical Economics and others.

Jalal Naser graduated from SciencesPo Paris in 2017. He holds a Master of Science (M.Sc.) in Applied Labour Economics for Development and a Bachelor of Science (B.Sc.) degree in Applied Statistics with honors from UAEU. He is a Graduate Statistician (GradStat) of the Royal Statistical Society in UK. He has over 17 years of experience as a Principal Consultant with JAFCON Consultants for Productivity Improvement and in using IBM SPSS. Also, he is a tutor with Strathclyde University and RCSI in Ireland – Bahrain. Jalal is a regular guest visitor to Sultan Qaboos University in Oman. He founded Bahrain Statistical Society electronically on Linkedin in 2012, graduated from the US Department of State cultural program IVLP in 2013 and was honors among the Faces of Exchange awardees in 2020. He has authored and published a book, articles, papers and researches.

Hamid Murad Özcan completed his undergraduate education at Hacettepe University, Department of Business Administration. He graduated from Eskişehir Osmangazi University Business Administration Doctorate Program. He works as a research assistant doctor in the department of management and organization in the same institution. Main fields of study: organizational behavior, human resource management.

Burak Özdemir received his PhD from Ekişehir Osmangazi University, Turkey. He is working as an assistant professor in Department of International Trade and Logistics at the Kastamonu University. Dr Ozdemir's research interests are in organizational behavior, organization theory and strategic management.

Bradley Saunders received his PhD from Loughborough University Business School, UK. Prior to joining the American University of Bahrain, Dr Saunders has held a number of academic posts in the Gulf region including four years as Lecturer at Zayed University in Dubai and most recently as an Assistant Professor at Prince Mohammad bin Fahd University, KSA, where he taught for five years. Dr Saunders also has wide experience in the UK, having taught Management at several UK universities, including the University of Northampton, University of Derby, and

Regent's University London. Dr Saunders' research interests include overeducation, migrant workers, self-initiated expatriates, job transitions, corporate expatriation and repatriation, and student employability.

Sana Shabir pursued her doctoral programme of study at the School of Business Studies, Central University of Kashmir, J&K, India. She acknowledges the support of Government of India's Maulana Azad National Fellowship (MANF) for her research, on which the present chapter is based. She has presented papers at various national and international conferences and also contributed research papers to many journals of international repute. Her research interests include Gender resource, OB, Work-life balance, Organisational commitment, Ethics, Spirituality, and leadership.

Ryan H. Sharp is an Assistant Professor at Brigham Young University. He completed his doctorate work at the University of Utah where his dissertation focused on positive organizational behavior. In addition to his research in organizational behavior, he also very active in both teaching and writing about religion. While he is passionate about his teaching and research, his greatest joy is working with his wife in raising their six energetic boys.

Index

A

B

C

D

E

H

I

K

L

M

N

O

P

R

S

V

W

Z

www.ingramcontent.com/pod-product-compliance
Lightning Source LLC
LaVergne TN
LVHW061549290926
849162LV00004B/956
* 9 7 8 1 7 9 9 8 9 3 1 9 6 *